A-Z 10TH EDITION OF CAREERS & JOBS

City & Guilds

*Learning for work,
life and leisure*

www.city-and-guilds.co.uk

THE TIMES

A-Z 10TH EDITION OF
CAREERS & JOBS

IRENE KRECHOWIECKA

KOGAN
PAGE

First published in 1984
Tenth edition 2002

Kogan Page Limited
120 Pentonville Road
London N1 9JN
UK

© 1984, 1986, 1988, 1991, 1992, 1994, 1995, 1997, 2000, 2002

The views expressed in this book are those of the author, and are not necessarily the same as those of Times Newspapers Ltd.

British Library Cataloguing in Publication Data

A CIP record for this book is available from the British Library.

ISBN 0 7494 3660 3

Typeset by Saxon Graphics Ltd, Derby
Printed and bound in Great Britain by Bell & Bain Ltd, Glasgow

City & Guilds – *qualifications for work, life and leisure ...*

Whatever your ambitions, City & Guilds has the ideal qualification for you. Learning new skills opens doors to new opportunities.

City & Guilds is a household name, according to Consumer Surveys carried out recently, one in five households has a City & Guilds.

More than 8,500 approved City & Guilds centres offer over 500 qualifications in sectors ranging from agriculture to hairdressing IT to care. Everyday over a million people are working towards their City & Guilds qualifications!

Chose the level of qualification that's right for you and progress as far as you want to go. We also have a range of basic and key skills. Skills essential for work, life and leisure!

Assessment ranges from traditional classroom-based methods to assessments in the workplace.

The City & Guilds Group

The City & Guilds Group incorporates some of the best known names in vocational education:

City & Guilds offers the widest range of vocational qualifications.

Pitman Qualifications provides qualifications covering office, secretarial, business and language skills.

NEBS Management is the largest provider of general and specialist management qualifications.

City & Guilds International operates in a hundred countries world-wide.

City & Guilds Affinity concentrates on childcare, health, care and community services.

Why chose vocational qualifications?

City & Guilds qualifications have been developed following consultation with industry, national training and employers. They are nationally recognised awards proving to employers that you have the skills and ability they are looking for.

You will be in good company too! Many well known TV personalities began their career with a City & Guilds qualifications, including: Gary Rhodes, Ainsley Harriet, Jamie Oliver, Nicky Clarke, Handy Andy Kane, Alan Titchmarsh, and Anita Roddick name just a few!

For information call 020 7294 2800 *or check out* www.city-and-guilds.co.uk

INTRODUCTION

There's never a good time to update a book like this because something crucial is always changing. The research for this edition was undertaken in the autumn of 2001, a period overshadowed by uncertainty. As stories of impending recession, redundancy and the effects of terrorism dominated the news, career areas that had previously shown promise of sustained growth, such as travel, leisure and IT, demonstrated the dangers inherent in trying to predict employment trends.

Smaller events such as the decision to replace National Training Organisations with Sector Skills Councils are paltry in comparison but nevertheless problematic when working to produce an accurate and up to date guide to careers. So it's fortunate that one of the major developments since the last edition has been that most professional organisations have made excellent use of the Web for promoting the careers they represent. Where previous editions suggested sending a stamped addressed envelope for information, the norm now is to provide Web-based resources. Changes in qualifications, salaries and many other employment related details are inevitable; it's a relief to know readers can check the latest developments on the sites attached to each career description.

Relevant sites have been added to most entries, but email addresses have only been included where the organisation has indicated willingness to respond to requests sent this way. Some organisations prefer enquirers to use online forms, others do not have the staffing to cope with email enquiries and make all necessary information available on their site.

A career may not be for life any more – although many still are – but finding the one that suits you makes life so much better. These short descriptions provide a flavour of what's involved for over 300 occupations. The aim is to provide an overview that makes it quick and easy to compare options and decide which are worth further investigation. In this book you will find an explanation of qualifications and their equivalents, along with a list of further useful Web sites.

If you have any comments or corrections please contact the publisher.

Irene Krechowiecka

ABBREVIATIONS

A level	Advanced level
AS level	Advanced Special level
CAM	Communication, Advertising and Marketing Foundation
CCETSW	Central Council for Education and Training in Social Work
Edexcel	Edexcel Foundation
Edexcel (BTEC)	Comprises of ULEAC (University of London Examination and Assessment Council) and BTEC (Business and Technology Education Council)
GCE	General Certificate of Education
GCSE	General Certificate of Secondary Education
GNVQ	General National Vocational Qualification
GSVQ	General Scottish Vocational Qualification
H grade	Higher grade (SCE)
HNC/HND	Higher National Certificate/Higher National Diploma
HTC	Higher Technical Certificate
NC/ND	National Certificate/National Diploma
NVQ	National Vocational Qualification
QCA	Qualifications and Curriculum Authority
SCE	Scottish Certificate of Education (equivalent to GCSE)
SNC/SND	Scottish National Certificate/Scottish National Diploma
SQA	Scottish Qualifications Authority
SVQ	Scottish Vocational Qualification
TEC	Training and Enterprise Council

QUALIFICATIONS

Scottish readers should be aware that in order to simplify the text the editor has referred to qualifications required in terms of GCSEs, A levels and NVQs or equivalent. NVQs are directly equivalent to SVQs but Scottish National and Higher Qualifications are not equivalent to GCSEs and A levels. A new qualification, the Advanced Higher, does equate to A level but most universities still express their entry requirements in terms of the Higher. Full details of all Scottish qualifications can be found on the SQA Web site. The easiest way to compare the points awarded for A levels and Highers is using the Universities and Colleges Admissions Service (UCAS) tariff calculator.

Relevant Scottish sources of further information have been included where appropriate.

USEFUL POINTS OF CONTACT

www.ucas.com
Details of, and current entry requirements for, most higher education courses in the UK. The tariff calculator that can be found in the News section removes the need to grapple with the new points system (www.ucas.com/higher/tariff/calc/index.html).

www.statistics.gov.uk
The current edition of *The New Earnings Survey* can be downloaded from the Labour Market section of the site and provides up to date information on salaries in the UK.

www.nto-nc.org.uk
Although National Training Organisations are being phased out, the sites of many will continue to provide excellent careers information in the interim. Details of all NTOs and links to their sites are available here.

www.ssda.org.uk
Information about the progress of the new sector skills network from the Sector Skills Development Agency.

www.qca.org.uk
The Qualifications and Curriculum Authority accredit and monitor qualifications in schools, colleges and at work in England, Wales and Northern Ireland. Details of the national qualifications framework showing the equivalence between all qualifications is available here.

www.sqa.org.uk
The Scottish Qualifications Authority is responsible for the development, accreditation, assessment, and certification of qualifications other than degrees in Scotland. Information on these and their equivalence to qualifications in the rest of the UK can be found on this site.

ACCOUNTANT

Accountants are trained to examine, interpret and plan all types of financial transactions. Those who work in accountancy firms deal with such matters as auditing, analysing, verifying and interpreting clients' accounts, advising on taxation, executorship and trusteeship, and liquidations. Accountants employed in industry and commerce or by local authorities are more concerned with financial planning and the allocation of funds. After qualifying, some accountants specialise in areas such as taxation, auditing or management consultancy. They may also specialise in clients from a particular field, for example music or the theatre. In the public sector, the range of career opportunities covers everything from central and local government to health and further/higher education.

Qualifications and Training

Accountants must obtain membership of one of the many professional bodies. Minimum educational requirements are GCSEs plus at least two A levels or equivalent. The majority of those training to be chartered accountants in England and Wales are graduates.

For those with at least two A levels or equivalent there is the Association of Accounting Technicians (AAT) to Associate Chartered Accountant (ACA) Fast-Track route. Students can enter the AAT at intermediate level and qualify as an ACA in four years.

For the Institute of Chartered Accountants of Scotland, all entrants must hold a degree. It is generally compulsory for students to undertake a period of practical training – of three to four years' duration – in addition to taking professional examinations before being admitted as a professional Member of an Institute.

Personal Qualities

Numeracy, careful attention to detail, logical and analytical skills are essential. Communication, problem solving, self-organization and good interpersonal skills are also important. Accountants need to be creative, discreet and trustworthy and able to work both independently and as part of a team.

Starting Salary

The average starting salary for graduate trainees is £15,500, and can be as high as £28,000 in London. Pay often doubles once training is completed.

| i |

The Institute of Chartered Accountants in England and Wales, PO Box 433, Chartered Accountants' Hall, Moorgate Place, London EC2P 2BJ; 020 7920 8100; www.icaew.co.uk; e-mail: careers@icaew.co.uk

The Chartered Institute of Public Finance and Accountancy, 3 Robert Street, London WC2N 6RL; 020 7543 5600; www.cipfa.org.uk; e-mail: choices@cipfa.org

The Institute of Chartered Accountants of Scotland, CA House, 21 Haymarket Yards, Edinburgh EH12 5HB; 0131 347 0162; fax: 0131 347 0108; www.icas.org.uk; e-mail: caeducation@ icas.org.uk

Accountancy National Training Organization, Viking House, Swallowdale Lane, Hemel Hempstead, Hertfordshire HP2 7EA; 01442 250525; www.anto.org

Association of Chartered Certified Accountants (ACCA), Student Recruitment and Training, 29 Lincoln's Inn Fields, London WC2A 3EE; 020 7396 5800; www.accaglobal.com; e-mail: info@accaglobal.com

The Chartered Institute of Management Accountants, 26 Chapter Street, London SW1P 4NP; 020 8849 2251; www.cima.org.uk; e-mail: student-services@cimaglobal.com

Careers in Accountancy (Kogan Page)

ACCOUNT EXECUTIVE

see *Advertising*

ACCOUNTING TECHNICIAN

Accounting technicians work in a variety of roles alongside professionally qualified Chartered Accountants. They are involved in the day-to-day practical work of accountancy and finance, including the preparation of information and accounts and the interpretation of computer information, such as audit tax and payroll. Accounting technicians are widely employed in public finance, industry and commerce, and private practice. Their roles range from accounts clerks to finance managers. A growing number of accounting technicians provide a range of services direct to the public and manage their own practice. Many go on to qualify with the senior chartered accountancy bodies.

Qualifications and Training

The Association of Accounting Technicians' (AAT) Education and Training Scheme offers open access, although candidates must demonstrate numeracy and literacy. The scheme, which usually takes three years part-time, is competence-based and accredited at NVQ levels 2 to 4. Central assessments are combined with relevant work-based assessments during the training period. The three stages of the scheme are Foundation (NVQ level 2 in Accounting), Intermediate (NVQ level 3 in Accounting) and Technician (NVQ level 4 in Accounting). The AAT also offers the following specialist qualifications: NVQ in Audit (Internal), available at levels 3 and 4; NVQ in Payroll Administration available at levels 2 and 3; AAT Diploma in Government Finance; AAT Bookkeeping Certificate.

Personal Qualities

The job requires a methodical, systematic approach and the ability to work with figures. Computer skills are an advantage.

Starting Salary

With experience £13,000 in London, £7,500 to £13,000 outside London; fully qualified £19,000 in London, £13,000–£14,000 outside London.

i

The Association of Accounting Technicians, 154 Clerkenwell Road, London ECIR 5AD; 020 7837 8600; www.aat.co.uk; e-mail: aatuk@dial.pipex.com

Accountancy National Training Organization, Viking House, Swallowdale Lane, Hemel Hempstead, Hertfordshire HP2 7EA; 01442 250525 ; www.anto.org

'Improve Your Prospects – Quality with AAT' (The Association of Accounting Technicians)

ACTOR

(see also *Theatre*)

Acting mainly involves the interpretation of someone else's work and the communication of it to an audience, although there are opportunities for actors to write their own material. Actors are employed in various types of theatre (commercial, subsidised, community, fringe theatre and theatre-in-education), and also in television, film, radio, and television and radio commercials. Competition is keen and, because it is such a precarious profession, those entering it must be prepared for long periods of unemployment.

Qualifications and Training

Most potential actors attend drama school. The National Council for Drama Training is a useful source for information on accredited courses. A good general education is important and some schools require GCSEs and A levels or equivalent. Training courses at established schools usually last two or three years. Entrance is by audition and is competitive. Further experience may be gained from working in a repertory company or in fringe theatre. This may be an alternative way of entering the profession, but it is becoming increasingly difficult to enter solely by this method.

Personal Qualities

Acting requires a combination of intelligence, sensitivity and imagination, together with a good memory, determination and physical stamina.

Starting Salary

Comparatively low: minimum weekly salaries are set by theatre employers after negotiations with Equity which has a number of different agreements for theatre, television and film work.

| i |

National Council for Drama Training, 5 Tavistock Place, London WC1H 9SS; 020 7387 3650; www.ncdt.co.uk; e-mail: ncdt@ lineone.net

Conference of Drama Schools, 1 Stanley Avenue, Thorpe, Norwich NR7 OBE; 01603 702021; www.drama.ac.uk; e-mail: enquiries@cds.drama.ac.uk

British Actors Equity Association, Guild House, Upper St Martin's Lane, London WC2H 9EG; 020 7379 6000; www.equity.org.uk

The Spotlight (casting directory), Charles House, 7 Leicester Place, London WC2H 7RJ; 020 7437 7631; www.spotlightcd.com

The Stage; www.thestage.co.uk (advertises jobs and auditions)

Careers in the Theatre (Kogan Page)

ACTUARY

Actuaries play a key role in businesses that require an understanding of finance, mathematics and risk management. The majority are employed by insurance companies and consultancies. Others work in areas such as investment, banking and healthcare. The work offers management opportunities, often at the highest level, with actuaries having a commercial as well as a technical role. It is a small but influential profession with good opportunities for career progression. Last year around 1,250 new entrants joined the existing 13,000 members of the Faculty and Institute of Actuaries. As the financial world becomes more complex, the skills of the actuary look set to be in demand both in the UK and overseas.

Qualifications and Training
The minimum entry requirements are A level maths (or equivalent) and proficiency in English, equivalent to GCSE grade C. However, most trainees have a good degree in maths, statistics or economics. Training is on the job, often with an insurance company or firm of consultants, and is combined with part-time study for the examinations of The Faculty or Institute of Actuaries. On average, it takes five to six years to complete all the examinations and become a qualified actuary.

Personal Qualities
Prospective actuaries should have an aptitude for maths, a practical outlook and an analytical mind, as well as the ability to express themselves clearly and accurately.

Starting Salary
Actuarial trainees earn in the region of £17,000–£27,000 and £38,000+ when qualified. London salaries are higher.

Institute of Actuaries, Napier House, 4 Worcester Street, Oxford
    OX1 2AW; 01865 268228; fax: 01865 268253;
    www.actuaries. org.uk; e-mail: careers@actuaries.org.uk
Faculty of Actuaries, Maclaurin House, 18 Dublin Street, Edinburgh
    EH1 3PP; 0131 240 1300; fax: 0131 240 1313;
    www.actuaries.org.uk; e-mail: careers@actuaries.org.uk
'A Head Start – Your Guide to Careers in the Actuarial
    Profession' (available from either the Faculty or Institute of
    Actuaries at the above address or by e-mail)
Actuaries – Inside Careers Guide, www.insidecareers.co.uk

ACUPUNCTURIST

Acupuncture is a system of healing which has been practised in China and other Far Eastern countries for thousands of years. It involves the insertion of fine needles into one or more points of the body to restore the overall health of the person and help alleviate symptoms from which they may be suffering. Acupuncture can also be used for relieving pain and in China is used to anaesthetise patients during operations.

Qualifications and Training
The training of acupuncturists is monitored by the British Acupuncture Accreditation Board (BAAB), an independent body which is allied to the British Acupuncture Council (BAcC). Training standards are detailed in the BAcC's Guidelines for Acupuncture Education and graduates of accredited or candidate colleges have automatic right of membership of the Council. Details of accredited, three-year full-time courses or their part-time equivalents are available from the Council.

Personal Qualities
Acupuncturists need the necessary practitioner skills, including a knowledge of western medicine appropriate to the practice of acupuncture. They must also be able to put patients at their ease and to gain their confidence.

Starting Salary
Salaries vary depending on location, number of patients and amount charged. After qualifying, most acupuncturists will be self-employed and may practise from home, in a clinic, or occasionally, within the NHS.

British Acupuncture Council (BAcC), 63 Jeddo Road, London
    W12 9HQ; 020 8735 0400; fax: 020 8735 0404;
    www.acupuncture.org.uk
The College of Integrated Chinese Medicine, 19 Castle
    Street, Reading RG1 7SB; 0118 950 8880; fax: 0118 950 8890;
    www.cicm.org.uk
The College of Traditional Acupuncture (UK), Tao House,
    Queensway, Royal Leamington Spa, Warwickshire CV31 3L;
    01926 422121; www.acupuncture-coll.ac.uk
The International College of Oriental Medicine UK, Green
    Hedges House, Green Hedges Avenue, East Grinstead, West
    Sussex RH19 1DZ; 01342 313106; www.orientalmed.ac.uk

The London College of Traditional Acupuncture, HR House, 447 High Road, Finchley, London N12 0AF; 020 8371 0820; www.lcta.com

The Northern College of Acupuncture, 61 Micklegate, York YO1 6LJ; 01904 343 305; www.chinese-medicine.co.uk

The School of Five Elements Acupuncture, 13 Mandela Street, London NW1 0DU; 020 7383 5553; fax: 020 7383 5503; www.sofea.co.uk

Traditional Chinese Medicine / Acupuncture, Centre for Community Care and Primary Health, University of Westminster, 309 Regent Street, London W1R 8AL; 020 7911 5066; www.westminster.ac.uk

Working in Complementary and Alternative Medicine (Kogan Page)

ADMINISTRATIVE MANAGEMENT

Information is central to all management processes, and administrative management represents an element of all managers' and most professionals' jobs, whether they are employed in finance, personnel, the arts, facilities management, purchasing, marketing or general administration. An organization's ability to manage its administrative operations effectively is often crucial to its success. This is a sector that offers potential for people to start in clerical and junior administrative jobs and to proceed to any level according to their capability and qualifications.

Qualifications and Training

NVQs in Administration are available at levels 1 to 4. Foundation and Advanced Modern Apprenticeships in Business Administration can help employees progress and develop in supervisory and management roles. The Institute of Administrative Management (IAM) offers a range of professional educational qualifications through colleges, universities and distance-learning providers. These include the certificate, diploma, advanced diploma and BA (Hons) in administrative management.

Personal Qualities

Good organizational, numeracy and communication skills are required. High levels of computer literacy are becoming increasingly important.

Starting Salary

Supervisory posts start at around £12,000–£15,000, depending on qualifications, experience and special expertise, such as a high levels of ICT skills. Managerial grades start at around £18,000.

The Institute of Administrative Management, 40 Chatsworth Parade, Petts Wood, Orpington, Kent BR5 1RW; 01689 875555; fax: 01689 870891; www.instam.org

The CfA – NTO for Administration, 18/20 Bromell's Road, London SW4 0BG; 020 7627 9876; www.cfa.uk.com

ADVERTISING

(see also *Artist, Marketing, Market Research* and *Public Relations*)

Advertising is a complex industry providing a wide range of openings, mostly with agencies that plan, organise and run advertising campaigns. Working on behalf of clients, advertising agencies study the product or service to be advertised and its market. They then plan how it should be sold and distributed and how the media might be used to the best advantage in this process.

Account Executive

Account executives are responsible within the agency for a particular client or group of clients. They interpret the client's wishes; coordinate and supervise the work of others within the agency, such as creatives, account planners, and copy- and scriptwriters; seek advice from other experts such as media executives and then present the ideas most likely to meet with the client's approval.

Account Planner

Some agencies employ full-time account planners. On the marketing side they are involved in annual planning and in making longer-range plans for the future. They may also plan future campaigns for particular accounts and consider the long-term position regarding media advertising. Apart from knowledge of the activities being planned, account planners need imagination, common sense and an ability with figures.

Media Executive

Media executives provide expert advice on the advertising medium – for example, television, cinema, posters, newspapers, journals – that will best suit a particular campaign, and negotiate the most economical rates.

Copy- and Scriptwriters

The writers in the agency produce headings, text, jingles and copy for articles in journals and scripts for films and commercials. Copywriters often work closely with the Art Editor and visualisers.

Art Editor/Executive

This position involves coordinating the work of the creative department, which converts the client's original intentions into a visual form for approval. Others, including copywriters, may elaborate upon this.

Artist

Agency artists prepare initial visual layouts of adverts, posters and displays, and produce final artwork for printing. They increasingly need competence in using design software.

Qualifications and Training

A number of universities offer degrees and HNDs in advertising and marketing which provide a useful background, but don't guarantee entry to a job in advertising. The Communication, Advertising and Marketing (CAM) Education Foundation runs certificate and diploma courses which provide the opportunity to specialise in areas such as marketing, advertising and public relations. Minimum entry requirements for the certificate are two A levels or equivalent. Business studies graduates and holders of a diploma in management or business studies may be exempt from the certificate. The diploma may be completed in one year by candidates who hold the certificate. It covers international, industrial and consumer advertising and marketing. Creative staff generally have a degree or HND in art and design.

Personal Qualities

Advertising account and media executives need to be persuasive, critical, enthusiastic, confident, well organised and able to get on well with the public. They need drive and stamina and considerable business acumen. Creative staff require imagination and ingenuity in order to express ideas and concepts accurately and economically, emphasizing the most important aspects of a product. Copy- and scriptwriters must have a flair for writing and communication.

Starting Salary

Trainees' salaries are £12,500+; experienced staff may earn very high salaries.

Advertising Association, Abford House, 15 Wilton Road, London SW1V 1NJ; 020 7828 2771; www.adassoc.org.uk; e-mail: aa@adassoc.org.uk (The AA's career guide 'Getting into Advertising' is only available from their Web site in the Information Centre section)

CAM Foundation Ltd Communications and Marketing Education Foundation Limited, Moor Hall, Cookham, Maidenhead, Berkshire SL6 9QH; 01628 427; www.camfoundation.com; e-mail: info@camfoundation.com

Institute of Practitioners in Advertising, 44 Belgrave Square, London SW1X 8QS; 020 7235 7020; www.ipa.co.uk

Careers in Marketing, Advertising and Public Relations (Kogan Page)
How to Get On in Marketing (Kogan Page)

ADVOCATE

see *Barrister/Advocate*

AERIAL ERECTOR

Aerial erectors fix aerials to roof structures along with the necessary cabling to feed televisions, VCRs and radio receivers. With the extension of broadcasting methods and the growth of multi-channel viewing, many installers offer cable and satellite dish alongside normal aerial installation. A number of businesses specialise in satellite dish as well as communication aerial installation.

Qualifications and Training

Formal qualifications are not necessary as training is often given on the job by experienced colleagues. Formal training is given in all aspects of aerial and satellite installation through the Confederation of Aerial Industries Ltd (CAI). The ability to drive is an advantage.

Personal Qualities

A head for heights plus the ability to work in a confined space (aerials and the relevant cabling are sometimes installed in lofts) is essential, as is good colour vision. As all the work takes place in customers' homes, it is necessary to be pleasant and polite.

Starting Salary

Low when training, varying according to experience and whether working in a firm. The majority of aerial installers are self-employed, sometimes working on a subcontract basis to establish a steady income.

i

Confederation of Aerial Industries Ltd (CAI), Fulton House Business Centre, Fulton Road, Wembley Park, Middlesex HA9 0TF; 020 8902 8998; www.cai.org.uk
Local Jobcentres and Careers/Connexions Centres

AERONAUTICAL ENGINEERING

see *Engineering*

AGENT, LITERARY

see *Literary Agent*

AGENT, THEATRICAL

see *Theatre*

AGRICULTURAL CONTRACTOR

Agricultural contractors employ experienced workers and managers to provide specific help to farmers at certain times of the year. About 60 per cent of farms use contractors from time to time.

Qualifications and Training

While qualifications are not essential, NVQs are available in relevant subjects. These, together with certificates at national or advanced national level in agriculture or agricultural contracting, from a college of agriculture, improve chances of finding employment.

Personal Qualities

Agricultural contractors must have an appreciation of farmers' needs, combined with efficiency, reliability and a good business sense.

Starting Salary

Variable, depending on whether or not the contractor is an employee or running his or her own concern, and the size of the operation.

Careers, Education and Training in Agriculture and the Countryside, Warwickshire Careers Service, 10 Northgate Street, Warwick CV34 4SR; 01926 401300

Lantra Connect, Lantra House, NAC, Kenilworth, Warwickshire, CV8 2LG; 0845 707 8007 (Lantra Connect – Helpline); www.lantra.co.uk; e-mail: connect@lantra.co.uk

AGRICULTURAL ENGINEERING

see *Engineering*

AGRICULTURAL SURVEYING

see *Surveyor/Surveying Technician*

AGRICULTURE

see *Farming*

AMBULANCE SERVICE

Most of the work in the ambulance service is directly with patients, providing pre-hospital care and transportation in response to emergency and urgent calls or providing transport for those unable, for medical reasons, to make their own way to hospital. There are two distinct areas of front-line work: Accident and Emergency and Patient Transport Services.

Ambulance Care Assistants

Ambulance care assistants are mainly concerned with transporting elderly, infirm or handicapped people to hospital. They work within Patient Transport Services (PTS) and are mainly involved in routine transportation work. Such work does not involve emergency duties but staff are trained in Basic Life Support Skills, First Aid and Patient Care. Staff may also work in hospital units.

Ambulance Paramedics

Paramedics are trained to use advanced life support techniques and administer a range of drugs for the emergency treatment of a number of conditions. In order for paramedics to maintain their qualification, they must update their skills regularly and prove their competence through examination, and are only allowed to practise if they are state registered. They must comply with Council for Professions Supplementary to Medicine (CPSM) regulations. There has to be a paramedic on each emergency ambulance.

Ambulance Technicians

Ambulance technicians work alongside paramedics responding to 999 and urgent calls. They make decisions on the treatment and transportation of ill and injured patients. Their work involves a wide range of skills, including resuscitation, oxygen and some drug therapy, fracture splintage, wound dressing and pain relief.

The type of work undertaken by both technicians and paramedics is varied and demanding. Both paramedics and technicians are trained in advanced driving skills and may work in ambulance motor vehicles, air ambulances or on motorcycles.

Emergency Medical Dispatcher

Emergency medical dispatchers work in central control rooms answering calls from GPs and the public and ensuring that resources are deployed effectively and efficiently. Some ambulance services run a despatch prioritizing system for emergency calls that are analysed and placed in order of priority. When a caller gives information about a life-threatening situation, staff give advice over the phone while the ambulance travels to the scene.

Ambulance Control and Communication staff requirements vary among ambulance services, although most require a good general standard of education. Control staff can move to ambulance duties providing they meet the entry requirements and successfully complete the selection process.

Qualifications and Training

Ambulance care assistants need to be over 18 years of age and to have had a full current UK driving licence for at least one year and often two. Some ambulance services simply require a good standard of education while others specify GCSEs or equivalent, including English and maths. Selection includes a medical assessment to ascertain that they are physically fit with good eyesight. Training takes up to three weeks, covering moving and handling techniques, first aid, basic patient care skills and safe driving techniques.

Technicians must meet the minimum ambulance care assistant requirements, although frequently services will require higher academic qualifications. Some services allow for direct entry technicians and others recruit internally from the ambulance care assistant grade. Technicians spend up to three weeks on an intensive driving course followed by six to nine weeks training in prehospital emergency care. This includes regular examinations and assessments. They then work under supervision for up to a year gaining experience completing competency assessments.

Paramedics must have at least one year of experience as a technician and then pass written and practical examinations. Intensive training lasts ten to twelve weeks. Technicians and paramedics are required to attend regular training and reassessment. Paramedics re-qualify every three years.

Control and Communication staff requirements vary among services; most require a good general standard of education. Control staff can move to ambulance duties providing they meet the entry requirements and successfully complete the selection process.

Personal Qualities

Ambulance personnel must be honest, show initiative, have good people skills, a caring personality and be prepared to work with all types of people. They have to be well organised and work well as part of a team, though able to make their own decisions when necessary. They must stay calm under pressure and be good communicators. Physical fitness is essential as staff regularly lift patients and equipment.

Technicians and paramedics require a high level of technical knowledge, a cool head in emergencies and the manual dexterity to carry out treatment in awkward conditions. Paramedics need to cope with advanced theoretical studies and be able to apply clinical judgement in emergencies.

Control and Communication staff need strong powers of concentration because calls involve assimilating a lot of information quickly and making decisions rapidly. They must be able to take clear notes and operate high technology equipment.

Starting Salary

The full-time pay for a qualified ambulance care assistant ranges from approximately £9,000 to £12,500 per year. Ambulance technicians earn a basic salary of around £17,500 when they are fully qualified and ambulance paramedics earn approximately £18,500.

i

Recruitment is managed by individual ambulance services which are listed in phone directories. Details are also available from the Ambulance Service Association.

Ambulance Service Association, Friars House, 157–168 Blackfriars Road, London SE1 8EU; 020 7928 9620; fax: 020 7928 9502; www.asa.uk.net

The Council for Professions Supplementary to Medicine, Park House, 184 Kennington Park Road, London SE11 4BU; 020 7582 0866; www.cpsm.org.uk (This will be replaced by the Health Professions Council in mid-2002)

ANALYST

see *Chemist*

ANIMAL NURSING AUXILIARY

see *Veterinary Nurse*

ANIMAL TECHNICIAN

Animal technicians are a specialised and distinct group of professionals who are responsible for the care and welfare of animals used in biomedical research. Governments around the world require that new medicines have been extensively tested on animals before allowing human clinical trials. Testing is also undertaken on veterinary medicines and other products which may have an effect on human health. Animal technicians are responsible for caring for the animals, undertaking observations, sampling for the scientific studies, and ensuring that the strict laws controlling their use are followed at all times. Applicants should have a genuine desire to work with animals and must demonstrate concern and respect for their well-being.

Qualifications and Training
Minimum requirements are four GCSEs, grades A to D, or equivalents. The subjects should include English, maths and biology, or two science subjects. Training includes in-house, day release and special seminars. Trainees may work towards the Certificate in Animal Technology (one year), the Membership diploma (two years), or the Fellowship diploma (five years). Edexcel/BTEC offer First, Ordinary and Higher National Certificates in Animal Technology.

Personal Qualities
The job requires people who have a genuine desire to work with animals and can handle them with confidence, care and concern. They must have a committed interest in animal welfare and an understanding of the requirements of scientific studies. Since the job requires close observation of the animals and accurate record keeping, the ability to give careful attention to detail is important.

Starting Salary
First-year trainee, £8,000–£12,000.

The Institute of Animal Technology, 5 South Parade, Summertown, Oxford OX2 7JL; www.iat.org.uk
The Association of the British Pharmaceutical Industry, 12 Whitehall, London SW1A 2DY; 020 7930 3477; www.abpi.org.uk
Universities Federation for Animal Welfare (UFAW), The Old School, Brewhouse Hill, Wheathampstead, Hertfordshire AL4 8AN; 01582 831818; www.ufaw.org.uk
Careers Working with Animals (Kogan Page)

ANTHROPOLOGIST

Anthropologists study the development of human societies, making comparisons between different communities and cultures. This academic discipline is linked with the other social sciences and with evolutionary biology. Much of the work still concerns non-industrial, 'primitive' or rural cultures, but changes brought about by contact with more sophisticated outside influences and pressures from 'modern' societies are an important aspect of study, and many anthropologists now undertake research in urban or industrial societies. The career involves a combination of research, teaching and finding out more about the people being studied by going to live with them over a period of time.

Increasingly, anthropologists are finding employment as consultants, for instance in the development, health and humanitarian fields and in such professions as journalism, human resource management, planning, tourism and heritage, museum curatorship and medicine.

Qualifications and Training
A good degree in anthropology. Postgraduate study is usually required.

Personal Qualities
Those wishing to embark on this career must normally be committed to an academic way of life, although there is growing demand outside universities. Field researchers must be prepared to spend long spells abroad, often in basic conditions. Physical and mental stamina is required, as well as independence and resourcefulness. Anthropologists must be prepared to work on their own. However, as anthropology has diversified, so the ways of working life adopted by anthropologists have become more varied too, and they now work in every imaginable setting, from offices and day-care centres to out in the field. Linguistic ability is useful.

Starting Salary
Salaries are variable, depending on the path chosen.

i

The Royal Anthropoligical Institute, 50 Fitzroy Street, London W1T 5BT; 020 7387 0455; fax: 020 7383 4235; www.therai.org.uk

ANTIQUE DEALER

The buying and selling of antiques for profit entails expert knowledge of the field, combined with sound managerial and business sense. Comparatively few people make a living at this trade and many businesses are family concerns. Dealers frequently specialise in particular types of antiques and trade among themselves as well as with private buyers and sellers. Dealers may sell from shops, antiques markets, antiques fairs and from home. An increasing number trade on the Internet using auction sites such as Ebay as well as their own Web sites.

Qualifications and Training

No specific qualifications are required, although a broad artistic background may be useful. The accepted route into the business is via a job with an established antique dealer, which provides an opportunity for learning the trade.

Personal Qualities

A good memory for detail, in order to acquire the expertise required, and good business acumen are necessary.

Starting Salary

Salaries vary; most dealers are self-employed.

British Antique Dealers' Association, 20 Rutland Gate, London
    SW7 1BD; 020 7589 4128; www.bada.org;
    e-mail: enquiry@ bada.demon.co.uk

ARBORICULTURIST

see *Horticulturist*

ARCHAEOLOGICAL SURVEYING

see *Surveyor/Surveying Technician*

ARCHAEOLOGIST

Archaeology – building up a picture of the past – is both an art and a science. Archaeologists use highly technical and scientific methods of discovery, analysis and identification to reconstruct and study men and women from the past using their material remains. The evidence is collected through fieldwork, including excavations, where clues are sought in objects, their sur- roundings, the ground itself and remains of living things. The evidence is analysed, subjected to experiment, assessed, identified, catalogued, conserved and possibly exhibited. Archaeologists usually specialise in a particular period, tech- nique or geographical area. Opportunities for full-time, perman- ent positions are limited, consequently competition is fierce for the few jobs available. These are to be found in central and local government, museums and universities, independent units and trusts, as well as a variety of positions in commercial opera- tions. Job availability is closely related to the building and devel- opment work. Some work includes the opportunity to spend time abroad.

Qualifications and Training

A good honours degree in archaeology is necessary for a position as a qualified archaeologist. Practical experience of archaeological fieldwork is advantageous.

A postgraduate qualification is becoming the norm for anyone hopeful of getting a permanent or long-term post without going through many years of short contract work, which can often mean week-to-week contracts.

The conservation of archaeological, historical and ethnographic - al artefacts requires a specialist training of its own. A Diploma in Conservation is offered by the Institute of Archaeology on a block- or day-release scheme. Degrees in conservation are also available. Those wishing to work in professional archaeology will increasingly be expected to be members of The Institute of Field Archaeologists.

Archaeological science also holds opportunities: bioarchae- ology is the study of animal and plant remains – bones, teeth, grain – found on an archaeological site; materials science allows precise dating of artefacts; geoarchaeology is the study of sedi- ments deposited on a site; forensic archaeology involves the use of archaeological techniques in police investigations.

Personal Qualities

Archaeologists need endless patience. They must pay great attention to detail, and have imagination and an enquiring mind. They must be able to use computers, write reports, plan and administer, work as a team with other academic experts and get on well with their workforce. Languages are useful, as is an ability to negotiate, and a talent for drawing or photography. Archaeologists should be healthy and willing to work in all conditions, situations and environments.

Starting Salary

£11,800–£17,500 for salaried posts; less for short contracts.

i

Council for British Archaeology (CBA), Bowes Morrell House, 111 Walmgate, York YO1 2UA; 01904 671417; www.britarch.ac.uk; e-mail: info@britarch.ac.uk

Training Online Resource Centre for Archaeology (TORC); www.torc.org.uk (This information service from the CBA and English Heritage includes a database of courses and provides fact sheets on learning, training and gaining experience in archaeology.)

The Institute of Field Archaeologists, University of Reading, 2 Earley Gate, PO Box 239, Reading RG6 6AU; www.archaeologists.net; admin.ifa@virgin.net

ARCHITECT

Architecture is a profession requiring the practical combination of imaginative design with scientific and technological principles, to produce designs for new buildings and for the extension, or renovation, of those already existing. In the first instance, conceptual design is based on information supplied by the client on the function of the building, the proposed budget and the site. When the design is agreed, working drawings are produced for the builder. These show dimensions, materials and how everything will be put together. On large jobs there will be a team of architects working with engineers and other specialists and it may take months to prepare all the drawings and schedules. Alternatively, very small jobs take only a few weeks. After the contract documents have been prepared and a builder selected, work begins on the site.

   The architect visits frequently as the building goes up. This can involve tramping around in boots and a hard hat, climbing up and down ladders as well as taking the chair at site meetings. Opportunities exist for employment in private practice, with local authorities, in research, teaching, central government and some industrial organizations. The use of computer-aided design packages now plays a significant part in the work of architects.

Qualifications and Training

Candidates should have passes in at least two subjects at A level or one A level and two AS levels, together with passes in at least five other subjects at GCSE level. Subjects should be drawn from academic fields of study and include maths, English language and a separate science (physics or chemistry), or a double certification in science. Training takes a minimum of seven years, but only five of those are spent at a school of architecture. After a three-year degree course, students spend a year in an architect's office. Students often work abroad during this year or work in other parts of the building industry. Another two years' further study to obtain a diploma or higher degree are followed by a further year of working in an office, ending with a professional practice exam to become registered as an architect with the Architects' Registration Board and a corporate member of the RIBA. This allows the use of the title Architect in business. Part-time training is an alternative offered by a few schools for students already working in an architect's office on a day-release basis. Membership of the Royal Institute of British Architects (RIBA) and Royal Incorporation of Architects, Scotland (RIAS) is open to students while studying and also to those who are fully qualified.

Personal Qualities

Architects must have artistic ability and be imaginative, but at the same time need to be able to understand and apply technical information. They must adopt a practical approach to their work and be able to communicate their ideas and instructions to a variety of people. Business acumen, a professional approach, discretion and willingness to conform to a strict code of conduct are very important.

Starting Salary

While completing their two years' practical training, architectural students may expect to earn between £12,000 and £16,000; when fully registered this will increase to about £21,000, and thereafter be dependent upon position, experience and employer. £32,000 is the average.

Royal Institute of British Architects (RIBA), Public Information Line, 66 Portland Place, London W1B 1AD; 0906 302 0400 (calls cost 50p per minute); www.architecture.com (There is a comprehensive careers section on this Web site.)

The Architects' Registration Board (ARB), 8 Weymouth Street, London W1N 3FB; 020 7580 5861; www.arb.org.uk

Royal Incorporation of Architects in Scotland (RIAS), 15 Rutland Square, Edinburgh EH1 2BE; 0131 229 7545; www.rias.org.uk

Careers in Architecture (Kogan Page)

ARCHITECTURAL TECHNOLOGIST

Architectural technologists work alongside architects and other professionals as part of the building design and construction team. Technologists can negotiate the construction project from inception to completion. Specific, specialist skills could include surveying land and buildings, preparing and undertaking feasibility studies, presenting design solutions, analysing and detailing drawings, managing and applying computer-aided design (CAD) techniques.

Qualifications and Training

A degree in architectural technology, an HNC/HND in Building Studies (with specific additional units) or an NVQ level 4 in Architectural Technology lead to Associate Membership of British Institute of Architectural Technologists (BIAT) and the designation ABIAT.

Personal Qualities

Architectural technologists should be able to work both as part of a team and on their own initiative. Attention to detail is necessary, as is the ability to take account of other professionals' needs. Effective communication skills are necessary when working as part of the team, liaising with clients or tendering for contracts and they should feel comfortable with new technology and innovative concepts.

Starting Salary
Junior technologists, £8,000–£10,000; qualified technologists with three years' experience, £12,500–£14,000; senior technologists with appropriate educational qualifications and ten years' experience, up to £22,000.

British Institute of Architectural Technologists (BIAT), 397 City Road, London EC1V 1NH; 020 7278 2206; Freephone (UK only) 0800 731 5471; www.biat.org.uk; e-mail: careers@biat.org.uk
Careers in Architecture (Kogan Page)

ARCHIVIST

In the course of business lots of organizations and people create or collect archives. These include government agencies, local authorities, universities, hospitals, businesses, charities, professional organizations and families and individuals. Archives may be books or papers, maps or plans, photographs or prints, films or videos, or computer-generated records. Archives are intended to be kept permanently, to preserve the past and allow others to discover it.

It is the job of the archivist to preserve and exploit this archival heritage and the information contained within it. This includes assisting visitors or users, promotional work including exhibitions, presentations or media liaison, as well as the curatorial skills of selecting archives for preservation and interpreting them for archive users.

Qualifications and Training
This is a small profession, requiring a strong academic background. Entrants should have a good degree and an interest in heritage and information management and good customer service skills. The recognised qualification is a postgraduate Diploma/ MA, usually taken as a one-year full-time course at one of five universities in the UK and Ireland.

The Society of Archivists also offers an in-service diploma to graduates who are currently employed in archives or records management. Competition for places on these courses is fierce and substantial practical paid or voluntary experience is required for applications to be successful. Lists of graduate placements are kept by the Society of Archivists' Training Officer and, in addition, many local archives are also prepared to accommodate occasional volunteers interested in a career in archives.

Personal Qualities

Archivists must be good communicators, able to relate to and encourage a wide variety of people. They must also be ready to accept and exploit the technological advances, which will continue to have a profound effect on demands for and use of information. A logical mind is essential for identifying and sorting archives before they can be effectively interpreted or used and, although archivists are not researchers, an understanding of research skills is helpful in all aspects of their work, particularly advising users. Archivists need to be prepared to continue their development after qualification, acquiring management, budgetary and other relevant skills.

Starting Salary

£15,000+.

Society of Archivists, 40 Northampton Road, London, EC1R 0HB; www.archives.org.uk

ARMY

The Army is the largest of the three armed forces and offers a wide range of opportunities to men and women, both in the UK and abroad. Regiments and corps provide opportunities in the Armoured Corps, Royal Artillery, Royal Engineers, Royal Signals, Infantry, Army Air Corps, Royal Logistics Corps, Military Police, in pay and administration, teaching, catering and for qualified doctors, dentists, vets, lawyers and chaplains.

Qualifications and Training

Officers
Officer recruits are normally aged 18–29 and of graduate calibre. The Army recruits graduates from all disciplines to all areas of the Army. All officers are awarded an initial three-year Short Service Commission (SSC) on commissioning from Sandhurst and this is the minimum length of commitment. An SSC can be extended up to a maximum of eight years. After two years' SSC service officers can apply to convert to an Intermediate Regular Commission (IRC), which provides up to 16 years' service. After two years' IRC service, officers can apply to convert to a Regular Commission, which provides service up to the age of 55.

Sponsorship
Cadetships and bursaries are available for those studying for a recognised first degree. All successful applicants complete 11 months' officer training at the Royal Military Academy, Sandhurst.

Soldiers and Servicewomen
Eligibility is determined by the results achieved on the Army Entrance Test (known as BARB). This assesses an applicant's ability for training by using computer touch-screen question and answer techniques. Entry is from age 16 to 30. Recruits usually enlist on an open engagement by which they agree to serve for 22 years, although it is possible to leave after a minimum of four years' service provided a year's notice is given.

Personal Qualities
Applicants must be British or Commonwealth citizens, born of British or Commonwealth parents and have been resident in the UK for the past five years. All candidates must be medically fit, intelligent, have the ability to work in a team and show dedication, courage, patriotism and a sense of responsibility.

Starting Salary
Soldiers, 16–17½, £8,000; over 17½, £10,344. Officers, £22,597.

The Army Recruiting Group, FREEPOST 4335, Bristol BS1 3YX;
08457 300 111; www.army.mod.uk
Local Army Career Information Offices

ART THERAPIST

Art therapy is used as a treatment for psychological and
emotional disorders. Drawing, painting, modelling and sculpture
are among the creative activities employed. Art therapy is a State
Registered Profession. All training courses need to be approved
by The Council for Professions Supplementary to Medicine
(CPSM) and the British Association of Art Therapy. Details are on
the CPSM Web site.

Most art therapists work in hospitals, some in special schools
and child guidance clinics and some in prisons, detention centres
and community homes. As posts are often part-time, therapists
usually work for more than one institution within an area.

Qualifications and Training

Entry to postgraduate courses requires a degree in art and design or
related subject, one years' clinical experience and a minimum age of
23. Candidates without a degree but with relevant working backgrounds are also considered. The postgraduate qualification is
usually a two-year full-time course or a three-year part-time course.

Personal Qualities

Art therapists should have the ability to apply art in a practical
way, together with a great deal of patience and the maturity to
work with people in emotional or psychological need. A background in art practice is also necessary.

Starting Salary

Salaries vary greatly according to the place of employment, but
start at around £17,000.

British Association of Art Therapists, Mary Ward House, 5
Tavistock Place, London WC1H 9SN; 020 7383 3774;
www.baat.co.uk

The Council for Professions Supplementary to Medicine, Park House, 184 Kennington Park Road, London SE11 4BU; 020 7582 0866; www.cpsm.org.uk (This will be replaced by The Health Professions Council in mid-2002)
Careers in Art and Design (Kogan Page)

ARTIST

(see also *Advertising, Interior Decorator, Interior Designer, Teacher*)

Only a very few artists are able to earn a living solely by the sale to clients of original work. Many more work as designers in advertising, industry and publishing, the latter also offering opportunities for illustrators, particularly for covers and jackets of children's books, or teach art in a school or college. Design work includes graphic design concerned with display, lettering, packaging – all aspects of visual communication; fashion and textile design; environmental design – office and shop interiors as well as some museums and galleries; interior design; and product design – the appearance of equipment such as televisions, cars and also more scientific apparatus.

There are limited opportunities for work as a community artist, community arts officer (encouraging art in the community) and artist-in-residence.

Qualifications and Training
For the majority of artists, academic qualifications are necessary. These range from two-year diploma courses for 16-year-olds with some GCSEs or equivalents, to degrees. Many degree courses require the completion of a one-year Foundation course. A portfolio of work is normally required alongside academic qualifications for entry to art-related courses. Art teachers require appropriate teaching qualifications; *see also* Teaching.

Personal Qualities
The qualities required vary according to the work undertaken. Creativity, talent and imagination are all important, as well as enthusiasm and, in some cases, the ability to work as part of a team and to meet deadlines.

Starting Salary
Designers, £13,000+. Teachers' salaries start at over £16,000.

i

National Society for Education in Art and Design (NSEAD), The
    Gatehouse, Corsham Court, Wiltshire SN13 OBZ; 01249
    714825; www.nsead.org
Design Council, 34 Bow Street, London WC2E 7DL; 020 7420 5200;
    www.designcouncil.org.uk and
    www.yourcreativefuture.org.uk;
    e-mail: info@designcouncil.org.uk
Careers in Art and Design (Kogan Page)

ARTS ADMINISTRATION

This is the administration and management of theatres, orches-
tras, opera houses, ballet companies and arts centres. The Arts
Council, responsible for the promotion of art throughout the
country, has its own administrative staff. The British Council,
responsible for displaying British arts abroad, also employs a
small number of staff.

Qualifications and Training
Experience is often more important than formal qualifications,
although a good general education is expected; many entrants are
graduates. Commercial awareness plus a knowledge of and interest in the arts is essential. Postgraduate courses such as an MA in
Arts Administration can be studied part- or full-time.

Personal Qualities
The ability to communicate and to get on with people is vital.
Practical administrative and organizational skills are also
required.

Starting Salary
£11,000–£15,000.

i

The Arts Council, 14 Great Peter Street, London SW1P 3NQ; 020
7333 0100; www.artscouncil.org.uk

Scottish Arts Council, 12 Manor Place, Edinburgh EH3 7DD; 0131
226 6051; www.sac.org.uk

Arts Marketing Association, 7a Clifton Court, Clifton Road,
Cambridge CB1 7BN; 01223 578078; fax: 01223 578079;
www.a-m-a.co.uk; e-mail: info@a-m-a.co.uk

ASTRONOMER

Astronomers study the sun, planets, stars, galaxies and other
objects in the sky, analysing the radio, infrared, optical, ultraviolet, X- and gamma-radiations they emit to find out how they
work. Some of these radiations do not penetrate the earth's atmosphere, so observations by satellite are necessary as well as from
the ground. Modern astronomical detectors are usually based on
electronic methods and give results which can be analysed by
computer.

Qualifications and Training

To become a research astronomer, a good degree in physics or
maths is necessary and it is possible to do degrees in astronomy or
astrophysics. This is normally followed by postgraduate study
and research. Various grants are available to support students
undertaking such courses.

Astronomy-related careers at an engineering or technical level
are also open to those with skills in applied physics, electronics,
computer hardware and software, optics and mechanical
engineering.

Personal Qualities

Astronomers need curiosity and imagination; they must be able to
make logical deductions from the available observations.
Working long and unusual hours and travelling to remote obser-
vatories may also be involved.

Starting Salary

Post-doctoral salaries start at around £18,000; technical salaries after training are around £15,500–£22,000, depending on qualifications.

The Library, Royal Astronomical Society, Burlington House, Piccadilly, London W1V 0NL; 020 7734 3307; www.ras.org.uk; e-mail: info@ras.org.uk

Public Information Officer, Royal Observatory Greenwich, National Maritime Museum, London SE10 9NF; 020 8312 6735; fax: 020 8312 6734; www.rog.nmm.ac.uk

AUCTIONEER

(see also *Estate Agent, Valuer*)

The auctioneer's work involves the sale by auction of property of all kinds, including buildings (houses, farms and estates), livestock, and goods such as furniture, antiques, paintings, glass, toys, carpets and china. The work also entails valuations for various purposes, including investment and insurance.

Qualifications and Training

An auctioneer's work involves the valuation of land and property, so surveying or valuation qualifications are necessary.

There are two components to qualifying as a Chartered Surveyor or Valuer. First, successful completion of a Royal Institution of Chartered Surveyors (RICS) accredited degree or diploma, followed by enrolment onto the Assessment of Professional Competence (APC). This is two years' practical training while in employment, finishing with an RICS professional assessment interview. One-year full-time and two-year part-time postgraduate conversion courses are also available.

Personal Qualities

Attention to detail is important for this job, together with a practical attitude and an aptitude for figures. In fine-art auctioneering, a certain flair and the ability to distinguish a fake from the genuine article are desirable.

Starting Salary
Trainees starting at 18, £8,000–£9,000; graduates with relevant degrees, £11,000–£13,800 rising to £19,000+ or higher in London.

The Royal Institution of Chartered Surveyors, 12 Great George Street, London SW1P 3AD; 020 7222 7000; www.rics.org.uk/afa

AUDIO ASSISTANT

see *Broadcasting*

AUDIOLOGY TECHNICIANS

Audiology technicians carry out tests to assess the presence, nature and extent of a hearing loss, using complex and advanced techniques. They take aural impressions for individual moulded ear inserts, fit and instruct the patients on how to use hearing aids, and review their progress.

Qualifications and Training
Four GCSEs at C grade or equivalent, in English, maths, physics and another science, and two A levels, one of which must be a science. Training involves two years of combined theory and practice while in employment, leading to an Edexcel (BTEC) qualification in medical physics and physiological measurement, or NVQ equivalent.

Personal Qualities
Candidates must be patient, have a clear speaking voice and the ability to get on with people.

Starting Salary
Trainee £8,000+. Once qualified, depending on grade, £10,000–£30,000+.

i

British Society of Audiology, 80 Brighton Road, Reading RG6 1PS; 0118 966 0622; fax: 0118 935 1915; www.b-s-a.demon.co.uk

British Society of Hearing Aid Audiologists, Bridle Croft, Burgh Heath Road, Epsom KT17 4LF; 01372 725348; www.bshaa. co.uk

AUDITOR

see *Accountant*

BAKER

The baking trainee learns the skills involved in the production of a wide variety of bread and confectionery. Master bakers have traditionally provided an ideal environment in which to acquire craft skills. Hours of work can be unsocial, with shifts or early starts.

Trainees can also enter the industry by working for a large manufacturing plant bakery or in-store bakeries in supermarkets. Opportunities in supermarkets have increased considerably over recent years. Plant bakeries can teach mass-production techniques, with the operation of highly sophisticated, though usually automated, equipment. In addition, many organizations employ research and quality control staff.

Qualifications and Training

No formal educational qualifications are required to enter the trade but GCSE grade C in English, maths and a science such as food technology are advantageous. Both large and small firms often operate schemes by which trainees can attend their local bakery college or train in the workplace for NVQs in Craft Baking at levels 2 and 3. Work-based training is becoming more common. Plant bakers would normally work towards NVQs in Food and Drink Manufacturing Operations. Modern Apprenticeships are available in craft baking and bakery service. Details of these and colleges that offer BTEC National Diploma in Science (Baking Technology) and SQA Scottish National Certificate in Craft Baking can be obtained from Anglo Welsh Bakery Training.

The University of Wales Institute at Cardiff and Thomas Danby College in Leeds offer full-time HNDs in Baking.

Personal Qualities

Willingness to learn the craft and the ability to work in a team, with an above-average concern for cleanliness and hygiene.

Starting Salary

New trainees start at around £7,600 a year, experienced bakers earn £10,700– £20,000 with extra pay for shift work and overtime.

Anglo Welsh Bakery Training, 21 Baldock St, Ware, Herts SG12 9DH; 01920 468061; fax: 01920 461632; www.masterbakers.co.uk
Scottish Association of Master Bakers, Atholl House, 4 Torphichen St, Edinburgh EH3 8JQ; 0131 229 1401; fax: 0131 229 8239
Federation of Bakers, 6 Catherine St, London WC2B 5JJ; 020 7420 7190; www.bakersfederation.org.uk

BALLET

see *Dancing*

BANKING

Banks provide a delivery point for financial services. The most obvious side of banking is the high-street branches but other work includes: international banking (financing foreign trade and providing an overseas banking service for UK customers); corporate finance (dealing with the requirements of large companies); human resources, recruitment, training and staff development; insurance; computer services; marketing; training; and trust work (when a bank is appointed as executor or joint executor of a will).

The recent reduction in the number of bank branches and the growth in Internet and telephone banking is a trend that is expected to continue, with more opportunities being offered in bank call centres.

High Street or Clearing Banks

They provide a financial service for customers, including maintaining accounts, making payments and arranging personal loans and mortgages. They also undertake the safe custody of valuables and act as executors and trustees of wills. The work involves: general office work, such as dealing with telephone enquiries, using computer systems, cashier work at the counter and foreign and securities work. Sales skills are also required to promote a range of other products such as credit cards. Specialization may take place in areas such as investment, computer operations, international sevices, personnel and marketing. Working for a British bank abroad, or for an overseas bank in London, requires specialization in international business, finance, and development projects. The ability to speak one or more languages is useful.

The Bank of England

This is the banker to the government. It is concerned with the financial structure of Great Britain, with other banks in the country and with operating accounts for overseas central banks. The Bank of England is responsible for the printing, issue and withdrawal of British banknotes and it also controls interest rates and raises short-term government finance. The monitoring of economic developments at home and abroad provides informa-tion for the Bank, the Treasury and other government depart-ments. It does not offer banking facilities to the general public. Specialists such as economists, statisticians and librarians are recruited in addition to other banking staff.

Investment Banks

These are generally financial houses, which started from trading as merchants and have expanded their role to financing the trading and commercial activities of others, especially in the inter-national marketplace. An investment banking group nowadays includes the following services for its clients: corporate finance and advisory work, banking for governments, institutions and companies, investment management and securities trading.

Qualifications and Training

Each bank has different entry points, recruiting school leavers after GCSEs and A levels as well as graduates. Structured training programmes often provide access to qualifications of the Institute of Financial Services in England and Wales or Chartered Institute of Bankers in Scotland (CIOBS). As well as covering traditional areas of banking there are a range of new qualifications such as certificates in Commercial Banking in the Networked World, Capital Markets, and the New Economy and E-Finance.

The Chartered Institute of Bankers in Scotland first-level qualification (The Certificate in Financial Services) requires no previous qualifications for entry. Students completing the certificate can progress to the Associateship and Membership examinations. NVQs level 2–4 in Providing Financial Services are available.

Most banks welcome applications from graduates who have qualified from a range of disciplines such as law, accountancy or business. There are also vacancies for individuals seeking a career in information technology.

Personal Qualities

Accuracy, integrity, good powers of concentration and a clear mind are essential for success in a banking career. It is important to be able to get on with people and to work as a member of a team.

Starting Salary

Salaries are dependent on the job and performance of the individual. Banks operate a job evaluation salary structure and promotion is on merit. Extra allowances are paid in London and some other towns and cities.

Institute of Financial Services, IFS House, 4–9 Burgate Lane, Canterbury, Kent CT1 2XJ; 01227 818609; www.ifslearning. com; e-mail: institute@ifslearning.com

London Investment Banking Association (LIBA), 6 Frederick's Place, London EC2R 8BT; 020 7796 3606; fax: 020 7796 4345; www.liba.org.uk

The Chartered Institute of Bankers in Scotland, Drumsheugh House, 38B Drumsheugh Gardens, Edinburgh EH3 7SW; 0131 473 7777; www.ciobs.org.uk

The Bank of England; www.bankofengland.co.uk (Excellent careers information and access to *The City Handbook* which is only available on the Internet. It provides information on over one hundred and fifty financial organizations mostly in the City of London.)

Careers in Banking and Finance (Kogan Page)

BARRISTER/ADVOCATE

The services of a barrister are required by solicitors (*see also* Solicitor), who deal with the clients and then 'brief' the barrister. Barristers plead counsel in the higher courts and may also appear in the lower courts, where they usually begin their careers. They give specialised advice on the law and may advertise their services to the public. Some are employed in the Army Legal Services, giving advice on all aspects of service and civil law that may affect the Army.

In Scotland, an advocate is the equivalent of a barrister. Advocates may not select their clients. Provided that a reasonable fee is tendered they may not, without good cause, refuse instructions to act in litigation. Advocates also work in the public sector, Crown Prosecution Service, the legal section of a government department or as parliamentary draftsmen.

Qualifications and Training

Full details of qualifications required for admission are available from the General Council of the Bar, but generally students are expected to hold a UK law degree with second class honours or better, or a non-law degree at the same standard plus a pass in a special one-year course known as the Common Professional Examination/Postgraduate Diploma in Law.

Every intending barrister must join one of the four Inns of Court. Students intending to practise must also attend a one-year full-time vocational course. A list of institutions offering this is available from the Bar Council. This is followed by a one-year pupillage under the personal instruction and guidance of a barrister. Pupillage may involve researching relevant details of a case, setting them out in detail and drafting documents. During the first six months, pupils may attend court but may not accept briefs.

After completing pupillage a barrister has to find a 'seat' in an existing set of barristers' chambers. Some may choose to work as employed barristers and enter the Civil Service, local government or commerce and industry. About 15 years after being established at the Bar, a barrister may apply for a 'patent' as a Queen's Counsel. Although 'taking silk' (as it is known) is usual (but not obligatory) if a barrister wishes to become a High Court Judge, it can have financial penalties and some barristers stay 'juniors' throughout their career at the Bar.

Full details of the qualifications and training required for advocacy in Scotland are available from the Clerk of Faculty. Generally speaking, applicants require a Scottish law degree with second class honours or better, or a degree in Scottish law together with an Honours degree, second class or better, from a university in the UK in another subject. In addition, they will have obtained a Diploma in Legal Practice from a Scottish university and served at least 12 months' traineeship in a solicitor's office in Scotland.

Personal Qualities

Since the work is confidential, an intending barrister needs to be trustworthy and discreet. An excellent command of the English language, which ensures the meticulous understanding and use of words, is essential. It will be necessary to understand and interpret complex legal wording in clear basic English. Barristers must understand and talk knowledgeably about technical matters in order to be able to cross-examine the most expert witness, for example, on complex aspects of technology. It is also useful if barristers can put on a 'good performance' in court and possess certain theatrical qualities.

Starting Salary

Barristers' earnings relate to the amount and type of their work, their reputation, and, if they share chambers, the apportionment and value of briefs. Barristers may find it a struggle to make a living at the beginning of their profession, but the rewards for those who succeed can be high.

i

General Council of the Bar, 2/3 Cursitor Street, London EC4A 1NE; 020 77440 4000; www.barcouncil.org.uk (Details of training from www.lawzone.co.uk/barcouncil.)

Faculty of Advocates, Advocates Library, Parliament House, 11 Parliament Square, Edinburgh EH1 1RF; 0131 226 5071; www.advocates.org.uk

Careers in the Law (Kogan Page)

BARRISTER'S CLERK/ ADVOCATE'S CLERK

The barrister's clerk is the administrator or manager of the business chambers, deciding which briefs to accept, which of the barristers in the chamber to give them to and negotiating the fees with the solicitor. The accounts, the barristers' appointment books and the efficient day-to-day running of the office are all part of the job of an experienced clerk.

Qualifications and Training

The necessary qualifications are four GCSEs, grades A to C, including maths and English. Training is on the job and juniors can apply through the Institute to attend a two-year part-time Edexcel (BTEC) national certificate course studying organization, finance, management, law, marketing and chambers administration. On obtaining the certificate, juniors may apply, after five years' service, for qualified Membership of the Institute of Barristers' Clerks.

The Bar in Scotland is divided into 10 'stables', each of which is served by an advocate's clerk and a deputy clerk employed by Faculty Services Ltd. Training is provided in service. The job of advocate's clerk is very similar to that of barrister's clerk in England and Wales. Their rates of pay are linked to the Civil Service scale on a level which roughly relates to a comparable post within the courts' administration. The 10 clerks have clerical and secretarial staff back-up.

Personal Qualities

In order to organise efficient chambers and the barristers who work from them, a barrister's clerk needs an orderly mind, the ability to work in a team and to get on with the general public. A good command of written and spoken English and an appreciation of the necessity for absolute confidentiality at all times are vital to success in this career.

Starting Salary

£8,500–£10,000. Juniors with two or three years' experience receive £11,500–£17,000, going up to £27,000 for very experienced juniors. Senior clerks may earn £60,000–£75,000 plus a performance-related bonus. Senior clerks were traditionally paid a fee which was a percentage of the barrister's own earnings. Some are still paid in this way and the fee is usually around 5 per cent.

i

Institute of Barristers' Clerks, 4a Essex Court, Temple, London EC4Y 9AJ; 020 7353 2699; www.instbclerks.org

Faculty Services Ltd, Advocates Library, Parliament House, 11 Parliament Square, Edinburgh EH1 1RF; 0131 226 5071; www.advocates.org.uk / web / fsl1.htm

Careers in the Law (Kogan Page)

BEAUTY THERAPIST

Therapists give treatments ranging from facials, make-up, manicuring and body treatments to electric depilation and waxing and the treatment of skin conditions such as open pores. A fully qualified therapist is capable of using various types of electrical apparatus. Therapists must know when to deal personally with skin complaints and when to refer a client to a doctor. It is usual to treat about eight clients a day in a treatment salon, which may be run by a cosmetic firm, an owner-manager, or occasionally as part of a hairdressing establishment.

Sales Consultant

Working in the perfumery department of a large store, in a luxury hotel at home and overseas, on a big liner or at airports, sales consultants sell and promote their firm's products, answering questions from potential buyers on skin care and make-up. They occasionally give talks at schools and colleges or to women's organizations and may travel for their companies at home and abroad.

Hairdresser/Beauty Therapist

The double qualification gives greater scope for employment, and some may work as make-up artists in radio or television. Some progressive psychiatric hospitals employ hairdressers / beauty therapists in rehabilitation centres and work of this nature plays an important part in treatment and recovery programmes. *See also* Hairdresser.

Qualifications and Training

Educational qualifications vary. The only officially recognised ones are NVQ level 3 Beauty Therapy, or a Modern Apprenticeship in Beauty Therapy, which is a three-year course available for 16–25-year-olds. Although there are no formal entry requirements, in practice GCSEs at grades A-C are often required.

Private schools run courses leading to the award of their own diplomas. Most good courses last from five to six months, although some are longer. Courses lasting a few weeks for sales consultants are usually at schools attached to cosmetic houses; some charge fees which may be refunded after a period of working for the firm. The minimum age is usually 21 and experience in selling is required.

Personal Qualities

A friendly, confident manner combined with a liking for women of all ages, tact and courtesy, good health and a good skin, and a smart and well-groomed appearance are all important. Beauticians need stamina, as they are on their feet for long periods.

Starting Salary

Trainee beauty therapists' earnings are low and later depend upon the number of clients; consultants earn from £7,500 upwards, plus commission on sales. A fully qualified and experienced therapist may earn between £10,000 and £12,000 a year.

Hairdressing And Beauty Industry Authority (HABIA), Fraser House, Nether Hall Road, Doncaster DN1 2PH; 01302 380000; www.habia.org.uk

Local Careers Offices/Connexions Centres and further education colleges

Careers in Hairdressing and Beauty Therapy (Kogan Page)

BIOCHEMIST

Biochemistry is the study of chemical substances and processes in living cells and tissues. Most biochemists work in laboratories;

however, some make their careers in education, or industry, in brewing, food technology, forestry, agriculture, dietetics, pharmaceuticals management and planning.

Many biochemists are employed in hospitals, where they manage and develop the service and carry out research into disease. Pharmaceutical firms also employ biochemists to develop new drugs and study their effects on diseases and patients. Qualified biochemists are also employed in research institutions funded by the Medical Research Council, the National Institute for Medical Research and Biotechnology and Biological Sciences Research Council, as well as some funded by charities such as the Imperial Cancer Research Fund (ICRF).

Laboratory Technician
Universities, Institutes of Higher Education and industry employ technical staff to support the work of scientists in teaching and / or research. In hospitals, technical staff (biomedical scientists) perform much of the analytical work of clinical laboratories, using a variety of manual and automated techniques.

Qualifications and Training
Biochemists entering the professions in universities, hospitals and industry will be graduates, usually with good honours degrees in biochemistry or a related science subject. Laboratory technicians in universities and industry often join with good GCSE passes in mathematics and science subjects, or A levels or equivalent. They will usually study part-time for Edexcel (BTEC) higher certificates in appropriate subjects. Biomedical scientists in hospital laboratories can enter with either degrees (usually an accredited BSc in biomedical science) or A levels, following which they will study part-time for a degree.

Personal Qualities
It is important to be able to work independently or as part of a team in any branch of science. Patience, powers of concentration and meticulous attention to detail are also important.

Starting Salary

Salaries vary with the type of employment and the responsibility involved. Graduates entering the professions as biochemists will start on £12,000–£18,000. Laboratory technicians with good GCSE passes have salaries of £6,000+ and trainee biomedical scientists will start at £11,000+. Additional academic and professional qualifications attained during employment will permit career development and usually lead to positions of greater responsibility with higher salaries.

Association of Clinical Biochemists, 130–132 Tooley Street, London SE1 2TU; 020 7403 8001; www.acb.org.uk

The Education Officer, The Biochemical Society, 59 Portland Place, London W1B 1QW; 020 7580 5530; www.biochemistry.org

The BioIndustry Association, 14–15 Belgrave Square, London SW1X 8PS; 020 7245 9911; www.bioindustry.org

Biotechnology and Biological Sciences Research Council, Polaris House, North Star Avenue, Swindon SN2 1UJ; 01793 413 301; www.bbsrc.ac.uk

A Career for Scientists in Clinical Biochemistry (Association of Clinical Biochemists)

Which Bioscience? (The Biochemical Society)

BIOLOGIST

see *Biochemist, Biomedical Scientist, Biotechnologist*

BIOMEDICAL SCIENTIST

Biomedical scientists (including medical laboratory scientific officers in the NHS) investigate specimens of body fluids and tissues, and play an important role in the diagnosis and treatment of diseases. Most are employed in hospital laboratories and pathology departments, but many also work for the blood transfusion service, in public health laboratories, for veterinary establishments, universities, pharmaceutical and other manufacturing companies. There are sometimes opportunities to assist in research and to teach.

Qualifications and Training

The profession has all-graduate entry. A guide to courses can be obtained from the Institute of Biomedical Science. Trainees in the NHS and related bodies have to proceed to state registration and need a degree to do so.

Personal Qualities

Biomedical scientists must be able to work quickly, accurately and methodically. Complicated and new equipment must be used, so technical as well as scientific ability is needed.

Starting Salary

£11,181–£12,527, depending on qualifications.

Institute of Biomedical Science, 12 Coldbath Square, London EC1R 5HL; 020 7713 0214; www.ibms.org

BIOTECHNOLOGIST

Biotechnology is the application of living organisms and biological systems to industrial processes. Various aspects of biological science are involved – biochemistry, microbiology and genetics. At present, the main industrial areas in which biotechnologists are employed are fermentation, waste-systems management, production of antibiotics, vaccines, hormones, and animal and human food production.

Qualifications and Training

Most new entrants are graduates. Degree entry requirements are a minimum of five GCSEs including maths, plus three A levels or equivalent including biology and chemistry.

Personal Qualities

A high degree of accuracy, thoroughness, lots of patience and the ability to check and recheck details are needed.

Starting Salary

£17,000 upwards for graduates.

The Education Officer, The Biochemical Society, 59 Portland Place, London W1B 1QW; 020 7580 5530; www.biochemistry.org

The BioIndustry Association, 14–15 Belgrave Square, London SW1X 8PS; 020 7245 9911; www.bioindustry.org

Biotechnology and Biological Sciences Research Council, Polaris House, North Star Avenue, Swindon SN2 1UJ; 01793 413 301; www.bbsrc.ac.uk

Institute of Biology, 20–22 Queensberry Place, London SW7 2DZ; 020 7581 8333; www.iob.org

BOOKMAKER

Bookmaking and betting shops can be small independent units or part of an international group of companies operating in the leisure industry. The work is varied, involving counter work and general administration.

Qualifications and Training

Trainee managers need GCSE passes or equivalent in maths and English. Most companies also require applicants to sit an aptitude test as part of the selection procedure. Trainee managers usually start behind the counter at age 21. Promotion follows basic on-the-job training and counter work.

Personal Qualities

Competence in dealing with cash and the general public are necessary.

Starting Salary

Starting salary £10,000 to £15,000.

British Betting Office Association, 5 St Michael's Court, Victoria
  Street, West Bromwich, West Midlands B70 8ET; 0121 525 7428;
  www.bboa.co.uk

BOOKSELLER

In a bookselling career the emphasis is on knowing the product
and being able to sell it. It is important to keep up to date by
reading new books and reviews, in order to assist customers and
to display the books to advantage. The ability to find information
in catalogues and directories, particularly on computer, is essential. Managers order new stock and work to give their shops an
image that will attract regular customers and help them compete
with the discounts offered by supermarkets. A growing number
of bookshops sell their products through the Internet.

Qualifications and Training

A good general education is essential. Some bookshops require a
degree. The industry-recognised qualification, the Diploma in
Professional Bookselling, is available through the Booksellers
Association of United Kingdom and Ireland, together with a
number of comprehensive training resources. An understanding
of e-commerce is an advantage.

Personal Qualities

A liking for books and people, good general knowledge and an
interest in reading and handling books are necessary, as are good
health and stamina for a job which involves much standing. An
interest in selling and customer care is essential to create a
friendly and reassuring atmosphere where book buyers know
that they are being looked after in an efficient manner by professional, knowledgeable staff.

Starting Salary

Salaries are usually negotiable in small shops and many booksellers work part-time. Salary ranges are (with London at the top
end of each range): sales assistants £9,000–£12,000, senior assis-

tants £10,000–£13,000, managers £14,000–£25,000. Managers of larger chains can earn up to £40,000.

Booksellers Association of United Kingdom and Ireland, Minster House, 272 Vauxhall Bridge Road, London SW1V 1BA; 020 7834 5477; www.booksellers.org.uk

BOX OFFICE

see *Theatre*

BREWING

Brewing is the complex process of making and packaging beer. Specialist technicians are responsible for the choice of all raw materials – malt, hops, and so on – and plant equipment. Brewing technicians and brewing scientists are required to maintain consistently high-quality products. There are opportunities for non-qualified people to work as plant operators.

Qualifications and Training

No formal qualifications are necessary for non-technical jobs in the brewing industry. For technical jobs, the main demand is for honours graduates in science and engineering, particularly if they have specialised in brewing, biochemistry or chemical engineering. Specialist degrees in brewing are available at Heriot-Watt University; these provides exemption from the Associate Membership examination of the Institute of Brewing which offers training and internationally recognised qualifications at various levels.

Personal Qualities

Good health is required for a job that will inevitably involve some night and shift work. The ability to organise and communicate effectively at all levels, and a keen interest in science and engineering, are the hallmarks of successful brewers and brewing scientists.

Starting Salary

Non-technical staff can earn from £13,000 to £15,000 once experienced; graduate trainees start on £15,000 – £22,000+.

The Institute and Guild of Brewing, 33 Clarges Street, London
   W1J 7EE; 020 7499 8144; fax: 020 7499 1156;
   www.igb.org.uk; e-mail: enquiries@igb.org.uk

BROADCASTING

(see also *Journalism*)

The aim of radio and television is communication. The range of programmes offered is enormous, including news, entertainment, sport and music. Most jobs in broadcasting require specialist knowledge, training and experience. A good working knowledge of digital equipment is an asset. Broadcasting companies prefer individuals who are multi-skilled; digital technology and Internet-related skills are in demand. It is important to demonstrate your enthusiasm through practical involvement in relevant activities such as writing for a local newspaper or Web site, or working behind the scenes in amateur theatre. Vacancies can be found on broadcasting company Web sites as well as in a number of national newspapers.

Journalist/Reporter

Journalists work in all forms of media, reporting on current affairs, events and general items of interest. They carry out research and interviews for newspapers, broadcast news programmes and online services. A candidate who is able to script, record and edit their own piece digitally would stand a stronger chance of gaining employment. There has been an increase in the number of journalists working for online publications.

Programme Assistant

They work in radio and are responsible for the technical and artistic presentation of programmes. They need to be able to operate the equipment and to be good at dealing with other people in the team and with the people who are interviewed or who work on the programmes.

Producer's Assistant/Secretary
They work for the producer, organizing all the administrative work. They retype scripts to incorporate any changes which have been made, ready for the next rehearsal or performance.

Floor Manager
Floor managers work in television doing a similar job to the stage manager in the theatre. The broadcasting floor manager's job can be strenuous – actors working on different sets cannot see each other and the floor manager's function is to cue and coordinate them all. The floor manager is also responsible for health and safety in the studio.

Studio Manager
Studio managers work in radio and are responsible for all issues relating to the artistic and technical operation of a programme. They must know how to interpret the producer's ideas correctly and how to achieve the best sound effects.

Assistant Floor Manager and Floor Assistant
These people carry out a variety of tasks according to each production. They are often in charge of the prompt book.

Production Assistant
The production assistant works as part of the production team. They must have good keyboard and organizational skills, be able to deal with a wide range of contacts and work to deadlines. Part of the job involves sitting in the control gallery timing the programme. In addition, they may do research for programmes.

Director/Producer
Directors and producers are often specialists in a specific area such as documentary, children's programming, drama, and so on. Both jobs require a good technical knowledge of the media, with financial management and budgeting skills as well as the necessary creative ability.

Broadcast Engineer
Engineers are involved in maintaining and testing the equipment used in studios and in outside broadcasts in radio and television,

together with operating and maintaining the transmission chain. They may also be involved in project development and research work. Recently there has been a shortage of skilled broadcast engineers owing to an ageing workforce and staff moving towards new media.

Vision Mixer
Vision mixers are responsible for recording the images from different cameras under the instruction of the director. They must have a strong concentration and the ability to work under pressure.

Film Editor/Video Editor
Film and video editors increasingly work with both formats. The editor must be able to visualise the director/producer's ideas and make the required creative decisions. Film and video editors have usually had experience in a technical/creative capacity before moving to an editor's position.

Television Make-up and Hairdressing
This is a highly skilled area of work, and competition for any vacancies is keen. It requires a thorough knowledge of period hairstyles and an understanding of the effects of lighting and camera on people's faces. In television, the make-up designer/assistant is responsible for both make-up and hair; in film, the jobs are separate.

Costume Designer
After gaining the relevant diplomas, costume designers should have theatrical experience. The work involves liaison with producers and make-up staff and responsibility, where necessary, for hiring and adapting costumes. They must have had basic training in pattern-making, cutting and dressmaking, and have gained practical experience in a fashion house or theatrical costumier.

Costume Dressmaker
The dressmaker carries out necessary alterations and adaptations on hired or existing costumes, as well as making up new designs.

Dresser

Duties involve the maintenance of costumes and the dressing of artists for performances. Requirements are sewing ability, and relevant experience in the theatre, the film industry or as a theatrical costumier.

Camera Operator

Camera operators work both in studios and on outside broadcasts. They have deep interest in subjects such as photography and lighting. An ability to establish good working relationships with other crewmembers and the director is necessary.

Audio Assistant

Audio assistants work on radio and television programme origination throughout the UK, doing similar jobs to sound operators and studio managers. There is a tendency now in BBC regions for the job to split into these two categories.

Sound Operator

They help to set up and operate sound equipment in studios and on outside broadcasts. An understanding of MD recording would be an advantage. They have a deep practical interest in subjects such as hi-fi and sound. The ability to establish good working relationships is necessary.

Secretaries and Clerks

There are a large number of administrative jobs available in broadcasting, and there is always the slight possibility of promotion from clerk-typist to secretary, and from secretary to producer's assistant.

Qualifications and Training

Many companies offer in-service staff training schemes which are advertised as they occur. Competition for a place on these schemes is fierce. The selection boards are impressed by good all-rounders as well as candidates with specialist knowledge.

In technical areas, engineers require, at trainee level, at least English GCSE plus A level maths and physics or a national diploma in electronics. Qualified engineers need to have a degree or HND in electronic engineering. There are a number of degree courses, including Foundation Degrees in Digital Broadcast Technology.

Technical operators require a good standard of education; at least GCSE grades A–C in English, maths and combined sciences (preferably physics). To improve their chances, candidates often progress their education further. Evidence of in-depth relevant practical involvement, often through amateur interests, always impresses. Many training courses now have an equivalent NVQ or Skillset Professional Qualification.

Trainee studio managers need to have knowledge of sound equipment together with practical involvement in radio. GCSEs in maths and physics are generally required. Production trainees must have practical experience of work directly related to production, either professionally or in an amateur capacity. No specific qualifications are asked for but applicants must have a wide range of interests.

Journalism training opportunities require applicants to have a demonstrable interest in news and current affairs, with evidence of practical involvement. Training schemes attract a large response and the standard is high.

Secretarial and clerical staff must have a good standard of education. Qualifications for clerical posts vary, depending on the department – for example, in finance an aptitude for figures is essential. Accurate keyboard skills are required for clerk-typist posts. Secretaries must have accurate typing; shorthand is an advantage.

Make-up trainees need to demonstrate involvement in professional or amateur theatre, and must have had formal training in make-up and hairdressing. Applicants should have A levels including art.

Personal Qualities
Qualities vary from job to job but all broadcasting staff must show commitment, enthusiasm, the ability to work as part of a team, and enormous stamina.

Starting Salary
The range of salaries in broadcasting is vast. Examples include: BBC production trainees, £17,000; broadcast journalist and New

Media trainees, £16,000; Web assistants, £12,500; researchers, £19,000. These are basic salaries, and allowances are often paid in addition.

BBC Recruitment Services, PO Box 7000, London W12 8GJ; www.bbc.co.uk/jobs

Skillset National Training Organization, 2nd Floor, 103 Dean Street, London W1V 5RA; 020 7534 5300; www.skillset.org; e-mail: info@skillset.org

BECTU, 111 Wardour Street, London W1F 0AY; 020 7437 8506; fax: 020 7437 8268; www.bectu.org.uk; e-mail: info@bectu. org.uk

Skills for Media, 111 Wardour Street, London W1F 0AY; 020 7437 0810; www.skillsformedia.com; e-mail: info@skillsformedia.com (New Media Careers Information Service from Skillset and Bectu)

ITV Network Limited, 200 Gray's Inn Road, London WC1X 8HF; www.itv.com

Channel 4 Television, Human Resources Department, 124 Horse-ferry Road, London SW1P 2TX; www.channel4.com; e-mail: careers@channel4.co.uk

Channel 5, 22 Long Acre, London WC2E 9LY; www.channel5.co.uk and; www.rtlgroup.com/careers; personnel@channel5.co.uk

Careers in Television and Radio (Kogan Page)

BUILDING

Building work involves the maintenance and construction of any structure. It is allied to civil and structural engineering, building and environmental engineering, municipal engineering, and highway and transportation engineering. There are a huge range of career options within the industry for graduates, technicians and at craft level.

Trades available include carpenters and joiners (*see also* Carpenter and Bench Joiner), formwork erectors, wood machin-ists, mastic asphalters, bricklayers, painters and decorators, crane drivers and mechanical equipment operators, electricians, refriger-ation fitters, thermal insulators, plumbers (*see also* Plumber) and gas fitters, plasterers, glaziers, scaffolders, paviours, steel erectors, stonemasons, roofing and wall tilers, floor and ceiling tilers, coiling fixers, heating and ventilation specialists. Each craftsperson is responsible for a specific part of the job but also works as part of a team whose collective responsibility is to produce high-quality work. The Construction Industry Training Board (CITB) predicts that the sector will need some 76,000 new recruits every year until 2006, to replace those leaving, and to fill new vacancies. Nearly 60 per cent of the new recruits needed are for trade occupations.

Contract Manager

The contract manager is the person responsible for the overall control of a building project. This means coordinating the subcontractors and specialist firms, the technical staff and the machine operatives, and making sure that the whole project is completed within the specified time limit and to budget.

Clerk of Works

The clerk of works undertakes independent inspection of the works in progress to ensure that they conform to the specification so that the client obtains value for money.

Site Manager

The site manager is the person responsible for all operations on a construction site, including the recruitment of skilled and semi-skilled workers. In a large construction company, the site manager works in conjunction with the personnel department.

Qualifications and Training

Formal educational requirements are not required. Training is by apprenticeship – usually of three to four years. Applicants for apprenticeship training take an aptitude test administered by the CITB. In England and Wales, apprentices work towards NVQs awarded jointly by the City and Guilds and the CITB. In Scotland, building apprenticeships are jointly awarded by Scottish Qualifications Authority (SQA) and Scottish Building Apprenticeship Training Council (SBATC).

Technician entrants to the building industry must have a minimum of four GCSEs grades A to C or equivalent, to include a science, maths and a subject showing the use of English.

Anyone wanting to become a clerk of works should have a sound technical education, ideally with a construction trade background. Students can progress through the Institute of Clerks of Works examinations (intermediate and final parts 1 and 2) or gain partial exemption through equivalent routes. Existing clerks of works can also gain an NVQ in Site Inspection at level 3. Clerks of works have normally spent a significant length of time working within industry prior to taking up this position. A thorough knowledge of building methods and appropriate experience are essential.

Site managers will have had several years' experience of working on a building site and will probably hold a Building Technician qualification. Managers come from a variety of backgrounds: some through a craft apprenticeship, some may start at technician level and some may come from university with a degree. Therefore, entry requirements will also vary enormously depending on the route chosen.

Personal Qualities

The construction worker needs to be committed and enthusiastic, able to work accurately from technical drawings using traditional or modern equipment, and to work as part of a team. Some jobs can be physically demanding. Contract managers need to be well organised in dealing with technical, financial and administrative issues. They must also have the ability to liaise with a variety of clients, from architects (*see also* Architect) and planners to craftspeople and the public.

Starting Salary

Salaries for those in craft occupations are normally paid according to nationally recommended industry rates; minimum rates for skilled workers start from £5.50 per hour. Apprentices are normally paid a percentage of the craftsperson's rate.

i

Construction Industry Training Board, Bircham Newton, King's Lynn, Norfolk PE31 6RH; 01485 577577; www.citb.org.uk

Education Unit, 4 Edison Street, Hillington, Glasgow G52 4XN;
    0141 810 3044; www.citb.org.uk
Scottish Building Apprenticeship Training Council (SBATC),
    Carron Grange, Carron Grange Avenue, Stenhousemuir FK5
    3BQ; 01324 555550
Institute of Clerks of Works of Great Britain Incorporated, 41 The
    Mall, Ealing, London W5 3TJ; 020 8579 2917;
    www.icwgb.sagehost.co.uk

BUILDING CONTROL SURVEYOR

Building control is undertaken by local authorities and Approved
Inspectors. The main activities involve the examination and assessment of plans, site visits to inspect work, and liaison with designers, builders, and other professionals within the construction team
and the fire authorities to ensure that new building construction
and alterations to existing buildings conform to building regulations. A broad knowledge of the many areas of building work, and
skills in dealing with people, need to be developed.

Qualifications and Training
There are two components to qualifying as a Chartered Building
Control Surveyor: first, successful completion of a Royal
Institution of Chartered Surveyors (RICS) approved degree or
diploma, followed by enrolment onto the Assessment of
Professional Competence (APC) which is two years' practical
training while in employment, concluding with an RICS professional assessment interview. Postgraduate conversion courses are
also available.

Personal Qualities
A knowledge of construction technology and legislation is necessary, plus the ability to state requirements firmly and to see that
they are carried out.

Starting Salary
Around £10,000 , increasing to £17,000 once fully qualified.

The Association of Building Engineers (ABE), Jubilee House, Billing
   Brook Road, Weston Favell, Northampton NN3 8NW; 01604
   404121; www.abe.org.uk; e-mail: building.engineers@abe.org.uk
Institute of Building Control, 92–104 East Street, Epsom, Surrey
   KT17 1EB; 01372 745577; fax: 01372 748282;
   www.rics.org/building_control

BUILDING SERVICES ENGINEERING

see *Engineering*

BUILDING SOCIETIES

(see also *Banking*)

Building societies are mutual organizations – they are owned by
those who invest in them; traditionally they functioned by attracting savings and investments from the public, and then using these
funds to make loans for home ownership. More recently building
societies have moved into offering a range of financial services,
such as insurance, credit cards, investment, estate agency and
unsecured lending, but the savings and loan activities remain the
most important. The number of building societies has decreased
since deregulation as many have converted to banks. There are
now just 66 in the UK

Building society assistants deal with customers' enquiries and
are expected to sell some of the Society's financial services, as well
as being responsible for routine and administrative tasks. With
the increase in telephone and Internet banking the number of jobs
in building society branches has decreased but there has been an
increase in related call centre work.

Building society managers work with customers on mortgage
and loan applications, financial planning queries and with
customers facing repayment difficulties. They may be in charge of a
single large branch or a number of small branches, where they have
responsibility for managing staff and ensuring targets are met.

Qualifications and Training

Assistants need four GCSEs or equivalent including English and
maths. Competency-based on-the-job training is common and can

include the opportunity to take Chartered Institute of Bankers (CIB) or Chartered Institute of Bankers in Scotland (CIOBS) modules or examinations. Those with CIB/CIOBS Associateship qualifications can move into management. Graduates are also recruited into management training posts; entry can be from any degree discipline and further professional training is available through CIB/CIOBS.

Personal Qualities

Honesty and discretion are essential as well as good communication, mathematical and IT skills. The ability to market financial products is becoming increasingly important. Managers need negotiating, decision-making and problem-solving skills.

Starting Salary

Assistants earn from £9,000 to £15,000 depending on qualifications and experience. Graduate trainees start on £16,000–£18,000+.

The Building Societies Association, 3 Savile Row, London W1X 1AF; 020 7437 0655; www.bsa.org.uk

Institute of Financial Services, 90 Bishopsgate, London EC2N 4AS; 020 7444 7115; www.ifslearning.com

The Chartered Institute of Bankers in Scotland, Drumsheugh House, 38B Drumsheugh Gardens, Edinburgh EH3 7SW; 0131 473 7777; www.ciobs.org.uk

Careers in Banking and Finance (Kogan Page)

BUILDING SURVEYING

see *Surveyor/Surveying Technician*

BUS AND COACH COMPANIES

About 65 per cent of personnel working in passenger transport on the roads are drivers. Many work on routes within one town or city, but some are employed by coach companies taking passengers from one town to another, across the country, or on international journeys. Other staff are employed as engineers, administrators, or managers.

Engineering work includes vehicle maintenance and repair in mechanical work, electrical and electronic systems and body structures, as well as technical research and design. Increasingly, companies are looking for employees with multiple skills or the willingness to undertake training in other occupational areas.

Administration covers route planning, traffic surveys, publicity, fare scales, computer operation, legal work and financial management.

Qualifications and Training

Modern Apprenticeships are available for engineers; some formal qualifications may be required depending on the scheme offered. NVQs are available at levels 1 to 5, which provide a career pathway within the industry. Semi-skilled engineers and engineers from other occupational areas are often recruited, and in-service training is provided.

There are Induction and Foundation programmes (5 modules) for coach drivers. Passenger-carrying vehicle (PCV) licence driver training is provided by all major companies. This may be supported by NVQs at levels 2 and 3 in Road Passenger Transport. Formal qualifications are not required.

School leavers and graduates are eligible for training in administration and management. In-service training is an integral part of all careers with the major bus and coach companies.

Personal Qualities

The work of bus drivers means dealing constantly with the general public, and a friendly attitude is important. Tact and good humour are essential, as well as a liking for the elderly and for young people, who form the majority of the bus-travelling public. Drivers need to be willing to work early and late shifts.

For engineering occupations, a sound mechanical ability and aptitude are preferred. A variety of skills are required within administration; information on these occupations can be obtained from individual companies.

Starting Salary

Salaries vary and applicants should enquire of the individual companies. The average for a driver is £14,500.

Local bus and coach companies
The Passenger Transport Forum for Employee Development (TRANSfED), Regency House, 43 High Street, Rickmansworth WD3 1ET; 01923 896607;
    www.transfed.org; enquiries@transfed.org

BUTCHER

(see also *Meat Industry*)

Career prospects are varied in the meat industry, extending from work in a small retail shop through to supermarkets; from meat buying for large organizations such as hotels and caterers, to the manufacture of meat and poultry products.

Qualifications and Training

A good general education is necessary but there are no formal educational requirements. Training is on the job and courses are available at further education establishments and technical colleges, leading to examinations of the Meat Training Council. NVQs are available at levels 1–4, and higher national diploma/certificate qualifications. Modern Apprenticeships are available. Further training, appropriate to the relevant sector of the industry, in management, meat technology, or small business ownership, may follow an apprenticeship.

Personal Qualities

An above-average attitude to hygiene is vital, as in all the food industries, plus a real interest in people and their eating habits, so that the meat products may be geared to the customers' needs.

Starting Salary

Trainees earn between £6,000 and £8,000; those with experience can earn up to £14,000.

Meat Training Council, PO Box 141, Winterhill House, Snowdon Drive, Milton Keynes MK6 1YY; 01908 231062; www.meattraining.co.uk

BUYER

see *Purchasing Officer*

C

CALL/CONTACT CENTRE

Contact Centre is replacing the term Call Centre as it more accurately describes the activities in places where customer support is provided by e-mail, fax and Web chat as well as by telephone. It's an expanding industry with nearly half a million people working in over 7,000 contact centres in the UK. The business and organizations behind these vary from local and national government (DVLA, NHS Direct) to charities (Childline, Oxfam) through to highly technical help desk functions (Microsoft, IBM, British Telecom). The work can be sales or advice oriented and in some centres language skills are essential as calls are taken from all over the world.

Management
Call Centre management can involve leading a small team of agents or managing a multi-site global operation which employs thousands. Managers need technical expertise and product knowledge as well as people skills. Opportunities to move into management from team leader or agent positions are common as this is a growing industry.

Call Centre Agents
The work involves dealing with queries and requests for information from the public, often in a very regulated environment with strict adherence to start, finish and break times. The role can be varied, with agents working across a number of departments to resolve the enquiry. Varied working patterns mean the opportunity to work part time or term time only is common.

Qualifications and training

Keyboard skills, good communication abilities and, for e-mail and Web chat, reasonable spelling and grammar. Increasingly the simpler activities in contact centres are becoming automated, leaving the human operator to deal with more complicated queries.

Many employers offer work-based training programmes in product knowledge, language skills, technical know-how and people skills; some offer Modern Apprenticeships. There are a growing number of Certificate, Diploma and Degree-level courses in Call Centre Management. These are often available through distance or Web-based learning.

Personal Qualities

The work requires patience, tolerance, level-headedness, a sense of humour, listening skills, flexibility and emotional self-management.

Salaries

Average wages for customer service advisers is £11,900. A fully trained agent can expect to earn between £11,200 and £15,000 per year. A Call or Contact Centre Manager's starting salary is usually between £22,000 and £32,000 depending on industry, experience and qualifications.

Call Centre Management Association (UK), International House, 174 Three Bridges Road, Crawley, West Sussex RH10 1LE; 01293 538400; www.ccma.org.uk

The Call Centre Association (CCA), Strathclyde House, 6 Elmbank Street, Glasgow G2 4PF; 0141 564 9010; www.cca.org.uk; e-mail: cca@cca.org.uk

CARDIAC PHYSIOLOGIST

Cardiac physiologists set up, calibrate and operate a wide range of highly sophisticated electro-medical equipment. They undertake clinical procedures which assist in the diagnosis and treatment of patients with known or suspected heart disease. These include the implantation and follow-up of permanent cardiac pacemakers, undertaking and reporting of cardiac ultrasound and monitoring of heart pressure during heart surgery. Their work ranges from outpatient clinics to operating theatres, cardiac catheterization laboratories and intensive/coronary care units. Some routine procedures are often handled by a cardiographer, who is less qualified.

Qualifications and Training

New applicants are expected to have a minimum of two A levels or equivalent. On-the-job training lasts a minimum of two years, but typically four, on a block- or day-release basis leading to the Edexcel (BTEC) National and Higher National Certificates in Medical Physics and Physiological Measurement.

Alternatively, an increasing number of trainees are registering for a four-year part-time BSc (Hons) Clinical Science (Cardiology) degree or 'topping-up' Edexcel (BTEC) qualifications with degree courses post-HNC. A number of trainees are recruited already holding relevant Edexcel (BTEC) qualifications or university degrees. From 2002 it is expected that the BSc in Clinical Physiology will replace the HNC.

Personal Qualities

Candidates need technical skills and interest as well as a high sense of responsibility, an ability to communicate sympathetically with patients and team-working skills.

Starting Salary

Trainee £8,163–£9,784; once qualified, depending on grade, £10,064–£30,877.

Society for Cardiological Science and Technology, British Cardiac Society, 9 Fitzroy Square, London W1P 5AH; www.scst.org.uk

CAREERS ADVISER

(see also *Personal Adviser*)

The role of careers advisers and the way in which guidance is delivered to those still at school in England is changing. A new service, Connexions, will be available to all by 2003. Until then, some areas will continue to be served by careers service companies. The Connexions Service will have responsibility for young people's personal development and provide intensive support to those who encounter barriers to learning as well as providing information, guidance and counselling on all aspects of education, training and careers. For details of careers adviser work within Connexions, *see* Personal Adviser.

In Scotland, a new all-age careers guidance service will be introduced from April 2002. This will incorporate careers service companies, adult guidance networks, education business partnerships and lifelong learning partnerships. In Wales, an all-age guidance and information service, Careers Wales, was introduced in April 2001. In Northern Ireland the careers service is part of the civil service and is reviewing its provision.

Careers advisers also work in further and higher education institutions and adult guidance services. They give guidance, information and advice about local and national employment and education opportunities. This is done through talks, involvement in the curriculum and organised events as well as through individual interviews. Advisers visit employers and educational establishments to gain first-hand knowledge of what is involved. There are opportunities to specialise in areas such as working with clients with special needs, students in higher education or with adults affected by redundancy, looking for a career change or returning to work after a break.

Careers advisers need to keep up to date with changes in employment law, academic and vocational qualifications. Being able to use ICT to research information, keep records and even provide guidance online is becoming increasingly important.

Qualifications and Training

The Diploma in Careers Guidance is being phased out and replaced by the Qualification in Careers Guidance (QCG), a one-year full-time or two-year part-time university course. This provides evidence for capability towards the NVQ level 4 in Advice and Guidance which is completed through supervised work-based training. Those with the QCG will be qualified to work as personal advisers in the Connexions Service once they have completed the Diploma for Personal Advisers. A list of institutions offering the QCG is available from the Institute of Career Guidance. Some employers offer a combination of work-based and off-the-job training leading to NVQs in Advice and Guidance at level 4. There are no specific entry requirements for the QCG or NVQs; however, the ability to cope with the academic nature of the course needs to be demonstrated.

For new advisers working in Higher Education there is a Certificate and a Diploma in Careers Education, Information and Guidance in Higher Education. Experienced careers staff can undertake an in-service MA in Careers Guidance in Higher Education. Details from AGCAS.

Personal Qualities

An ability to communicate sympathetically with people of all ages and from a range of backgrounds, including those with disabilities, is essential. Advisers must also be able to establish good working relationships with other professionals such as teachers, employers, training providers and social workers. Careers advisers have to assimilate and organise a large amount of constantly changing information. They must be able to work to targets, cope with pressure, work on their own initiative and as part of a team.

IT skills are becoming increasingly important for record keeping, research and making use of databases and guidance programs.

Starting Salary

Starting salaries for newly qualified advisers are around £15,000, rising to £21,500 for those with experience. Managers' salaries range from £27,000 to over £40,000.

Association of the Graduate Careers Advisory Services (AGCAS) Administration Office, c/o Careers Service, University of Sheffield, 8–10 Favell Road, Sheffield S3 7QX; 0870 770 3310; www.agcas.org.uk; e-mail: mike.proctor@agcas.org.uk

Institute of Career Guidance, 27a Lower High Street, Stourbridge,
    West Midlands DY8 1TA; 01384 376 464; www.icg-uk.org
Connexions: www.connexions.gov.uk
'Careers Adviser/Careers Consultant/Higher Education Careers
    Adviser/Adult Guidance worker' (AGCAS – all available on
    www.prospects.ac.uk or via HE Careers Services)
'A Career in Careers Guidance' (Institute of Careers Guidance)
'The Qualification in Careers Guidance' (Institute of Career
    Guidance)

CARPENTER AND BENCH JOINER

Traditionally, joiners were responsible for smaller, more intricate
jobs, and carpenters for larger jobs such as laying floorboards.
Nowadays, the terms are synonymous. The work involves making
and fitting doors, windows, staircases, cupboards and shuttering;
fitting structural joists, roof timbers, door frames, skirting boards,
doors, handrails, wardrobes, and so on. Carpenters may also be
called upon to wall up excavations and erect shoring during demolition. Opportunities exist with a wide range of employers of all
sizes, such as building and civil engineering contractors, specialist
carpentry and joinery firms, local authorities, in industrial and
commercial maintenance, shipbuilding, shopfitting and vehicle
manufacture, or as a self-employed craftsman.

Cabinet Maker

Cabinet makers use traditional hand skills to make, finish or
restore high-quality items of wooden furniture. They may work in
factories for furniture manufacturers or be self-employed in small
workshops.

Qualifications and Training

A general education to secondary level is the only academic
requirement, although some arithmetical ability is useful. Training
is over a two- to three-year period with courses leading to NVQs.

Personal Qualities

As qualified craftspeople, carpenters and joiners must be able to
work from technical drawings or notes without close supervision and to produce neat accurate work. They must be manually

skilled, possessing a steady hand and a head for heights. A good eye for form is necessary, plus a willingness to work outside in all weathers.

Starting Salary
When qualified, the craftsman rate is around £230 per week; some employers pay more, offering bonuses and overtime.

Construction Industry Training Board, Bircham Newton, King's Lynn, Norfolk PE31 6RH; 01485 577577; www.citb.org.uk

Institute of Carpenters, Central Office, 35 Hayworth Road, Sandiacre, Nottingham NG10 5LL; 0115 9490641; www.central-office.co.uk; e-mail: mail@central-office.co.uk

A range of information leaflets is available from the Institute of Carpenters (address above)

CARPET FITTER

Carpet retailers, furniture stores and department stores all employ their own trained personnel who deliver and fit carpets and other floor coverings to customers' homes, shops, offices or hotels. Many fitters are also self-employed.

Qualifications and Training
GCSE English and maths or equivalents are usually required. Training is mainly given on the job, working with an experienced fitter, although in some firms there are possible opportunities for day-release courses leading to the examinations of the National Institute of Carpet Fitters and Floorlayers.

Personal Qualities
Strength and fitness are important in order to handle heavy rolls of carpet. A good head for calculations and an eye for detail (such as matching patterns) are also essential. Generally, too, it is necessary to be able to drive.

Starting Salary
Around National Minimum Wage rates.

Local Jobcentres and Careers/Connexions Centres
National Institute of Carpet and Floorlayers, 4D St Mary's Place,
The Lace Market, Nottingham NG1 1PH; 0115 958 3077;
www.nicf.carpetinfo.co.uk

CARTOGRAPHY

(see also *Ordnance Survey Work*)

Cartography embraces all aspects of map-making, from the initial
collection and editing of material (by cartographers) to the actual
generation and production of the finished product (by cartographic draughtsmen, workstation operators and assistants). It
also covers the making of charts, globes and models of the earth or
heavenly bodies. Most cartographic work is undertaken in
government departments such as the Ministry of Defence, the
Meteorological Office and the Department of the Environment,
Transport and the Regions. The Ordnance Survey no longer
employ cartographic draughtsmen or assistants as their mapping
is produced digitally, but they do recruit trainee surveyors.

Vacancies sometimes occur in local authority planning departments and with specialist publishing houses or survey companies. Computers are reducing the need for manual draughtsmen, especially in repetitive work, and the increasing application
of Geographical Information Systems (GIS) via a graphics workstation is significantly changing the work of professional cartographers. There is substantial growth in the number of map/chart
products becoming available on CD, many of which are designed
for interactive use.

Qualifications and Training
Cartographers are increasingly graduates with a relevant undergraduate or postgraduate qualification. Universities offering
courses in cartography, GIS, topographic science or surveying
and mapping science include Newcastle, Oxford Brookes and

East London. Admission requirements vary, but are likely to include geography A level.

Personal Qualities

Neatness, precision, aesthetic appreciation and a fine attention to detail are important, as are mathematical awareness and an ability to analyse visual judgements on graphic efficiency.

Starting Salary

For a graduate, from £14,500; mapping and charting technicians, from £11,000; and assistants, £8,500+.

i

British Cartographic Society, School of Planning, Oxford Brookes University, Gipsy Lane Campus, Headington, Oxford OX3 0BP; 01865 483346; www.cartography.org.uk

CATERING AND ACCOMMODATION MANAGEMENT

(see also *Chef/Cook, Health Service, Hotel Work*)

There is a wide variety of job opportunities in this category at all levels, from managers and supervisors to craft workers. Sometimes the dividing lines are not clear-cut, and it is quite usual for individuals to move up from one to another.

Management

Catering management can cover work in a roadside or motorway restaurant, a luxury restaurant, a hospital meals service, a snack bar, a take-away service, university and college restaurants, the armed forces, outdoor events or contract catering (providing meals and snacks to the management and staff of the contractor, for example a bank or insurance company). The manager in charge is normally responsible for budgeting, menu planning, stock monitoring, seeing that good food is served as and when it is required (often round the clock), keeping customers satisfied and supervising staff.

Accommodation management is concerned with the domestic side of colleges and universities (where managers are sometimes known as bursars), hospitals, local authority day centres and residential homes (for the aged or disabled, for instance). The demanding duties of such managers include responsibility for accommodation and catering (particularly in halls of residence, which may be used as conference centres during the vacation). The work can involve personal contact with the residents (in homes, for instance, where the population is fairly permanent) or be more in the nature of housekeeping (as in hospitals where the patients are constantly changing and are not the direct concern of the domestic staff).

Kitchen

In the kitchen there are opportunities at all levels, from the chef in charge of a select restaurant to the dish-washer in a snack bar. There are also opportunities for freelance work – catering for directors' dining rooms, private parties and business lunches, for instance. It is demanding work, often in 'unsocial hours', when most people are out enjoying themselves. Some cooking can be repetitious (such as take-away menus), some creatively satisfying.

Food Service Assistants

Waiters and waitresses, as well as serving, may cook special dishes at table or specialise in particular skills such as wine-waiting. As well as serving food and drink, they have to maintain contact with their customers; unfriendly servers may ruin the reputation of a restaurant. Promotion is to head waiter / waitress.

Qualifications and Training

There are two main routes to qualification: attending a college or university as a full-time student, or joining a training programme operated by an employer or an organization that works with employers to provide training, such as the Hotel and Catering Training Company (HCTC). In the latter case, entrants learn on the job and attend college or a training centre on a short-course or day-release basis. Recruits on the work-based training programme will generally acquire NVQ awards. An increasing number of employers are offering Modern Apprenticeships which provide a route to higher-level technical or supervisory posts and NVQs at level 3.

Full-time courses are available, including HNDs, Foundation Degrees and degree courses in hospitality-related subjects.

Personal Qualities

Craft workers usually need physical fitness and stamina as well as high standards of personal hygiene. Skin complaints may disqualify entrants. Managers need to be well motivated with good interpersonal and team skills. All staff have to be prepared to work split shifts and antisocial hours.

Starting Salary

Average wages for qualified hotel and restaurant staff are £14,500. Salaries for managers start around £16,000 but vary depending on the size of the business.

i

Hotel and Catering Training Company; 0500 832 300; www.hctc.co.uk

Springboard UK, 1 Denmark Street, London WC2H 8LP; 020 7497 8654; www.springboarduk.org.uk

Hotel and Catering International Management Association, 191 Trinity Road, London SW17 7HN; 020 8772 7400; www.hcima.org.uk; e-mail: info@hcima.co.uk

Careers in Catering and Hotel Management (Kogan Page)

The Caterer and Hotelkeeper; www.caterer.com (job adverts)

CHARTERED CLINICAL PSYCHOLOGIST

see *Psychologist*

CHAUFFEUR

Chauffeurs are skilled car drivers who are employed either by one person or by companies or organizations where senior personnel need their own reliable transport on hand at all times. Private chauffeurs may live in accommodation provided and have various other duties. Apart from the actual driving, the job will also involve making sure the cars are well maintained and clean. Some chauffeurs have a security role and may also act as bodyguards.

Qualifications and Training
Proven driving experience and a 'clean' driving licence, with no endorsements, are essential. Mechanical and/or geographical knowledge may be required, depending on the individual demands of the job. Some of the better-known car manufacturers run their own training schemes; Rolls-Royce, for instance, has its own driving school, *see* below.

Personal Qualities
Essential attributes are a calm, unflappable nature when under pressure such as being stuck in heavy traffic when late for an appointment, patience, politeness and the discretion not to repeat confidential conversations which may well be overheard.

Starting Salary
£15,000+. Accommodation may be provided.

School of Instruction, Rolls-Royce Limited, Crewe, Cheshire CW1 3PL; 01270 534957; fax: 01270 535454; www.rollsroycemotorcars.co.uk; e-mail: dealer.academy@bentley.co.uk

The Lady, 39–40 Bedford Street, London WC2E 9ER; 020 7379 4717 (job advertisements); www.lady.co.uk

The International Guild of Professional Butlers and Private Personnel; www.butlersguild.com

Local Jobcentres and Careers/Connexions Centres

CHEF/COOK

In addition to creating and supervising the preparation of all kinds of different dishes, a head chef/cook has to be trained in the management of a kitchen, being responsible for the staff and the organization of their workload, planning the menus, budgeting, ordering and approving the necessary ingredients and maintaining high standards of efficiency and hygiene. Chefs are employed in hotels, restaurants, industrial organizations (such as offices or factories), institutions (such as hospitals, schools and universities or colleges) and in the armed forces. In large establishments the *chef de cuisine* is in overall charge while there may be a number of *chefs de partie* (in charge of their part of the kitchen) and a number of *commis chefs* (still learning the trade).

Qualifications and Training
Qualifications are the same as for Catering and Accommodation Management, *see* page 73.

Personal Qualities
Requirements include the ability to work under pressure in hot and noisy conditions and to enjoy practical as well as creative work. The higher chefs rise in their profession, the more they need to be able to take responsibility and the more management skills they require.

Starting Salary
Salaries are similar to those indicated for Catering and Accommodation Management, *see* page 74. Experienced chefs may command very high salaries.

i

Hotel and Catering Training Company; 0500 832 300;
  www.hctc.co.uk
Springboard UK, 1 Denmark Street, London WC2H 8LP; 020 7497
  8654; www.springboarduk.org.uk
Hotel and Catering International Management Association, 191
  Trinity Road, London SW17 7HN; 020 8772 7400;
  www.hcima.org.uk; e-mail: info@hcima.co.uk
Careers in Catering and Hotel Management (Kogan Page)
The Caterer and Hotelkeeper; www.caterer.com (job vacancies)

CHEMICAL ENGINEERING

see *Engineering*

CHEMIST

Chemistry is the basis of a wide range of careers. The majority of trained chemists work in the manufacturing industries within organizations producing such materials as foodstuffs, plastics, pharmaceuticals, cosmetics, petroleum, detergents and fertilisers. Large numbers teach in schools, colleges and universities, generally combining teaching with research work; there are also openings with local authorities, the Health Service, the Civil Service and the nationalised industries, as well as in marketing and sales, information and patents and specialised publishing. Professional chemists are often assisted by laboratory technicians and assistants. Chemistry is essential in many other careers such as medicine or veterinary science.

Analysts

Analysts work in industry providing a service for research, development and production departments. They analyse the results of experiments and advise what a newly produced substance may be. An analyst may check the quality of raw materials bought in by a company and examine the quality of the company's own products. Public analysts are employed by local authorities to examine, for example, the state of the water supply; the adequacy of the sewage treatment system; toxic and suspect materials and leachate from landfill sites. They may also be asked to examine food from a suspect restaurant. Public analysts are frequently required to give witness on their findings in courts of law and should be familiar with the law relating to goods and services.

Qualifications and Training

Most professional chemists and analysts have membership of the Royal Society of Chemistry, for which a degree or equivalent qualification is necessary. Entry requirements for degree courses generally include at least two A levels or equivalent in science subjects, including chemistry and another scientific or mathematical subject. To become a public analyst it is necessary to hold the

Mastership in Chemical Analysis (MChemA), a qualification awarded by the Royal Society of Chemistry.

Chemistry technicians usually need three GCSE or equivalent for entry to an national certificate in science or chemistry – these are generally day-release courses. This can be followed by a higher certificate or degree level qualification.

Personal Qualities

Chemists usually form part of a team, so an ability to work alongside others is essential. The actual work varies enormously but generally a chemist also needs an enquiring mind and practical experimental ability and experience. Attention to detail and a sense of responsibility are important.

Starting Salary

Varies according to type of employment. Technicians start on £8,000–£10,000, newly qualified graduates can generally expect £15,000–£18,000+.

The Royal Society of Chemistry, Burlington House, Piccadilly, London W1V 0BN; 020 7437 8656; http://chemistry.rsc.org

CHILD CARE

see *Nursery Nurse*

CHILD GUIDANCE

see *Psychologist, Psychotherapist, Social Work and Social Care – Children and Young People*

CHIROPODIST

Chiropodists are also known as podiatrists; the profession is in the process of changing its name. They are concerned with the health of feet. Those working in the NHS deal with problems caused by diabetes or arthritis and may work with those suffering from sports injuries. Ailments such as corns, bunions and malformed nails are more likely to be dealt with by those in private practice.

Chiropodists perform minor operations under local anaesthetic. They may work in the NHS in hospitals, clinics or health centres; or in private practice or large organizations. Many undertake postgraduate training to specialise in areas such as sports medicine, biomechanics and podiatric surgery.

Qualifications and Training

To work within the NHS chiropodists must have completed a degree approved by The Council for Professions Supplementary to Medicine. Degrees in chiropody/podiatry or podiatric medicine are offered by 13 chiropody/podiatry schools attached to universities and institutions throughout the UK (contact the Society of Chiropodists and Podiatrists for details). Normally, five GCSEs plus two A levels or equivalent are needed, but individual institutions may have their own requirements. In private practice it is essential to belong to a reputable chiropodial association which operates a strict ethical code and offers professional liability insurance.

Personal Qualities

Chiropodists in the NHS work as part of multidisciplinary teams. They need good business sense and organizational skills as well as the ability to relate to those they are treating. Organizing ability is essential in private practice.

Starting Salary

£15,920 for a chiropodist in the NHS, plus London weighting of around £3,000 for inner London. Salaries can rise to £35,260 for a District Senior Chief Chiropodist.

The Society of Chiropodists and Podiatrists, 1 Fellmonger's Path, Tower Bridge Road, London SE1 3LY; 020 7234 8620; www.feetforlife.org

The Council for Professions Supplementary to Medicine, Park House, 184 Kennington Park Road, London SE11 4BU; 020 7582 0866; www.cpsm.org.uk (This will be replaced by the Health Professions Council in mid-2002.)

CHIROPRACTOR

Chiropractic is a health-care profession concerned with, but not limited to, the diagnosis, treatment and prevention of structural and functional disorders affecting the musculo-skeletal system. Common complaints include low back and leg pain, headaches, and neck and arm pain, as well as sports injuries. Working in a primary contact profession, a qualified chiropractor may be approached directly, without a medical referral, by patients seeking help.

Chiropractors are trained to utilise a wide variety of diagnostic techniques, including X-ray. Manual manipulation (adjustment) of spinal and extremity joints as well as soft-tissue structures is the most common treatment method employed. They will also offer advice on nutrition, rehabilitative exercises and modifications to activities of daily living. There is an increasing demand for chiropractic services and employment prospects are good both in the UK and in Europe.

Qualifications and Training

Chiropractors are subject to statutory regulation by the General Chiropractic Council (GCC). It is illegal for anyone to describe themselves as a Chiropractor if they are not registered with the GCC. Recognised courses are provided by the Anglo-European College of Chiropractic, McTimoney College of Chiropractic and the Universities of Glamorgan and Surrey. Entry requirements vary but normally include two science A levels or equivalent. Fees for courses vary considerably because some colleges are private.

Personal Qualities

Manual dexterity and practical skills as well as a sound theoretical knowledge of the body are necessary. An ability to communicate with patients and inspire confidence is important.

Starting Salary

Salaries vary according to number of patients and how well established the practice is. Patients are usually charged per session.

i

General Chiropractic Council, 344–354 Gray's Inn Road, London
WC1X 8BP; 020 7713 5155; fax: 020 7713 5844; www.gcc-uk.org;
e-mail: enquiries@gcc-uk.org

British Chiropractic Association, Blagrave House, 17 Blagrave
Street, Reading, Berkshire RG1 1QB; 0118 950 5950;
fax: 0118 958 8946; www.chiropractic-uk.co.uk;
e-mail: enquiries@chiropractic-uk.co.uk

Anglo-European College of Chiropractic, 13–15 Parkwood Road,
Bournemouth, Dorset BH5 2DF; 01202 436200;
fax: 01202 436312; www.aecc.ac.uk

The McTimoney College of Chiropractic, The Clock House, 22–26
Ock Street, Abingdon, Oxfordshire OX14 5SH; 01235 523336;
www.mctimoney-college.ac.uk;
e-mail: chiropractic@mctimoney-college.ac.uk

University of Glamorgan, Chiropractic Field, School of Applied
Sciences, Pontypridd, Glamorgan, CF37 1DL; 01443 482287;
www.glam.ac.uk

University of Surrey, European Institute of Health and
Medical Sciences, Duke of Kent Building, Stag Hill,
Guildford, Surrey, GU2 5XH; 01483 879770;
fax: 01483 259395; www.eihms.surrey.ac.uk

CHOREOGRAPHY

see *Dancing*

CINEMA MANAGEMENT

A cinema manager is responsible for the smooth running of a
cinema, the box-office takings and the staff. Most cinemas are now
controlled by major distribution companies and the manager has
little say about what films are shown, but there are also some
independent cinemas. There may be special functions to organise,
such as live performances and late-night shows.

Cinema Projectionist
A projectionist is responsible for showing the correct films, in the
correct sequence, and for maintaining the necessary equipment.

The work may often be repetitious and the hours 'unsocial' (mainly afternoons and evenings).

Cinema Attendant

Staff are also needed in cinemas to assist the public to their places, check and sell tickets, distribute refreshments and keep public rooms clean and tidy. This kind of work can be full- or part-time.

Qualifications and Training

Formal qualifications are not always specified but candidates for managerial positions need to show intelligence and aptitude (often working their way up from more junior positions). The main distributing companies have their own training programmes for cinema managers and projectionists and most of the training is done on the job.

Personal Qualities

A cinema manager needs to enjoy responsibility, be able to handle a variety of demands and / or complaints with courtesy and tact. A projectionist needs technical ability, organization and should not be bored by repetitive work. Attendants need to have a pleasant personality as they will be dealing with the general public.

Starting Salary

Salaries vary according to organization and there is often a supplement for Sunday working.

Local Jobcentres and Careers / Connexions Centres

CIVIL AVIATION

Pilot

Commercial pilots in the UK fly fixed-wing aircraft and helicopters. Before take-off the pilot must prepare a flight plan, study the weather, make sure that the craft is airworthy, check that the cargo and fuel are safely loaded and work out estimated arrival times. Little time is spent actually flying the aeroplane manually.

The pilot spends most of the time carefully monitoring sophisticated computer-controlled automatic flying, navigational and communications systems. Pilots keep in touch with air traffic control and must be prepared to deal with sudden changes in weather and other conditions. Pilots work irregular hours but their actual flying time is strictly controlled.

Most UK pilots are employed by one of the major carriers of passengers and goods, and when flying large aircraft they are part of a team. Opportunities for pilots of small aircraft and helicopters are to be found in flying executive jets, in the field of air taxiing (especially in the North Sea), conducting aerial surveys or as test pilots or flying instructors.

Air Cabin Crew

Stewards and stewardesses look after the safety, comfort and welfare of passengers. Before a flight they check stocks of equipment, welcome passengers on board and go through safety routines. During the flight they will serve ready-cooked meals and drinks, sell duty-free goods and deal with any problems passengers have. Flight reports are prepared by senior stewards, who also attend to first-class passengers and supervise junior staff.

Aircraft Maintenance Engineer

Aircraft maintenance engineers make sure that aircraft are airworthy. They maintain, service and overhaul the aircraft, their engines and equipment, working to very high standards set by the Civil Aviation Authority (CAA). Every part of every job is checked and certified. Engineers usually specialise in either mechanics or avionics and work on major overhaul or in 'turnarounds' – the work carried out after each flight. Apart from working with the airlines, other opportunities are found with firms that specialise in aircraft maintenance. There are also a few openings for professional engineers in works management, production, planning, and research and development.

Air Traffic Control

The safe and efficient movement of all aircraft through British air space and airports is the responsibility of National Air Traffic Service (NATS) air traffic control officers and assistants. With the aid of sophisticated radio, radar and computer systems and with visual checks on visibility and weather conditions made from the control tower, they ensure that aircraft are kept a safe distance apart and that pilots are well advised as to their position and prevailing conditions, give clearance to land and directions to loading bays. Air traffic controllers mainly work for work for NATS, although there may be limited opportunities with other employers, such as local authorities or aircraft manufacturers. All must hold a CAA licence stipulating the service they are qualified to give and where they can operate. Some of the more routine tasks, such as checking flight plans, updating weather information, logging aircraft movements and keeping runways clear, are carried out by the air traffic control assistants. Prospects for promotion to officer level are good, but air traffic control staff are employed to work at any location within the country.

Air Traffic Engineer

Air traffic engineers are responsible for the efficient operation of the wide range of sophisticated telecommunications, electronic systems and specialist equipment needed in air traffic control centres, airports and other specialist centres. This involves the installation, calibration and maintenance of radar, air-to-ground communication systems, navigational and landing aids, computer data and processing equipment and visual display units. Opportunities may exist for engineers to look after day-to-day maintenance, and, at graduate level, for field management, installation and development work.

Qualifications and Training

Pilot

UK pilots are required to hold a licence issued by the Joint Aviation Authorities (JAA) which represent the civil aviation departments of a group of European States who have collaborated to set common safety standards called Joint Aviation Requirements. Licence holders can work as pilots in any of the JAA member states. Full details of licensing requirements and organizations providing approved courses can be obtained from the CAA (*see* further contacts). Training to be a commercial pilot costs £50,000–£60,000 and may be integrated (ab initio) or modular. Helicopter courses tend to be more expensive. Most applicants wishing to undertake integrated courses are sponsored privately or by an airline. Such sponsorship is highly competitive and difficult to obtain. Trainees are generally expected to contribute to training costs either whilst training or by repaying some of the fees once in employment. An alternative entry route is via a short service flying commission with either the RAF or Royal Navy. All pilots are expected to attend retraining and refresher courses throughout their careers.

Entry requirements for sponsored pilot training vary between airlines, but most ask for a minimum of 2–3 A levels or equivalent, including maths and physics. Many airlines recruit graduates up to the age of 26. Eyesight must be of a very high standard. Normal colour vision and an excellent level of health and fitness are essential.

Air Cabin Crew

Airlines usually train their own cabin crews at special centres on courses lasting four to six weeks. Applicants should be over 18, have a good level of general education to GCSE standard, preferably including English and maths, and have conversational fluency in at least one European language. Experience in a customer care setting can be helpful.

Aircraft Maintenance Engineer

Entry to aircraft maintenance engineering is via craft, technician or student apprenticeships; entry qualifications depend upon the type of apprenticeship. The apprenticeships take the form of on-the-job training and part-time study at local colleges to prepare for aeronautical engineering / aircraft maintenance engineering qualifications offered by City and Guilds and Edexcel (BTEC)/ SQA or the CAA. Qualified aircraft engineers (including those from the armed forces) have to meet certain practical experience requirements before they can take examinations to become licensed aircraft maintenance engineers. There are some full-time courses in aeronautical engineering and aircraft maintenance, usually lasting two and a half years.

Air Traffic Control

Entrants for the NATS scheme must be eligible for work within the UK, have security clearance, be aged between 18 and 29 and pass a medical. The training lasts just under 18 months and includes practice at Bournemouth Airport. This is followed by an extensive period of practical training at a designated site.

Air Traffic Engineer

NATS runs a training scheme for graduate electrical/electronic engineers lasting a minimum of 15 months. The training is approved by the Institute of Electrical and Electronic Engineering and will lead after approximately three years to chartered engineering status.

Personal Qualities

Pilot

Pilots must be very well balanced, physically fit, have stamina, be mentally and physically alert and ready to respond quickly to changing conditions. They must be unflappable, confident, self-assured leaders with considerable technical skill.

Air Cabin Crew

Air cabin crew must be reassuring and approachable, smart, have lots of energy and stamina, confidence and the ability to act quickly, decisively and in a firm but polite and tactful manner.

Maintenance Engineer

Maintenance engineering requires a combination of practical interest, mechanical aptitude, accuracy and manual dexterity. Engineers must be willing to adapt and to retrain. Very high standards and a responsible attitude are also most important.

Air Traffic Control Officer

The work is stressful; officers need to be able to assimilate and interpret a great deal of information and instantly act upon it. They must be able to react quickly if conditions suddenly change, be healthy, reliable and emotionally well balanced; good eyesight and colour vision are also important.

Air Traffic Engineer

Normal colour vision, great care, accuracy and a basic understanding of the practical applications of electricity and magnetism are required.

Starting Salary

Salaries vary between airlines but the following is a guide: pilot £25,000+; cabin crew £9,000+; air traffic controllers £22,000+.

Civil Aviation Authority, 45–59 Kingsway, London WC2B 6TE; 020 7379 7311; www.caa.co.uk

Recruitment Services, National Air Traffic Services (NATS), T1213, CAA House, 45–59 Kingsway, London WC2B 6TE; 020 7832 6696; www.nats.co.uk

The Royal Aeronautical Society, 4 Hamilton Place, London W1J 7BQ; 020 7499 4300; www.aerosociety.com

British Helicopter Advisory Board, Graham Suite, Fairoaks Airport, Chobham, Woking, Surrey GU24 8HX; fax: 01276 856126; www.bhab.demon.co.uk

British Women Pilots Association (BWPA), Brooklands Museum, Brooklands Road, Weybridge, Surrey KT13 1QN; www.bwpa.demon.co.uk

'A Career in Aviation' is available from BWPA for £5.50 including postage and packaging

Oxford Aviation Training; www.oxfordaviation.net

Cabair; www.cabair.com

Individual airlines

CIVIL ENGINEER

see *Engineering*

CIVIL SERVICE

The Civil Service is a multi-million pound business made up of many departments and agencies. Each department is responsible for a different field (for example, health or education) and together they employ around half a million people. Many still associate the Civil Service with middle-aged men wearing bowler hats and spending their days shuffling vast reams of paper, but this is not the reality. The Civil Service actively recruits a diverse range of people to reflect the make-up of the country it serves and has undergone huge changes as a result of the Modernizing

Government initiative. Many civil servants do not work in offices but may be engineers, lawyers or scientists working anywhere from laboratories to prisons. One in five civil servants works in London, where most of the departments have their headquarters. The rest are employed in towns and cities nation-wide and across the world. Some regularly travel to Brussels if their work involves business with the European Union. Members of the Diplomatic Service spend much of their careers living abroad as representatives for British interests in foreign countries.

Administrative Staff

This is the largest group whose members work in all depart-ments, carrying out the work of government. At the top level it is responsible for policy and management. Many new entrants are junior staff dealing with customers and administrative work. Others join at Junior Manager level (sometimes known as Executive Officers) and may be in charge of a team of people or one particular area, such as fraud investigation. There is a Fast Stream Development Programme offering accelerated training and development to around 500 graduates a year who are mainly recruited into positions in central government departments (for example, the Home Office, Cabinet Office or the Foreign and Commonwealth Office). It's possible to 'hop-on' to this scheme (known as In-Service Nomination) if you enter the Civil Service via a different route.

Scientific Staff

Scientific staff are employed in government laboratories and research establishments, working in research, design and devel-opment. Most opportunities here are in physics and engineering, although there are also opportunities in maths and computing, chemical and life sciences. The majority of candidates are recruited at Scientific Officer grade (working on routine testing and analysis). Those with fewer qualifications can join as Assistant Scientific Officers.

Professionally Qualified Staff

Professionally qualified staff (particularly in the field of technol-ogy) are employed as the government needs its own archi-tects, accountants, computer personnel, lawyers, librarians, statisticians, photographers, surveyors, draughtsmen, valuers and veterinary surgeons in the various departments.

Qualifications and Training

Requirements vary from GCSE passes or equivalent for junior posts to an honours degree for professional and higher administrative posts. For example, a good honours degree (or equivalent) is essential for the Fast Stream Development Programme, scientific and other professional posts. Candidates with Edexcel (BTEC)/SQA higher awards may be considered for some scientific jobs. A levels or equivalent are required for Executive Officers. Appropriate NVQs may be acceptable for many posts. Much of the training is given on the job and supplemented by attendance at formal courses (for example, in managerial or tax skills) when necessary. A large number of in-service training courses are also available (part-time, full-time and sandwich) to assist in gaining appropriate qualifications.

Personal Qualities

Qualities required vary considerably from department to department. Much of the work of civil servants involves dealing with the public either face to face or by telephone, so good communication skills are essential. As the work is often of a confidential nature, loyalty and discretion are important.

Starting Salary

Salaries compare favourably with those for similar work in other organizations. Some departments may pay a retention and recruitment allowance.

---

i

Individual Web sites for all departments can be accessed via the Recruitment Gateway at www.civilservice.gov.uk/ jobs

Jobs in the Civil Service are routinely advertised in both local and national press and can also be found on www.rasnet.co.uk

For further information about the Fast Stream Development Programme, see www.faststream.gov.uk

For jobs in Europe see www.euro-staff.gov.uk

CLOTHING INDUSTRY

(see also *Fashion*)

The clothing industry is diverse and complex, with products ranging from off-the-peg garments that are turned out in thousands, to exclusive haute couture designs from top fashion houses. There are job opportunities in large factories, small workrooms, with large wholesaling firms, in small family businesses and on production lines. The most important sections of the industry are men's and boys' outerwear, women's and girls' outerwear, children's clothing, bespoke tailoring (made to measure) and dressmaking. More specialised areas such as millinery and glove making are relatively small. Skilled workers are generally in great demand in most areas.

The main craft jobs are pattern cutting and grading, lay making (positioning the pattern to make the most economical use of the cloth), cutting, marking or fixing (putting the different pieces of an individual garment together and marking the stitch lines), hand sewing and pressing. There are also opportunities for semi-skilled workers and operators, particularly machinists. Much of this work can be repetitive. Production lines are arranged so each machinist sews only one part of a garment. However, opportunities exist to move into more skilled work later, such as sample machining. Technology is changing the clothing industry with more advanced sewing machines, computer-controlled pattern laying and die cutting of bulk quantities. The industry needs skilled operatives and mechanics to work with, maintain and care for these increasingly sophisticated machines.

The clothing industry also employs people in its commercial sections – marketing and sales, or purchasing and supply – where there are often close links with the major textile and fibre companies. As more and more companies outsource their production overseas, the need for additional garment technologists has become apparent. This involves overseas travel and the use of a wide range of technical skills.

Qualifications and Training

Formal educational qualifications are not always needed to train for the craft skills. These are traditionally learnt by courses leading to City and Guilds and Edexcel (BTEC) examinations. The

Foundation Modern Apprenticeship scheme which leads to NVQ level 2 qualifications and the Advanced Modern Apprenticeship scheme which leads to NVQ level 3 awards are available. Machinists are generally trained on the job by the employing company.

An alternative route to learn is via further and higher education. Courses are run at many colleges and universities across the UK leading to National Diplomas, Higher National Diplomas or degrees in a variety of clothing related disciplines.

Personal Qualities

These vary according to the particular sector of the industry concerned. It is generally advantageous to have deft hands and high standards of neatness and precision. In factories, a willingness to be part of a team is needed, while in bespoke tailoring a candidate should have a pleasant manner and be able to put potential customers at their ease.

Starting Salary

Depends upon individual employers. Graduates generally start on £13,000.

CAPITB Trust, 80 Richardshaw Lane, Pudsey, Leeds LS28 6BN; 0113 239 3355; www.careers-in-clothing.co.uk

COACH

There are many opportunities for coaches, both voluntary and paid, in a wide variety of sports provided by sports centres, clubs, schools and swimming baths. Some local authorities employ coaches to offer facilities for local schools at one or more centres in the authority. Such coaches are expected to be able to coach in most of the following sports: badminton, basketball, climbing (on indoor walls), ice skating, swimming, squash, tennis, trampolining and weight training. Increasingly, there is a need for coaches in the summer months to work in outdoor activity centres.

Qualifications and Training

Coaches must gain recognised coaching qualifications, which are awarded by the governing bodies of the various sports and acquired either at evening class or weekend school. Swimming coaches must also hold a national lifeguard award.

Personal Qualities

Coaches need the ability to communicate, as well as perseverance, patience and tact. The ability to inspire children or adults of very different abilities, often in less than ideal situations, is also needed.

Starting Salary

Salaries vary greatly. Local authorities' coaches receive £11+ an hour.

Sport England, 16 Upper Woburn Place, London WC1H 0QP; 020 7273 1500; www.sportengland.org.
Sport Scotland, Caledonia House, South Gyle, Edinburgh EH12 9DQ; 0131 317 7200
Sports Wales, Sophia Gardens, Cardiff CF1 9SW; 029 2039 7571
Sports Coach UK; www.sportscoachuk.org

COACH DRIVER

see *Bus and Coach Companies, Road Transport*

COASTGUARD

HM Coastguard coordinates maritime search and rescue for the UK. Their area of responsibility, which covers approximately 10,500 miles of coastline and a million square miles of sea, is divided into four Search and Rescue Regions. Each is headed by a Regional Inspector, and within each Region are Maritime Rescue Coordination Centres and Sub Centres from which searches and rescues are coordinated.

At these centres, a constant watch is kept on international distress frequencies, satellite, radio and telephone communications, all of which are responded to immediately. HM Coastguard can call upon a wide range of facilities for search and rescue, including lifeboats, helicopters, tugs and local rescue organizations for rescues at sea. On-shore rescues from cliffs and mud are carried out by teams of Auxiliary Coastguards.

Qualifications and Training

Most coastguard officers are ex-seamen who have done previous marine work in services such as the Royal Navy or the Merchant Navy. Coastguard Watch Officers should have a minimum of 4 years' professional maritime/navigational experience evidenced by qualifications such as laid down for Accreditation of Prior Learning for VTS (Vehicle Traffic Separation) Module 4 – Nautical Knowledge (Class 4 (deck)), OOW (Officer of the Watch) Unlimited, Master (less than 500 gt) Near Coastal, Class 2 (fishing) or acceptable equivalent.

All candidates will require GCSE grade C or above in both English and maths. If candidates do not have these or equivalents, competency tests can be taken as part of the assessment process.

Personal Qualities

Good eyesight and hearing are essential. Candidates are expected to pass a strict medical and must be prepared to work shifts and serve anywhere in the UK.

Starting Salary

£11,281 plus 25 per cent shift allowance.

The Maritime and Coastguard Agency, Personnel Section, Spring Place, 105 Commercial Road, Southampton SO15 1EG; 023 8032 9461; www.mcagency.org.uk

COLOUR SCIENCE AND TECHNOLOGY

Colour technologists are concerned with producing dyes and pigments that have a wide range of applications, including the textile, paint, rubber, plastics, paper, leather and foodstuffs industries. They must ensure that exact colours can be produced at an economic price and in the right quantities whenever they are needed. They are often involved in research and development projects. Technologists are also employed in sales, management, buying, development and research, quality control, customer liaison and technical services departments (depending on the industry involved and the expertise needed).

Textile technologists may work in the design, manufacture and operation of textile machinery, and in the design, production, coloration, finishing and manufacture of fibres, yarns and fabrics of all types.

Qualifications and Training

Two, preferably three, A levels or equivalents, one of which must be chemistry or a subject including chemistry, are required for entry to a degree course in colour chemistry or textile chemistry. Minimum entry requirements for part-time technician courses leading to the Edexcel (BTEC)/SQA certificate and higher certificate in textile coloration (textile dyeing) are GCSE or equivalent in maths, an appropriate science and English.

For textile technologists, the basic professional qualification is the Associateship and Chartered Textile Technologist (CText ATI) of the Textile Institute, awarded on the fulfilment of the academic and industrial/professional experience requirements. The professional qualification for a specialist in colour technology is the Associateship and Chartered Colourist of the Society of Dyers and Colourists (CCol ASDC) or the Licentiateship of the Society of Dyers and Colourists (LSDC).

Personal Qualities

Good colour vision is essential, as is scientific or technical ability and the ability to work as part of a team.

Starting Salary

£14,000+ with a degree; £8,500+ for a textile technologist.

The Society of Dyers and Colourists, PO Box 244, 82 Grattan Road, Bradford, West Yorkshire BD1 2JB; 01274 725138; www.sdc.org.uk

COMPANY SECRETARY

The Company Secretary plays a major part in the organization's governance. Duties include ensuring that the company complies with relevant legal and regulatory matters, administration of mergers and acquisitions, drafting contracts, advising the board of directors on company law and procedures and maintaining company records. Other duties can include pensions administration, personnel matters, shareholder issues, property management and finance.

Qualifications and Training

The law recognises the importance of the Company Secretary role, mandatory for every company, by requiring the Company Secretary of a public limited company (plc) to have specific knowledge and experience. Only the Institute of Chartered Secretaries and Administrators (ICSA) qualification specifically addresses the requirements of the role.

The ICSA Qualifying Scheme comprises three programmes: Foundation, Pre-Professional and Professional. Graduates and holders of recognised postgraduate qualifications are eligible for direct access on to the Professional Programme. It consists of core modules in Corporate Governance, Corporate Administration, Corporate Secretaryship, Corporate Financial Management, and top-up modules in Corporate Law, Management Accounting, Financial Accounting and Strategic Management.

Upon completion of the ICSA Qualifying Scheme, candidates become Graduates of the Institute (Grad ICSA). To become a Member, an ICSA Graduate has to demonstrate three years' relevant experience and have two sponsors of professional status to confirm their fitness to practise. There are two grades of Membership: Associate and Fellow.

Personal Qualities

The Company Secretary must possess integrity and sound judgement, with the ability to act with authority for the good of the company. High-level organizational skills and a flair for administration are also important, along with strong communication skills, numeracy and ICT skills.

Starting Salary

Those with little previous experience can expect a starting salary of between £18,000 and £22,000. A salary above £70,000 is not uncommon for an experienced, fully qualified Company Secretary. Salaries will vary depending on the size and location of the company.

Graduate Recruitment Managers, The Institute of Chartered Secretaries and Administrators (ICSA), 16 Park Crescent, London W1B 1AH; 020 7612 7028/26; fax: 020 7612 7027; www.icsa.org.uk; e-mail: gradrec@icsa.co.uk

COMPUTING

(see also *Call Contact Centre, Information and Communication Technology*)

Work that involves using a computer is common in all career areas; computer literacy is an asset for most jobs and essential in a growing number. The uses of computers are almost limitless; there are applications in industry (on production lines), in commerce (for preparing salaries, invoices and business-to-business transactions via the Internet), in retailing (for stock control, customer databases and online selling), in scientific research (for analysing and comparing results), in travel (for making and confirming bookings and flight reservations) and in banking (for storing information about accounts and providing Internet banking services).

The majority of UK businesses and organizations now have a Web site and a growing number do business on the Web. This has created a range of new jobs, from developing e-commerce sites to running online communities. However, it is an extremely fast-moving area with many people working on short-term contracts and the demand for skilled workers fluctuates. The initial growth in dot com companies led to large numbers of jobs being created for designers, writers, salespeople and customer support staff. This has been followed by a large number of redundancies as companies closed or slimmed down. Although the boom in Internet-related work seems to be over, there is still a steady demand for those with creative, technical and e-marketing skills.

Computer Service Technician

Employed by retailers, manufacturers and organizations which make extensive use of computers in their business. Regular upgrading of office systems means a substantial amount of time is spent on installing and checking new systems, the rest being spent on diagnosing and correcting faults.

Database Administration

Organizations obtain and store information about their customers, accounts, orders or stock levels on computers. The database manager takes responsibility for maintaining these and for security, access and the legal use of information held.

Hardware Engineer

Engineers design, develop and undertake research into computers and the computerised components of cars and appliances. They are involved in manufacture, installation and testing. As well as dealing with engineering issues they need to be aware of safety, efficiency and environmental factors.

Network Engineer

A network is a system of computers and other communication equipment linked to exchange information. This could be used to enable staff to share information through a company intranet or for global communication via the Internet. Network engineers advise clients on options and benefits, as well as installing and testing equipment. They also diagnose faults and maintain the hardware, software and cabling systems.

Programmers

These are the people who write software such as operating systems. They may be employed by software manufacturers or in the computer departments of large organizations. As well as creating new programs they can be involved in identifying bugs in existing programs, modifying them, testing new programs and preparing user manuals.

Software engineers

They have a similar role to that of programmers but use this in technical and engineering settings. They may, for example, work on systems for contact centres or air traffic control. Most have a degree in software engineering or a related computer science. Many universities ask for maths A level or equivalent for entry to such courses. As most commercial and manufacturing functions now have established IT systems, the work undertaken by software engineers has shifted emphasis from creating new systems to using existing software and devising appropriate interfaces to integrate it with new products.

Systems Analysts

Systems analysts work on delivering the best IT solutions for an organization's needs. They examine how and where computerised systems would be of benefit, assess the hardware needed and look at the most cost-effective solutions. Systems analysts then work with programmers and supervise software production.

Systems Support Staff

Systems support staff work for suppliers of software and hardware, Internet service providers or the computer departments of large companies. They provide technical support to users, often via the phone or e-mail. The work involves establishing what the problem is, helping the client put things right or deciding to refer the problem to other specialists. It requires detailed product knowledge as well as extreme patience and excellent communication skills. Training is often on the job, with entrants coming from a variety of backgrounds in which they have been able to demonstrate high levels of computer literacy.

Trainers

Software packages are increasingly complex and users require training to get the best out of them. Trainers are employed by software vendors, training consultancies and user companies for their own staff. Trainers need to be familiar with the packages at all levels, and have excellent communication and teaching skills. They may also be required to develop and write materials.

Web Designers

Web designers design and plan Web sites either for their own company or for clients. The complexity of the task varies according to the nature of the site and can include extensive use of multimedia or implementing secure systems for financial transactions. A considerable amount of time is spent testing sites and checking they are user friendly. Once the site is working properly, designers upload it to a server and may be responsible for registering it with search engines in order to drive traffic to the site. In some cases designers are involved in keeping the site up to date in terms of both content and design.

Designers need an in-depth knowledge of the Internet and must be up to date with technological developments. Many designers work on a freelance basis. The availability of jobs in this area is decreasing as increasingly sophisticated software packages are making Web design less of a specialist area.

Qualifications and Training

Many employers set their own entry requirements, but are increasingly asking for academic or vocational qualifications from NVQs to degrees. Applicants for posts may be asked to take aptitude tests to assess their numeracy, logic, accuracy, thinking speed and verbal reasoning. Systems analysts and programmers are generally expected to be graduates. Entry to computer science degrees is normally with 2–3 A levels or equivalent, including maths. Web designers need a knowledge of HTML and Java as well as familiarity with Web design software such as Dreamweaver and Flash. Technicians and network engineers usually have a related National Diploma or vendor qualifications.

There are a large number of computer-related courses and entry requirements vary according to the nature of the course. A growing number of Foundation Degrees with flexible entry requirements are becoming available. Product-specific and professional qualifications are offered by companies such as Microsoft, Cisco and Novell and by professional bodies such as the British Computer Society, the Help Desk Institute and the Institute for the Management of Information Systems.

Employment-based training opportunities include Modern Apprenticeships for school leavers and Graduate Apprenticeships for those from non-IT disciplines. Many companies run their own programmes as well as sending trainees on relevant external courses.

Personal Qualities

All the above roles require an analytical and creative approach to problem solving. Excellent team working and communication skills are equally essential.

Starting Salary

Graduate trainees £16,000–£22,000+; technicians and support staff £15,000–£21,000; both vary depending on location, size and type of employer.

i

e-skills NTO, 1 Castle Lane, London, SW1E 6DR; 020 7963 8920; www.e-skillsnto.org.uk; e-mail: info@e-skillsnto.org.uk

British Computer Society, 1 Sanford Street, Swindon, Wiltshire SN1 1HJ; 01793 417424; www.bcs.org.uk

Help Desk Institute, 21 High Street, Green Street Green, Orpington, Kent BR6 6BG; 01689 889 100; www.hdi-europe.com; e-mail: support@hdi-europe.com

Institution of Analysts and Programmers, Charles House, 36 Culmington Road, London W13 9NH; 020 8567 2118; www.iap.org.uk

Institute for the Management of Information Systems, 5 Kingfisher House, New Mill Road, Orpington, Kent BR5 3QG; 0700 00 23456; www.imis.org.uk; e-mail: central@imis.org.uk

British Interactive Media Association, Briarlea House, Southend Road, South Green, Billericay CM11 2PR; 020 7436 8250; www.bima.co.uk

CONFERENCE ORGANISER

In many companies, conference organization is combined with other promotional or administrative duties. Large organizations and industrial concerns may have their own conference departments with staff responsible for coordinating the necessary arrangements for regular sales conferences, staff conferences, product launches and special events. These will employ staff specializing in the organization of meetings and events. Other firms employ professional conference organisers.

Conference organisers select and book the most suitable venue, organise the invitations and where necessary, accommodation for participants. They also deal with the relevant paperwork, catering and reception facilities, any specialist equipment necessary (such as video, microphones, projectors and closed-circuit television), media coverage and a host of minor details. Some firms of professional organisers have a small core staff and employ temporary freelancers.

Conference centres and hotels specializing in conference facilities have their own staff who are responsible for arrangements for conferences already booked and for advertising and encouraging further bookings.

Qualifications and Training
There are no formal educational requirements, but NVQs are available. Useful experience could include sales and marketing, knowledge of hotel and venue operations, and language skills, as well as secretarial duties. Computer literacy is important.

Personal Qualities
A flair for organization and forward planning is needed, as are tact, discretion and the ability to talk to all kinds of people and anticipate their various demands. In addition, some conference organisers should be prepared to work abroad.

Starting Salary
Large firms offer £15,000–£17,000. Salaries for freelancers vary according to the type and amount of work undertaken.

Association for Conferences and Events, ACE International, Riverside House, High Street, Huntingdon, Cambridgeshire PE29 3SG; 01480 457595; www.marktex.co.uk/ace; e-mail ace@martex.co.uk

How to Organise Effective Conferences and Meetings (Kogan Page)

CONSERVATION (ENVIRONMENTAL)

Environmental conservation covers a range of activities from recycling waste to habitat management. It does not just involve green issues but is about making the best use of scientific knowledge to produce solutions for a sustainable environment. Conservation includes the protection of rural and urban landscapes, plants and animals and countryside recreation. This includes protection and management of rivers, coastal zones and waterways, together with their fisheries and fish stocks.

There are opportunities in a range of organizations from government departments to the voluntary sector. Competition for jobs is high but there can be a lack of applicants with experience, which often needs to be gained through voluntary work. A large proportion of those working for conservation organizations do so on a voluntary, casual or part-time basis. It's estimated that 47,000 paid employees work in this sector alongside 200,000 volunteers. The majority of those in permanent jobs have higher education qualifications. Many of the permanent jobs are with government agencies, which include the following.

The Countryside Agency is the statutory body working for people and places in rural England. It aims to conserve and enhance the countryside, to promote social equity and economic opportunity for the people who live there, and to help everyone, wherever they live, to enjoy this national asset. This is achieved by leading via research and advice, influencing others, especially central and local government, and by demonstrating ways forward through practical projects.

English Nature, the statutory adviser to government on nature conservation in England, promotes the conservation of wildlife and natural features. Its work includes the selection, establishment and management of national nature reserves and marine nature reserves, the identification and provision of advice and information about nature conservation and the support and conduct of relevant research. The Countryside Council for Wales and Scottish Natural Heritage fulfil similar roles in those countries.

The Department of the Environment, Transport and the Regions supervises and advises upon land reclamation and coastline protection schemes carried out by local authorities. It is also involved with national parks projects and the restoration of derelict sites.

The Natural Environment Research Council involves itself in a broad range of activities concerned with conservation (mainly involving scientists), including geological surveys, studies of the ocean, terrestrial ecology and the British Antarctic Survey, which studies atmospheric, earth and life sciences.

In addition, conservation is carried out by a large number of voluntary societies, such as the Councils for the Protection of Rural England, Wales and Scotland, the Commons Open Spaces Trust, British Trust for Conservation Volunteers and The Wildlife Trusts Partnership. Such organizations have a few full-time posts, mainly confined to administrative staff.

The National Trust is the largest single private landowner in the country. It is concerned with the conservation of places of natural beauty and historic buildings, employing land agents and various specialist staff to care for such sites and to supervise the visiting public. The Royal Society for the Protection of Birds has its own protected reserves and employs nature wardens, researchers and surveyors in reserve management, although such posts are relatively few.

Qualifications and Training

Qualifications vary, as there are many different jobs. Conservation officers and science specialists need relevant degrees or equivalent; much of the training is done on the job with the opportunity to gain related NVQs at levels 1–4 in a range of specialisms, including landscapes and ecosystems, maintaining and conserving rivers, coasts and waterways and environmental management.

Personal Qualities

Conservationists must show dedication in their chosen field and be prepared to work as part of a team.

Starting Salary

Salaries vary but are in the region of £13,000 for Assistant Ecology and Conservation Officers; scientists and engineers can earn more.

i

Lantra Connect, Lantra House, NAC, Kenilworth, Warwickshire
   CV8 2LG; 0845 707 8007 (Lantra Connect – Helpline);
   www.lantra.co.uk; e-mail: connect@lantra.co.uk
The Countryside Agency, John Dower House, Crescent Place,
   Cheltenham GL50 3RA; 01242 531381;
   www.countryside.gov.uk; e-mail: info@countryside.gov.uk
Countryside Council for Wales, Plas Penrhos, Ffordd Penrhos,
   Bangor, Gwynedd LL57 2LQ; 01248 370444; www.ccw.gov.uk
English Nature, Northminster House, Peterborough PE1 1UA;
   01733 455000; www.english-nature.org.uk;
   e-mail: enquiries@english-nature.org.uk
National Trust, 36 Queen Anne's Gate, London SW1H 9AS;
   020 7222 9251; fax: 020 7222 5097;
   www.nationaltrust.org.uk;
   e-mail: enquiries@ntrust.org.uk
Natural Environment Research Council, Polaris House,
   North Star Avenue, Swindon SN2 1EU; 01793 411500;
   www.nerc.ac.uk
The Royal Society for the Protection of Birds, The Lodge, Sandy,
   Bedfordshire SG19 2DL; 01767 680551; www.rspb.org.uk
Scottish Natural Heritage, 12 Hope Terrace, Edinburgh EH9 2AS;
   0131 447 4784; www.snh.org.uk
Environment Agency, Rio House, Waterside Drive, Aztec West,
   Almondsbury, Bristol BS32 4UD; 01454 624400;
   fax: 01454 624409; www.environment-agency.gov.uk
BTCV, 36 St Mary's Street, Wallingford, Oxfordshire OX10 0EU;
   01491 821600; www.btcv.org
The Wildlife Trusts Partnership; www.wildlifetrusts.org
Careers in Environmental Conservation (Kogan Page)

CONSERVATION (HERITAGE AND ARTS)

Conservation is the ethical preservation of works of art and
historic objects such as paintings and sculpture, historic buildings,
furniture, textiles (such as costumes and tapestries), manuscripts,
clocks and china. Some museums and art galleries employ specialist conservators who are responsible for conserving, repairing and

protecting the exhibits in their charge, using the latest scientific techniques. Such work generally calls for scientific training and historical knowledge. A large number of conservators and restorers also work in the private sector, usually in small workshops of 2–5 people, sometimes larger units of up to 30. These serve private owners, historic house owners, dealers and auctioneers. Increasingly, museums and art galleries are sending out more of their objects to private conservators rather than taking on their own staff.

Qualifications and Training

Training courses accept students from a wide variety of backgrounds. An art, crafts or history background is a good starting point, and although familiarity with a science is desirable this is often provided on the course. The most important thing is demonstrating being good at working with one's hands. The training courses for conservators, whether employed by museums or in private practice, are increasingly at degree or postgraduate level, though a number are at HND level.

Personal Qualities

Those working in this area need scientific ability, good problem-solving skills, a strong sense of ethics, meticulous attention to detail and patience.

i

Cultural Heritage National Training Organization (CHNTO) 1st Floor, Glyde House, Glydegate, Bradford BD5 0UP; 01274 391056; fax: 01274 394890; www.chnto.co.uk

UK Institute for Conservation of Historic and Artistic Works, 109 The Chandlery, 50 Westminster Bridge, London SE1 7QY; 020 7721 8721; www.ukic.org.uk; e-mail: ukic@ukic.org.uk

Historic Scotland, Scottish Conservation Bureau, Longmore House, Salisbury Place, Edinburgh EH9 1SH; 0131 668 8668; www.historic-scotland.gov.uk

The Institute for Paper Conservation, Leigh Lodge, Leigh, Worcester WR6 5LB; 01886 832323; www.ipc.org.uk

CONSTITUENCY AGENT

see *Politics*

COURIER (MESSENGER)

Couriers deliver and collect parcels, generally in larger towns and cities. Around ten thousand couriers work in Central London. Mostly, the delivery or collection is in the same city, sometimes in a different one and, very occasionally, another country. Most couriers use a motorbike, which they may be required to buy. Couriers carrying packages abroad travel by air.

Qualifications and Training

No formal educational qualifications are necessary. An NVQ level 2 qualification is available. Motorbike couriers must be 17 and hold a clean licence.

Personal Qualities

Couriers are generally required when speed is important or when the package cannot be entrusted to the post. Reliability is most important, as is the ability to arrive without undue delays. Common sense and initiative are also useful. It is an outdoor job so couriers must be prepared to work in all weathers.

Starting Salary

Some couriers are self-employed, with the firm paying a certain amount per mile, and the messenger being responsible for petrol, insurance and other overheads. Others are employees. Starting salaries vary, but an employed courier can earn between £180 and £350 a week.

Local Jobcentres and Careers/Connexions Centres
Camelot Training, 1st floor, Green Man Tower, 332 Goswell Road, London EC1V 7LQ; www.couriertraining.com; e-mail: mail@couriertraining.com

COURIER (TRAVEL)
see *Tour Managers*

COURT STAFF
(see also *Barrister's Clerk*)

Court Reporter
Court reporters attend court sittings and take down a complete report of all the evidence, the summing-up or judgment and, on occasions, the speeches of counsel in the various cases. Formerly, the proceedings were taken down in shorthand; now a palantype or stenograph is used. This is a typewriter-like machine which enables the reporter to achieve 200 words per minute. In addition, computers may be used to prepare transcripts with all the advantages of on-screen editing and speed of preparation. The work sometimes involves travelling to a number of different courts. The majority of verbatim reporters begin their careers in the courts but can also work for *Hansard*, producing reports of proceedings in the House of Commons and the House of Lords. Television subtitlers also use the skills of verbatim reporting.

Justices' Clerks' Assistant
Administrative assistants and administrative officers assist Justices' Clerks in the administration of the magistrates' courts. Their work involves the preparing of summonses and warrants, the issuing of licences and fine notices and seeing that correct court procedures are followed.

In Scotland, the administration of the court comes under the province of the Scottish Court Administration, which is part of the Civil Service. This includes staff who do a similar job to Justices' Clerks' assistants.

Qualifications and Training
No specific academic qualifications are demanded for court reporters, although GCSE and A level passes can be an advantage. Applicants need to have proven ability in shorthand or stenotyping (usually over 150 words per minute), good typing speeds,

and a thorough knowledge of grammar and punctuation. Legal experience can also be an asset. Details of full-time, part-time and distance learning courses are available from the British Institute of Verbatim Reporters. In Scotland, there are no college courses but training is provided on the job by working alongside an experienced reporter.

Administrative Officers need five GCSE passes (grade C or above), one of which must be English. The Scottish Court Service look for applicants with Highers. Training lasts for two to three years, during which time trainees work and undertake courses run by the Court Service.

Personal Qualities

Anyone concerned with the courts must be discreet, honest and trustworthy, as most of the work is confidential. Reporters must show a high degree of accuracy.

Starting Salary

Qualified court reporters earn around £13,000. Freelancers can earn £140+ a day.

i

British Institute of Verbatim Reporters, 61 Carey Street, London WC2A 2JG (for court reporters; send an sae)

Individual Courts of Law

Northern Ireland Court Service, Windsor House, Bedford Street, Belfast BT2 7LT; 028 9032 8594; www.nics.gov.uk/pubsec/courts/courts.htm

The Law Society of Scotland, 26 Drumsheugh Gardens, Edinburgh EH3 7YR; 0131 226 7411; www.lawscot.org.uk

Careers in the Law (Kogan Page)

CROUPIER

Croupiers work at gaming tables in clubs and casinos. They are in charge of accepting the bets, allocating chips, spinning the roulette wheel or dealing the cards, and giving out the winnings, or gathering in what customers have lost.

Qualifications and Training

No formal educational qualifications are needed but a good head for figures is vital, and GCSE level maths is an advantage. A smart appearance and pleasant personality are assets. No one with a criminal record can be granted a gaming licence by the Government Gaming Board, and without such a licence it is impossible to be legally employed as a croupier in Britain.

Most of the major casinos have their own training schools where candidates are taught how to dress, behave and treat the customers, as well as the rules of the various games, special skills for counting chips, memorizing and calculating the bets. It takes six weeks to train as a croupier

Personal Qualities

The job involves working with people so good communication skills and an ability to defuse potentially awkward situations are needed. Manual dexterity and mental agility are essential. Croupiers need to take pride in their appearance and have an unflappable nature. They must also be scrupulously honest, willing to work shifts and unsocial hours. Most casinos are open until 6 am, and staff may be required to work this shift up to twice a week. Greater deregulation is expected in coming years

Starting Salary

Salaries vary, with starting salaries between £9,000 and £11,000; experienced staff can earn £10,000–£14,000.

The Gaming Board for Great Britain, Berkshire House, 168–173 High Holborn, London, WC1V 7AA; www.gbgb.org.uk www.e-casinoworld.co.uk (Details of training schools, casino head offices and jobs.)

Local Jobcentres and Careers/Connexions Centres

CURATOR

see *Museum and Art Gallery Work*

CUSTOMS AND EXCISE

HM Customs and Excise is responsible for collecting about 40 per cent of central government taxation and protects society against illegal importations of drugs and other prohibited goods.

Most new entrants to the Department are at Executive Officer level and begin their career in a local VAT office. They give advice to local businesses and are responsible for ensuring that the correct amount of tax is paid. Executive officers are likely to spend four days out of five visiting companies to find out what they do and to audit their records.

The Department is also responsible for collecting excise duties; for example, on petrol, spirits, cigarettes, and betting and gaming. Again, the Department's role is to ensure that businesses understand their responsibilities.

Probably the most familiar role is the control of imported and exported goods at ports and airports throughout the UK. As well as checking passengers' baggage, commercial importations of cargo are examined. The work is interesting and varied, with opportunities to get out of the office. With offices all over the UK, there are often opportunities to work in a choice of locations.

Qualifications and Training

There are three main entry levels into Customs and Excise. Administrative Assistants need two GCSEs at C grade or above, including English language. Administrative Officers require five GCSEs at C grade or above, including English language. Alternatively, with two A levels and three GCSEs, including English language, it is possible to join at junior management level as an Executive Officer. Full training is given as necessary. This may involve a combination of classroom training, self-learning packages and on-the-job training.

Personal Qualities

An ability to get on with people, tact, sensitivity and firmness are all useful qualities. Candidates also need to be able to use their initiative and common sense.

Starting Salary

Varies depending on age and location but an indication is: Administrative Assistant £9,891–£13,002; Administrative Officer £12,220–£16,136; Executive Officer £15,400-£20,699. Rates are higher in London.

HM Customs and Excise, New King's Beam House, 22 Upper Ground, London SE1 9PJ; 020 7620 1313; www.hmce.gov.uk

DANCING

Dance can be divided into the two main categories of theatre dance (ballet, modern and contemporary dance, jazz, and tap) and social dance (ballroom, folk dance and disco). However, there are no hard and fast divisions between the different forms.

The profession of dancing consists of two main areas: performing and teaching. Choreography, notation, dance animation and dance therapy are related areas of work.

Performing
Many of those who wish to perform have had early training in ballet and/or other forms of theatre dance. Opportunities in ballet and contemporary companies are limited and many dancers find their first employment in companies abroad. Dancers also work in pantomimes, shows and musicals, and on cruise ships. Professional performers find it useful to be members of the British Actors' Equity Association.

Teaching
Teachers of dance can specialise in one area of dance teaching or teach in a variety of areas. The demand for teachers is high, especially as dance is now seen as a form of recreation. Teachers may work in commercial dance studios and professional dance schools both in the UK and abroad.

Dance Notator
Notators are employed by dance companies to record their repertoire and assist choreographers and rehearsal staff in the revival of choreographic works. Most notators are graduates of voca-

tional dance schools or ex-professional dancers as the work involves close and informed observation of the choreography, the ability to demonstrate the movement accurately and the ability to work effectively with professional dancers.

Dance Animateur

Dance animateurs work in the community or education to encourage participation and involvement and to raise the profile of dance activity locally. Their precise role is dependent on the funding organization and the needs of the community in which they work.

Dance Therapy

Dance movement therapy uses movement and dance as a medium through which the individual can engage creatively in a process of growth and personal integration. Dance movement therapists work with individuals and groups in health, education and social service settings. Their clients include people who are emotionally disturbed or have learning difficulties, and those who want to use this therapy for personal growth.

Qualifications and Training

Ideally, ballet students should attend a recognised residential establishment such as the Royal Ballet School from the age of 11 to 18. Means-tested financial assistance may be available to UK students. Dancers who want to become teachers must obtain the relevant qualifications, for which full-time or part-time courses are available. These generally have an entry requirement of four to five GCSEs at grade C and above. The Royal Academy of Dancing offers certificates, diplomas and degrees in classical ballet teaching. The courses are available on a part-time and full-time basis.

Personal Qualities

Dancers need to be hard working, self-disciplined both physically and mentally, dedicated and determined. They must be imaginative, able to express themselves artistically, have a good sense of timing and an ear for music.

Starting Salary
Starting salaries vary according to the organization or company.

The Royal Ballet School, 155 Talgarth Road, London W14 9DE;
020 8748 6335; www.royalballetschool.co.uk
Royal Academy of Dancing, 36 Battersea Square, London SW11
3RA; 020 7223 0091; fax: 020 7924 3129; www.rad.org.uk
Council for Dance Education and Training (CDET), Toynbee
Hall, 28 Commercial Street London E1 6LS; 020 7247 4030;
fax: 020 7247 3404; www. cdet.org.uk; e-mail: info@cdet.org.uk
Association of Dance Movement Therapy UK, c/o The Quaker
Meeting Rooms, Wedmore Vale, Bedminster, Bristol BS3 5HX;
www.admt.org.uk
Dance UK, Battersea Arts Centre, Lavender Hill, London
SW11 5TN; 020 7228 4990; www.danceuk.org; e-mail:
info@danceuk.org

DENTISTRY

Currently all dentists, dental hygienists and dental therapists must
be registered with the General Dental Council in order to practise in
the UK. The GDC plans to extend statutory professional regulation
to include all members of the dental team, dental nurses and technicians and other professionals complementary to dentistry.

Dentist
Dentists aim to prevent gum disease and tooth decay and to identify and treat such diseases. This involves filling, crowning and
extracting teeth, scaling and cleaning teeth and gums. They design
and fit dentures and plates and take corrective measures for teeth
growing abnormally. They are also involved with the rectification
of fractured jaws and surgery of the mouth. Opportunities exist
both in the UK and abroad. In general dental practice, dentists
work on contract to the NHS, but growing numbers work in
private clinics. Some work in hospitals, community services, school
services or the armed forces. There are also opportunities for
dentists to work in university dental teaching and research.

Dental Hygienist

Dental hygienists clean, polish and scale teeth and, in some cases, prepare patients for oral operations. Through lectures and practical experience they also endeavour to educate children and adults on the importance of proper dental care. Dental hygienists work to the written prescription of a dentist.

Dental Nurse

Dental nurses prepare the surgery and get the appropriate instruments ready. During treatment, they assist the dentist by passing instruments, mixing materials, taking notes from the dentist's dictation for records and making sure the patient is comfortable at all times. Once the patient has left, the dental nurse tidies the surgery and sterilises all the instruments. Sometimes, particularly in general practice, dental nurses also help with reception work – making appointments, taking payments, dealing with the paper work, meeting and reassuring patients.

Dental Technician

Dental technicians design and fabricate a wide variety of different materials and equipment to make crowns, dentures, metal plates, bridges, orthodontic braces and other appliances prescribed by a dentist.

Dental Therapist

Dental therapists work in local authority clinics and hospitals assisting dentists by carrying out simpler forms of treatment such as fillings and the extraction of first teeth. They also give guidance on general dental care. Dental therapists must always work to the written prescription of a dentist.

Qualifications and Training

Dentist

To qualify, a dentist must have a degree in dental surgery. All dentists must be registered to the Dentists' Register, which is maintained by the General Dental Council. Competition for degree course entry is stiff, requiring good A level grades in physics, chemistry and biology. Entry requirements vary; some schools have pre-dental courses for students who have not studied science A levels. All applicants are expected to have spent time work-shadowing a dentist.

The undergraduate course lasts at least five years. It incorporates a sound academic education combined with theoretical and practical training in all aspects of dental practice.

In the armed forces, dental cadetships leading to a commission are open to candidates who have completed part of their training at a dental school.

Dental Hygienist

Applicants for the Diploma in Dental Hygiene must be over 18 with five GCSE passes, including biology and English. They also need two years' experience as a dental nurse or two A levels or equivalent. Manchester University offers a three-year BSc in Oral Health Science. Graduates work as Oral Health Therapists which combines the skills of a hygienist and therapist.

Dental Nurse

Many dentists like to train their own assistants and expect applicants to be educated to GCSE standard. Currently dental nurses in general practice do not need to have undertaken specific training; however, compulsory registration will be introduced in the near future. This will require students to have obtained NVQ level 3 or passed the National Certificate of the Examining Board for Dental Nurses. Preparation for this exam can be obtained either at evening or day-release classes or via full-time attendance on a course lasting between one and two years. A certificate is awarded on passing the exam and completing 24 months' practical experience. Courses are offered by colleges of further education and dental hospitals. Courses offered by dental hospitals usually require four GCSE passes, including English and biology.

Dental Technician

The usual entry requirements for courses are five GCSEs or equivalents (English, maths, physics and chemistry). The Edexcel (BTEC) diploma in dental technology is a full-time three-year course but can also be studied part-time.

Dental Therapist

To become a dental therapist it is necessary to take a 27-month full-time course. The minimum course entry requirement is five

GCSE passes or equivalents; these should include English and biology. Applicants should also hold the National Certificate for Dental Nurses, which requires at least two years' practical experience. As competition for places is fierce, actual requirements are likely to be higher than this.

Personal Qualities
Manual and visual dexterity combined with medical knowledge and clinical skills are essential. Candidates should be equable, sympathetic and have an agreeable nature and an ability to communicate. Good administrative and managerial skills and the ability to work in a team are important.

Starting Salary
General dental practitioners earn the fees that they receive from patients or the NHS; these start from £24,500. Salaries for senior posts are over £50,000. Dental hygienists earn £13,500 +; dental technicians £7,500–£9,000 whilst training, rising to £10,000–£18,000 when qualified. Salaries for dental nurses vary greatly depending on the type of practice and its location. Some employers pay around the national minimum wage; others pay more and include additional benefits.

> [i]

British Association of Dental Nurses, 11 Pharos Street, Fleetwood, Lancashire FY7 6BG; 01253 778631; www.badn.org.uk; e-mail: admin@badn.org.uk

The British Dental Association, 64 Wimpole Street, London W1M 8AL; 020 7935 0875; www.bda-dentistry.org.uk

National Examining Board for Dental Nurses, 110, London Road, Fleetwood F17 6EU; 01253 778417

British Dental Hygienists' Association, 13 The Ridge, Yatton, Bristol BS19 4DQ; 01934 876389; www.bdha.org.uk

The Dental Technicians' Education and Training Advisory Board (DTETAB), 5 Oxford Court, St James Road, Brackley, Northamptonshire NN13 7XY; 01280 702600; www.dtetab.co.uk

General Dental Council, 37 Wimpole Street, London W1G 8DQ; 020 7887 3800; www.gdc-uk.org

DESIGNER

see *Artist, Fashion, Industrial Designer, Interior Designer, Jewellery Trade, Publishing, Theatre*

DETECTIVE/PRIVATE INVESTIGATOR

A private detective can either be self-employed or work as part of an agency. The investigation profession has a diverse workload and it is therefore difficult to generalise. A small cross-section of the subjects that an investigator may be instructed to assist with are tracing missing persons and debtors; finding witnesses and taking statements; undertaking video and photographic surveillance for matrimonial cases or insurance company fraud investigations; process serving (the correct delivery of legal documents); pre sue and means enquiries; verification of credit worthiness; road traffic and industrial accident investigations involving sketch plans and photographs; land registry searches; land and property repossession and test purchases.

Qualifications and Training

No formal qualifications are necessary but a good standard of education will be an advantage in the preparation of reports and the taking of statements. Training seminars are run by the Association of British Investigators. A sound knowledge of computers, experience in credit control or in a service industry providing direct contact with the public is useful. NVQs level 3 and 4 are available in Investigation Techniques.

A private detective needs personal indemnity and public liability insurance, and should also register with the Office of Fair Trading and the Data Protection Registrar. It is also advisable to obtain membership of a recognised association.

Personal Qualities

Honesty, integrity, and discretion are vital. Patience, perseverance, self-motivation, ability to work on one's own initiative, adaptability and a good outgoing personality are all useful qualities.

Starting Salary

This depends upon experience and location. An agency charges £20+ per hour but pays lower rates to staff. The self-employed may be able to charge similar rates.

Association of British Investigators, 48 Queens Road, Basingstoke, Hampshire RG21 7RE; (The General Secretary can assist with finding a local agency that may offer further information.); www.assoc-britishinvestigators.org.uk
Local Jobcentres and Careers/Connexions Centres
Libraries hold directories of investigators

DIETITIAN

A dietitian is an authority on diet and the application of the principles of nutrition. Dietitians working in hospitals collaborate with medical staff, other healthcare professionals and catering staff in planning the correct balance of foods for all the patients, depending on their general state of health and medical requirements. Dietitians are also employed by local health authorities to work with general practitioners, in health centres and clinics dealing with infant welfare and antenatal treatment. Some dietitians may now be employed directly by fund-holding GPs. They are also called upon to educate other healthcare professionals in nutrition. Other opportunities for dietitians exist in education, research, the food industry and the media. Increasingly, dietitians work in a freelance capacity.

Qualifications and Training

Dietetics is an all-graduate profession; entry to degree courses requires GCSEs in maths and English plus two or three A levels, preferably chemistry and another science. Edexcel (BTEC) qualifications may be acceptable and entry requirements may be relaxed for mature students.

Graduates with a relevant degree such as human physiology and biochemistry can take a postgraduate diploma course in dietetics at a number of universities.

Personal Qualities

A dietitian's special skill is to translate scientific and medical decisions relating to food and health into terms which everyone can understand. An interest in food, coupled with an understanding of how different cultural, social and economic factors can determine a person's dietary requirements, is needed in the dietitian. Dietitians must therefore be interested in people, not just the scientific aspects of their problems, and have a non-judgmental approach.

Starting Salary

£15,000+; senior dietitians earn £20,000–£24,000 and managers up to £33,000.

British Dietetics Association, 5th Floor, Charles House,
   148/9 Great Charles Street, Queensway, Birmingham B3 3HT;
   0121 200 8080; www.bdacareerchoices.com

DIPLOMAT

see *Civil Service*

DIRECT MARKETING

The increased sophistication of databases has led to the growth of niche marketing. Information gathered is used, subject to industry codes of practice, to make direct contact between companies and prospective customers. Direct marketing is based on providing relevant, timely products and services and then developing an ongoing relationship with customers and encouraging loyalty. The industry makes use of all communications channels, including mail; telephone; door-drops; fax; field marketing; direct response TV, radio and press advertisements and inserts; the Internet; mobile phone SMS and interactive TV.

   Job roles within industry include creative/copy writing, production, account planning, data planning, and account handling (also known as client service). The most frequently chosen path for people with good marketing qualifications (*see* below under Qualifications and Training) is account handling. New entrants tend to be graduates, with some work experience in a marketing or sales-led organization.

Other career opportunities include specialist areas such as field marketing (demonstrations, merchandising; road shows), tele-marketing, mailing, e-mail and SMS marketing which can require some technical ability and knowledge.

Qualifications and Training

Entry qualifications can vary considerably, depending on the products or services being sold. Good GCSEs are the minimum, but employers are increasingly demanding an appropriate degree or diploma such as the Chartered Institute of Marketing's gradu-ate Diploma in Marketing. Colleges, universities and education and training organizations, such as the Chartered Institute of Marketing, offer a wide range of marketing courses, or courses including marketing options. Additionally, most companies give some sort of in-house training in product knowledge, selling tech-niques, customer relations and order processing.

Personal Qualities

Account handlers need to be well presented, have an outgoing personality and be willing to work hard. They should also be excellent communicators (both written and verbal), diplomatic (particularly when dealing with clients), good negotiators, highly organised and able to deal with a wide variety of people at different levels. They also need to be numerate and have good business acumen in order to help their clients retain a competi-tive edge. There are also many technical roles within the direct marketing industry for people with computer and data process-ing skills.

Starting Salary

Entry level is usually at Junior Account Executive or Account Executive level and carries a salary of between £12,000 and £18,000, according to experience. Account managers with 2–3 years' experience can earn £20,000–£28,000; a Client Services Director can earn £65,000+.

i

The Direct Marketing Association (DMA) UK Ltd, Haymarket House, 1 Oxendon Street, London SW1Y 4EE; 020 7321 2525; www.dma.org.uk; e-mail: dma@dma.org.uk

DISC JOCKEY

Disc jockeys provide music and entertainment at a range of venues such as clubs, private parties and radio stations. They use a variety of high-tech equipment for mixing, pitch control, and cross-fading and may also be responsible for lighting and multimedia effects.

Qualifications and Training

A strong interest and enjoyment of different music styles is essential and it's useful to have an interest in technology and electronics. Some DJs specialise in specific music genres such as soul, funk, hip-hop and pop. Most are self-taught and usually begin their career by volunteering their services at clubs, radio stations or to friends. It is useful to send a tape demonstrating DJ skills when asking for work.

Personal Qualities

DJs must have a lively personality, a sense of fun, and natural creativity. They need to have a good knowledge of and genuine interest in music, and be able to interact effectively with an audience.

Starting Salary

This varies enormously, depending on the hours worked and the venue. Successful DJs are offered lucrative financial deals.

i

Local and national radio stations
Clubs and social venues

DISPENSING OPTICIAN

(see also *Optometrist*)
Dispensing opticians do not examine eyes or test sight, but supply and fit spectacles and other aids prescribed by an optometrist. They usually work in general practice, including independent businesses, partnership, as an employee of corporate bodies or as a franchisee. There are also job opportunities in hospitals and clinics. Once registered, dispensing opticians can undertake further training to enable them to fit contact lenses.

Qualifications and Training
A dispensing optician must be a Fellow of the Association of British Dispensing Opticians and have gained registration with the General Optical Council to practise in the UK. Minimum educational standards required for training are five GCSEs which must include English, maths and science each at grade A to C. For degree courses, minimum entry is two A levels or equivalent. Degrees are offered by Glasgow Caledonian University (BSc in ophthalmic dispensing); Bradford and Ilkley Community College (BSc Hons in ophthalmic dispensing with management) and Anglia Polytechnic University (BSc in optical management). All three include the full syllabus in ophthalmic dispensing leading to the Association's Fellowship Examination. A distance learning course is run by the Association of British Dispensing Opticians.

Personal Qualities
An ability to get on with patients of all ages and backgrounds and to be able to put them at their ease.

Starting Salary
£14,000–£18,000+.

Association of British Dispensing Opticians, c/o FODO,
113 Eastbourne Mews, London W2 6LQ; 020 7706 0289;
www.abdo.org.uk; e-mail: general@abdo.org.uk

ABDO College of Education, Godmersham Park Mansion, Godmersham, Canterbury, Kent CT4 7DT; 01227 738829; www.abdo.org.uk; e-mail: education@abdo.org.uk
'A Career in Vision Care' is available for download from www.college_optometrists.org

DISPLAY DESIGNER

Display designers are responsible for shop windows and displays inside stores. These may be to attract customers into a shop, promote a new product or reinforce a company image. Displays are often seasonal or themed. Some designers work to instructions from head office, others create their own designs. The work may include making props, arranging lighting and general care of the display areas. Some shops also employ visual merchandisers who arrange products according to an organization's display policy.

Qualifications and Training

Some companies have their own training schemes but these are generally intended to supplement previous training. Many designers have completed a higher-level course in design. Specialised courses in Visual Merchandising Management and Retail Design are available at degree, foundation degree and HND level at The London Institute. Other higher education courses in retail management can include a design option. Entry requirements for degrees are normally 2–3 A levels or equivalent; for Foundation Degrees and HNDs, 1–2 A levels or equivalent. Some art courses require applicants to have completed a foundation course in art and design. NVQs in Visual Merchandising at levels 2, 3 and 4 are available.

Personal Qualities

Display managers must have an interest in art and fashion and skill in handling materials, as well as an appreciation of colour, design and texture. They must have an understanding of sales techniques, be resourceful and have the ability to produce scale drawings. Ability to use computer-aided design packages is becoming increasingly important.

Starting Salary
£8,500–£10,000 whilst training, rising to £15,000+ once experienced.

Distributive NTO, Mardall House, 9–11 Vaughan Road,
 Harpenden, Hertfordshire AL5 5HU; 01582 760809;
 www.dnto.com
National Society for Education in Art and Design (NSEAD), The
 Gatehouse, Corsham Court, Wiltshire SN13 OBZ; 01249
 714825; www.nsead.org
Local Jobcentres and Careers/Connexions Centres

DISTRICT NURSE

(see also *Nurse*)
District nurses are employed by NHS Community Trusts. They
work closely with GPs, health visitors, practice nurses and other
community nurses, providing skilled nursing care for patients
and their families in their own homes, in surgeries and in other
health and community centres. The district nurse is the leader of
the district nursing team, which includes staff nurses, district
enrolled nurses and care assistants.

Qualifications and Training
Applicants must be registered general/adult nurses, usually with
post-registration experience. Since October 1998, all qualifications
have been replaced by the new Specialist Practitioner (District
Nursing) qualification, for which degree-level courses are available
at institutions of higher education.

Personal Qualities
The district nurse must have good leadership skills, the ability to
understand the needs of individuals and families in the community, the confidence to work independently and relate well to
other members of the primary healthcare team. As well as the
ability to work efficiently and manage their own workload,
district nurses need good communication skills and a sense of
humour.

Starting Salary

Dependent upon previous experience, but from around £21,000 and up to £30,000 in inner London.

NHS Careers, PO Box 376, Bristol BS99 3EY;
　　www.nhscareers.nhs.uk/home.html
Careers in Nursing and Related Professions (Kogan Page)

DIVER

(see also *ROV Pilot Technician*)
Professional divers are mainly employed by commercial diving contractors in the North Sea, ports and docks. There are also opportunities in the armed services and police forces. The growth of diving as a popular sport has created a number of positions for instructors worldwide. Currently there are many more qualified divers looking for work than there is work available.

Qualifications and Training

Diving is potentially hazardous and it is essential for anyone who wishes to become a commercial diver to attend and satisfactorily complete a course of training at a diver training school which has been approved by the UK Health and Safety Executive (HSE) and leads to certificates of competence relevant to offshore and inland/inshore commercial diving. All commercial offshore divers need to hold a current first aid certificate. In addition, other skills are required, including welding, cutting, and underwater tools

The Royal Navy and the police force give training for their own personnel. In the case of the latter, pupils must have a minimum of two years' experience as a constable. BSAC or other sport diving qualifications do not qualify divers for commercial diving.

Personal Qualities

Divers must be sound swimmers and physically fit; all professional divers have to pass a full commercial diving medical, which complies with HSE Diving Operations at Work regulations. They must be able to tolerate hard exercise, extreme conditions and recognise and work within their own personal limits. They must be very responsible and willing and able to work as part of a team. Initiative and the ability to sell their own skills to a potential employer are essential.

Starting salary

There is no uniform pay rate for divers who work inland / inshore; it varies from £50–£120 per day. Divers who work in the UK sector of the North Sea on oil- or gas-related activities are paid around £160 per day, which rises to about £260 once they have spent 300 days offshore as members of a diving team and have completed 150 'approved' dives. Sport diving instructors work largely for travel and enjoyment and pay can be low.

i

Health and Safety Executive, Row Court, 1 Southwark Bridge, London SE1 9HS; 020 7717 6000; www.hse.gov.uk
The International Marine Contractors Association, Carlyle House, 235 Vauxhall Bridge Road, London SW1V 1EJ; www.imca-int.com / careers; e-mail: imca@imca-int.com
Fort Bovisand Underwater Centre, Plymouth, Devon PL9 OAB; 01752 408021; www.fortbovisand.com; e-mail: dive@fortbovisand.com
Society for Underwater Technology, 80 Coleman Street, London EC2R 5BJ; 020 7382 2629; www.sut.org.uk
The Underwater Centre, Fort William, Inverness-shire, Highland PH33 6LZ; 01397 703768
British Sub Aqua Club, Telford's Quay, South Pier Road, Ellesmere Port, Cheshire, CH65 4FL; 0151 350 6200; fax: 0151 350 6215; www.bsac.org
Local police forces
Royal Navy Careers Offices

DOCTOR OF MEDICINE

see *Medicine*

DOG GROOMER

Dog grooming is a growing industry, with more and more dog owners using the services provided by grooming salons of which there are 2,000 in the UK. Most are small, private businesses and some are part of other establishments, including pet shops, garden centres, boarding and breeding kennels. Some mobile groomers visit animals in their own home.

Each breed has different requirements and there are many types of coat, which all require specialist skills and techniques. The work involves bathing, shampooing, drying, clipping, trimming and brushing a variety of long- and short-coated dogs. Specialist procedures include nail clipping, teeth cleaning, ear care and treatments for parasites.

Qualifications and Training

There are two main routes into training: a fee-paying course at a private grooming training centre or learning on the job. Candidates with practical dog-grooming experience may enrol for the City and Guilds Dog Grooming Certificate 775. This two-part exam, with a written paper and a practical element, tests candidates' skills on three different types of dog. This qualification shows employers that the groomer has had correct training and gives customers confidence that the groomer is competent.

The Advanced Grooming Diploma tests the expertise and skill required of the experienced groomer working in a commercial environment. A good working knowledge of the Kennel Club Breed Standards, styles and trimming techniques is required in order to pass all components. The exam consists of a written paper and seven practical modules, which can be taken over a period of time until all seven are complete, working at a timescale to suit the individual.

Personal Qualities

A love of animals is essential, as is a good deal of patience and a firm but gentle way of handling. Good customer care plays a large part and a pleasant, courteous manner, combined with a neat and tidy appearance, is essential. Dog groomers should have good hand–eye coordination and an eye for detail. Artistic flair is an advantage.

Starting Salary

This varies from area to area, and hours and rates of pay are negotiable.

| i |

British Dog Groomers Association, Bedford Business Centre, 170
Mile Road, Bedford MK42 9TW; 01234 273933; fax: 01234
273550; www.petcare.org.uk; e-mail: info@petcare.org.uk
Lantra Connect, Lantra House, NAC, Kenilworth,
Warwickshire CV8 2LG; 0845 707 8007 (Lantra Connect –
Helpline); www.lantra.co.uk; e-mail: connect@lantra.co.uk
Local Jobcentres and Careers/Connexions Centres

DOMESTIC SERVICE

Although this sounds like something from the Victorian era, there
is still a demand for butlers, cooks, housekeepers, maids and occasionally, footmen and valets. Butlers' duties involve announcing
guests, serving drinks and supervising other staff; cooks are
responsible for preparing food; housekeepers for the general
running of a household, often in the absence of the owner; while
maids wait at table, clean and/or look after the lady of the house's
clothes.

Some jobs such as buttling can be done on a temporary basis,
and agencies exist to provide domestic staff for special occasions.

Qualifications and Training

Formal educational qualifications are not necessary, although
catering qualifications may be a bonus. Experience and good
recommendations are important.

Personal Qualities

Discretion, tact and the ability to put someone else first are important.

Starting Salary

Salaries vary depending on whether full board and lodging are
provided, hours worked and individual employers.

| i |

Local Jobcentres and Careers/Connexions Centres

The Lady, 39–40 Bedford Street, Strand, London WC2E 9EN; 020
    7379 4717; www.lady.co.uk (job advertisements)
The International Guild of Professional Butlers; www.butlers-
    guild.com

DRAMA THERAPIST

The main focus of drama therapy involves working and playing
using action methods to facilitate creativity, imagination, learning, insight and growth. It is used in many different settings,
including mental health-care centres, training centres, education,
prison and probation, child care and private practice.

Qualifications and Training

Trainee drama therapists usually need a relevant first degree in
drama, theatre or performing arts, or a nursing qualification. Six
UK institutions currently offer postgraduate training courses in
drama therapy: University of Hertfordshire, College of Art and
Design, St Albans; University College of Ripon and York, St John,
York; South Devon College of Arts and Technology, Torquay;
Sesame/Central School of Speech and Drama, London; Institute
of Dramatherapy at Roehampton, London; and City College
Manchester. A new course is planned at the University of Derby.

Personal Qualities

This is demanding work, which requires awareness, insight,
integrity and compassion.

Starting Salary

Salaries vary according to whether the work is full- or part-time
and the type of setting. Many drama therapists work on a freelance basis, or practise drama therapy while employed in some
other capacity, perhaps as a teacher, social worker, nurse, occupational therapist, psychiatrist or manager.

British Association for Drama Therapists, 41 Broomhouse Lane,
    London SW6 3DP; 020 7731 0160; www.badth.co.uk

DRESSER

(see also *Broadcasting, Theatre*)

Dressers may find employment in theatre, television, films and fashion houses. They prepare and maintain costumes and help the performers and models to dress, especially where quick changes are needed.

Qualifications and Training

No formal qualifications are necessary. Experience, especially in the theatre, is helpful as is sewing ability.

Personal Qualities

Calmness and speed, a soothing and sympathetic nature, discretion and tact are all helpful.

Starting Salary

Dependent on age, experience and employer, but generally relatively low.

The Stage, 47 Bermondsey Street, London SE1 3XT; 020 7403 1818; www.thestage.co.uk (job advertisements)

DRESSMAKER

(see also *Theatre*)

Opportunities for dressmakers occur in *couture* houses which make specially designed costumes for a particular collection or customer, in wholesale fashion houses making mass-produced garments, and in theatres both making and adapting costumes. Dressmakers may also be employed by large stores to carry out alterations, or they may be self-employed making clothes either from home or from a workshop. Teachers of dressmaking are employed in schools, colleges and by adult education centres.

Qualifications and Training

No formal qualifications are necessary; but City and Guilds qualification and NVQs are available. Some degrees and HNDs in
clothing design or fashion have a dressmaking option.

Personal Qualities

Dressmakers need to combine artistic and practical skills with an
ability to follow instructions and to recognise problems as they
arise and make the necessary adaptations. They may have to deal
with temperamental designers and their customers.

Starting Salary

Dependent on experience, practical ability and specializations.
Trainees can earn £8,000–£10,000. Experienced dressmakers can
earn up to £50,000 in London.

i

Local Jobcentres and Careers / Connexions Centres
CAPITB Trust, 80 Richardshaw Lane, Pudsey, Leeds LS28 6BN;
0113 239 3355; www.careers-in-clothing.co.uk

DRIVING EXAMINER

Driving examiners must ensure that candidates are competent to
drive without endangering other road users and demonstrate due
consideration for other drivers and pedestrians. The examiner
directs learner drivers over an approved route and asks them to
carry out various exercises. While doing this, the examiner must
take notes without distracting the candidate's concentration and
must make a fair assessment of the learner's ability.

Qualifications and Training

Driving examiners are required to complete a strict selection
process, followed by four weeks' training. They must have
detailed knowledge of the *Highway Code* and road and traffic
safety problems, some mechanical understanding, have held positions of responsibility and dealt with the public. Driving examiners must be over 25 and have had extensive experience of a variety

of different vehicle types. Vacancies are advertised both locally and nationally by the Driving Standards Agency. Selection is dependent upon passing a special driving test and interview. For those who are successful, there are continuous checks by a supervising examiner to ensure the maintenance of a high standard.

Personal Qualities
Examiners should be fair, sympathetic, friendly, clearly spoken and have a calm, unflappable nature. The ability to work to a strict timetable is important.

Starting Salary
Varies depending on hours worked. Examiners generally have annualised hours contracts and minimum working hours are guaranteed on entry into employment.

Driving Standards Agency, Stanley House, Talbot Street,
    Nottingham NG1 5GU; 0115 901 2805; www.dsa.gov.uk
Local Jobcentres and Careers / Connexions Centres

DRIVING INSTRUCTOR

Driving instructors teach clients how to drive in preparation for all categories of the Driving Standards Agency's theory and practical driving tests. Instructors can also provide post-test training for the Pass Plus scheme as well as prepare clients for advanced driving tests, such as the DIAmond Advanced Motorists test.

The industry is now very much structured to self-employment, with instructors either having their own business or existing as an independent operation within a franchise agreement.

Qualifications and Training
In order to be allowed by law to accept payment for teaching people to drive, car driving instructors must either be registered or licensed by the Registrar of Approved Driving Instructors (ADIs) at the Driving Standards Agency. This requires them to have passed the three-part qualifying test within the space of two

years. The ADI exam consists of a written test, a practical driving test and a practical test of the ability to instruct. Training is available from any of the establishments listed in the Official Register of Driving Instructor Training (ORDIT), which is included in the starter pack (*see* below). ORDIT establishments are regularly required to satisfy the inspection criteria under the voluntary scheme of minimum required standards set up and agreed by the Driver Training Industry and the Driving Standards Agency.

Personal Qualities

Driving instructors must have a calm and friendly nature, be very alert and quick to react, should be clearly spoken and able to express themselves well. Patience, confidence and tact are also important characteristics, as is the willingness to abide by a professional Code of Practice.

Starting Salary

Typical earnings, after business or franchise fees, will vary widely, depending on tuition hours worked and operating costs.

$\boxed{\text{i}}$

Driving Instructors' Association, Safety House, Beddington Farm Road, Croydon CR0 4XZ; 020 8665 5151; fax: 020 8665 5565; www.driving.org

Driving Standards Agency, Stanley House, 56 Talbot Street, Nottingham NG1 5GU; 0115 901 2500; fax: 0115 901 2940; www.dsa.gov.uk

Your Road to Becoming an Approved Driving Instructor, AD114 starter pack, including application forms, for £3.00, from DSA

Local driving schools, Jobcentres and Careers Offices

The Driving Instructor's Handbook (Kogan Page)

The Driving Instructor's Manual (DIA Publishing)

E

ECOLOGIST

see *Conservation (Environmental)*

ECONOMIST

Economists study the use, organization and distribution of the world's resources. The field of investigation is very wide, but may include the study of such topics as the reasons for balance of payments crises, the effects of different forms of taxation, international trade or business economics. Economics is not a precise science; it is only possible to forecast the degrees of probability of a particular economic model having certain results. The Government Economic Services (GES) is the largest employer of professional economists in the UK, with nearly 600 people working in 30 government departments and agencies. Economists also work in industry, teaching and research, banking and stockbroking, journalism, international organizations and independent consultancies.

Their primary task is to give advice on the probable consequences of a course of action; for example, they might advise a company on the effects of a rise in the price of its products. Economists are also concerned with collecting data, preparing reports, and, to an increasing extent, with building complex mathematical models.

Qualifications and Training

A good honours degree in economics, or in one of the specialised branches of the subject, is needed. In addition, many economists take a postgraduate qualification. Some degree courses are mathematically biased, and for these an A level pass in maths is essential. For most other courses, GCSEs in maths or English are required and A levels in arts subjects, such as history and modern languages, are useful.

Personal Qualities
An analytical mind, numeracy and the ability to express oneself clearly, both verbally and in writing, are required.

Starting Salary
£20,000–£22,000; the average for experienced staff is £35,000 but some can earn substantially more.

i

Government Economic Service, Economist Group Management Unit, HM Treasury, Parliament Street, London SW1P 3AG; 020 7270 4835/4581/5073/4571; www.ges.gov.uk e-mail: egmu.int@hm-treasury.gov.uk
HM Treasury, Parliament Street, London SW1P 3AG; 020 7270 4835/4581/5073/4571; www.hm-treasury.gov.uk/careers
Society of Business Economists, 11 Bay Tree Walk, Watford WD1 3RX; 01923 237 287; www.sbe.co.uk

EDUCATION WELFARE OFFICER
(see also *Social Work* and *Social Care – Children and Young People*)

Education welfare officers are employed by local authorities to liaise between schools and families, providing support where necessary. EWOs deal with problems affecting children's behaviour. One of their main roles is to ensure regular school attendance and to deal with persistent cases of truancy. There are relatively few posts for education welfare officers in Scotland, where the responsibility for school welfare is shared between social work and education departments.

Qualifications and Training
The main professional qualification is the DipSW, which can be studied part time while working, or full time at a college. Entry

requirements are two A levels or equivalent, but services will appoint from a variety of backgrounds which include relevant degrees, teaching and youth-work experience.

Personal Qualities
Maturity, emotional stability, tact, patience and a sense of humour are necessary.

Starting Salary
£14,500 rising to £25,000 for those with experience.

TAG – Training for the Education Welfare Service;
   www.eduwelfaretag.force9.co.uk
General Social Care Council, Goldings House, 2 Hay's Lane,
   London SE1 2HB; 020 7397 5800;
   www.doh.gov.uk/gscc; e-mail: info@gscc.org.uk

ELECTRICIAN

Electricians are needed in a number of different areas, and a variety of jobs come under the title of 'electrician'.

Installation
The installation industry has the biggest electrical training scheme in the country. In the main it comprises thousands of private firms of electrical contractors; some installation apprenticeships are also offered by electricity boards and local councils. The electrical installation industry works on new construction and refurbishment sites and also on contract repair and maintenance work.

Factory Maintenance
Most factories employ maintenance electricians.

Servicing
Service engineers usually concentrate on a particular range of equipment, travelling from house to house, or firm to firm. They repair domestic equipment such as televisions, office equipment or electrical equipment in factories.

Manufacturing
Electricians are involved in inspection and testing.

Auto Industry
Auto electricians check, repair and replace the electrical/electronic circuiting and components in all types of motor vehicle.

Theatre Industry
Theatre electricians are responsible for operating theatre lighting and dealing with any problems.

Qualifications and Training
At craft level, GCSEs in maths, science and English are helpful. Training is normally by Modern Apprenticeship and lasts three to four years. NVQs are available in Electrical Installation Engineering and Electricity Generation, Supply and Distribution. Technician engineers need four GCSEs or equivalents, including maths, a science subject and English. Training takes four years and usually leads to an Edexcel (BTEC)/SQA certificate.

Installation apprenticeships include City and Guilds qualifications and a comprehensive practical Achievement Measurement Test is also taken. Success in all elements leads to NVQ level 3.

Personal Qualities
Technical aptitude is essential, and service electricians must also have the ability to deal with the public. The work can be strenuous and it may be necessary to work from heights. Colour blindness prevents entry to the industry.

Starting Salary
Low to start with, but upwards of £21,000 when qualified.

i

National Electrotechnical Training, 34 Palace Court, London W2 4HY; 020 7313 4846; helpline: 0800 3288475; www.net-works.org.uk/careers.htm; info@net-works.org.uk

JT Ltd, Stafford House, 120/122 High Street, Orpington, Kent BR6 0JS; 01689 884100; fax: 01689 891658; www.JTLimited.co.uk; e-mail: enquiries@jtlimited.co.uk

ENGINEERING

The British engineering industry is a major wealth producer and almost every other industry depends upon engineering in some way. Engineering provides a challenging career for men and women, with employment offered by industry, universities and colleges, consulting engineers, contractors, local authorities and the armed forces. The Engineering Council gives a simple definition of engineering, saying that it involves 'the application of science and maths to the solving of practical problems and the making of useful things'. The variety of specializations are covered by over 20 professional institutions. A selection are described below.

Aeronautical Engineering

Aeronautical engineering is one of the most technically advanced areas of engineering. It is both exciting and rewarding, involving leading-edge technology, variety, skill and innovation. This diversity means that career opportunities can be found across the entire global aerospace spectrum, from research, design, manufacture and maintenance, through to operation and support. However, the dramatic downturn in the aeronautical industry in 2001 significantly reduced opportunities and it may be some time before the good employment prospects once offered by the industry return.

Agricultural Engineering

The main fields in which agricultural engineers are involved are: design and production of agricultural machinery; planning, design and construction of farm buildings and associated equipment; field engineering – irrigation, drainage and land resource planning and service engineering, involving the sale, servicing, repairing and installation of farm machinery. They are also involved in forestry engineering, amenity and ecological engineering, and precision farming using satellite positioning systems.

Air Conditioning, see Building Services Engineering

Automobile Engineering

In the vehicle manufacturing industry engineers may be employed in design, development, production, operations management and maintenance activities. In motor vehicle servicing, the work tends to be at craft level, with some engineers using their technical base to develop into motor vehicle engineering management. Currently, NVQs in Vehicle Mechanical and Electronic Systems Maintenance and Repair are offered at levels 2 and 3.

Biochemical Engineering

This involves the application of engineering principles to industrial processing. Biochemical engineers are involved in the research, design, construction and operation of plant used for the processing of biochemicals such as those used in effluent treatment, fermentation and the production of drugs.

Biomedical Engineering

Most biomedical engineers are employed in hospitals or by companies manufacturing medical equipment. Their work involves applying engineering techniques and principles to medicine and biology.

Building Services Engineering

Building services engineers are concerned with heating and ventilation, refrigeration, lighting, air conditioning, electrical services, internal water supply, waste disposal, fire protection, lifts, and acoustic and communication systems. The work involves the planning and design of engineering systems, and supervision of contracts, working in collaboration with architects, surveyors, structural engineers and builders.

Chemical Engineering

Chemical engineers are concerned with large-scale processes, not always in the chemical industry. The term 'process engineering' is often used to describe their work, as they are more interested in the physical factors involved in a process than in the chemical reaction itself. Chemical engineers are employed in the oil, chemical, pharmaceutical, food, brewing and process industries.

Civil Engineering

Civil engineering plays an important part in everyday life. Civil engineers devise, plan and manage development in vital areas – the design and construction of state-of-the-art roads, dams, harbours, railroad systems, bridges and airports. Civil engineers also play an important part in the provision of electricity and water supplies, and in managing traffic and transport. Every project is unique and involves the expertise of a team of people who plan, design, build and maintain these essential assets.

Control Engineering

This is a multidisciplinary field involving electrical and electronic engineering, maths, computer science, instrument and mechanical engineering. Specialization in control engineering often follows the study of another branch of engineering.

Electrical and Electronic Engineering

The technology of electrical engineering deals with heavy current, while electronic engineering deals with light current. Applications of heavy current include electrical machinery of all kinds, generating stations and distribution systems. Light current is used for such products as transistors, microprocessors and telecommunications equipment. The two fields are often interdependent and training is closely related. Electronics is a rapidly developing field and offers excellent opportunities, as do the allied disciplines of computer and software engineering.

Energy Engineering

This branch of engineering is concerned with the use, production, distribution, conversion and conservation of energy, with due regard to the environment. Energy engineers are employed across the whole spectrum of industry, as energy management and control are essential elements in containing costs, reducing pollution and addressing environmental concerns. The majority of openings are in major fuel industries (including renewables), consultancy and research.

Environmental Engineering, see Building Services Engineering

Fire Engineering

This involves the application of engineering principles to the assessment, prevention and inhibition of fire risk within buildings, manufacturing plant and industrial processes. The various stages include the use of mathematical principles in the assessment of fire risk, the application of scientific principles to fire safety practices and the use of management techniques to the inhibition and prevention of the onset and spread of fire.

Fire engineers are employed in the fire services, architectural and building design, project management, insurance assessment, industrial processing, the aircraft industry, environmental health and any area of safety where the possibility of fire or combustion represents a hazard.

Gas Engineering

Gas engineering involves specialization in the use, transmission and distribution of gas (natural or manufactured), or in the production of gas, or in related fields such as exploration.

Heating and Ventilation Engineering, see Building Services Engineering

Highway Engineering, see Transport Engineering

Instrument Engineering

Instrument engineers are concerned with the measurement of pressure, temperature, and so on, designing, installing and maintaining instrument systems. *See also* Control Engineering.

Manufacturing Systems Engineering

This branch of engineering deals with the skills required to operate new manufacturing systems: computerised production, computer-controlled assembly, robotic systems and flexible manufacturing systems.

Marine Engineering

This discipline is related to offshore engineering under the general title of 'maritime engineering', which involves engineering systems and equipment in a maritime environment. Both marine and offshore engineers are involved in design, research, consultancy, survey, manufacture, installation and maintenance activities, the former with vessels of all sizes and types, the latter with offshore platforms, sub-sea installations and under-sea vehicles. Employment opportunities exist within firms offering design and research activities, engine- and shipbuilding firms, classification societies, government bodies, the Merchant Navy and the Royal Navy.

Mechanical Engineering

Mechanical engineering is the biggest branch of the engineering industry. It involves the skills of designing, developing, producing, installing and operating machinery and mechanical products of many types. The field is enormous in scope, and most engineers specialise in a particular area. Other branches of engineering, such as electrical and civil engineering, overlap with mechanical engineering to a certain extent.

Mechanical engineers are employed in almost every sector of industry. Some of the largest areas of employment are machine tools, railway engineering, aerospace and the automobile industry.

Mining Engineering

In Britain, most mining engineers are employed by companies in mining areas, working for consultants who monitor mining activity and subsidence. They need some knowledge of related disciplines such as mechanical, electrical and civil engineering, and to understand geology and surveying in relation to mining. The majority of openings in metal mining are overseas.

Municipal Engineering

Municipal engineering is the application of civil engineering to the public service. Municipal engineers are employed by local authorities or other public bodies. They work on a wide range of projects concerned with public works, and in such fields as traffic engineering, environment, land reclamation, marine works (harbours and jetties), and building and infrastructure maintenance.

Nuclear Engineering

Nuclear engineering involves the applications of nuclear energy and associated research and development. The work of designing and constructing nuclear reactors and the management of nuclear power stations through waste management and storage and decommissioning of plant is carried out by nuclear engineers.

Offshore Engineering

Offshore engineers are concerned with the construction and operation of drilling platforms and wellheads, and other engineering problems related to the exploitation of offshore oil and gas.

Operations Engineering

Operations engineers are concerned with specifying, evaluation, acquisition, commissioning, inspection, maintenance, asset management and disposal of facilities, systems, vehicles and equipment. Career opportunities exist at craft and technician level in the servicing and maintenance of a wide variety of industries, of which transport is the largest. Chartered and incorporated engineers may be engaged in asset or fleet engineering management, requiring multidisciplinary engineering, commercial and legal knowledge and encompassing health and safety, reliability, environmental and economic factors, or in specialised inspection roles. Many technicians build on their practical skills by further career development to aspire to these more senior positions.

Petroleum Engineering

Petroleum engineers are concerned with exploration and drilling for oil. They obtain and interpret information – for example, the quantities and quality of oil discovered.

Production Engineering

Production engineers develop and improve manufacturing techniques. They are responsible for designing production systems to ensure that products can be manufactured to the specified design, in the right quantities, at the right price and by the required date. Their work overlaps with production management.

Recording Engineering

Recording engineering is a specialised branch of electronic/radio engineering. Recording engineers are mainly employed by broadcasting authorities and recording studios, and vacancies are limited. *See also* Broadcasting.

Refrigeration Engineering, see Building Services
Engineering

Structural Engineering
Structural engineers are concerned with the design and maintenance of the framework and fabric of large structures such as
bridges, motorways and office blocks.

Transport Engineering
Transportation (or traffic) engineers are concerned with managing the best use of roads and related facilities and work mainly
with road traffic. Transportation planners, who are not necessarily engineers, are concerned with the provision of all types of
transport. The current priority is to provide an integrated transport system.

Water Engineering
Water engineers mostly work for water companies and river
authorities, ensuring the supply of fresh water, and dealing with
the reclamation and disposal of water which has been used.

Qualifications and Training
Professional qualifications are important throughout the industry
as they are an independent review by peers to confirm both technical and managerial competence and the professional experience of
individuals. The Engineering Council sets standards for the registration of Chartered Engineers (CEng), Incorporated Engineers
(IEng) and Engineering Technicians (EngTech) in all disciplines.
There are five main categories of employment in the engineering
industry, as follows:

Chartered Engineers
Chartered engineers are concerned primarily with the progress of
technology through innovation, creativity and change. They
develop and apply new technologies; promote advanced designs
and design methods; introduce new and more efficient production
techniques and marketing and construction concepts; and pioneer
new engineering services and management methods. They may be
involved with the management and direction of high-risk and
resource-intensive projects. Professional judgement is a key feature

of their role, allied to the assumption of responsibility for the direction of important tasks, including the profitable management of industrial and commercial enterprises. Entry to a career as a chartered engineer is via a four-year MEng degree accredited by one of the engineering institutions, followed by a period of initial professional development combining training and professional experience. Some disciplines specify a Professional Qualification Scheme – details are available from the engineering institutions. For those not holding a MEng alternative routes are available. These include an honours degree followed by a Matching Section equivalent to one year of further learning and the Mature Candidate Routes offered by most engineering institutions.

Incorporated Engineers

Incorporated engineers (IEng) are specialists in the development and application of today's technology, managing and maintaining applications of current and developing technology at the highest efficiency. With their detailed knowledge and understanding of current engineering applications, they have the skills and know-how to make things happen and often have key operational management roles. They have a detailed understanding of a recognised field of technology and exercise independent judgement and management in that field. They add substantial value, independently and as leaders, to any organization where technology is a core activity or supports the business. Entry to a career as an incorporated engineer is via a degree accredited by one of the engineering institutions. Initial professional development, combining training and professional experience, is also required. For those who do not hold a degree alternative routes include an HND plus a Matching Section equivalent to a further year of learning and the Mature Candidate Routes offered by most engineering institutions.

Engineering Technicians

Engineering technicians (EngTech) are creative and skilled engineering practitioners, often with responsibility for operational engineering and other staff. They apply knowledge and proven techniques and procedures to the solution of practical problems in a wide variety of contexts. They carry a measure of supervisory and technical responsibility and are competent to exercise creative aptitudes and skills within defined fields of technology.

They make a key contribution to a range of functions, including design, development, manufacture, commissioning, operation and maintenance of products, equipment, processes and services. Engineering technicians require a National Certificate/Diploma or equivalent qualification, combined with initial professional development. This may be achieved through an Advanced Modern Apprenticeship or similar training scheme.

Craft Workers

Craft workers specialise in a particular practical skill, such as tool-making or welding. They must be able to interpret engineering drawings, and to work with a minimum of supervision. Entry is normally at 16 or 17, to an apprenticeship lasting three to four years. GCSEs in maths, science and English are an advantage, although not absolutely essential. On-the-job training, together with day or block release, leads to NVQs awarded by the City and Guilds and the Engineering Industry Training Board. With very good exam results, transfer to Technician courses is possible.

Operators

Operators are employed in a wide range of jobs, and make up about a third of the engineering industry's labour force. Their work is often simple and routine, but in some cases they may require some skill or skills similar to those of craft workers.

No specific academic requirements are needed, but aptitude in English and arithmetic and knowledge of metalwork or technical drawing are useful. Operators may work towards NVQs at an appropriate level.

Aeronautical Engineering

There are four main routes to registration as an Incorporated Engineer in aeronautical engineering: the Standard Route, Registration for Licence Holders, the Mature Candidate Route and the Mature Servicemen's Route. Details are available from the Royal Aeronautical Society (address below).

Personal Qualities

Graduate and Chartered Engineers need academic ability, an imaginative and problem-solving approach and social and communication skills. Incorporated Engineers and Engineering Technicians should have reasoning ability, numeracy and the ability to communicate. Craft workers, as well as manual dexterity, need basic mathematical ability, patience and self-discipline. Operators should show reliability, patience and the ability to work with others.

Starting Salary

Newly qualified graduate engineers start at £15,000–£18,000 and can expect to earn over £30,000 once experienced. Craft workers and technicians start at around £13,000 but can earn up to £22,000 after a few years' experience.

i

Engineering Careers Information Service, EMTA, 14 Upton Road, Watford, Hertfordshire WD1 7EP; 0800 282 167; www.emta.org.uk/enginuity; e-mail: ecis@emta.org.uk

Careers Department, The Institution of Civil Engineers, 1 Great George Street, Westminster, London SWIP 3AA; 020 7665 2106; fax: 020 7233 0515; www.ice.org.uk; e-mail: careers@ice.org.uk

The Chartered Institution of Building Services Engineers, Delta House, 222 Balham High Road, London SW12 9BS; 020 8675 5211; www.cibse.org; e-mail: info@cibse.org

The Engineering Council, 10 Maltravers Street, London WC2R 3ER; 020 7240 7891; www. engc.org.uk; e-mail: staff@engc.org.uk

The Institute of Energy, 18 Devonshire Street, London W1N 2AU; 020 7580 7124; www.entech.co.uk/ioe/ioe.htm; e-mail: eworld@ioe.org.uk

The Institute of Marine Engineers, The Memorial Building, 76 Mark Lane, London EC3R 7JN; 020 7481 8493; www.imare.org.uk; e-mail: imare@imare.org.uk

The Institute of Measurement and Control, 87 Gower Street, London WC1E 6AA; 020 7387 4949; www.instmc.org.uk

Society of Operations Engineers, 22 Greencoat Place, London SW1P 1PR; 020 7630 1111; www.soe.org.uk; e-mail: soe@soe.org.uk

The Institution of Agricultural Engineers, West End Road, Silsoe, Bedford MK45 4DU; 01525 861096; www.iagre.demon.co.uk; e-mail: secretary@iagre.demon.co.uk

The Institution of Chemical Engineers, 165–171 Railway Terrace, Rugby CV21 3HQ; 01788 578214; fax: 01788 560833; www.icheme.org.uk

The Institution of Electrical Engineers, Michael Faraday House, Six Hills Way, Stevenage, Hertfordshire SG1 2AY; 01438 313311; www.iee.org.uk

The Institution of Incorporated Engineers, Savoy Hill House, Savoy Hill, London WC2R 0BS; 020 7836 3357; www.iie.org.uk; e-mail: info@iie.org.uk

The Institution of Fire Engineers, 148 New Walk, Leicester LE1 7QB; 0116 255 3654; fax: 0116 247 1231; www.ife.org.uk

The Institution of Gas Engineers, 21 Portland Place, London W1N 3AF; 020 7636 6603; fax: 020 7636 6602; www.igaseng.com

The Institution of Highway Incorporated Engineers, 20 Queensbury Place, London SW7 2DR; 020 7823 9093; www.ihie.org.uk

The Institution of Mechanical Engineers, 1 Birdcage Walk, London SW1H 9JJ; 020 7222 7899; www.imeche.org.uk; e-mail: enquiries@imeche.org.uk

The Institution of Mining and Metallurgy, Danum House, South Parade, Doncaster DN1 2DY; 01302 320486; www.imm.org.uk; e-mail:hq@imm.org.uk

The Institution of Nuclear Engineers, 1 Penerley Road, London SE6 2LQ; 020 8698 1500; www.inuce.org.uk

The Institution of Structural Engineers, 11 Upper Belgrave Street, London SW1X 8BH; 020 7235 4535; fax: 020 8235 4294; www.istructe.org.uk; e-mail: mail@istructe.org.uk

The Royal Aeronautical Society, 4 Hamilton Place, London W1V 0BQ; 020 7499 4300; www.aerosciety.com

The Royal Institution of Naval Architects, 10 Upper Belgrave Street, London SW1X 8BQ; 020 7235 4622; www.rina.org.uk e-mail: hq@rina.org.uk

ENVIRONMENTAL HEALTH OFFICER

Environmental health officers are enforcers, educators and advisers. They are employed in both the public and private sectors, and their aim is to protect the public from environmental health risks. Their responsibilities include pollution control, including noise control, environmental protection, the inspection of food and food premises, health and safety in workplaces and in the leisure industry, and the control of housing standards, particularly in the private rented sector. Much of their time is spent out of the office, dealing with the public and visiting premises of all types.

Qualifications and Training

Training in England, Wales and Northern Ireland involves a four-year sandwich course leading to a degree in environmental health, or a two-year postgraduate sandwich course, for those with a good honours degree in a natural science. The course must be accredited by the Chartered Institution of Environmental Health (CIEH). Degree entry qualifications vary between institutions.

In Scotland, candidates for the professional qualification (Diploma in Environmental Health, awarded by REHIS) must hold a BSc honours degree in environmental health from the University of Strathclyde or Edinburgh. Currently only the University of Strathclyde offers a course for new entrants. Applicants for this four-year degree course need four H grade passes in maths, chemistry, biology or physics and one other subject. Details of current requirements should be checked with the university as there can be flexibility for mature students. Before being awarded the diploma, candidates must have undergone a minimum of 48 weeks' training with a local authority and have passed professional exams.

Personal Qualities

These should include social responsibility, tact, integrity, an enquiring mind and good communication skills.

Starting Salary
Trainee grade £10,000–£14,000+; qualified officers £18,000+.

Chartered Institute of Environmental Health, Chadwick Court,
15 Hatfields, London SE1 8DJ; 020 7928 6006;
www.cieh.org.uk; education@cieh.org
The Royal Environmental Health Institute of Scotland, 3 Manor
Place, Edinburgh EH3 7DH; 0131 225 5444;
www.rehis.org; e-mail: rehis@rehis.org.uk

ESTATE AGENT

Estate agents are responsible for the sale, letting and management
of any kind of property – factories, shops, offices and farms as well
as residential property. They also, in many cases, deal with valuation and survey work and offer other services such as auctioneering
and financial services advice. Large firms provide a wide range of
these services through specialist departments employing qualified
professionals, particularly in the area of surveying and valuation.
Dedicated sales staff fulfil the role of property negotiators and in
the majority of smaller firms with just one or two branches, a
combination of these functions will be found.

Qualifications and Training
The principal professional bodies are the National Association of
Estate Agents (NAEA) and the Royal Institution of Chartered
Surveyors (RICS). Membership of RICS is normally attained
through graduate entry coupled with a period of accredited prac-
tical training. NVQs in Residential Estate Agency and Lettings
and Management are available through the NAEA's National
Assessment Centre. The NAEA also offers examination-based,
nationally recognised qualifications in Residential Sales (CREA),
Lettings and Management (CRLM) and Commercial and Business
Transfer (CCBT). These qualifications also provide the route to
membership of the Association at the senior level of Fellow.

Professional qualifications are an asset and becoming more
sought after by employers. However, anyone can set up in business as an estate agent unless they have been banned from doing

so by the Director General of Fair Trading, are bankrupt or guilty of a range of other criminal offences proscribed under the 1979 Estate Agents Act.

Established firms will very often provide opportunities for unqualified beginners within the field of property negotiation but at the same time encourage the attainment of a more formal qualification.

Personal Qualities

For most people the purchase or sale of a house is the biggest financial transaction they will ever make and there are bound to be attendant worries and problems. Estate agents must be able to deal with their clients' problems sympathetically, but in a businesslike way. In addition to being numerate and literate, they should possess an outgoing personality, coupled with the energy and enthusiasm to work in a competitive, fast-moving environment where customer care is of paramount importance.

Starting Salary

On target earnings of £7,000–£8,000 per annum are available to school leavers with A levels, whereas graduates and late entrants may well find that they will start at around £12,000–£15,000. In both cases a large element of earnings will be commission related. Firms of estate agents charge a commission for selling or letting property; the rate for a sale is usually in the region of 1.5 to 3 per cent of the selling price and for lettings and management a combined fee of between 12 and 15 per cent.

The National Association of Estate Agents, Arbon House, 21 Jury Street, Warwick CV34 4EH; 01926 496800; fax 01926 400953; www.naea.co.uk; e-mail: info@naea.co.uk

Royal Institution of Chartered Surveyors, Surveyor Court, Westwood Way, Coventry, West Midlands CV4 8JE; 024 7622 7000; www.rics.org/com

ESTATE MANAGER

see *Land Agent*

EVENTS ORGANISER

Events organisers generally work for a place visited by the public such as a national park or a stately home. They may also be appointed on a temporary basis to cover a festival lasting one or two weeks.

They are responsible for organizing long-standing events such as a series of waymarked walks and activities such as a music festival or summer holiday entertainment for children. If appropriate, the organiser will be in contact with the local education department to encourage school visits.

Those working for a large concern will coordinate their work with other members of staff such as the information and press officers.

Qualifications and Training

Events organisers do not necessarily need formal qualifications but a background in marketing and experience at promoting events and campaigns are useful. A knowledge of simple financial planning is looked for, plus experience in preparing material for print. The ability to drive is essential.

Personal Qualities

Events officers should be energetic, sociable and adaptable, able to talk to a variety of people, and have the ability to think up new ideas and organizational skills.

Starting Salary

£12,500+.

Association for Conferences and Events, ACE International, Riverside House, High Street, Huntingdon, Cambridgeshire PE29 3SG; 01480 457595; www.marktex.co.uk/ace; e-mail: ace@martex.co.uk

Jobs advertised in the Monday edition of the *Guardian*; www.jobs.guardian.co.uk

EXHIBITION ORGANISER

Exhibition organisers usually work for specialist companies. They plan and coordinate exhibitions, negotiating with all those concerned – managers of the exhibition, exhibitors, stand suppliers, and designers and caterers. With overseas exhibitions, government departments are often involved.

Qualifications and Training

Training is usually on the job and graduates or those with HNDs in business or marketing are preferred. CAM or Institute of Marketing qualifications are also useful. Several universities and colleges offer degree or HNDs courses in events management.

NVQs 2–4 are available but have no industry recognition so there has been little take-up.

Personal Qualities

Applicants should be good at dealing with people and at administration, with the ability to keep a large amount of information at their fingertips. Physical and mental stamina is essential.

Starting Salary

£12,000–£16,000.

Association of Exhibition Organisers, 113 High Street, Berkhamsted, Hertfordshire HP4 2DJ; 01442 873331; fax: 01442 875551; www.aeo.org.uk; e-mail: info@aeo.org.uk

Chartered Institute of Marketing, Moor Hall, Cookham, Maidenhead, Berkshire SL6 9QH; 01628 427137; www.cim.co.uk

F

FACTORY WORKER

Factories employ people in three different areas: production, research and development, and administration. In production, depending on the product being made and the processes involved, varying proportions of skilled, semi-skilled and unskilled workers may be employed.

Skilled craftsmen operate sophisticated machines such as lathes and precision grinders; they may be welders, sheet metal workers, toolmakers or fitters responsible for the assembly of precision engines and machines. Tool setters may 'set' assembly lines ready for operation by semi-skilled workers who feed in materials and semi-finished components and who ensure that the production process runs as smoothly as possible.

Unskilled labourers are mainly employed to fetch, carry and clean. There are many other jobs related to the production process such as store keeping, purchasing, tool-room maintenance and repair, transportation and quality control. Prospects for promotion are often good in factories and legislation ensures that conditions of working and engagement are fair.

In research and development, opportunities exist for scientists, engineers, technicians, designers and draughtsmen, and for general office workers; financial, marketing and sales staff are employed in administration. The functions carried out in these two areas are similar to those performed in other job areas and individual entries should be referred to for further details.

Qualifications and Training

To work in a factory as an unskilled or semi-skilled worker formal qualifications are not required. Training is given on the job and may vary in length from one hour to weeks or months, depending on the type of work.

Those wishing to follow a career as a skilled craftsman must follow a three- to four-year apprenticeship which requires two or three GCSE grades D–E (or equivalent) in maths and science. Other useful subjects are technical and engineering drawing, metalwork, woodwork and English. Apprenticeships take the form of training at work towards NVQs or day release to attend colleges and study for City and Guilds or other craft certificates.

Personal Qualities

Craftsmen must have a sound understanding of machinery, manual dexterity, a good eye for shape, sound eyesight, patience and concentration. Semi-skilled workers, especially on production lines, must be able to cope with repetitive work and to work quickly. All factory workers must be safety-conscious and able to tolerate dirt and noise.

Starting Salary

Dependent upon industry but those with some experience can earn between £7,000 and £14,500, more with bonus schemes and shift allowances.

Local Jobcentres and Careers/Connexions Centres

FARMING

In recent years, economic conditions and animal health crises have had significant effects on jobs in this sector. Incomes have fallen and opportunities become more limited. There is increasing mechanization and a tendency towards greater specialization and larger farms. Mixed farms are now in a minority and most farmers choose to specialise in one or two areas of production. The most common of these are milk, cereals, poultry, sheep, pigs or beef. In order to make a farm profitable, the modern farmer needs a thorough working knowledge of the type of farming to be undertaken, an understanding of general agricultural science, and years of practical experience as well as an aptitude for farming and farm management.

Opportunities are few, land and equipment are expensive. Land prices have made the chances of a beginner becoming a tenant farmer almost impossible. Most of those who go into farming come from farming families.

Farm Manager
Farm managers are employed by the landowner and are responsible for all aspects of the day-to-day working of the farm. They must plan ahead, organise the staff and work schedules, decide which crops to plant or which animals to rear and keep a check on buildings and machinery. In addition, they must deal with the office work and accounts.

Farm Worker
Specialization and large-scale farming have led to a fall in demand for the farm worker who can turn his or her hand to anything. There is now a need for highly skilled personnel and new entrants should aim at becoming skilled in a special area such as animal husbandry, mechanics or food, flower or fruit production.

Qualifications and Training
There is a range of qualifications related to farming, including degrees in agriculture or agricultural science, and National Diplomas in general agriculture. Various NVQ awards are available at different levels, such as Crop and Livestock Production, levels 1, 2 and 3.

Starting Salary
Salaries for farmers are set by the Agricultural Wages Board (see below) and vary depending on qualifications, age and responsibility. Standard workers earn just over £100 a week at 16; at 19 with NVQ level 3 the basic rate of pay is around £210 a week.

Careers, Education and Training in Agriculture and the Countryside, Warwickshire Careers Service, 10 Northgate Street, Warwick CV34 4SR; 01926 401300

Lantra Connect, Lantra House, NAC, Kenilworth, Warwickshire
    CV8 2LG; 0845 707 8007 (Lantra Connect – Helpline);
    www.lantra.co.uk; e-mail: connect@lantra.co.uk
Royal Agricultural Society of England, National Agricultural
    Centre, Stoneleigh Park, Warwickshire CV8 2LZ;
    01476 696969; www.rase.org.uk
Agricultural Wages Board, Nobel House, 17 Smith Square,
    London SW1P 3JR; Agricultural Wages Helpline:
    0845 0000134;
    www.defra.gov.uk/farm/agwages/ agwages.htm

FASHION

(see also *Clothing Industry*)
Clothing is one of the UK's largest manufacturing industries and
employs over 145,000 individuals. The fashion industry covers all
aspects of clothing and accessories for men, women and children
and falls into three main sectors: *haute couture* houses, where original model garments are made for individual customers; wholesale *couture*, where trends set by the *haute couture* houses are
closely followed, and limited numbers of model garments in stock
sizes are made for retail; and wholesale manufacture, which occu-
pies the largest sector of the fashion industry. Here, the latest
trends are adapted to styles that are attractive to the main market,
and mass produced at acceptable prices.

Designer
Designers do more than produce stylish sketches. Their work will,
depending on the size and organization of the particular establishment, include a wide variety of tasks. The work of the *haute couture*
designer is both highly creative and intricate. Unfortunately, there
is little scope for young designers or assistants as many houses are
designer owned; they are nevertheless an excellent training ground
for future designers willing to work as sketchers, stylists, fitters,
hands, and so on. In wholesale couture, designers produce original
garments, but they generally follow the instructions of an
employer as far as style and cost are concerned.
    The wholesale manufacture designer must be able to predict
future trends, combine this with the firm's own 'brand image',
match it to available fabrics and produce a garment which can be

produced economically and will appeal to its particular section of the market. When sketches have been drawn, it is necessary to produce working drawings and translate these into flat patterns, so sample garments can be made to show to retail buyers and garment costs in fabric and manufacturing time estimated.

Pattern Cutter/Grader

Pattern cutters make the patterns that enable a designer's sketch to be made into a garment. Pattern graders work from a pattern representing a basic size and create the patterns needed for a range of sizes. Jobs vary from company to company. The two ways of making patterns are by flat pattern cutting, when the cutter works from the designer's sketches or working drawings and makes a pattern for each part of a garment, or by modelling on to a stand, when the cutter works from the designer's drawings and drapes and pins fabric on to a dummy and fits it in accordance with the drawings. Computers are increasingly used to help in designing garments, creating patterns and for pattern grading.

Cutter/Spreader

The cutter or spreader checks that the cloth is smooth and free of wrinkles and flaws, and that patterns or other features will match when it is sewn together. The laying-up process is done manually by two people or by machine. Once it is ready, the fabric can be cut using a number of methods. Hand cutting is done using shears, an electric knife or a vertical band knife. Die-cutting is done by machine. Computer-controlled cutting is also being introduced, with machines capable of cutting up to 250 inches per minute, depending on the depth of the lay. In laser cutting computer images are used to operate the cutter with great accuracy.

Qualifications and Training

Pattern Cutter/Grader

An Advanced Modern Apprenticeship in Apparel Manufacturing Technology leading to an NVQ level 3 in one of four routes (Pattern Cutting and Grading, Sample Technician, Garment Technologist, Hand Craft Garment Making is available). This is a work-based route providing an alternative to further and higher education.

Cutter/Spreader

Training is largely given on the job. Some employers offer the NVQ level 2 qualification for Cutters or the Foundation Modern Apprenticeship route.

Personal Qualities

Pattern cutters/graders should have an interest in fashion and an appreciation of what their designers are aiming for. Numerical ability is essential for measurement and calculation. Some technical drawing skills and an aptitude for working on computers are also useful.

Spreaders/cutters need to be physically fit. They must have good eyesight and perfect colour vision. Some numerical ability is required.

Starting Salary

For a pattern cutter/grader, earnings vary tremendously, from £10,000 to £20,000, depending on qualifications and experience. Experienced cutters/spreaders are paid according to their skill and the level of responsibility in their job.

CAPTIB Trust, the National Training Organization for the UK apparel and allied products industries, 80 Richardson Lane, Pudsey, Leeds LS28 6BN; 0113 227 3345; www.careers-in-clothing.co.uk

The National Textile Training Organization, Edwinstowe House, High Street, Edwinstowe, Nottinghamshire, NG21 9PR; 01623 825500; www.textilecareers.org

FILM PRODUCTION

(see also *Broadcasting*)

Opportunities to work in film production arise in television, film companies and advertising. Most people who work in this area are self-employed freelancers. Film production involves both studio and location work. Jobs within film production are much sought after, vacancies are few and competition is consequently fierce. Individuals who are serious about working in this area will need to develop personal marketing skills in addition to their creative craft skills.

Animation
Animation involves the design, creation and operation of animated production and effects. Much of the work is done using computer animation techniques, although there are still opportunities for traditional 'cell' animation.

Announcers
Announcers work to detailed and carefully timed scripts, communicating information to the viewer from a soundproof 'behind the scenes' office. They sometimes write or adapt their own material and need to be able to work on their own.

Archivists/Librarians
Archivists and librarians collect, collate, preserve and make available collections of recorded visual, sound, written and other materials for use by various productions. Archives are valuable business resources and some archivists are now involved in selling and marketing materials.

Art and Design
The art and design function is to create a visual effect to meet the needs of the production, creating manual or computer-generated graphics.

Costume/Wardrobe
The wardrobe department interprets the production requirements in terms of costumes and accessories to ensure historical accuracy and an accurate portrayal of the style and ethos of the period.

Direction
The director is responsible for achieving the creative, visual and auditory effect of a production and, equally importantly, motivating a team.

Engineering
Engineers provide a design, maintenance and installation service to the production site and equipment. Research specialists are

usually employed by the equipment manufacturers or design consultancies.

Film, Video and Audio Tape Editing
Raw tape or film is shaped to interpret the requirements of the director, either by physical cutting (film) or by selecting sequences and re-recording on to a master tape using sophisticated computer equipment.

IT Specialists
IT specialists support many aspects of broadcasting, film and video, either within the companies or as consultants, providing and maintaining relevant systems and software.

Journalists
Journalists generate and report on local, national or international stories, and research relevant background information. Bi-media (radio and TV) contracts are increasing. Some journalists present their own work.

Laboratory
Lab technicians develop and process film, duplicate and check video tapes, ensuring high technical quality.

Lighting
Lighting specialists ensure that the stage or set is correctly lit to meet the needs of the production.

Make-up and Hairdressing
Make-up and hairdressing professionals interpret the requirements of the production and research to ensure accurate representation of the historical or design concept. They maintain a continuity of approach throughout the production in studio or on location.

Management
Management directs and coordinates the different elements of the industry to ensure their efficient function – ranging from commissioning a production to negotiating international rights. Specialists work in a full range of business areas.

Marketing and Sales

Marketing and sales staff work in an international marketplace to raise revenue for broadcasters or film makers. Airtime is sold, sponsorship and co-production rights are negotiated and spin-off products, such as books, toys and videos, are developed.

Producers

Producers perform a variety of management and operational roles to bring together the many elements of a production, either in a studio or on location. Often responsible both for the initial concept and raising the essential finance, they are the team leaders.

Production Assistants

Production assistants provide high-quality administrative and secretarial support to the producer and director at every stage of production, coordinating all activities and preparing schedules and scripts.

Production Management

Production managers organise all essential support facilities for the team, from accommodation and transport to on-set catering. They will also roster crews and arrange payments.

Production Operatives

Production operatives perform the operational duties of the production such as vision mixing and autocue operations.

Researchers

Researchers support the producer, helping to turn ideas into reality – providing and following up ideas, contacting and interviewing people, acquiring relevant factual material, and writing briefings for presenters.

Recording Still and Moving Images (Camerawork)

Workers in this area operate and assist with still, film and video cameras to record images as directed, using different techniques.

Runners/Gofers

The traditional entry-level job for the industry. Bright, highly motivated – often highly qualified – people act as general assistants, taking messages, making deliveries, being indispensable... and learning the basics of the commercial business.

Setcraft/Props

People working in this area construct the scenery, sets and backdrops to meet the production brief, reflecting both historical accuracy and required design and style. They also maintain sets during a production, and operate any mechanical features as directed. Props (hired or made) are used to dress the set.

Sound

Sound craftspeople interpret the requirements of a production in terms of sound collection. During post-production they may be involved in recording, editing and dubbing, using a range of sophisticated equipment.

Special Effects

Special effects designers create and operate effects for a production, within technical limitations and budget, and operate the necessary machines.

Support Staff

Many people working in film, video, television and radio fulfil essential support roles, including administration, catering, driving and cleaning.

Transmission

Technicians and engineers work to exhibit the production in a high-quality form, which can involve projecting images or operating transmission equipment linking electronic signals from the studios to a transmitter.

Writers

Writers work to produce or edit scripts for a variety of radio, TV, video or film productions.

Qualifications and Training

New-entrant training is offered by FT2; competition for places is fierce. Their new entrant technical training programme covers art department assistant, props assistant, camera assistant, grips, assistant editor, sound assistant, production/continuity assistant and make-up/hair assistant. They also offer a set crafts apprenticeship training scheme for fibrous plasterers, carpenters and painters.

Skillset, the National Training Organization for Broadcast, Film, Video and Multimedia, offers NVQs level 2–4 in areas such as camera, costume, editing, production, make-up and hair. These are available to those employed in the industry.

The National Film and Television School offers a two-year MA in film and television in ten professional disciplines: Directing (Animation, Documentary or Fiction); Screenwriting; Producing; Cinematography; Screen Design; Editing; Screen Sound; and Screen Music. Students specialise in one of these. NFTS courses are not for complete beginners and although many of the applicants for the 60 places available are graduates, relevant knowledge and practical experience are essential and treated as equivalent to academic study. Other institutions offering film related courses can be found on the UCAS Web site.

Personal Qualities

In film work it is important to combine artistic ability with technical expertise, to pay attention to detail, to have patience, good powers of concentration and an interest in colour and design. An even-tempered, logical and visually imaginative approach is necessary. It is important to keep in touch with what is happening in the industry, and to be able to create a network of friends and contacts. Absolute reliability is essential, especially at the start of a career.

Starting Salary

Salaries are too varied to give an appropriate indication. Many people negotiate their own salary and there is an increase in freelance working.

Broadcasting Entertainment, Cinematograph and Theatre Union (BECTU), 111 Wardour Street, London W1V 4AY; 020 7437 8506; www.bectu.org.uk

National Film and Television School, Beaconsfield Studios,
    Station Road, Beaconsfield, Bucks HP9 1LG; 01494 671234;
    www.nftsfilm-tv.ac.uk; e-mail: admin@nftsfilm-tv.ac.uk
Skillset, National Training Organization for Broadcast, Film,
    Video and Multimedia, 2nd Floor, 91–101 Oxford Street,
    London W1R 1RA; 020 7534 5300; fax: 020 7534 5333;
    www.skillset.org
Skills for Media, 111 Wardour Street, London W1F 0AY;
    020 7437 0810; www.skillsformedia.com;
    info@skillsformedia.com (New Media Careers Information
    Service from Skillset and Bectu)
FT2 (Film and Television Freelance Training), Fourth Floor,
    Warwick House, 9 Warwick Street, London W1R 5RA; 020
    7734 5141; www.ft2.org.uk
BBC Talent run an annual competition for those trying to break
    into this area of work; www.bbc.co.uk/talent
Careers in Film and Video (Kogan Page)
Great Careers in Film, Video and Photography (Kogan Page)

FIRE SERVICE

Firefighters save and rescue life and property in emergencies.
Fighting fires is only one aspect of their work; other emergencies
they deal with are tanker spillages, car, train and aeroplane
crashes, flooding, building collapse, and explosions where people
and animals may have to be rescued. Some firefighters specialise
in particular areas such as training or communications. The Fire
Service also promotes fire safety through education programmes,
and advice on fire protection and prevention for existing properties and new buildings. In addition they enforce legal regulations
to reduce risks of injury by fire, such as the provision of secure
escape routes.

The Fire Service is administered by local authorities in the UK.
Recruitment is undertaken by each local brigade which is responsible for its own recruitment procedures.

The Ministry of Defence, Army, Royal Air Force, Royal Navy
and the British Airports Authority all have their own brigades.

Qualifications and Training

Firefighters should have a good general level of secondary education. Qualifications in English, maths and science are useful but not essential. The minimum age is 18 and there are strict requirements for entrants concerning physical fitness, hearing, colour vision and physique. All applicants must pass a medical and series of selection tests that measure initiative and team-working skills as well as physical fitness. Initially training takes place in a training school and is followed by regular courses of instruction for special situations and the use of specialist equipment.

Personal Qualities

Members of the Fire Service must be practical, courageous, able to use their own initiative, prepared to work shifts and work as part of a team. Some scientific understanding is helpful when dealing with dangerous chemicals.

Starting Salary

Just over £16,000 on entry rising to around £21,000 after four years. Salaries for Senior Divisional Officers are from £37,623 to £40,584.

The Fire Service College, Moreton on Marsh, Gloucestershire
GL56 0RH; 01608 650 831; www.fireservicecollege.ac.uk;
e-mail: enquiries@fireservicecollege.ac.uk
Scottish Executive Justice Department, Fire Service and
Emergency Planning Division, Room F1–5, Saughton House,
Broomhouse Drive, Edinburgh EH11 3XD; 0131 244 2167
Local Chief Fire Officer/Firemaster, Fire Brigade Headquarters
(address in local phone book)
Ministry of Defence (contact the nearest Ministry of Defence
establishment with a fire service); www.mod.uk
BAA Plc, Jubilee House, Furlong Way, North Terminal,
Gatwick Airport, Gatwick, West Sussex RH6 0JN; 01293
595323; www.baa.co.uk
The Chief and Assistant Chief Fire Officers' Association;
www.fire-uk.org provides links to brigades with Web sites

'A Career in the Fire Service' produced by the Department for
   Transport, Local Government and the Regions;
   www.safety.dtlr.gov.uk/fire/fepd/cifs.htm

FISH FARMER

In Britain, around 500 fish farms produce fish, mainly rainbow trout
and Atlantic salmon, for consumption and sport. Pacific oysters,
mussels and scallops are also farmed. This is a growing activity and
although most farms are owner-run, there are opportunities for
farm managers and workers. Scientists also work in the industry,
testing new methods for improving conditions, stocks and disease
control. Bailiffs are employed to look after the general welfare of the
fish from hatchery to harvesting. As more food manufacturers move
into fish farming, there is a need for marketing staff.

Qualifications and Training

NVQs in Fish Husbandry at level 2 and in aquaculture at levels 2
and 3 are available. Certificates, diploma and degree courses in
fish farming and agriculture are offered by universities and
specialist colleges. The Institute of Fisheries Management (IFM)
organises correspondence courses leading to Certificates in
Fisheries Management and in Fish Farming, and to a Diploma in
Fisheries Management.

   No formal qualifications are required to become a bailiff,
although correspondence courses are available from the IFM.
Graduate and postgraduate biologists are employed on the scientific side and specialist degrees are available, as are courses
dealing with the sporting aspect of fish farming.

Personal Qualities

Physical fitness, a willingness to work outside, in remote areas
and in all conditions, plus an ability to think ahead and act independently are necessary.

Starting Salary

£10,000+ for technicians, £11,000+ for bailiffs, £14,000–£15,000+
for scientists, and £15,000–£20,000 for managers.

British Trout Association, 8 Lambton Place, London W11 4PH;
020 7221 6065; fax: 020 7221 6049; www.britishtrout.co.uk

The Institute of Fisheries Management (IFM), 22 Rushworth
Avenue, West Bridgford, Nottingham NG2 7LF; 0115 982 2317;
fax: 0115 945 5722; www.ifm.org.uk; e-mail:admin@ifm.org.uk

Lantra Connect, Lantra House, NAC, Kenilworth, Warwickshire
CV8 2LG; 0845 707 8007 (Lantra Connect – Helpline);
www.lantra.co.uk; e-mail: connect@lantra.co.uk

Careers, Education and Training in Agriculture and the
Countryside, Warwickshire Careers Service, 10 Northgate
Street, Warwick CV34 4SR; 01926 401300

Vacancies are generally advertised in local newspapers and in the
specialist magazines such as *Fish Farmer* and *Fish Farming
International.*

FISHERMAN

Fishermen perform many tasks: they cast out and haul in the nets
when they are full; gut, clean and stow away the catch; mend nets;
maintain the tackle and wash down the decks. Fishermen may
work on deep-sea trawlers in the North Sea or on 'factory' stern
vessels which prepare and deep-freeze the catches of cod,
haddock, plaice, halibut and sole at sea. Fishing boats operate
close to shore as well as in distant fishing grounds such as
Greenland, the North Atlantic and Norway. Crews may stay at
sea for weeks at a time. While fishing is actually taking place, all
hands must work for stretches of up to 18 hours. On the older
ships all work is done on the decks but the more modern factory
ships process the catch below decks. Catering staff, engineers and
radio operators are also employed on these large vessels.

Fishermen on drifters carry out similar tasks but these boats
follow fish around the coast and land a catch every day. Small
seine-net boats with a crew of only four stay at sea for two weeks.
Inshore fishing boats are usually family concerns using a variety
of different methods to catch white fish, herring, cod, haddock,
whiting, shrimps, lobster and crab.

Although the fishing industry is in decline, there are still
employment opportunities at the five main ports of Grimsby,
Hull, Lowestoft, Fleetwood and Aberdeen.

Qualifications and Training

No formal education qualifications are necessary for a career in fishing, although an understanding of maths would be helpful. Colleges generally require applicants to have spent time at sea before entry on to a pre-seagoing course. Courses are available at colleges in Hull, Fleetwood, Grimsby, Lowestoft and Aberdeen. Further training is gained in employment. NVQs in Marine Vessel Operations are available, as is an Advanced Modern Apprenticeship in Sea Fishing.

Personal Qualities

Physical fitness, stamina and courage are essential for fishermen, who may have to withstand terrible Arctic conditions and long periods of very hard work. They must also be good sailors, able to turn their hand to any task, react quickly to emergencies, and be able to work in a team.

Starting Salary

Fishermen all take a share of the catch; the more they catch, the more they earn.

Jobcentres and Careers/Connexions Centres in port towns
Seafish Training, Seafish House, St Andrew's Dock, Hull
    HU3 4QE; 01482 327837; www.seafish.co.uk/

FLIGHT ENGINEER

see *Civil Aviation*

FLORIST

The florist's job involves designing and creating flower arrangements and displays such as table decorations, bouquets, sprays and wreaths as well as selling cut flowers and plants. Some florists buy from flower markets; others have stock delivered from wholesalers, local nurseries or overseas producers. The work can include providing office displays, making arrangements for banquets, functions and receptions, and decorating hotels and public buildings. Florists generally work a 40-hour week, including Saturdays.

Qualifications and Training
Edexcel (BTEC) qualifications are offered by a number of colleges, at First Diploma, National Diploma and HND level. The Society of Floristry offers two professional qualifications – the Intermediate Certificate (ICSF) and the National Diploma (NDSF); these are for experienced florists. NVQs in Floristry are available at levels 2 and 3.

Personal Qualities
Imagination and creative flair, colour sense, organizational ability, an ability to work to deadlines, a friendly manner, patience and dexterity are necessary. Good health and stamina are essential because the work can be physically demanding.

Starting Salary
Rates of pay vary according to size and location of the business, and according to the individual's own skills and qualifications, experience and seniority. Salaries are similar to those in other retail work. Part-time work may be available.

Lantra Connect, Lantra House, NAC, Kenilworth, Warwickshire CV8 2LG; 0845 707 8007 (Lantra Connect – Helpline); www.lantra.co.uk; e-mail: connect@lantra.co.uk

The Secretary, The Society of Floristry, Meadowside, Hall Road, West Burgholt, Colchester, Essex; 0870 241 0432; fax: 01202 855520; www.societyoffloristry.org

FOOD SCIENCE AND TECHNOLOGY

Food scientists study the properties and behaviour of foods from raw materials through processing to the final product, using a variety of scientific disciplines, notably chemistry and biology, but also physics and nutrition. Food technologists use food science and other technological know-how to turn raw materials into finished products for the consumer in an industry which is becoming increasingly sophisticated.

The majority of those qualifying in food science or technology will readily find employment in a variety of positions in the food industry, which covers not only the manufacture of food but its ingredients, food packaging and the manufacture of food-processing machinery. Positions exist in production, quality assurance or in product or process development. The growth of 'own label' products has led to additional opportunities in the food retailing sector where technologists are responsible for developing new products, identifying suppliers, and ensuring the quality of the product from manufacture, through distribution to the store and, ultimately, to the consumer's table. Those keen to secure a career in research will find opportunities in government service, in research associations, as well as commercial organizations and the universities. There are additional opportunities in environmental health, education, consultancy, public health laboratories and in technical publishing and journalism.

Qualifications and Training

Food science and technology qualifications may be gained via NVQs (levels 1–4), Edexcel (BTEC)/SQA national certificates and diplomas, HNC, HND and degree courses. There is also the opportunity to train while in a job. Qualifications at all levels can be taken as full-time and sandwich courses. There are also a few part-time courses. For minimum entry requirements, contact colleges directly.

Membership of the Institute of Food Science and Technology depends upon satisfying both academic qualifications (minimum HND) and having several years' experience at a responsible level for higher grades.

Personal Qualities

Food scientists and technologists require a sound theoretical knowledge and scientific ability, a practical approach, an ability to communicate with people and a willingness to work as part of a team.

Starting Salary

Graduates would expect to start at around £15,000 in a small company. A large retailer may pay up to £25,000.

The Food and Drink National Training Organization, 6 Catherine Street, London WC2B 5JJ; 020 7836 2460; www.foodanddrinknto.org.uk
Institute of Food Science and Technology, 5 Cambridge Court, 210 Shepherds Bush Road, London W6 7NJ; 020 7603 6316; www.ifst.org; e-mail: info@ifst.org

FORENSIC SCIENTIST

The Forensic Science Service (FSS), an agency of the Home Office, employs scientists both for research and operational forensic science. Forensic scientists examine and try to identify, by means of analytical chemistry, molecular biology and microscopic analysis, samples of materials such as clothing, hair, blood, glass, paint and handwriting, in order to provide evidence to expose criminals, the location of a crime, the weapons used, and other relevant details.

Qualifications and Training

Forensic scientists are graduates; laboratory experience and post-graduate qualifications are an advantage as there is considerable competition for jobs. Relevant degrees include physical, mathematical or applied science. The universities of Bradford, Strathclyde and Cranfield offer degrees and postgraduate qualifications in forensic science but these do not guarantee a job.

Personal Qualities

Forensic scientists should be analytical, able to work as part of a team and have good communication skills. They also need to be logical and methodical, paying great attention to detail. A naturally inquisitive, unsqueamish nature and a concern for accuracy are also important.

Starting Salary

Starting salaries for graduates are around £14,000, increasing to £18,000 after a year's training and experience. There are additional allowances for those working in London.

i

The Forensic Science Service, Norfolk House, Smallbroook Queensway, Birmingham B5 4LJ; 0121 607 6800; www.forensic.gov.uk

The Forensic Science Society, Clarke House, 18a Mount Parade, Harrogate HG1 1BX; 01423 506068; www.forensic-science-society.org.uk

Forensic Science Northern Ireland, 151 Belfast Road, Carrickfergus, Northern Ireland BT38 8PL; 028 9036 1888; www.fsni.gov.uk

A Career in Forensic Science (The Forensic Science Society)

Vacancies and graduate recruitment schemes are advertised in the national press

FORESTRY

Tree, woodlands and forests cover some 13 per cent of the land area of Britain. The job of the forester is to manage this resource to achieve multiple objectives, balancing competing factors. Forests and woodlands give society many things; they create employment, give space for recreation ranging from rallying to solitary strolls in ancient woodlands whilst providing a home for a vast array of plants, birds and animals and producing timber for construction, paper and a multitude of other uses.

Forestry needs people with a vast range of skills and abilities ranging from manual workers who tend and manage forests by planting, fencing and felling, to machine operators who drive very sophisticated machines which fell and extract timber from woodlands. These operations are managed by foremen and foresters who plan and oversee forests and woodlands. Their work is very varied and includes tasks such as managing habitats for bio-diversity, planning the felling and planting of forests along with the management of staff and supervision of large contracts.

Qualifications and Training

Forest workers must have nationally recognised chainsaw and pesticide application qualifications, such as those provided by the National Proficiency Tests Council (NPTC). A number of training schemes are available leading to NVQs in forestry at levels 1–3.

Foresters normally start their career with a degree or HND in forestry and then progress their career with membership of their professional body, the Institute of Chartered Foresters. Entry to courses normally requires a period of work experience in forestry as well as the relevant academic qualifications.

Personal Qualities

Forestry work requires a good standard of physical fitness, a willingness to work outside, all year round, in all weathers and in remote areas. A driving licence is usually essential. Foresters and managers should be able to organise others and be prepared to do varying amounts of office work.

Starting Salary

Trainee forest workers earn about £100 a week at 16, rising to £150–£180 at 18. Forestry machine operators are normally paid on piece work but can earn in excess of £20,000. Graduate foresters are likely to start on around £15,000 which could rise to around £24,000. If further management responsibilities are taken on this could rise considerably.

Forestry Commission, Personnel Division, 231 Corstorphine
    Road, Edinburgh EH12 7AT; 0131 334 0303;
    www.forestry.gov.uk
Institute of Chartered Foresters, 7a St Colme Street, Edinburgh
    EH3 6AA; 0131 225 2705; www.charteredforesters.org
The Royal Forestry Society of England, Wales and Northern
    Ireland, 102 High Street, Tring, Hertfordshire HP23 4AF;
    01442 822028; www.rfs.org.uk

The Royal Scottish Forestry Society, Hagg-on-Esk, Canonbie, Dumfriesshire DG14 0XE; 01387 371518; fax: 01387 371418; www.rsfs.org

National Proficiency Tests Council, Avenue 'J' , National Agricultural Centre, Stoneleigh, Warwickshire CV8 2LG; 024 7669 6553; www.nptc.org.uk; e-mail: information@nptc.org.uk

Lantra Connect, Lantra House, NAC, Kenilworth, Warwickshire, CV8 2LG; 0845 707 8007 (Lantra Connect – Helpline); www.lantra.co.uk; e-mail: connect@lantra.co.uk

Forestry Contracting Association, Dalfling, Blairdaff, Inverurie, Aberdeenshire AB51 5LA; 01467 651368

Careers Working Outdoors (Kogan Page)

FOUNDRY WORK

(see also *Engineering*)

Foundry work is craft-based. The industry provides for a wide range of industries, metal-cast components such as propellers, turbines, crankshafts, all types of machinery, and domestic items such as fireplaces.

Craftsmen are employed in foundry work as pattern, mould and model makers and to maintain the equipment. The introduction of computerised processes means foundries also employ machine operators with a range of different skills. Technical engineering staff are concerned with estimating, inspection and laboratory work. There are many opportunities for operatives in foundry work as die casters, dressers, finishers, moulders, coremakers and in metal melting.

There are also limited openings for foundry technologists, metallurgists, chemists and engineers in research and development. Graduate trainees are recruited to production and administrative management posts.

Qualifications and Training

Craftsmen and operatives do not require formal qualifications. Foundation and Advanced Modern Apprenticeships are available and training is work based, leading to NVQs level 1–3. Technicians study on a day-release or full-time basis for the Higher

National Certificate/Diploma, in cast metals technology, mechanical or electrical engineering. Management trainees need HNDs or degrees in a relevant subject.

Personal Qualities

Workers in the foundry industry must be fit and strong as the work is heavy. They should have good eyesight and be skilful in the use of tools. They must be willing to work in noisy conditions and to work shifts.

Starting Salary

Operatives earn £10,000–£12,500; craftsmen, once trained, earn £15,000+; technicians start at around £14,000.

i

Local Jobcentres and Careers/Connexions Centres

Cast Metals Federation, National Metalforming Centre, 47 Birmingham Road, West Bromwich B70 6PY; 0121 601 6390; www.castmetalsfederation.com; e-mail: admin@cmfed.co.uk

FREIGHT FORWARDING

(see also *Logistics*)

A freight forwarding firm will arrange for the most efficient means of the international transport of goods and will ensure that all documentation, legal and insurance requirements are met, and customs duties paid. Freight forwarders may be individuals or firms; they may specialise in a particular method of transportation, certain goods or countries. They may arrange for a number of different shipments to be grouped together for more economical transport. Some very large organizations have their own freight forwarding department or a subsidiary company.

Freight forwarders are usually located near ports or airports and in provincial centres. They employ people to deal with a wide range of clerical and administrative tasks such as sales, personnel, timetabling, accounting and computer work.

Qualifications and Training

School leavers can enter the industry through the Modern Apprenticeship route. NVQs are available in International Trade and Services, Distribution and Warehousing Operations and Organizing Road Transport. There are several degree courses in international trade, logistics, supply chain management, transport, export studies and overseas business. Large companies may offer graduate training schemes for those with relevant degrees.

The Institute of Freight Forwarders offer an Advanced Certificate in International Trade that can be studied full- or part-time or by correspondence. The Institute of Logistics and Transport offer a range of professional qualifications from introductory to MSc level which can be studied by distance learning.

Personal Qualities

People working in freight forwarding need excellent problem-solving and communication skills. Accuracy and clarity are essential as misunderstandings can cause major problems. IT skills are essential with a growth in Internet trading and greater use of technology such as global position satellite systems to plan and manage journeys. Geographical, cultural and religious awareness is also important.

Starting Salary

Clerical salaries are similar to those in other industries. Graduate salaries can be between £12,000 and £18,000 and increase significantly with experience.

i

British International Freight Association, Institute of Freight Forwarders, Redfern House, Browells Lane, Feltham, Middlesex TW13 7EP; 020 8844 2266; www.bifa.org; e-mail: bifa@bifa.org

The Institute of Logistics and Transport, Logistics and Transport Centre, PO Box 5787, Corby, Northamptonshire NN17 4XQ; 01536 740100; www.iolt.org.uk; e-mail: careers@iolt.org.uk

Instititute of Transport Administration, Mill House, 11 Nightingale Road, Horsham, West Sussex RH12 2NW; www.iota.org.uk

The 'Logistics and Transport Management Careers Guide' is available for download from www.insidecareers.co.uk

FUNERAL DIRECTOR

Funeral directors collect the deceased from hospital or their residence and prepare them for burial or cremation; this may include embalming. Most funeral premises include private viewing rooms for family visitations. On behalf of the family the funeral director often makes all the funeral arrangements such as the date, time and place of any ceremony and interment or cremation. The funeral director places the relevant notice of death and acknowledgement of thanks for sympathy in newspapers, pays all the fees, arranges flowers, transports the coffin and mourners to and from church, and will act as a collection point for flowers, or donations in lieu, if desired.

Funeral directors may be employed by large firms such as cooperative societies, or by small family-run concerns. In remote rural areas, the local carpenter or other craftsman may also work as a funeral director.

Qualifications and Training

Those wishing to obtain their Diploma in Funeral Directing must register with the National Association of Funeral Directors (NAFD) and will also have student membership of the British Institute of Funeral Directors (BIFD). Full details of the diploma course are forwarded to each student. Every student must follow the foundation module – there are no exceptions.

A satisfactory standard must be reached in the foundation module before proceeding to the diploma. A student will be required to have 24 months' experience and have arranged 25 funerals before the diploma is awarded. NVQs levels 2 and 3 in Funeral Services are available for those employed within the profession.

Personal Qualities

Tact, sympathy and a reassuring, helpful nature are essential to funeral directors when they are advising the bereaved. They also need to combine administrative ability with technical expertise in the varied preparations of funeral arrangements. On-call and out-of-hours work is an integral part of the job and an ability to adapt to irregular hours is essential.

Starting Salary

Salaries vary greatly depending on size of firm, many of which are family concerns.

British Institute of Embalmers, Anubis House, 21c Station Road, Knowle, Solihull, West Midlands B93 0HL; 01564 778991; www.bioe.co.uk; e-mail: info@bioe.org.uk

National Association of Funeral Directors, 618 Warwick Road, Solihull, West Midlands B91 1AA; 0121 711 1343; www.nafd.org.uk; e-mail: slats@nafd.org.uk

FURNITURE AND FURNISHING

(see also *Upholsterer*)

Furniture manufacturing and repair companies exist in all parts of the country. The industry maintains much of its craft base, with skilled people carrying out many of the tasks needed to create a piece of furniture. Within larger factories some of this has been mechanized, making use of computerised production methods. At the other end of the scale many small designer/makers bring together the designs, materials, machinery and knowledge of today coupled with the skills from a previous age.

Modern furniture is made from timber, textiles, steel, glass, plastics, stone and a range of polymers. Skilled frame makers provide frames to be filled, sprung and covered by upholsterers. The machining part is increasingly done by use of IT-driven processes, but other work is still done by hand.

There are opportunities to work on a freelance or self-employed basis, or for one of the many manufacturing units which may specialise in particular items, or materials, or in certain types of furniture such as school, office or domestic furniture. In the design of furniture, carpets, fabrics, curtaining and wall coverings, opportunities exist to work freelance, in studios and in the retail trade.

There are also a number of openings for teachers; craft, design and technology teachers are in short supply.

Qualifications and Training
Craft training is generally gained through a three- to four-year Modern Apprenticeship including NVQs at level 3. Other training is available, from beginner-level courses (City and Guilds / OCN Craft Certificates) through more advanced knowledge-based programmes (City and Guilds Progression Awards) to HND / Cs, foundation and full degrees. Entry to many of these courses is dependent on practical ability, although some courses do have specific academic requirements.

Personal Qualities
Furniture craftsmen must be neat, accurate and able to follow drawings exactly. They must be interested in practical work which requires great precision, have care and patience, and sufficient strength to lift heavy furniture. Good eyesight is an advantage. Designers are required to work as part of a team to a busy schedule and present their work well; a sound knowledge of how furniture is made is most valuable.

Starting Salary
Salary rates vary but pay is generally good with apprentices at 16 earning £70+ a week. By 19 many are earning in excess of £300 a week. Qualified and experienced staff can earn a lot more. Individual craftsmen working for themselves set their own rates.

i

The Furniture, Furnishings and Interiors National Training Organization, The Poplars, Off Wollaton Rd, Beeston, Nottinghamshire NG9 2PD; 0115 9221200; fax: 0115 9223833; www.ffinto.org; e-mail: info@ffinto.org

G

GAMEKEEPER

Gamekeepers work on large country estates for private landlords, management firms and private syndicates who wish to organise a shoot. They rear the game birds and fish, and protect them from poachers and predators. They must ensure that the proper environment for the game is maintained and, on shooting days, organize the beaters.

Qualifications and Training
No formal qualifications are necessary, although a keeper should be able to use a gun, handle a dog and have a driving licence. Training is usually on the job, with the opportunity to complete related NVQs. A number of colleges offer full-time courses at a range of levels from first diploma to HND.

Personal Qualities
Gamekeepers should love the outdoor life, be self-reliant and independent.

Starting Salary
Based on agricultural wages (*see* Agricultural Training Board details below), generally with a house provided.

| i |

Agricultural Wages Board, Nobel House, 17 Smith Square, London SW1P 3JR
Agricultural Wages Helpline, 0845 0000134; www.defra.gov.uk/ farm/agwages/agwages.htm

The Game Conservancy Trust, Fordingbridge, Hampshire SP6
1EF; 01425 652381; fax: 01425 651026; www.gct.org.uk; e-mail:
info@gct.org.uk

Lantra Connect, Lantra House, NAC, Kenilworth, Warwickshire
CV8 2LG; 0845 707 8007 (Lantra Connect – Helpline);
www.lantra.co.uk; e-mail: connect@lantra.co.uk

The National Gamekeepers' Organization PO Box 107, Bishop
Auckland DL13 5YU; www.nationalgamekeepers.org.uk

GARAGE WORK

(see also *Vehicle Technician*)

This involves selling and buying cars, supplying car parts, selling
petrol, repairing and maintaining cars and other vehicles and the
overall management of the garage.

Qualifications and Training

No specific educational qualifications are necessary for people
working on a petrol forecourt as training is given on the job, but an
aptitude in dealing with cash transactions and good numeracy
skills are generally required. Mechanics generally need to have at
least three GCSEs (grade C or above) preferably in maths, science
or a craft subject. Training via Modern Apprenticeship usually
leads to NVQ level 3. Preferred qualifications for salespeople and
parts people are four GCSEs (grade C or above). A range of NVQs
is available as qualifications in these areas. Managers are recruited
with varying qualifications and some have a degree. Membership
of the industry's professional institute is encouraged.

Personal Qualities

Mechanics must have a high level of responsibility, be strong and
get on well with people. Salespeople need to be friendly, polite
and have a good sense of humour. Parts people need to be well
organised with good administrative skills. Managers need to have
all the above qualities plus the ability to inspire confidence and
gain respect.

Starting Salary
Varies across the country and is dependent on experience and level of responsibility.

Retail Motor Industry Training (ReMIT), 201 Great Portland Street, London W1N 6AB; 0207 307 3413; fax: 0207 307 3425; www.remit.co.uk

MITC Motor Industry Training Council, 201 Great Portland Street, London W1N 6AB; 0207 436 6373; www.mitc.co.uk; e-mail: info@mitc.co.uk

GARDENER

(see also *Horticulturist, Landscape Architect, Market Gardening*)

Gardening, also known as amenity horticulture, involves not only planting and caring for flowers, trees and shrubs, but also the routine jobs of cleaning out beds, sweeping leaves and, in the winter, shovelling snow.

Gardeners may be employed by local authorities to care for parks, school and hospital grounds, work for a garden centre or landscape contractor, or be self-employed. Heritage gardening is a growth area and involves working for organizations such as the National Trust, English Heritage, and other private gardens.

Qualifications and Training
It is desirable but not always necessary to have formal qualifications to become a gardener. Training is given on the job, often as part of an apprenticeship; NVQ levels 1–3 are available. Full-time training courses in horticulture are available at colleges throughout the country, from First Diploma level. The Royal Horticultural Society offers a limited number of opportunities for practical training and plantsmanship at its gardens at Wisley, Rosemoor and Hyde Hall. Voluntary Internships for four or more weeks are available for those studying horticulture at college and at a number of schools work experience placements are available for secondary pupils.

Personal Qualities
Gardeners should enjoy working outdoors in all weathers and be patient and caring. The ability to drive is essential in many jobs.

Starting Salary
For commercial horticulture salaries are set by Agricultural Wages Board (*see* below). Qualified gardeners can earn between £13,000 and £17,000.

i

Local Jobcentres and Careers/Connexions Centres
Agricultural Wages Board, Nobel House, 17 Smith Square,
    London SW1P 3JR
Agricultural Wages Helpline, 0845 0000134;
    www.defra.gov.uk/farm/agwages/agwages.htm
Institute of Horticulture, 14–15 Belgrave Square, London SW1X
    8PS; 020 7245 6943; www.horticulture.org.uk;
    e-mail: ioh@horticulture.org.uk
Royal Horticultural Society, 80 Vincent Square, London SW1P
    2PE; 020 7834 4333; www.rhs.org.uk; e-mail: info@rhs.org.uk
Careers Working Outdoors (Kogan Page)
Leaflets on RHS courses/exams and 'Come into Horticulture'
    available from The Education Department, RHS Garden
    Wisley, Woking, Surrey GU23 6QB (send SAE)

GAS SERVICE ENGINEER

The work involves fitting and repairing appliances such as cookers, boilers and water heaters, the installation, maintenance and replacement of gas appliances, and conducting safety inspections. Service engineers are employed by British Gas, Transco, CORGI registered gas companies, independent gas contractors or utility companies.

Qualifications and Training
Training is through modern apprenticeships; NVQs in Gas Servicing and Installation are available. No formal qualifications are necessary but a good general education with some knowledge of maths and physics is advantageous. Registration with the

Council for Registered Gas Installers (CORGI) is a legal requirement for businesses and self-employed people working on gas
fittings or appliances.

Personal Qualities
As much of the work takes place in private houses, fitters must be
friendly, polite and honest. It is necessary to be able to drive.

Starting Salary
£16,000+ once qualified.

[i]

Gas and Water Industry NTO, The Business Centre, Edward
Street, Redditch, Worcestershire B97 6HA.
www.ginto.co.uk; e-mail:enquiries@ginto.co.uk
The Council for Registered Gas Installers (CORGI);
www.corgi-gas.com

GENEALOGIST

Genealogists trace lines of descent from ancestor to ancestor and
also study pedigrees. Their work is useful to the legal profession
in cases of intestacy or disputed will claims and, sometimes, to
doctors when trying to establish the origins of a disease.
However, the vast majority of genealogists work for private
clients who are interested in tracing their family trees. Some
genealogists work for companies but many more are self-
employed and work from home.

Qualifications and Training
Genealogists must have knowledge of the content and location of
the diversity of documentary sources held in public and private
archives and libraries. A good understanding of history, Latin and
expert palaeographical skills are essential to enable the geneal-
ogist to read and interpret original documents.

The Institute of Heraldic and Genealogical Studies provides
full-time, part-time and correspondence courses leading to
professional qualifications. There are also short courses on

ancestry for beginners provided by the Institute, certain local authorities and the Society of Genealogists. The Association of Genealogists and Researchers in Archives (AGRA) is the main professional organization. Membership is restricted to those who are suitably qualified and experienced.

Personal Qualities

Integrity, honesty, patience, inquisitiveness, curiosity, attention to detail, intuitiveness and determination are all useful attributes.

Starting Salary

There is no set salary scale and there are few full-time genealogists. AGRA's recommended minimum hourly rate is £18 plus disbursements.

i

Association of Genealogists and Researchers in Archives, 29 Badgers Close, Horsham, West Sussex RH12 5RU; www.agra.org.uk; e-mail:agra@agra.org.uk
The Institute of Heraldic and Genealogical Studies, 79–82 Northgate, Canterbury, Kent CT1 1BA; 01227 768664; fax: 01227 765617; www.ihgs.ac.uk; e-mail: ihgs@ihgs.ac.uk
The Society of Genealogists, 14 Charterhouse Buildings, Goswell Road, London EC1M 7BA; 020 7251 8799; www.sog.org.uk; e-mail: genealogy@sog.org.uk
Association of Scottish Genealogists and Record Agents, 51/3 Mortonhall Road, Edinburgh EH9 2HN; www.asgra.co.uk

GENERAL PRACTITIONER

see *Medicine*

GEOLOGIST

Geoscience is fundamental, as all energy resources and raw materials come from the Earth. Keeping these resources available and safe relies upon the expertise of the geoscientist. There are many different disciplines within geoscience.

Geologists study the Earth's crust, its materials, their origin, formation and composition. The work involves examining rocks and mineral deposits; some deposits (for example, coal) are assessed for their value. Specimens of rock, soil, water, fossils and minerals are collected for laboratory analysis and preserved for future reference. Geology not only includes fieldwork but much laboratory work, testing and analysing, often using computers. Geologists work mainly for oil, mining, quarrying or engineering firms and government establishments, and are becoming increasingly involved in environmental issues.

Closely allied to the work of the geologist is that of the geophysicist (*see* Oil/Gas Rig Work), geochemist and hydrogeologist, who use field and laboratory-based techniques to better understand the earth's physical and chemical properties and its underground water supplies. Hence, most of their work is related to the resources and the environment.

Qualifications and Training

The common route for entry into a professional geoscience career is a first degree (BSc/BA) in one of the geosciences. Such a degree also forms the basic qualification for Fellowship of the Geological Society of London, and for becoming a Chartered Geologist.

Personal Qualities

Geologists must be fit, as they are often required to work in difficult climatic conditions or even underground. They must be able to work both as team members and as team organisers when required. Relevant foreign languages are useful.

Starting Salary

£ 15,500+ to £19,500+; higher abroad.

The British Geological Survey, Nicker Hill, Keyworth,
   Nottingham NG12 5GG; 0115 936 3100; fax: 0115 936 3200;
   www.bgs.ac.uk; e-mail: enquiries@bgs.ac.uk
The Geological Society of London, Burlington House, Piccadilly,
   London W1J OBG; 020 7434 9944; www.geolsoc.org.uk;
   e-mail: enquiries@geolsoc.org.uk

GEOPHYSICIST
see *Oil/Gas Rig Work*

GLAZIER
Glaziers fit glass into both domestic and commercial buildings, some of which require the use of enormous sheets. They work for private contractors, local authorities and independently, in private homes and on building sites.

Qualifications and Training
There are no formal educational requirements. Training is on the job by three-year apprenticeship. It is usual for time off to be allowed to attend classes leading to NVQs, levels 2 and 3.

Personal Qualities
Useful attributes are strength, a liking for being outdoors, a steady hand, neatness and agility.

Starting Salary
Once trained, salaries are around £12,000.

i

Construction Industry Training Board, Bircham Newton, King's Lynn, Norfolk PE31 6RH; 01485 577 577; www.citb.org.uk

GROOM
Grooms look after all aspects of the horse's welfare. Their duties include grooming and strapping, mucking out, feeding, cleaning tack, saddling up, exercising and leading both mounted and dismounted, elementary veterinary care and sick nursing, preparation for and travelling with horses by road, sea and air, and care of the horse when at grass. Grooms work in racing stables, hunting establishments, private stables, studs and breeding concerns, riding schools, occasionally (seasonally) with polo ponies and at trekking centres.

Qualifications and Training

No formal qualifications are necessary but it is recommended that grooms take the British Horse Society examinations stages 1, 2 and 3 in Horse Knowledge and Care, which comprise the Grooms Certificate. Alternative options are NVQs in Horse Care, levels 1, 2 and 3.

Training is usually on the job and should be sufficient to prepare students for exams. There are also courses of varying lengths to prepare students for particular exams; however, the fees are often high. Funding may be available for the achievement of British Horse Society qualifications providing that the person is not eligible for any other type of funding.

Personal Qualities

A love of horses is essential, plus patience and the willingness to work long hours and perform many routine tasks. A heavy goods vehicle driving licence may be an advantage.

Starting Salary

Stable staff generally earn the national minimum wage. In some cases, food and accommodation may be free, in others they may be deducted from the wage. The hours may be long. The BHS issue guidelines on salaries for those with BHS qualifications; details are on their Web site.

i

The British Horse Society, Stoneleigh Park, Kenilworth, Warwickshire CV8 2LR; 01926 707700; www.bhs.org.uk; e-mail: enquiry@bhs.org.uk

The BHS Guide to Careers with Horses £3.50 plus 50p p&p. Available from the BHS Bookshop (address as above); Order line: 08701 201918; Online bookshop: www.britishhorse.com

Lantra Connect, Lantra House, NAC, Kenilworth, Warwickshire, CV8 2LG; 0845 707 8007 (Lantra Connect – Helpline); www.lantra.co.uk; e-mail: connect@lantra.co.uk

GROUNDSMEN/WOMEN

Groundsmen and women prepare, maintain and care for the various types of sports surfaces, both natural and synthetic turf on cricket and football pitches, bowling greens, athletic tracks, tennis courts, racecourses, polo grounds and amenity areas. They need to be familiar with scientific and technological developments relating to the machinery and materials used in the ground's maintenance. Employment opportunities exist in both the private and public sectors with local authorities, sports clubs and schools.

Qualifications and Training

Training can take place either on the job, or through colleges on residential or day-release courses. The Institute of Groundsmanship (IOG) organises courses and has its own examination structure. There are a number of routes to gain qualifications, including NVQs, HNCs and HNDs.

Personal Qualities

Groundsmen/women needs to be resourceful and happy to work outdoors regardless of the weather. An enjoyment of the physical challenge plus an interest in sport is an advantage.

Starting Salary

Salaries range from £8,000 at 16, £9,500 at 18, to £22,000 for a head groundsman and up to £28,500 for grounds managers.

Institute of Groundmanship, 19–23 Church Street, The Agora, Wolverton, Milton Keynes MK12 5LG; 01908 312511; www.iog.org.uk; e-mail:iog@iog.org

HAIRDRESSER

Hairdressers offer a variety of services involving hair, such as cutting, styling, perming and colouring. Salons or individual stylists may specialise in male or female hairdressing, or a niche market such as specialist colouring, Afro-Caribbean or ethnic hairstyles. Hairdressers may also be responsible for answering the telephone, making appointments, serving drinks to clients, cleaning and stock control. They work in salons, hotels, airports, cruise liners, hospitals and prisons. Some hairdressers work as freelancers. There are over 170,000 hairdressers in the UK.

Qualifications and Training

Most trainees combine on-the-job training with part-time study at a college or training centre towards an NVQ in Hairdressing at levels 1, 2 and 3. Salons may offer a three-year apprenticeship which includes training alongside experienced stylists and day release at college. Some colleges also offer full-time NVQs and full- or part-time BTEC courses in Design Fashion Styling for Hair and Make-Up. Full-time courses usually last for two years and include work experience in a college and external salon. Colleges may also offer the National Diploma of Hairdressing, awarded by the Guild of Hairdressers.

After training, hairdressers are expected to work for at least a year as an improver before being considered experienced. Hairdressers who want to enter salon management, become self-employed or teach hairdressing may need further qualifications in business studies or teaching. It may soon become necessary for all hairdressers to be state registered with the Hairdressing Council.

Personal Qualities

Hairdressers should have a genuine interest in people, a natural friendliness, the ability to stay calm under pressure, creative ability and an eye for detail. A presentable personal appearance is also essential. Hairdressers must not have skin conditions that can be affected by chemicals.

Starting salary

Trainees earn around £2,300, which rises according to qualifications obtained. Experienced hairdressers earn £8,000–£12,000, although some may earn considerably more. Hairdressers may be paid commission for selling hair products and some receive tips from clients.

Hairdressing Council, 12 David Street, 45 High Street, South
    Norwood, London SE25 6HJ; 020 8771 6205;
    www.haircouncil.demon.co.uk;
    e-mail: registrar@haircouncil.org.uk
Hairdressing and Beauty Industry Authority (HABIA), Fraser
    House, Nether Hall Road, Doncaster DN1 2PH; 01302 38000;
    www.habia.org.uk
National Hairdressers Federation, 11 Goldington Road,
    Bedford MK40 3JY; 01234 360332; www.nhfuk.com;
    e-mail: nhf@tgis.co.uk
Careers in Hairdressing and Beauty (Kogan Page)

HEALTH SERVICE (NON-MEDICAL JOBS)

There are over 70 non-medical career options within the health service, employing a wide range of skills.

Management

Health service managers work with professional staff, patients and the public to ensure efficiency and cost effectiveness at all levels of the health service. This involves forward planning, finance, personnel management, purchasing and supply, building maintenance, and the organization of laundry, catering and cleaning. At district and regional health authority levels, the responsibilities are for ascertaining the health needs of the local population and monitoring the quality of provision.

Catering

In hospitals, ordinary meals are provided for both patients and staff, as well as special diets. The catering officer supervises the kitchen, plans menus in consultation with the dietitian and is in control of ordering the food as well as its preparation.

Domestic Services

This covers all grades from basic domestic cleaner level to domestic supervisors and housekeepers. This section is responsible for cleaning groups of beds and areas within the hospital under the charge of the domestic superintendent. It includes district and area domestic managers who coordinate the hospital domestic services.

Laundry

This department deals with the supply of sterilised sheets, towels, blankets and overalls; the number of items handled weekly within one hospital may run into millions.

Medical Records (Patient Services)

Clerks arrange appointments, patients' registration, maintain waiting lists and filing systems, keep patients' records and maintain statistical data. The medical records officer may work within the hospital, in charge of the clerks and medical secretaries, or may work at regional or district authority level.

Ancillary Staff

Includes porters, who move supplies and people around the hospital, general building maintenance staff, and ambulance services.

Qualifications and Training

Staff are recruited and trained by the hospitals and health authorities. Some may work towards NVQs levels 1–4. Graduates are eligible to apply for two-year General and three-year Financial Management Training Schemes.

Personal Qualities

Working for the health service requires a real and sympathetic concern for people. Management trainees need good organization and communication skills.

Starting Salary

Salaries for some non-medical posts start at national minimum wage levels but increase according to responsibility and experience. Graduate management trainees start on £17,500 + London allowance.

NHS Careers; PO Box 376, Bristol BS99 3EY;
    www. nhscareers.nhs.uk; www.futureleaders.nhs.uk
    (for graduate management training)
Institute of Healthcare Management, 46 Grosvenor Gardens,
    London SW1; 020 7881 9235; www.ihm.org.uk/home.cfm
Local Jobcentres and Careers/Connexions Centres

HEALTH VISITOR

Health visitors promote health and contribute to the prevention of mental, physical and social ill health in the community. This involves educating people in ways of healthy living and making positive changes in the environment. Education may be achieved by teaching individuals or families in their own homes, in health centres, clinics, in informal groups, through campaigns for the promotion of good health practices through local or national mass media.

The health visitor may work with people who are registered with a GP or who live within a defined geographical area. The work includes collaboration with a wide range of voluntary and statutory organizations.

Qualifications and Training

Applicants must hold a first-level nurse or midwifery qualification with post-registration experience. One-year health visitor courses are provided at institutions of higher education.

All approved programmes now lead to the award of Specialist Practitioner (Public Health Visiting/Health Visiting). These programmes are at a minimum of first degree level.

Personal Qualities

Health visitors must have a desire to help people. They should be friendly and able to respond tactfully. An ability to communicate with all types of people and to speak in public is useful.

Starting Salary

Approximately £21,605–£25,420.

| i |

NHS Careers; PO Box 376, Bristol BS99 3EY;
   www. nhscareers.nhs.uk
Community Practitioners and Health Visitors Association,
   40 Bermondsey Street, London SE1 3UD; 020 7939 7000;
   www.msfcphva.org

HEALTHCARE ASSISTANT

Healthcare assistants work alongside nurses and provide basic care for patients. They help with treatments, keep wards tidy and complete basic paperwork. They work on general hospital wards, in clinics and outpatient departments, psychiatric hospitals, hospices and care homes. There are also opportunities for community-based work as well, providing physical care to individuals who may otherwise need to go into hospital or residential care homes.

Qualifications and Training

No qualifications are required for entry to the work and hospitals provide on-the-job training that can lead to related NVQs.

Personal Qualities

Like qualified nurses, healthcare assistants must have patience, tact, tolerance and an ability to communicate with the patients in their charge. Physical fitness is essential as the job sometimes involves heavy work (such as lifting and turning patients).

Starting Salary
£9,000 to £11,000.

Local Jobcentres and Careers / Connexions Centres
NHS Careers, PO Box 376, Bristol BS99 3EY; Careers helpline:
    0845 60 60 655; www.nhscareers.nhs.uk / home.html

HOME ECONOMIST

Home economics covers a variety of subjects connected with the
home, family life and consumer issues. This includes nutrition
and health, the preparation of food, equipment used in the home,
home management and budgeting. Home economists can find
themselves writing instructions for new food products, recipe
leaflets and cookery books or dealing with consumer affairs.
There are several levels of training, from certificate to degree
courses.

Demonstrator
Home economists demonstrate products for manufacturers in
shops or exhibitions, organise exhibitions and train demonstrators.
Their work can include giving talks to institutions or in the home
on products or services, or giving advice on home management.

Industry
Many home economists are employed in the food industry in
marketing and / or the research and development of new products
to supply retailers. Their counterparts in retailing are the home
economists who, as buyers / selectors, choose the products to be
stocked. Home economists are similarly employed in the domestic appliance manufacturing industry and with those retailers.

Local Authorities
Home economists are used by local authorities in the social
services, housing departments, consumer services and health
promotion units.

The Media
Some home economists work for magazines, journals, radio and television, where they are concerned with fact-finding and assessment, answering enquiries and preparing articles for publication or broadcast.

Teaching
A knowledge of science, particularly chemistry, is advisable for teaching. There are openings for teachers in colleges and universities, as well as in schools. Food and textiles are taught under technology.

Qualifications and Training
Degree courses and HNDs available in this area have a range of titles, for example Home Economics, Consumer Studies and Applied Consumer Sciences. Entry to these is with two A levels or equivalent. For those interested in teaching, a one-year Postgraduate Certificate in Education (PGCE) in Home Economics is available to graduates.

Personal Qualities
Home economists care about people and their quality of life, and need therefore to have an interest in the quality, performance and safety of goods and services related to the people who use these products. Much of the work involves communicating with the general public on the one hand and specialists on the other, so home economists must be confident and have the ability to express themselves verbally and in writing. Good self-management and interpersonal skills are needed.

Starting Salary
From £13,500–£15,000 for those with a degree.

Institute of Consumer Sciences, 21 Portland Place, London W1B
    1PY; 020 7436 5677; fax: 020 7436 5677;
    www.institute-consumer-sciences.co.uk
National Association of Teachers of Home Economics and
    Technology, Hamilton House, Mabledon Place, London
    WC1H 9BJ; 020 7387 1441; e-mail: nathe@globalnet.co.uk

HOMOEOPATH

Homoeopathy is a method of treating the whole person to create a healthy individual. There are three main principles of homoeopathy. First, treating like with like – what produces the symptoms of a disease may also cure it; the patient is treated by a small amount of the substance causing the symptoms and the natural defences are stimulated. Second, the lower the dose the better the result. Third, the remedy should be unique to the particular patient at a particular time. Homoeopathic remedies may be used to treat almost any reversible illness in adults, children or animals.

Many newly qualified homoeopaths set up in partnership in a clinic with other homoeopaths and some now work with GPs in fund-holding practices. Homoeopathic patients may come privately or be referred by GPs. Medical homoeopaths (doctors who have trained in homoeopathy) work as GPs, private practitioners or in one of the NHS homoeopathic hospitals.

Qualifications and Training

Medical doctors who have been qualified for a minimum of two and a half years may take a postgraduate course at one of the five teaching centres accredited by the Faculty of Homoeopathy.

Non-medically qualified candidates have a choice of institutions and courses. Several organizations register homeopaths as professionally competent. The largest, The Society of Homeopaths, is involved in developing professional education and is currently establishing a formal procedure for accrediting courses in homeopathy. There is a database of recognised courses on their Web site.

Personal Qualities

Homoeopaths must have an interest in people, an ability to consider and interpret information and be good listeners and communicators.

Starting Salary

Varies greatly, depending on hours worked and number of patients.

i

Faculty of Homoeopathy, Royal London Homoeopathic Hospital, Great Ormond Street, London WC1N 3HR; 020 7566 7810; www.trusthomeopathy.org (For medically qualified homoeopaths)

Society of Homoeopaths, 2 Artizan Road, Northampton NN1 4HU; 01604 621400; www.homoeopathy-soh.org (For non-medically qualified homoeopaths)

Working in Complementary and Alternative Medicine (Kogan Page) (contains details of courses)

HORTICULTURIST

(see also *Gardener, Market Gardening, Landscape Architecture*)

Commercial Horticulture

Commercial horticulturists grow crops, such as vegetables, on open land, and tomatoes, lettuce and cucumbers in glasshouses. Both orchard and soft fruits account for over one-fifth of the value of all horticultural production. Commercial horticulture also covers the growing of flowers and ornamental plants, including chrysanthemums, roses and carnations under glass and, for the gardening market, nurseries, landscaping and seedsmen.

Amenity Horticulture

Landscape architects, parks directors, landscape gardeners and groundsmen maintain public and private gardens and parks, sport and recreational facilities, industrial and residential areas, and landscape and plant roadsides. Employers may be local authority public parks and recreation departments, commercial landscaping or contract garden maintenance firms, or owners of major gardens.

Arboriculturists, who care for and maintain trees, are mainly employed by local authorities, although there are some opportunities in private firms. The term 'tree surgeon' is often used for a commercial arboriculturist.

Research

Horticultural scientists work on pests and diseases and general research to produce better and healthier plants, in industrial and government organizations and in universities and colleges. There is a wide range of prospects for graduates.

Advisory Work

The adviser provides a link between research workers and the grower, to pass on the result of experimental work. The commercial and consultancy firms and producer organizations provide opportunities for advisers. A degree plus practical experience is necessary.

Teaching

Opportunities for teaching in horticulture occur in universities, colleges and schools. A degree or diploma is required.

Qualifications and Training

There are openings in horticulture for all standards of education. No GCSEs are required for part- or full-time initial training courses, although beginners should be competent in biology, chemistry and maths. Applicants may work towards NVQs levels 1 to 4.

Those with five GCSEs, including science and maths plus one A level pass or equivalent, and one year's experience can study for the Higher National Diploma, specializing in commercial or amenity horticulture. Two A levels or equivalent are necessary to study for a degree in horticulture.

The Royal Horticultural Society offers a limited number of opportunities for practical training and plantsmanship at its gardens at Wisley, Rosemoor and Hyde Hall. Committed gardeners aged between the ages of 19 and 35 can apply for the two-year Wisley Diploma in Practical Horticulture and the one-year certificate course. Students receive £10,300 per year and accommodation.

Voluntary Internships for four or more weeks are available for those studying horticulture at college and at a number of schools work experience placements are available for secondary pupils.

Personal Qualities

A passion for plants is essential. For commercial horticulture, business acumen is essential, and artistic ability is important in the field of landscape gardening.

Starting Salary
For commercial horticulture salaries are set by the Agricultural Wages Board (see below). Qualified staff can earn between £13,000 and £17,000.

| i |

Local Jobcentres and Careers/Connexions Centres
Agricultural Wages Board, Nobel House, 17 Smith Square,
    London SW1P 3JR
Agricultural Wages Helpline, 0845 0000134;
    www.defra.gov.uk/ farm/agwages/agwages.htm
Institute of Horticulture, 14–15 Belgrave Square, London SW1X
    8PS; 020 7245 6943; www.horticulture.org.uk;
    e-mail: ioh@horticulture.org.uk
Lantra Connect, Lantra House, NAC, Kenilworth, Warwickshire
    CV8 2LG; 0845 707 8007 (Lantra Connect – Helpline);
    www.lantra.co.uk; e-mail: connect@lantra.co.uk
Royal Horticultural Society, 80 Vincent Square, London SW1P
    2PE; 020 7834 4333; www.rhs.org.uk; e-mail: info@rhs.org.uk
'Come into Horticulture' and 'Education and Training Courses in
    Horticulture' (available free from the Institute of Horticulture)

HOTEL WORK

(see also *Catering and Accommodation Management*)

Cooking
Depending on the type and size of hotel, cooking may involve traditional British and International cookery, large-scale kitchen production or the re-heating of pre-cooked meals. It may entail working under pressure in a hot and noisy kitchen, but leads to good career opportunities as a chef.

Food and Drink Service
Staff serving food, beverages and alcoholic drinks may have to work on early or late shifts and carry out weekend duties, but there will be compensating time off.

Housekeeping
Room staff, cleaners and other support staff keep the hotel clean and comfortable. The head housekeeper is in charge of this side of hotel life.

Reception
Receptionists receive guests, handle reservations and perform bookkeeping duties, so it is important to be good at figures, able to handle cash and use computers. Languages are an advantage. Working hours are arranged to deal with early and late arrivals and departures, so may entail shift and weekend work.

Management
Large hotels have a general manager, food and beverage manager, personnel and training manager and house manager, and there may also be heads of departments or sections. There are specialised opportunities in the fields of finance, administration, food and beverage operations, accommodation services, sales and marketing product development, public relations, personnel and training.

Qualifications and Training
Qualifications are the same as for Catering and Accommodation Management (*see* page 73).

Personal Qualities
Depending on which aspect of hotel work is undertaken, candidates need an understanding of food and drink, good social skills and an ability to establish relationships with staff and colleagues, and with customers and guests. Those serving food and drinks will benefit from a pleasant personality, alertness and a good memory for customers. Some may need a good head for figures and a grasp of statistics.

Starting Salary
Salaries vary according to the field of work and degree of responsibility. Many employees live in hotel accommodation and have food provided. Salaries are similar to those given for Catering and Accommodation Management (*see* page 74).

i

Hotel and Catering International Management Association,
191 Trinity Road, London SW17 7HN; 020 8772 7400;
www.hcima.org.uk; e-mail: info@hcima.co.uk

Hotel and Catering Training Company; 0500 832 300;
www.hctc.co.uk

Springboard UK, 1 Denmark Street, London WC2H 8LP;
020 7497 8654; www.springboarduk.org.uk

Careers in Catering and Hotel Management (Kogan Page)

The Caterer and Hotelkeeper; www.caterer.com (for job vacancies)

HOUSING OFFICER

Housing officers work mainly for local authorities and housing associations, but there are also opportunities in voluntary and private housing concerns. The work covers a broad range of areas that will vary by organization and sector. In catering for the demand for rented accommodation, the housing officer will manage and maintain properties, which includes dealing with rent arrears, reporting repairs, applications, allocations and arranging property exchanges and transfers. Housing officers often work with social and welfare agencies and need to have a basic understanding of the different welfare benefits.

Qualifications and Training

The basic qualifications needed for professional training in housing are three GCSEs and one A level or equivalent. Students over the age of 21 who do not meet these requirements but have relevant work experience may be considered as exceptional entrants. Contact local colleges to discuss this in more detail.

Those employed in housing follow a day-release or distance-learning course to study for the Chartered Institute of Housing's professional qualification (PQ). NVQs levels 2, 3 and 4 in Housing are available, and anyone working in housing is eligible to do these; NVQ level 4 allows candidates to proceed to stage 2 of the Chartered Institute of Housing's PQ.

In addition to the course, candidates also need to do the work-based Test of Professional Practice (TPP), normally completed within two years. The PQ can take three or four years to complete, depending on whether the graduate or non-graduate route is taken.

Graduates or mature entrant candidates are required to study a one-year graduate foundation course followed by a two-year professional diploma. Non-graduates are required to complete an Edexcel (BTEC)/SQA HNC in housing studies followed by a two-year professional diploma. There are also full-time degree courses and full- and part-time postgraduate diplomas. The Test of Professional Practice will still need to be undertaken with these alternative routes.

Personal Qualities
An interest in improving people's living conditions, good inter-personal skills, effective organization skills, sensitivity to an individual's needs and flexibility are all important.

Starting Salary
Trainee posts are offered in the range of £9,500 to £14,000. A standard Housing Officer/Manager post (requiring one to five years' experience) will have a salary of £14,000 to £22,000 (the higher figure includes London weighting).

i

Chartered Institute of Housing, Octavia House, Westwood Business Park, Westwood Way, Coventry CV4 8JP; 024 7685 1700; www.cih.org; e-mail: careers@cih.org

Chartered Institute of Housing in Scotland, 6 Palmerston Place, Edinburgh EH12 5AA; 0131 225 4544; www.cih.org; e-mail: scotland@cih.org

Chartered Institute of Housing Cymru, 4 Purbeck House, Lambourne Crescent, Cardiff Business Park, Llanishen, Cardiff CF14 5GJ; 029 2076 5760; www.cih.org; e-mail: cymru@cih.org

Chartered Institute of Housing in Northern Ireland, Carnmoney House, Edgewater Office Park, Dargan Road, Belfast BT3 9JQ; 028 9077 8222; www.cih.org; e-mail: ni@cih.org

HUMAN RESOURCE ADVISER/ MANAGER

The role of an HR professional can vary and is largely dependent on the individual organization's needs and the value that the organization's senior managers place on the HR function. It can include working at a strategic level on a range of HR policies, processes and practices in relation to the business needs of the organization. More commonly, however, HR advisers work on day-to-day issues such as recruitment, contracts of employment, payroll, training, induction, disciplinary and grievance procedures, redundancy programmes, equal opportunities policies and setting up staff support systems.

In large organizations, individuals may specialise in one of these areas, but in smaller companies they will deal with all aspects of the job.

Qualifications and Training

A good general education is essential and most HR professionals will have NVQ at level 3 or above, or a first degree in an appropriate area. A range of appropriate qualifications includes NVQs in Training and Development, Management or Administration, and postgraduate qualifications are also increasingly available. The Chartered Institute of Personnel and Development (CIPD) provide a range of professional qualifications.

Personal Qualities

A good understanding of business needs is essential at strategic level. An honest, straightforward and approachable manner is essential when dealing with colleagues. HR professionals need to be clear thinking and able to help implement changes effectively.

Starting Salary
Dependent on qualifications, experience, expertise and the business sector. HR advisers £17,000 to £30,000; HR managers £20,000 to £50,000.

Chartered Institute of Personnel and Development, CIPD House, Camp Road, Wimbledon SW19 4UX; 020 8971 9000; www.cipd.co.uk

I

ILLUSTRATOR

see *Artist, Medical Illustrator, Technical Illustrator*

INDEXER

Indexers provide a systematic arrangement of the terms appearing in a book, journal or other publication, which could be electronic or paper-based. They also work with page numbers or other locators in order to ensure the information can be easily found. Indexers are generally employed by publishers or authors. Most are freelancers working from home.

Qualifications and Training
No formal qualifications are required but a good education, normally to degree level, is necessary plus subject knowledge in the case of specialist books. Training is by open-learning course leading to accreditation. Registered indexers prove their experience and competence through an assessment procedure and admission to the Register of Indexers.

Personal Qualities
An ability to analyse a text and meticulous attention to detail are essential, plus the ability to work to set requirements and time limits.

Starting Salary
Payment may be by lump sum or by the hour. The minimum rates recommended by the Society are £15–£20 per hour or £1.20–£2.00 per page.

Society of Indexers, Globe Centre, Penistone Road, Sheffield S6
3AE; 0114 201 3060; fax: 0114 281 3061;
www.socind.demon.co.uk;
e-mail: admin@socind.demon.co.uk

INDUSTRIAL DESIGNER

Trained designers work within industry with engineers who have
created products. These range from household goods and furniture to specialised equipment for science, industry and commerce.
Designers are concerned with creating products that both look
attractive and are efficient and convenient in use. The competition
for the sale of new goods, from suitcases or spectacles to cassette
players or cars, has resulted in an increased demand for the
services of industrial designers.

Qualifications and Training

Employers recruit from those with an HND or degree in a design-
related subject; some courses offer specialist modules in industrial
design. Entry to such courses is normally via a National Diploma
course after GCSEs or a foundation course at an art college after A
levels. Applicants for art and design courses are expected to have
a portfolio of their artwork when interviewed.

Personal Qualities

As well as artistic ability, an understanding of mass-production
processes is necessary; the industrial designer should also be able
to work as part of a team, to schedule and recognise the needs of
the consumer.

Starting Salary

£13,000–£20,000.

National Society for Education in Art and Design (NSEAD), The
Gatehouse, Corsham Court, Wiltshire SN13 OBZ; 01249
714825; www.nsead.org

Design Council, 34 Bow Street, London WC2E 7DL; 020 7420
    5200; www.designcouncil.org.uk and
    www.yourcreativefuture.org.uk; e-mail:
    info@designcouncil.org.uk
Local Jobcentres and Careers/Connexions Centres

INFORMATION SCIENTIST

(see also *Librarian/Information Manager*)

The work of the information scientist is similar to that of a librarian and involves collecting, indexing and classifying information for experts such as scientists, engineers or economists. However, in information science more emphasis is placed on current technology, and information is supplied online or by other electronic media. Information scientists work for industrial concerns and research organizations in their information departments or 'special libraries'. The information scientist often needs to have specialist knowledge and must be able to keep up to date with technical information by reading journals and papers. Their work can include summarizing relevant articles, indexing and researching information from a variety of sources.

Qualifications and Training

Degrees and HNDs in Information Science are available at a number of universities. Entry requirements vary. Full- or part-time postgraduate courses are available to those with a relevant degree. First degree courses, postgraduate diplomas and masters are jointly accredited by The Library Association and the Institute of Information Scientists. A full list of the courses offered by 17 universities is available through Library Association Web site (see below). The Library Association and Institute of Information Scientists have joined together to create a new organization, the Chartered Institute of Library and Information Professionals.

Personal Qualities

A methodical approach and accuracy, the ability to retain information, and an interest in the appropriate field of research, plus a desire to help people to find the information they want, are all important attributes.

Starting Salary
Between £11,000 and £16,000.

Institute of Information Scientists, 39–41 North Road, London
  N7 9DP; 020 7619 0624/5; fax: 020 7619 0626;
  www.iis.org.uk; e-mail: iis@dial.pipex.com
The Library Association, 7 Ridgmount Street, London
  WC1E 7AE; 020 7636 7543; www.la-hq.org.uk;
  e-mail: Careers@la-hq.org.uk

INFORMATION AND COMMUNICATION TECHNOLOGY

(see also *Computing*)

Information and Communication Technology has an effect on all
aspects of our lives. Almost all businesses and services make use
of ICT to reach more customers, offer better services, reduce costs,
and improve efficiency. In the airline industry, for example, ICT
underpins everything from selling and allocating seats to calculating fuel and filing flight plans. In the UK alone, 1 million people
work as ICT professionals; 45 per cent in the ICT industry itself,
and 55 per cent working in an ICT role in other industries. The e-
skills NTO estimates that around 150,000 to 200,000 additional
ICT professionals are needed every year. A career in ICT can
mean working in any industry – from the media to healthcare,
education to financial services. Most jobs need a combination of
technical, business and personal skills and can be divided into the
following categories:

IT Services
This covers a range of customer facing roles and could include
developing Web sites, designing and installing IT systems for
customers, supporting customers with software or hardware
problems, managing projects. Job titles include Software Support
Professional, Technical Architect and Hardware Engineer.

IT Operations
This involves working in an IT department, running the computer systems. The work could include making sure the IT system is working properly, solving problems with it, helping those having trouble using the IT system, upgrading to add new functions and deciding how best to use IT to meet your organization's goals or enhance their business. Job titles include Applications Programmer, Systems Analyst, Network Manager and Database Administrator.

IT Sales and Marketing
This covers promoting or selling products, services and IT solutions. You may be assigned to a particular customer or group of customers, or specialise in particular products or services.

IT Research and Development
Those who work in this sector create new technologies or new products. This could mean researching new approaches to mobile communications, or developing software packages. Job titles in this area include Software Developer, Product Tester and Technical Author.

Qualifications and Training
Many employers set their own entry requirements, but 41 per cent of existing IT professionals are educated to degree level. New entrants increasingly have academic or vocational qualifications at degree or equivalent level. Applicants for posts may be asked to take aptitude tests to assess their numeracy, logic, accuracy, thinking speed and verbal reasoning.

There are a large number of relevant courses and entry requirements vary according to the nature of the course. Potential systems analysts are generally expected to hold degrees and/or programming and/or business qualifications (entry for such courses requires A levels, often in mathematical subjects). Programmers are usually expected to have A level/H grade or HNC/HND passes as well as GCSEs or equivalent in English and maths. A growing number of Foundation Degrees with flexible entry requirements are becoming available.

In addition, there is also a range of product-specific and professional qualifications, which have been developed by corporate organizations, such as Microsoft, Cisco and Novell, and by professional bodies such as the British Computer Society, the Help Desk Institute or the Institute for the Management of Information Systems.

Employment-based training opportunities are varied. Some firms recruit graduates from a range of degree disciplines as trainees for IT-related work and a number offer Modern Apprenticeship or Graduate Apprenticeship schemes. Many companies run their own programmes as well as sending trainees on relevant external courses.

Personal Qualities

Different jobs have very different skills requirements; however, most need good interpersonal skills, team-working and problem-solving ability. Some such as software developer require technical skills whereas for project management roles, communication and organizational skills are essential.

Starting Salary

This varies according to the type of employer and the work undertaken. Starting salaries in IT Operations range from £16,000 to £27,000. Help desk operators average £14,000; programmers with two years' experience can earn up to £40,000; in IT Sales and Marketing from £16,000 to £22,000 + bonus or commission.

i

e-skills NTO, 1 Castle Lane, London SW1E 6DR; 020 7963 8920; www.e-skillsnto.org.uk; info@e-skillsnto.org.uk

British Computer Society, 1 Sanford Street, Swindon, Wiltshire SN1 1HJ; 01793 417424; www.bcs.org.uk

Help Desk Institute, 21 High Street, Green Street Green, Orpington, Kent BR6 6BG; 01689 889 100; www.hdi-europe.com; e-mail: support@hdi-europe.com

Institution of Analysts and Programmers, Charles House, 36 Culmington Road, London W13 9NH; 020 8567 2118; www.iap.org.uk

Institute for the Management of Information Systems, 5 Kingfisher House, New Mill Road, Orpington, Kent BR5 3QG; 0700 00 23456; www.imis.org.uk; e-mail: central@imis.org.uk

INSURANCE

(see also *Actuary*)

Apart from statutory obligations, insurance is a way of covering the costs arising from disasters of various kinds. Many people pay into a common pool, and those who incur losses can draw money from the pool. The four main areas are personal lines (motor, household, travel), commercial lines (fire, liability, goods in transit), life assurance and reinsurance. Work undertaken in the office includes assessing risks, policy drafting, underwriting (the acceptance and rating of business) and claims settling, and often involves computers. Sales staff work outside the office, as do surveyors and claims inspectors who assess losses on site. Other aspects of insurance include investment, legal and accountancy work. Insurance companies also operate pension funds for businesses. Lloyd's of London is a group of private insurers and is traditionally connected with international insurance, offering all types of cover.

Broker

As the link between client and insurer, the broker advises on and arranges policies for a wide range of businesses.

Loss Adjuster

They work independently, and are appointed by insurers to negotiate settlement of insurance claims. Most chartered loss adjusters used to operate in private practice 'adjusting' claims to ascertain the proper liability of an insurer. Increasingly, loss-adjusting companies are just as likely to provide cost-effective claims and risk-management services to large corporations, local authorities, health services or brokers.

Agents and Inspectors

Agents call on people in their homes, selling insurance and collecting premiums; inspectors are salespeople and may also supervise agents and areas. The increase in Internet and contact centre insurance sales means many companies have reduced the number of traditional sales staff they employ. Opportunities in contact centres are increasing.

Qualifications and Training

Those with three GCSEs at grade C or above, including English and maths, may enter a company and at the same time study part time at a college for an Edexcel (BTEC)/SQA national certificate or diploma. Most insurance employers run a minimum basic training scheme, and candidates can also attend courses run by the employer or at the College of Insurance, leading to the examinations of the Chartered Insurance Institute. To take the initial qualifying exam of the Institute, candidates need three A levels or equivalent. Other routes to professional qualifications are available for those entrants without such qualifications.

The Chartered Insurance Institute's Certificate of Insurance Practice (CIP) can be taken by applicants over 21 without specific qualifications or by those under 21 with four GCSEs grades A to C or Edexcel (BTEC) equivalent. NVQs are available at levels 2, 3 and 4 for General or Life Insurance and intermediaries. The CII's Insurance Foundation Certificate (IFC) provides the insurance knowledge base for the level 2 NVQs, which then require individuals to prove their competence in insurance disciplines.

Personal Qualities

Absolute integrity is necessary, as well as some mathematical ability and an interest in people. Communication skills in speech and writing are also necessary.

Starting Salary

Salaries vary from employer to employer depending on qualifications and location. Some examples are: £8,000–£11,000 for clerks at 16 and claims officials; insurance salespeople £12,000 + commission; loss adjusters, underwriters and brokers £10,000–£12,000 to start, but paying more highly later.

The Chartered Institute of Loss Adjusters, Peninsular House,
    36 Monument Street, London EC3R 8LJ; 020 7337 9960;
    www.cila.co.uk; e-mail: info@cila.co.uk
The Society of Claims Technicians, Peninsular House,
    36 Monument Street, London EC3R 8LJ; 020 7337 9960;
    www.cila.co.uk; e-mail: info@cila.co.uk

The Chartered Insurance Institute, Careers Information Service, 20 Aldermanbury, London EC2V 7HY; 020 7417 4793; www.cii.co.uk; e-mail: michael.khan@cii.co.uk

INTERIOR DECORATOR

(see also *Interior Designer, Painter and Decorator*)

Decorators are craftsmen who paper and paint in private homes, or larger buildings. They may also give advice on colour schemes, including carpets, curtains, paint, wall coverings and fittings. They may be employed by large stores, manufacturers, architects, specialist shops or private individuals and companies.

Qualifications and Training

Craftsmen decorators can learn the trade without formal educational qualifications through apprenticeships working towards NVQs. Advisory decorators can learn by working in a workroom or studio of a store, specialist shop or architect's office as a junior, and taking suitable evening classes and City and Guilds courses. Unlike interior designers, interior decorators do not need to hold art and design qualifications.

Personal Qualities

Manual dexterity is necessary for craftsman decorators; artistic sense is imperative for advisers and useful for craftsmen too.

Starting Salary

Training allowance at 16; around £12,000+ when qualified.

Construction Industry Training Board, Bircham Newton, King's Lynn, Norfolk PE31 6RH; 01485 577577; www.citb.org.uk

INTERIOR DESIGNER

(see also *Interior Decorator*)

Interior designers work for commercial organizations as well as undertaking private commissions. They are responsible for the interiors of buildings (whereas an architect is responsible for its shell). Interior design can cover materials for floors and ceilings, fitments and fittings, and colour schemes, along with electrical and spatial planning. The commercial organizations may be offices, hotels, pubs, stores or banks. Interior designers may work with architects, have their own consultancies, or work in design units within large organizations.

Qualifications and Training
Entry to art school and college via a foundation course is the same as for an industrial designer (*see* page 209). Once at art college, the student may specialise in interior design.

Personal Qualities
A natural aptitude for art, the ability to work as part of a design team, and to present work to customers are necessary.

Starting Salary
£13,000–£20,000 according to experience and ability.

National Society for Education in Art and Design (NSEAD), The
    Gatehouse, Corsham Court, Wiltshire SN13 OBZ;
    01249 714825; www.nsead.org
Design Council, 34 Bow Street, London WC2E 7DL;
    020 7420 5200; www.designcouncil.org.uk and
    www.yourcreativefuture.org.uk;
    e-mail: info@designcouncil.org.uk
Careers in Art and Design (Kogan Page)

INTERPRETER
(see also *Translator*)

Interpreters communicate between people who do not share a common language. They use two main techniques: simultaneous and consecutive interpreting. Conference interpreters usually work using the simultaneous method in a booth with headphones and communicative technology, allowing them to hear the speaker and interpret to their audience.

Very few openings are available for interpreters, even world-wide. Conference interpreters work at international conferences such as the United Nations or the European Commission and at the International Court of Justice, using simultaneous or consecutive interpreting. Some work for international agencies; others are freelance. Demand for conference interpreters in particular languages may fluctuate depending on the political and economic requirements of the day. Interpreters with specialist knowledge, such as engineering or economics, may have the chance to work at conferences on their subject. Interpreters may also work as guides in tourist centres, and to do this they must usually be accredited and trained as guides.

Demand for interpreting in the public services (police, courts, public health and local government) has led to the creation of the National Register of Public Service Interpreters covering a wide range of African, Asian, European and Far Eastern languages. This register is supported by the Home Office and the UK legal agencies. The Institute of Translation and Interpreting (ITI) can also help source qualified public service interpreters from its membership, as can numerous other commercial agencies.

Qualifications and Training

To take a degree course, two GCE A levels or equivalent, including a foreign language, are normally required. At the newer universities and colleges, training in interpreting and translating is offered, combined with regional studies or technological or business studies, aimed at industry, commerce and international organizations. A list of these courses is offered by the Institute of Linguists and the Institute of Translation and Interpreting (ITI). Such degree courses usually involve work or study abroad. The Institute of Linguists Educational Trust also offers the only qualification in public service interpreting – the Diploma in Public Service Interpreting, which is mapped at between NVQ level 4 and 5.

Personal Qualities

Fluency in two or more languages should be allied with a natural feeling for words and phrases and a good ear. It is necessary to be able to think quickly, to remain alert for long periods, and to be socially confident. Subject knowledge is essential, especially for simultaneous interpreting which requires a degree of understanding and anticipation of subject matter and context.

Starting Salary

Interpreters working in business earn £200+ per day. Hourly rates for some public service agencies can be lower.

Institute of Linguists, Saxon House, 48 Southwark Street, London SE11 1UN; 020 7940 3100; fax: 020 7940 3101; www.iol.org.uk; e-mail: info@iol.org.uk

Institute of Translation and Interpreting (ITI), Exchange House, 494 Midsummer Boulevard, Milton Keynes, Buckinghamshire MK9 2EA; 01908 255905; fax: 01908 255700; www.iti.org.uk; e-mail: info@iti.org.uk

'Average Rates for Translation' (Institute of Linguists)

Careers Using Languages (Kogan Page)

Great Careers for People Interested in Languages (Kogan Page)

'Some courses in translation and Interpreting in the UK', fact-sheet from ITI (address above)

'2001 Rates and Salaries Survey', available from ITI (address above)

INVESTMENT WORK

Analyst

Investment analysts analyse the financial markets to advise on the best investments for clients. Investment managers rely on their information.

There are two main types of investment analyst. First, those who work for stockbrokers and undertake their own analysis to provide information for fund manager clients. The aim is to generate 'buy and sell' orders for the stockbrokers for whom they work. This is known as the 'sell side'. Second, there are those who work for investment management institutions. They provide ideas and information to enable their in-house fund managers to make the best decisions for their clients. This is known as the 'buy side'. The majority of investment analysts work on the 'sell side'.

Fund Manager

Investment fund managers invest the funds of other people – private clients and institutions, such as insurance companies, charities, independent schools and specialised research institutions. Managers must keep their clients' interests continually under review, offering advice on how to retain their clients' income and when to change investments. Investment fund managers may be employed by the larger institutions or work in specialist firms that tend to serve smaller clients.

Qualifications and Training

Entrants generally have a degree and often a professional qualification. The accepted global professional qualification is that of Chartered Financial Analyst (CFA). This is set by the Association for Investment Analysis and Research (AIMR), an international organization which has over a hundred constituent societies worldwide. The UK Society of Investment Professionals is the second largest of these societies.

Personal Qualities

Entrants must be able to work as part of a team as well as on their own initiative. Considerable time is spent on the telephone, so communication skills are important. Naturally, a keen interest in world financial and current affairs is essential.

Starting Salary

Trainees in investment analysis work draw a fairly modest salary, but with experience may earn £50,000+.

The Society of Investment Professionals, 21 Ironmonger Lane, London EC2V 8EY; 020 7796 3000; fax: 020 7796 3333; www.uksip.org; e-mail: uksipstaff@uksip.org

JEWELLERY TRADE

Design

Jewellery designers craft a wide variety of items either by hand or using methods of large-scale production. These may be very expensive, traditionally styled pieces using gold or platinum, cheaper costume jewellery using synthetic stones and base metals, or fashion accessories made from beads, plastic or wood.

Although there are a few openings for designers of expensive jewellery, the more costly costume jewellery and mass-produced jewellery, there is more scope for original designers on either a freelance or artist/craftsman basis, making fashionable ranges with semi-precious stones.

Manufacture

The jewellery, silverware and allied industries encompass a vast range of specialist skills. Apart from mounting and silver-smithing, other skills needed to support these occupations include gem setting, engraving (hand and machine), enamelling, chasing, engine turning, spinning, electro-plating and polishing.

Qualifications and Training

Those wishing to follow a career in jewellery design need specialist training before looking for employment. Full-time three-year, and some sandwich-based, degree courses in three-dimensional design have options in jewellery and silversmithing. The minimum entrance requirements are usually two A levels and three GCSEs or equivalents, plus satisfactory completion of an art foundation course.

Manufacturing training can be by traditional trade apprentice-ships, lasting between three and five years. NVQs in Manufacturing Jewellery and Allied Products are available.

The Gemmological Association and Gem Testing Laboratory (GAGTL) have two diploma qualifications – the Diploma in Gemmology (taken in two parts), and the Gem Diamond Diploma (one part). These may be studied by correspondence, or as daytime or evening courses at GAGTL and allied technology centres worldwide. There are also two examinations conducted by the British Horological Institute – the certificate for clockmak-ers and the diploma for salesmen.

Personal Qualities

People in the jewellery trade must have a sense of design and an appreciation of quality. Designers must be prepared to work hard and keep to a busy schedule. Self-employed or independent designers will need determination to keep going and unflagging enthusiasm to sell their products. Manufacturing employees and craftspeople must possess good manual dexterity, creativity, integrity, attention to detail, initiative and self-motivation.

Starting Salary

Shopworkers earn about £170 a week. Individual craftsmen set their own rates.

i

British Jewellers' Association, 10 Vyse Street, Birmingham B18
    6LT; 0121 237 1109; www.bja.org.uk
Gemmological Association and Gem Testing Laboratory of Great
    Britain, 27 Greville Street, London EC1N 8TN; 020 7404 3334;
    fax: 020 7404 8843; www.gagtl.ac.uk / gagtl
National Association of Goldsmiths, 78a Luke Street, London
    EC2A 4XG; 020 7613 4445; www.progold.net;
    e-mail: nag@jewellersuk.com

JOBBER

see *Market Maker*

JOCKEY

Jockeys are employed by trainers of flat racing and National Hunt (jump) racehorses to ride horses at race meetings. They may ride for one trainer or for several. To become a jockey it is necessary first to work in a racing stable as an apprentice jockey or stablehand.

Only those showing most talent – about one in ten – are chosen to ride in a race. The others remain as stablehands, and may be promoted to Head Lad (this title applies to boys and girls).

Stable Lad

Stable lads (who may be boys or girls) do a lot of labouring work: mucking out, fetching straw, filling haynets and sweeping. They must also learn to groom and exercise the horses, and usually become responsible for a certain number of their 'own'. On race days, a stable lad will accompany a horse, groom him, walk him round before the race and lead him into the winner's enclosure if he wins.

Qualifications and Training

No specific educational qualifications are needed to become a jockey. Some experience of riding is useful but serious training is given by the stable. The racing industry has introduced NVQs, levels 1, 2 and 3 in Racehorse Care and Management. Flat-racing apprenticeships start at 16 and last until the age of 24. National Hunt apprenticeships start at 17–18 and last until the age of 25.

There is a nine-week training course available at the British Racing School in Newmarket, funded by racing, and open to school leavers who wish to work in a racing yard. Pupils are taught to ride, look after horses and carry out elementary stable management. The Northern Racing School at Doncaster runs a 10-week residential course for school leavers who wish to work in a racing yard and for those already in the industry who wish to further their training as stable staff. Training is compulsory for all 16- to 19-year-olds employed by the industry.

Personal Qualities

Apprentice jockeys must be prepared to work long hours in all weather conditions. At 16, flat-racing apprentices should weigh 7–8 stone (44–51 kilograms), girls 8–9 stone (51–57 kilograms); National

Hunt jockeys may be heavier. Jockeys need strong hands and arms and must be able to deal with nervous horses in a calm, confident and unemotional way. Jockeys must also be able to work within the strict, rather conservative traditions of the racing world.

Starting Salary

Apprentice jockeys and stablehands over 19 with a year's experience earn about £140 a week. Apprentice and conditional jockeys receive their normal wage plus half the riding fee when racing. Racing jockeys' salaries vary according to their success; there is a rate per ride plus a percentage of the prize money.

i

British Racing School, Snailwell Road, Newmarket, Suffolk
  CB8 7NU; 01638 665103; www.brs.org.uk;
  e-mail: careers@brs.org.uk
The Jockey Club, 42, Portman Square, London WIH 6EN;
  0207 343 3236; www.thejockeyclub.co.uk
The British Horseracing Training Board (BHTB), 42 Portman
  Square, London W1H 6EN; 020 7396 0011;
  www. bhb.co.uk/ careers.asp, e-mail: info@bhb.co.uk
'Careers in the Horseracing Industry' can be downloaded from
  the Web site
The Northern Racing School, The Stables, Rossington Hall, Great
  North Road, Doncaster DN11 0HN; 01302 865462;
  www.northernracingcollege.co.uk

JOINER

see *Carpenter and Bench Joiner*

JOURNALIST

The title 'journalist' covers a variety of jobs. Journalists increasingly write for Web sites as well as paper publications.

Reporter
Reporters find, research and write news articles and features for newspapers, magazines, special-interest periodicals, news agen-

cies, radio and television. They work irregular hours to meet deadlines and must be able to produce accurate, interesting and readable copy quickly, often in noisy offices or even public places. Reporters cover all kinds of stories, from weddings and council meetings (at local level) to world events and sensational murder cases (for the national papers). Opportunities exist for foreign correspondents and freelance journalists.

Sub-Editor

Sub-editors reduce or, if necessary, rewrite articles to an appropriate size depending upon importance and position in the paper. They also deal with continuing stories which come in a bit at a time, write the headlines and, in between editions, may amend stories to accommodate sudden developments or change the page layout if required. Sub-editors may specialise; for example, dealing only with the sports-page production or page design.

Feature Writer/Columnist

Feature writers suggest subjects for research and produce longer than average articles dealing with topics not necessarily of current news value but of general interest, such as an interview with a public figure, an article about debt or planning laws. Columnists often write about subjects from a personal point of view.

The Editor

The editor of a publication is responsible for its policy, content and the appointment and organization of staff.

Qualifications and Training

Most journalists begin their career by serving for two or three years on a provincial newspaper. Minimum entry requirements are five GCSEs and two A level passes, but more than 65 per cent of all entrants are now graduates. There are also a number of degree courses in journalism but many entrants have a degree in other disciplines plus on the job or postgraduate training.

Approximately 1,000 school/college leavers undertake NCTJ pre-entry courses each year at some 30 colleges/universities accredited by the NCTJ. Direct entrants must complete a two-year on-the-job training period which includes either a 12-week block-release or day-release to an approved course.

Personal Qualities

Journalists must possess powers of self-expression, observation, accuracy, patience and tact. They must take pride in their work, be resourceful, willing to travel and to work under pressure and irregular hours; stamina is required, as is confidence, great curiosity and the ability to put people at their ease. It helps to be able to write fast in long hand; word-processing and Internet research skills are also important.

Starting Salary

Salaries vary greatly. Trainees on a small weekly paper earn about £10,000, more in London. Experienced journalists earn from £18,000–£23,000+.

National Council for the Training of Journalists, Latton Bush Centre, Southern Way, Harlow, Essex CM18 7BL; 01279 430009; www.nctj.org.uk; e-mail:info@nctj.com

Careers in Journalism (Kogan Page)

K

KENNEL WORK

(see also *Dog Groomer*)

Kennel staff ensure that the animals in their care have clean accommodation, are fed a regular and nutritious diet, kept clean and well groomed and given sufficient exercise. Where animals are sick or recovering from an operation, the kennel staff must also be able to provide adequate nursing care.

There are a number of different types of kennel – greyhound kennels train dogs for racing, hunt kennels for hunting – and they involve a lot of outdoor work, exercising the dogs, and perhaps travelling to meetings. There are quarantine kennels licensed by the Department for Food, Rural Affairs and Agriculture (DFRA) and breeding kennels where duties will also include weaning and training puppies, preparing dogs for shows, and possibly handling them. Boarding kennels look after animals while their owners are away. Some of the racing and quarantine kennels are large operations situated near racing stadia, airports and ports but others may be smaller, family-run concerns.

Qualifications and Training

No formal qualifications are needed to work in kennels, and most employers prefer school leavers to train on the job. The NVQ level 2 in Animal Care and the National Small Animal Care Certificate are nationally recognised by the industry and provide a good base for further study. Many training organizations and agricultural colleges throughout the country offer this qualification. Entry requirements vary depending on the institution.

Personal Qualities

Good health, general fitness and stamina are required for this manual, physically demanding outdoor work. Kennel staff must be unsentimental about animals but at the same time have a genuine concern for their well-being; they require patience and a placid but firm nature. A willingness to work long days, weekends and public holidays is also required.

Starting Salary

£150–£200+ a week.

Lantra Connect, Lantra House, NAC, Kenilworth, Warwickshire CV8 2LG; 0845 707 8007 (Lantra Connect – Helpline); www.lantra.co.uk; e-mail: connect@lantra.co.uk

Animal Care College, Ascot House, High Street, Ascot, Berkshire SL5 7JG; 01344 628269; www.animalcarecollege.co.uk

Our Dogs, 5 Oxford Road, Station Approach, Manchester M60 1SX; 0161 228 1984 (weekly magazine featuring job offers and advertisements from kennels. Also publishes *Cats*)

Local Jobcentres and Careers/Connexions Centres

Careers Working with Animals (Kogan Page)

Running Your Own Boarding Kennels (Kogan Page)

L

LABORATORY TECHNICIAN

(see also *Biomedical Scientist*)
Laboratory technicians support scientists, technologists, lecturers and medical staff by enabling practical work to be carried out in laboratories and related areas. Their work may include: preparation, cultivation, maintenance, use and disposal of specimens and samples used for analysis or other work; care of animals, insects and plants; design, construction, maintenance and use of equipment; obtaining, evaluating and reporting on results. A range of materials, procedures and equipment may be used, including sophisticated instruments with dedicated computers.

Laboratory technicians work in a range of industries, including petrochemical, food, textiles, pharmaceutical and engineering for national and local government, research organizations, in all sectors of education and in medical services.

Qualifications and Training
The minimum entry requirements are four or five GCSEs at grade C or higher, or equivalent, including maths and science. Training is usually provided on the job. NVQs are available for laboratory technicians working in the chemical and pharmaceutical industries and in education.

The Institute of Science Technology offers its own work-based qualification for laboratory technicians through a network of registered centres. NVQs at levels 1–4 in Laboratory Operations are available for those working in the chemical and pharmaceutical industries, and at level 2 to 3 for those working in education.

Personal Qualities

Laboratory technicians must be practical, numerate, methodical, conscientious, discreet and accurate. Good colour vision is essential.

Starting Salary

£10,000 rising to £14,000 with experience.

i

Institute of Science Technology, Stowe House, Netherstowe, Lichfield, Staffordshire WS13 6TJ; 01543 251346; fax: 01543 415804; www.istonline.org.uk

Science, Technology and Mathematics Council, 20–22 Queensberry Place, London SW7 2DZ; 020 7225 1155; www.sstmc.org.uk; e-mail: enquiries@stmc.org.uk

LAND AGENT

(see also *Surveyor/Surveying Technician*)

Land agents work for estate owners and for large institutional owners. Their work overlaps to some extent with that of agricultural surveyors in that they are both concerned with the use and development of land and may advise owners on agricultural methods, forestry, accountancy, building or improving of farm buildings. In addition the land agent may be responsible for stocking and for employing estate staff, as well as attending to the owner's personal business matters.

Qualifications and Training

Formal qualifications are not always necessary for a land agent who is employed by a private owner. However, it is advisable to become professionally qualified as a surveyor (*see* Surveyor/ Surveying Technician).

Personal Qualities

Necessary requirements include a love of the land and being out of doors, a practical approach and the ability to direct one's own work.

Starting Salary

A school leaver could expect about £8,000, whereas a newly qualified surveyor with professional competence would receive about £15,000–£20,000.

The Royal Institution of Chartered Surveyors, 12 Great George
    Street, London SW1P 5AD; 020 7222 7000; www.rics.org.uk

LANDSCAPE ARCHITECT

Landscape Architecture as a profession covers the three divisions of design, management and science.

Landscape Designers

Designers are trained in the planning and design of all types of outdoor spaces. They use design techniques based on their knowledge of the functional and aesthetic characteristics of landscape materials, and of the organization of landscape elements, external spaces and activities. Their work ranges from large-scale landscape planning to the preparation of schemes for the short- and long-term development of individual sites. It also includes preparing detailed designs, specifications, contract drawings and letting and supervising contracts. Some practitioners are also qualified in other disciplines such as planning and architecture and the landscape designer draws on many fields in order to promote new landscapes, and sustain existing ones.

Landscape Manager

Landscape managers employ management techniques in the long-term care and development of new and existing landscapes and also in determining policy and planning for future landscape management and use. They have particular expertise in the management and maintenance of landscape materials, both hard and soft, based on established principles of construction, horticulture and ecology. In addition, the landscape manager will have a thorough knowledge of budgetary control procedures, property and resource management, especially related to manpower and machinery and of letting and administration of contracts.

Landscape Scientist

Landscape scientists have a specific understanding of the principles and process of natural biological and physical systems. They relate their training and experience in subjects such as ecology, conservation, biology, soil science and botany to the solution of practical landscape problems, providing both traditional and innovative input to landscape design, planning and management work. Evaluation of the significance and effects of planning proposals, along with creating new habitats and environments in association with mineral workings, forestry and agriculture, make up a considerable amount of the work of landscape scientists. Smaller-scale ecological and habitat surveys, species assessments, wildlife management plans and the appraisal and preparation of conservation schemes are frequents tasks. Some landscape scientists are involved in research and teaching.

Qualifications and Training

The recognised professional qualification for those working in all aspects of Landscape Architecture is Member of the Landscape Institute (MLI), which entitles the use of the title Chartered Landscape Architect. There are three divisions, Design, Management and Science. Associate Membership, the first step towards achieving this, is gained after completing an accredited degree. Two years' relevant work is required as an Associate Member before taking the Institute's Professional Practice Examination and progressing to full Professional Membership. A list of accredited courses is available from the Landscape Institute.

Personal Qualities

Those working in design need creativity, imagination, a practical outlook, interest in the landscape and an enthusiasm for working outdoors. Those in management require good organizational and interpersonal skills, consistent application and a practical outlook. Scientists need enthusiasm for the subject, technical commitment and good communication skills.

Starting Salary

A recent graduate could expect to earn around £20,000. A fully qualified chartered member could expect to start on approximately £23,000.

The Landscape Institute, 6/8 Barnard Mews, London SW11 1QU; 020 7350 5200; fax: 020 7350 5201; www.l-i.org.uk; e-mail: mail@l-i.org.uk

Careers Working Outdoors (Kogan Page)

'Professional Careers in Landscape Architecture' (The Landscape Institute)

LAW COMMISSION (RESEARCH ASSISTANT)

The statutory government advisory body on law reform, the Law Commission, is currently working on projects in a variety of fields including common law, company and commercial law, crime and property law, and on general revision of statute law. The work is carried out in small teams, each under the direction of a Commissioner, consisting of qualified lawyers and research assistants. Draft Bills are prepared by Parliamentary Counsel on loan to the Commission. Extensive consultation and investigation takes place before proposals are formulated; a sizeable proportion result in legislation. Projects range from major investigations of controversial areas of law to the consideration of a specific problem.

Qualifications and Training

Law graduates and graduates of other disciplines who have completed the Legal Practice Course or the Bar Vocational Course are recruited annually to work as research assistants. The work offers the opportunity to take part in the creation of new legislative measures, as well as the in-depth development of skills in a particular area of law. Former research assistants have found their experience a valuable asset in their subsequent legal careers, whether in practice or in academic posts. The initial appointment is for one year with the possibility of extension for a further period up to a maximum of three years in all.

Personal Qualities

Entrants should have a good knowledge of and genuine interest in the law, and be able to think and write clearly.

Starting Salary

About £13,500.

The Law Commission, Conquest House, 37–38 John Street, Theobalds Road, London WC1N 2BQ; 020 7453 1210; www.lawcom.gov.uk

LAW COSTS DRAFTSMAN

Legal costs are a complex and developing subject. The costs that may be charged by a solicitor or recovered against an unsuccessful party in litigation depend on many different factors. Frequently the amount of costs payable is disputed.

Many solicitors employ law costs draftsmen to prepare their bills, to justify the costs claimed or to challenge the amount of costs payable by their client to another party to litigation. Some law costs draftsmen are employed in solicitors' offices whilst others work independently.

Qualifications and Training

To become a student with the Association of Law Costs Draftsmen an applicant must have a minimum of four GCSEs at Grade C or higher, including English and maths, be in employment predominantly concerning law costs and able to provide employment and character references. Students are required to enrol on the Association's training course. Exemptions may apply to parts of the course for those with legal qualifications.

Personal Qualities

Law costs draftsmen need to be patient, able to cope with detail and be methodical and careful in their work.

Starting Salary

From £11,000–£16,000, but in this work there is a range of payments and some people may earn much more than this.

Association of Law Costs Draftsmen, c/o S A Chapman, Church Cottage, Church Lane, Stuston, Diss, Norfolk IP21 4AG; 01379 741404; www.alcd.org.uk; e-mail: enquiries@alcd.org.uk

LEATHER PRODUCTION

Leather is produced from skins and hides to make shoes, bags, gloves, clothes, upholstery and saddlery. Modern leather production is based on up-to-date science (particularly chemistry) and technology with a responsible regard for environmental factors. There is a worldwide shortage of well-qualified leather technologists.

Qualifications and Training

Vocational qualifications are available for operatives and craftspeople through part-time, full-time and open-learning courses. Technicians require a good general education and GCSEs should include maths, science and English. Recognised qualifications include NVQs in Leather Production, BSc in leather technology and MSc in leather technology. Entry to a specific course is dependent on the entry requirements of the institution.

Personal Qualities

Operatives and craftsmen must be physically fit and possess stamina. Technologists must have a practical, responsible approach to their work and be prepared to travel abroad if required.

Starting Salary

The basic salary for operatives is around £140 a week and increases through piecework or incentive bonus to between £250 and £400. A leather technologist could expect an initial annual salary of approximately £16,000.

i

BLC, Leather Technology Centre, Leather Trade House, Kings
Park Road, Moulton Park, Northampton NN3 6JD; 01604
679999; fax: 01604 679998; www.blcleathertech.com;
e-mail: info@blcleathertech.com

British School of Leather Technology, University College,
Northampton, Bo Green Road, Northampton NN2 7AL;
01604 735500; fax: 01604 711183;
www.northampton.ac.uk/aps/bslt/ bslt.html

LECTURER

Higher Education

Lecturers in universities and other higher education institutions
(HEIs) teach mainly undergraduates. As well as teaching, many
carry out research, write articles and books, give outside lectures
and broadcasts. Competition is fierce and it is unlikely that a new
graduate will be able to enter higher education as a first job.

Further Education

Lecturers in this field may teach anyone over the age of 16. The
range of subjects taught in further education is diverse and
growing rapidly. Most lecturers have a particular expertise but
are increasingly expected to teach outside of their specialist area.
They may work on vocational and/or academic courses. In order
to meet the demands of their clients, further education colleges
offer courses on a full- or part-time basis. These include evening
courses and short courses.

Qualifications and Training

Lecturers in HEIs must have first or upper second class degrees;
many have postgraduate qualifications, and some have further
degrees. In the new universities, lecturers may be drawn from
industry or commerce.

Qualifications for lecturers in further education vary, depending on the subject taught. A degree, a professional qualification
and a teaching qualification are all acceptable and desirable.
There are one-year full-time and two-year part-time courses available for those intending to teach in further education.

Personal Qualities

All teachers/lecturers must have a high level of knowledge of, and enthusiasm for, their subject, combined with a desire to communicate this to others. They must have the ability to organise and deliver their material in a way that is understandable to their students.

Starting Salary

Starting salaries in higher education are from £17,600 upwards. Full-time lecturers in further education can expect a starting salary at £13,000+.

Association of University Teachers, Egmont House,
   25–31 Tavistock Place, London WC1H 9UT; 020 7670 9700;
   www.aut.org.uk; e-mail: hq@aut.org.uk
Individual universities and colleges

LEGAL CASHIER/ADMINISTRATOR

Legal cashiers and administrators work in solicitors' offices and are responsible for dealing with the accounts and administration. Legal cashiers may work as the sole bookkeeper, administrator or manager, or, in a big firm, be responsible for a large number of staff. The Institute of Legal Cashiers and Administrators keeps a register of vacancies, providing a free service to solicitors and members.

Qualifications and Training

The Institute of Legal Cashiers and Administrators has three levels of qualification: Diploma, Associateship and Fellowship. It offers correspondence courses leading to the Diploma and Associateship examinations. Formal academic qualifications are not required to take these. The diploma is a qualification in its own right and covers the maintenance of a solicitor's internal financial records. It is particularly aimed at those without book-keeping knowledge. The Associateship is for those who wish to make a career as a legal cashier or administrator and enables them to advise and manage financial and administrative affairs in any solicitor's office. The Fellowship, available to Associates, is the highest qualification, offering a deeper insight into the profession.

Personal Qualities

Entrants must have a high standard of integrity and reliability and be very discreet.

Starting Salary

£10,000–£16,000

The Institute of Legal Cashiers and Administrators, 146–148 Eltham Hill, Eltham, London SE9 5DX; 020 8294 2887; www.ilca.org.uk; e-mail: info@ilca.org.uk

LEGAL EXECUTIVE

A Legal Executive is a professional lawyer employed in a solicitor's office or in the legal departments of commerce and central and local government. The training and academic requirements in a specified area of law are at the same level as those required of a solicitor. Consequently, with few exceptions, a Legal Executive is able to carry out tasks which are similar to those undertaken by solicitors. The main areas of specialization are conveyancing, civil litigation, criminal law, family law and probate. In addition to providing a worthwhile career in its own right, the Legal Executive qualification provides access to those wishing to qualify as solicitors via the Institute route. In Scotland, the term Legal Executive is not used, but solicitors engage assistants to do similar work.

Qualifications and Training

The minimum entry requirement is four GCSEs to include English, but A level students and graduates are welcome. As an alternative, the Institute accepts a qualification in vocational legal studies and has special arrangements for students who are over 21. In the main, training is on a part-time basis so that there is potential for trainees to 'learn while they earn'. For those already working in a legal environment, but with no formal legal qualifications, an NVQ (level 4) in Legal Practice is available and ILEX is the awarding body.

Personal Qualities

An ability to communicate, both verbally and in writing, with people at all levels, absolute discretion and trustworthiness, together with meticulous attention to detail, are essential.

Starting Salary

Varies according to age and qualification, and the type of work undertaken. The average starting salary is around £12,000. Many established Legal Executives receive salaries in excess of £50,000.

The Institute of Legal Executives, Kempston Manor, Kempston, Bedford MK42 7AB; 01234 841000; www.ilex.org.uk; e-mail: info@ilex.org.uk

Careers in the Law (Kogan Page)

LEISURE AND AMENITY MANAGEMENT

(see also *Sport and Recreation Facility Management*)

People employed in this field may work in leisure centres, Outward Bound centres, theatres and arts centres, historic houses and ancient monuments, country areas offering nature trails, fishing and camping facilities to the public, or even be in charge of bingo or dance halls. Managers, as well as being interested in their particular leisure activity, must be responsible for the administrative and financial running of the enterprise. Many in this field are employed in local government, but there are also opportunities in private sports centres, health and fitness clubs and tourist attractions.

Qualifications and Training

The Institute of Leisure and Amenity Management (ILAM) offers five levels of qualification based upon the completion of work-based projects: the ILAM first award for candidates who are new to the industry and who hold junior positions within leisure organizations; the ILAM Certificate in Leisure Operations, for candidates who have a working knowledge of the industry and hold junior supervisory positions; the ILAM Certificate in Leisure Management for candidates with a good understanding of the industry and who hold junior or middle management jobs; the ILAM Diploma in Leisure Management for candidates who have successfully demonstrated their managerial ability at a senior level; and the Advanced Diploma in Leisure Management for those with substantial experience.

HND courses and a range of degree courses, including foundation degrees in leisure studies/recreation management and sports sciences, are available.

Personal Qualities
A strong interest in the particular area of leisure is necessary, as is the ability to organise, administer and manage people.

Starting Salary
Assistant managers earn £15,000–£20,000, depending on the size and type of establishment.

Institute of Leisure and Amenity Management, ILAM House, Lower Basildon, Reading, Berkshire RG8 9NE; 01491 874800; www.ilam.co.uk; e-mail: education@ilam.co.uk

LIBRARIAN/INFORMATION MANAGER

Librarians and information managers anticipate the information needs of their clients, acquire that information by the most efficient means possible on behalf of their clients, and may well analyse it and repackage it for the client. Information may come in the form of a book or journal, or may be extracted from databases in-house, on CD ROM or online. Librarians and information managers need to be able to use the Internet themselves and show others how to do so.

Information needs to be organised to make it accessible to users by indexing, cataloguing and classifying. Librarians and information managers promote and exploit the library's collection to the library or information source users and assist them with any enquiries. They work in public libraries and schools, universities and colleges, in government, in the law, in hospitals, business and industry, and also in accountancy, engineering, professional and learned societies and in virtually all areas of economic activity.

Qualifications and Training

Library assistants are usually required to have four to five GCSEs or equivalent, to include English language; training is on the job. Part-time or distance-learning vocational courses leading to City and Guilds and SQA qualifications are available to library assistants in post. NVQs levels 2–4 in Information and Library Services are also available. To qualify as a professional librarian or information officer and gain Chartered Membership of the Library Association, a degree or postgraduate qualification accredited by the association is necessary.

First degree courses, postgraduate diplomas and masters are jointly accredited by The Library Association and the Institute of Information Scientists. A full list of the courses offered by 17 universities is available through the Library Association Web site. The Library Association and Institute of Information Scientists have joined together to create a new organization, the Chartered Institute of Library and Information Professionals.

Personal Qualities

Librarians and information managers need to be well educated, with an outgoing personality, and able to communicate with people at all levels with clarity, accuracy and tact. They need intellectual curiosity, breadth of knowledge and a logical and methodical approach to seeking out, organizing and presenting information. A good memory is also useful. Management skills and an interest in working with computers are important assets.

Starting Salary

Depending on age and experience, library assistants' salaries range from £8,000 to £16,500; newly qualified librarians earn from £11,900 to £16,500, and middle managers from about £17,000 to £27,000. The most senior qualified library managers of large services can earn above £32,000.

i

The Library Association, 7 Ridgmount Street, London
WC1E 7AE; 020 7636 7543; www.la-hq.org.uk;
e-mail: Careers@la-hq.org.uk

LINGUIST

see *Interpreter, Translator*

LITERARY AGENT

Literary agents act as negotiators between authors and publishers, film producers and theatre managements. Initially they read authors' manuscripts and decide whether or not to accept an author as a client. Once accepted, an author may be guided by an agent about ideas for books and changes to existing manuscripts. The agent then finds a publisher or producer for the author's work and negotiates the best possible terms. The agent deals with the publisher on all matters that will affect the client, including the contract, manuscript delivery, follow-up titles, advertising, publicity, paperback, television and film rights, and obtaining payments when due.

Some literary agents also act for foreign publishers attempting to find British publishers who will bring out an English edition of a book already published abroad. Like publishers, agents tend to specialise in areas such as fiction, general non-fiction and specialist publishing.

Qualifications and Training

No particular educational qualifications are necessary. Experience of the book trade is the most important factor, and most literary agents have gained this by working in a publishing house. Foreign languages are an asset, particularly in the international field.

Personal Qualities

Agents need shrewd literary judgement and a knowledge of worldwide market conditions, negotiating and legal skills, business and financial ability. They must be hard working, persistent, adaptable and sympathetic towards their authors.

Starting Salary

Agencies receive a percentage of the money earned by the author – usually 10–20 per cent. Literary agents working for these companies would receive a salary plus annual bonuses related to the level of commission they bring in.

Association of Authors' Agents; www.agentsassoc.co.uk
The Writers' and Artists' Handbook, A&C Black (annual publication)

LOCAL GOVERNMENT

Local authorities provide a range of services that affect the daily lives of people living in their area, from sports centres to refuse collection; schools to homes for the elderly; fire services to libraries. They also have responsibility for ensuring that food sold in shops and restaurants is fit to eat; that streets are lit; that land is developed with environmental considerations and the needs of the local population in mind. All of these services rely on the collection of local revenues, and for the less well off, the efficient administration of housing and Council Tax benefits is essential. Consequently there are many varied areas of work to consider and over 500 different careers to choose from.

Local government employs over two million staff in England, Scotland and Wales, some of whom are administrators who supervise, coordinate and organise the provision of services to the community. They also employ professional and technical staff, for instance, architects, accountants, engineers and electricians.

Qualifications and Training

There are a variety of paths to follow to obtain a position in local government, because of the range of careers on offer. GCSE and A level passes may be necessary, or a degree, with some posts requiring professional qualifications. Training is seen as an important commodity in local government and as such is available through both internal and external courses.

Personal Qualities

These vary according to the job to be performed, but in general local government employees should be able to communicate effectively both with colleagues and with the community at large, work well in a team, be professional in their approach and have good customer service skills.

Starting Salary

Salaries in local government can be competitive. There may also be a variety of benefits, including relocation packages, as well as flexible working arrangements.

Institute of Revenues, Rating and Valuation, 41 Doughty Street, London WC1N 2LF; 020 7691 8980; www.irrv.org.uk (for information on qualifications in revenues and benefits administration)

Local Government Careers; www.LGcareers.com – for further careers information; www.LGjobs.com – for current job vacancy adverts in local councils all over the country

Personnel Officers of individual local authorities

LOGISTICS

(see also *Freight Forwarding*)

When a customer places an order, a chain reaction – the supply chain – is started. The supply chain ensures that the product that has been ordered, whether it is a car for an individual, or a thousand bars of chocolate for a retailer, reaches the customer who placed the order.

Logistics is the management of the supply chain. The professionals working in logistics are responsible for warehouse management, distribution and transport management, inventory (stock) control, information systems, transport, logistics planning and analysis and supply-chain management.

Qualifications and Training

Entry with GCSEs or A levels is still possible but many new entrants to managerial posts now have a degree or professional qualification. There are several degree courses in international trade, logistics, supply-chain management, export studies and overseas business. Large companies may offer graduate training schemes for those with relevant degrees. The Institute of Freight Forwarders offers an Advanced Certificate in International Trade that can be studied full- or part-time or by correspondence.

An MSc in logistics or supply-chain management may be an advantage when seeking progression into senior management positions in some organizations. The Institute of Logistics and Transport offers a range of professional qualifications from entry level upwards, which includes a distance-learning MSc offered in conjunction with Aston University.

Personal Qualities

Logistics can offer early responsibility, so trainee managers should be responsible, able to motivate others and enjoy a challenge. Organizational, numeracy and people-management skills are essential. Foreign language skills are an advantage. The ability to use IT packages and electronic communication has become increasingly important with the growing use of the Internet. The supply chain is at the centre of many e-commerce developments.

Starting Salaries

Graduate management trainees start between £18,000 and £22,000. Managers' salaries are variable and can reach £60,000, rising as high as £100,000 for directors with board-level responsibility in large organizations.

British International Freight Association, Institute of Freight
    Forwarders, Redfern House, Browells Lane, Feltham,
    Middlesex TW13 7EP; 020 8844 2266; www.bifa.org;
    e-mail: bifa@bifa.org
The Institute of Logistics and Transport, Logistics and Transport
    Centre, PO Box 5787, Corby, Northants, NN17 4XQ; 01536
    740100; www.iolt.org.uk; e-mail: careers@iolt.org.uk
Institute of Transport Administration, Mill House, 11 Nightingale
    Road, Horsham, West Sussex RH12 2NW; www.iota.org.uk
The 'Logistics and Transport Management Careers Guide' can be
    downloaded from www.insidecareers.co.uk

LORRY DRIVER

This work ranges from driving conventional flat-bodied lorries that can carry a variety of loads to driving lorries designed for one purpose, such as car and animal transporters and milk tankers. Drivers often take a load from A to B and then carry one back from B to A in the UK or across Europe. As well as driving, lorry drivers may have to help with the loading and unloading of goods. Drivers of potentially dangerous products must know how to handle them safely, and certification is required.

Qualifications and Training

No formal educational requirements are necessary, but drivers must have a good enough education to be able to do simple sums, read maps, follow instructions and handle documents concerned with the delivery of goods. An LGV licence at either Category C (rigid vehicles over 7.5 Tonnes) or C+E (articulated vehicles) is essential. These licences can only be applied for at age 21, although the Young LGV Drivers Scheme, operated through RHDTC (see below), enables a young person to obtain a Category C licence at 18 years old. Some firms will not take on drivers until they are 25, when the cost of insurance is reduced. A range of S/NVQs have been developed by the industry along with Foundation and Modern Apprenticeship frameworks.

Personal Qualities

Drivers spend much of their time on their own, so must be self-reliant. They also need to be physically strong, responsible, and careful drivers. Driving hours are strictly controlled, but overall hours tend to be above the national average. Night working is common and some jobs involve nights spent away from home. Implementation of the EU Working Time Directive has reduced working hours in the industry.

Starting Salary

A newly qualified driver will earn around £10,000–£12,000; an experienced driver can earn £25,000+.

| i |

Road Haulage and Distribution Training Council, 14 Warren Yard, Warren Farm Office Village, Stratford Road, Milton Keynes MK12 5NW; 01908 313360; www.rhdtc.co.uk; e-mail: info@rhdtc.co.uk

LOSS ADJUSTER

see *Insurance*

MAKE-UP ARTIST

see *Broadcasting, Film Production*

MANAGEMENT CONSULTANT

Management has been defined as the art of getting results through other people, and consultancy as giving professional advice. Management consultants are employed to provide a higher degree of expertise than is available in a particular company; to recommend business solutions and assist in their implementation; to assist in cultural change and to provide expertise to solve specific business issues.

Firms of management consultants specialise, tending to divide their activities into the following areas: organization, development and policy formation – long-range planning and re-organization of a company's structure; production management – production control arrangements; marketing, sales and distribution; finance and administration – installation of budgetary control systems; personnel management selection; management of information systems – the provision of software, systems analysis; economic and environmental studies – urban and regional development planning, work for overseas organizations. With the growth in e-commerce many consultancies are providing advice on e-business solutions.

Qualifications and Training

Recruits generally have a first degree, sometimes a PhD, MA or MBA. Additional training is on the job. The Institute of

Management Consultancy promotes the Certified Management Consultant (CMC) qualification which is competency-based. It draws on the work of the Management Charter Initiative in the UK, as well as the International Committee of Management Consulting Institutes (ICMCI) Global Body of Knowledge. This is a level 5 postgraduate qualification and requires at least three years' management consulting experience. A consultant must provide evidence of learning and competence in four quadrants of expertise: consultancy, management, technical specialism (such as Finance or IT) and PESTLE (Political, Environmental, Social, Technological, Legal and Environmental).

Personal Qualities

The following personality traits have been identified as essential: humour and perspective; ability to influence; confidence and self-esteem; the ability to summarise a situation quickly; active listening; responsiveness; and good organization.

Starting Salary

Starting salaries for graduates £25,000 to £30,000+. Once qualified, earnings can be very high.

Institute of Management Consultancy, 3rd Floor, 17–18 Hayward's Place, London EC1R 0EQ; 020 7566 5220; fax: 020 7566 5230; www.imc.co.uk; e-mail: consult@imc.co.uk

Institute of Management Services, Stowe House, Netherstowe, Lichfield, Staffordshire WS13 6TJ; 01543 251346; http://imgtserv.co.uk/imgtserv; e-mail: IMS@ISMStowe.demon.co.uk

Management Consultancies Association, 49 Whitehall, London SW1A 2BX; 020 7321 3990; fax: 020 7321 3991; www.mca.org.uk

MAPPING

see *Cartography, Ordnance Survey Work*

MARINE BIOLOGIST

Marine biology is a relatively new and expanding area of biology, and as yet offers few job opportunities. It is a science that studies the ecology of the sea and coastal waters and is particularly concerned with food stocks and the effects of pollution. Marine biologists are employed by government departments, the Natural Environment Research Council and in the marine laboratories of private organizations.

Qualifications and Training

Two or three A levels or equivalents in biology, chemistry and maths or another science, plus GCSE level or equivalent in maths and physics are necessary for entry to a first degree course in biology. Some universities offer degrees in marine biology, but it may be advisable to take a broader degree in applied biology first.

Personal Qualities

Biologists need the same characteristics as all scientists: patience and the willingness to repeat experimental work and measurements to check results, a methodical way of working, good observation and accuracy.

Starting Salary

£15,000+.

Institute of Biology, 20–22 Queensberry Place, London SW7 2DZ; 020 7581 8333; www.iob.org; e-mail: education@iob.org
Marine Biological Association of UK, The Laboratory, Citadel Hill, Plymouth PL1 2PB; www.mba.ac.uk; e-mail: sec@mba.ac.uk
The Scottish Association for Marine Science, PO Box 3, Oban, Argyll PA34 4AD; 01631 562244; www.sams.ac.uk

MARINE ENGINEERING

see *Engineering*

MARKET GARDENING

(see also *Gardener, Horticulturist*)

Crops grown in market gardens are vegetables, salad crops – such as lettuces and tomatoes – and flowers and ornamental plants. The work consists of preparing the soil, and working by hand on such jobs as transplanting young plants and thinning growing plants, and grading, washing and packing the produce after harvesting so that it can be sold.

Qualifications and Training

Qualifications in horticulture are desirable but not always necessary. Training programmes are provided through apprenticeship, and it is also possible to gain NVQ qualifications.

Personal Qualities

The enjoyment of growing plants is important, as is an ability to use the necessary machinery, plus physical strength, and a willingness to work outdoors whatever the weather.

Starting Salary

Market gardeners can earn between £13,000 and £17,000 once qualified and experienced.

Local Jobcentres and Careers / Connexions Centres

Institute of Horticulture, 14–15 Belgrave Square, London SW1X 8PS; 020 7245 6943; www.horticulture.demon.co.uk

'Come into Horticulture' and 'Education and Training Courses in Horticulture' (available free from the Institute of Horticulture)

MARKET MAKER

(see also *Stockbroker*)

Market makers, sometimes known as traders, conduct their business on the Stock Exchange, the market where industrial and commercial organizations raise finance through the sale of stocks and shares to individuals or institutions willing to invest capital.

They are employed by merchant banks. Market makers aim to make their profits by buying and selling securities to other market makers and stockbrokers, and some now deal directly with the public. It is usual for firms to employ individual market makers who have specialist knowledge of all the factors which may influence prices, and the ability to judge and predict the performance of companies within that particular field.

Qualifications and Training

Market makers are generally graduates from a range of disciplines but economics or business and finance related subjects are an advantage. Training is on the job, working alongside experienced dealers. To conduct business, market makers must be placed on the Stock Exchange's list of those eligible to trade, having passed exams set by the Stock Exchange and Securities Institute.

Personal Qualities

An ability to keep abreast of current affairs and any factors that may affect the price of shares, to make decisions very quickly and a willingness to take calculated risks. They must be able to work hard and to conduct business verbally. A good memory and a flair for dealing with people are helpful.

Starting Salary

Salaries are low initially, but there are eventual opportunities to earn upwards of £60,000.

i

The Securities Institute, Centurion House, 24 Monument Street, London EC3R 8AJ; 020 7645 0600;
   www.securities-institute.org.uk;
   e-mail: info@securities-institute.org.uk
The London Stock Exchange; www.londonstockexchange.com
Individual merchant banks (*see also* Banking)

MARKET RESEARCH

Market research is the collection and analysis of information about markets, organizations and people to support better business decisions. It's used to discover gaps in the market, to ensure customer satisfaction and to plan effective marketing campaigns. In a competitive environment, the more knowledge a business has about its customers, the more likely it is to succeed.

Over the past few decades, market research techniques have developed significantly, making it a more precise science. Methods used depend on the requirements of the business and the budget available, and include interviews with individuals, surveys by telephone, post and via the Internet and increasingly using mobile phone text messaging. These are used to gather quantitative (numerical) data. Qualitative research by face-to-face interviews with individuals or groups is geared to providing insight into why people hold the views they do, and provides greater understanding of customers. Interviewers are known as field workers, and their work, and that of the analysis personnel, is organised by the Research Executive, who is in overall charge of the project for a Marketing Executive or client, and is responsible for interpreting the results.

Every year, The Market Research Society (MRS) publishes the *Research Buyer's Guide*, which lists the majority of market research agencies in the UK and outlines the size of each agency, together with their areas of specialization. The *Guide* also details other organizations which can offer advice on getting started in market research; the online version of the *Guide* is free at www.rbg.org.uk.

Qualifications and Training

Field workers do not need qualifications but must be articulate, persuasive and presentable. Applicants for research and executive positions will be expected to hold a degree. The majority of market research graduates are drawn from disciplines that require strong communication or analytical skills, such as languages, English literature, maths, psychology, geography, history, politics, science and IT. However, graduates with degrees as contrasting as zoology and theatre studies are also welcomed by the industry.

The Market Research Society offers a Graduate Development Scheme in conjunction with some of the industry's leading agencies. The three-year scheme incorporates on-the-job training and assessment with two examinations, a project and self-managed learning.

Personal Qualities

Excellent communication skills and ability to get on with people of all types. Analytical skills, numeracy and data interpretation are important.

Starting salaries

Field workers are paid a day rate of £30+ for a six- to seven-hour day; permanent staff, analysis personnel and trainee executives earn £16,000+.

| i |

Market Research Society, 15 Northburgh Street, London EC1V 0JR; 020 7490 4911; www.mrs.org.uk; info@mrs.org.uk

MARKETING

(see also *Advertising, Direct Marketing, Events Officer, Market Research, Retailing*)

Marketing is concerned with undertaking research, identifying consumer needs and demands relative to product or service, price, place and time, organizing their production and promoting them to the appropriate customer segment. It includes new-product development, packaging, advertising, pricing, sales, distribution and after-sales service.

People usually come into marketing either from sales or from the market research side, or they may have worked for an advertising agency before joining the marketing team of a manufacturing company. Some enter as graduate trainees. There are a growing number of posts in e-marketing.

Qualifications and Training

Entry qualifications vary considerably, depending on the products or services being sold. Good GCSEs would probably be the minimum, but employers are increasingly demanding an appropriate degree or diploma, such as the Chartered Institute of Marketing's Diploma. Colleges and universities offer a wide range of marketing courses, or courses including marketing options. Additionally, most companies give some sort of in-house training in product knowledge, selling techniques and customer relationship management.

E-marketing is a growth area and degree courses increasingly include modules on this. The Chartered Institute of Marketing offers a 12-week course leading to an e-marketing award. This can be completed by part-time evening classes, distance learning or through weekend workshops. Assessment is through a business-based management report on e-marketing and a short online examination held in a CIM accredited centre.

Personal Qualities

All types of skills and abilities can be usefully employed in marketing; however, outgoing personality, good appearance, resilience, tact and a certain toughness are required in all selling jobs.

Starting Salary

A newly qualified entrant can expect to earn around £15,000.

| i |

Chartered Institute of Marketing, Moor Hall, Cookham,
  Maidenhead, Berkshire SL6 9QH; 01628 427500;
  www.cim.co.uk;
  www.connectedinmarketing.com; training@cim.co.uk
Careers in Marketing, Advertising and Public Relations (Kogan Page)
How to Get On in Marketing, Advertising and Public Relations (Kogan
  Page)

MASSAGE THERAPIST

Massage is the scientific manipulation of the soft tissues for a therapeutic effect, such as encouraging relaxation, relieving musculo-skeletal aches and pains or promoting healing. Massage therapists work in a range of settings such as health centres, hospitals, in professional sport, beauty clinics or as freelancers. The growth in alternative therapies has increased the demand and acceptance of massage therapy.

Qualification and Training

There is a wide range of massage courses available and most specialise in specific types of massage, although there are some general massage courses too. Every mode of delivery is available, from part- and full-time, to distance learning, weekend and block courses. There are also some postgraduate courses in sports therapy, electrotherapy and manual lympathic drainage. NVQs are available at levels 2 to 5 in a range of institutions and further education colleges.

Personal Qualities

Massage therapists must be physically strong, have good inter-personal skills and the ability to make people feel comfortable. They must also be good listeners and have excellent personal hygiene habits.

Starting Salary

Varied, depending on employer. Freelancers charge £15+ an hour.

The Northern Institute of Massage, 14–16 St. Mary's Place, Bury, Lancashire BL9 0DZ; www.nim56.co.uk; e-mail: information@nim56.co.uk

London School of Sports Massage, 28 Station Parade, Willesden Green, London NW2 4NX; 020 8452 8855; www.lssm.com; e-mail: admin@lssm.com

MATERIALS MANAGER

see *Purchasing Officer*

MATERIALS SCIENTIST

Materials science is the study of a wide variety of materials, including plastics, glass, ceramics, natural materials and metals, that are used in modern technology. The scientist or technologist is responsible for selecting materials for a specific job, or for finding uses for a material. There are opportunities in many industries such as sport, aerospace, transport, electronics and in nuclear power, research, development and production work.

Qualifications and Training

Technicians should have a good education to GCSE level to include studies in maths, a science and English in order to take the technician's certificate in metal finishing. An Edexcel (BTEC) certificate and diploma are available in metals technology, with the technician's certificate counting towards the units.

Two A levels or equivalent are necessary for entry to degrees in subjects such as metallurgy and materials science.

Personal Qualities

An interest in the scientific and technological problems posed, and the ability to find constructive solutions, must be allied to the scientific qualities of orderly and logical thought.

Starting Salary

This varies, depending on the level of employment and its nature, but is around £15,000–£16,000.

The Institute of Materials, 1 Carlton House Terrace, London SW1Y 5DB; 020 7451 7300; www.instmat.co.uk; www.materials-careers.org.uk

The Institution of Mining and Metallurgy, Danum House, South Parade, Doncaster DN1 2DY; 01302 320486; www.imm.org.uk; e-mail:hq@imm.org.uk

MEAT INDUSTRY

(see also *Butcher*)

As well as retail and supermarket work as a butcher, or working for large organizations such as hotels, there are other openings in the meat industry. Some wholesale establishments selling pre-packed meat need teams of butchers for boning, cutting and packing the meat, or processing it into pies. Wholesale butchers do not meet the general public but deal with other butchers and retailers. Workers are also needed in abattoirs, to handle and kill the animals, and to inspect and deal with the meat.

Qualifications and Training

A good general education is necessary but there are no formal educational requirements. Training is on the job and courses are available at further education establishments and approved training organizations, leading to NVQs levels 1 to 4, and exams of the Meat Training Council. Some Modern Apprenticeships are available; details are available from the Meat Training Council.

Personal Qualities

An above-average attitude to hygiene is vital. In addition, workers in the meat industry must be strong enough to cope with heavy lifting and fit enough to work in cold conditions.

Starting Salary

Around £14,000 once qualified.

The Meat Training Council, PO Box 141, Winterhill House, Snowdon Drive, Milton Keynes MK6 1YY; 01908 231062; www.meattraining.org.uk

MECHANICAL ENGINEER

see *Engineering*

MEDICAL ILLUSTRATOR

A career in medical illustration combines the requirement to work precisely to record medical conditions whilst using flair and initiative to help other visualise their ideas.

The profession provides specialist photographic, graphic design, art and video services tailored to patient care, pre/postgraduate medical education, research and medico-legal needs. As a collective body, medical illustrators form an integral part of the clinical healthcare team. Members of the profession include:

Medical Photographers

They are responsible for recording clinical conditions, working within the studio, clinic, ward and operating theatre environments. Specialised areas include diagnostic services within ophthalmology and planning images for craniofacial surgery.

Graphic Designers
They specialise in the design, layout and production of artwork, brochures, scientific posters and other visual material, primarily for patient information or marketing.

MEDICAL ARTISTS

Medical artists produce highest quality artwork for publication and medical education purposes.

Medical Videographers
Medical videographers produce high quality programmes for teaching and research purposes.

Qualifications and Training
Many trusts and health authorities now ask for a BSc in Medical Illustration. A prospective candidate may, however, be working towards the BSc, or commit to undertake the BSc upon commencement of employment. Trainees need at least a media qualification to HND level (or equivalent) in photography, video or graphic design.

The Glasgow Caledonian University/Institute of Medical Illustrators (GCU/IMI) BSc in Medical Illustration can be taken as a full-time course or as a three-year distance-learning course.

With a first degree in photography, video, graphics, art or media studies, such graduates may apply to undertake the IMI Post Experience Certificate (PEC).

Other degree courses available nationally are an MSc in Medical Illustration at the University of Wales College of Medicine and a BSc (Hons) in Biomedical Imaging at the University of Derby.

The Institute of Medical Illustrators is the leading professional body. Members qualify at degree level with the BSc in Medical Illustration, are actively involved in Continuing Professional Development and are registered with the National Board of Registration of Medical Illustrators (NBRMI). They are governed by a Code of Conduct, a Code of Responsible Practice and relevant law, for example the Data Protection Act. These measures cover legal and ethical aspects such as consent, confidentiality and copyright, and are designed to protect both patients and healthcare organizations from the misuse of medical images.

Personal Qualities
As well as having a natural artistic ability, the medical illustrator must be prepared to draw, or photograph, any part of the body in any condition.

Starting Salary
About £13,500.

British Institute of Professional Photography, Fox Talbot House, Amwell End, Ware, Hertfordshire SG12 9HN; 01920 464011; www.bipp.com; e-mail: bipp@compuserve.com
Institute of Medical Illustrators, Bank Chambers, 48 Onslow Gardens, London SW7 3AH; www.imi.org.uk

MEDICAL TECHNICAL OFFICER
see *Cardiac Physiologist*

MEDICINE
Most doctors work for the NHS in some capacity, in hospital services, general practice or in public health medicine and community health. Some doctors work exclusively in private practice.

General Practitioner
Family doctors, or GPs, may form a long-standing relationship with their patients. They must be able to diagnose and deal with a broad spectrum of illnesses and disorders, mainly those common within the community, but also to recognise those that are rare. Increasingly, doctors are asked to help their patients to cope with

personal and emotional problems. They have to be aware of and take into account physical, psychological and social factors when looking after their patients About 90 per cent of GPs now work together in group practices, allowing some specialization.

Public Health and Community Health

Public health medicine is concerned with preventive medicine, environmental health, the prolongation of life and the promotion of health. Public health physicians generally work in Health Authorities. Community health doctors deal with child health, family planning, social services, special hostels and day centres and other roles as advisers to the authority. The career structure is similar to that within a hospital.

Hospital

Doctors who wish to work in hospital medicine as a consultant will apply for a post as a Specialist Registrar (SpR) on completion of general professional training. All SpRs are issued with a national training number (NTN) which helps postgraduate deans keep track of trainees and to guarantee them a continued place in a Certificate of Completion of Specialist Training (CCST) training programme. In addition, it ensures that both nationally and within specialities the right number of doctors are being trained to meet the demand for consultants. Once SpRs are awarded completion of the CCST they can be included on the specialist register and apply for consultant posts.

If a doctor is unable or unwilling to become a consultant but wishes to remain in hospital medicine he or she is able to apply for a Staff Grade post on completion of the SHO post (*see* qualifications). Staff Grades are responsible to a consultant and have intermediate responsibility for patients.

Research and Teaching

Research work is carried out in universities, hospitals, public health laboratories, and other research establishments and pharmaceutical manufacturing companies. There are opportunities too for teaching in universities. Teaching may involve very little or no contact with patients, or it may be similar in content to hospital doctors' work. An academic career in medicine either through teaching or research is possible in practically all hospital specialities, general practice and public health medicine.

Occupational
Occupational physicians identify and investigate health problems at work and advise both management and employees on the prevention of hazards of occupations and the effects of work on health. Occupational physicians are usually employed by small to medium-sized companies at a grade equivalent to that of hospital consultant.

Qualifications and Training
Medical training in the UK is designed to meet the needs of the NHS and its length and structure may differ from those in countries with different healthcare systems.

A minimum age of 18 and excellent A level passes in chemistry and two other science subjects (biology, physics or maths) are necessary for entry to medical school. Most medical school courses last five years. Some, however, offer a six-year course, which includes a pre-medical year. This year, intended as a foundation year in basic sciences, gives students with good non-science grades and some non-science graduates a way into the medicine degree course. Medical schools now run accelerated four-year graduate entry courses for both science and arts graduates. Once a medical student graduates, he or she must apply to the General Medical Council for provisional registration.

All (not just hospital) doctors then begin their career in medicine as a Pre-registration house officer (PRHO) to complete their general clinical training. The PRHO year is generally split into two six-month periods of surgical disciplines and medical disciplines. Once doctors successfully complete their PRHO year they will be fully registered with the GMC. They then progress to senior house officer (SHO). This 2–3-year period is called general professional training and aims to equip doctors with the knowledge, skills and aptitudes required for entering a range of speciality training programmes. A large part of this training can be spent in the speciality of the doctor's choice. Doctors wishing to become GPs undertake a GP vocational training scheme where they spend two years as an SHO in selected specialities, followed by one year as a GP Registrar within general practice. On completion they will become a GP Principal – the career post for general practice.

Personal Qualities

Those who want to become members of the medical profession must have a caring and responsible attitude to other people, as well as ability in scientific subjects.

Starting Salary

Pre-registration house officer £17,935; senior house officer £22,380; GP £56,610; Consultant £50,810.

British Medical Association, BMA House, Tavistock House,
London WC1H 9JP; 020 7387 4499; www.bma.org.uk;
e-mail: info.web@bma.org.uk
Careers in Medicine, Dentistry and Mental Health (Kogan Page)

MEMBER OF PARLIAMENT

see *Politics*

MERCHANT NAVY

The 'Merchant Navy' is the collective term for the British shipping industry, which operates worldwide and includes the ferry sector, containership companies, cruise companies, oil, gas and chemical tankers, bulk carriers of ores, grain and coal and support vessels for the offshore exploration industry.

The Engineering Department

Engineer officers are responsible for the provision and mainte-nance of all technical services on board, including the propulsion and auxiliary machinery in the engine room. They are responsible for the work of engine-room staff, so managing people is part of the job, as with all ships' officers. An Engineer officer is a step on the way to becoming Chief Engineer officer.

Engineer ratings are involved in routine maintenance, engine operation and repairs.

The Deck Department

Deck officers are responsible for controlling the navigation of the ship, communications, cargo handling and ship stability. A Deck officer is a step on the way to becoming Captain (Master).

Deck ratings assist on the navigation of the ship, are involved in operating deck machinery such as winches, cranes and carry out maintenance tasks. There are also some dual officer roles, covering both deck and engineering departments.

Communications

Electro-technical officers are responsible for the maintenance and efficient operation of complex electrical, electronic and control systems on board ship.

Hotel and Entertainment Services on cruise ships and ferries

This includes pursers/receptionists, restaurant and bar staff, chefs, housekeepers, cruise directors, entertainments team etc, hairdressers, beauticians, photographers and retail staff. Those recruited are qualified and experienced within their own specialism.

Qualifications and Training

Training for careers at sea is provided by shipping companies or group training organizations. It usually consists of programmes of learning and experience based on a sandwich pattern of alternating periods at college and at sea, leading to nationally recognised qualifications and professional maritime certificates of competency. There are four main entry routes, each with deck and engineering options. Each provides progression opportunities to the next stage and, through the ranks, to Captain (Master) or Chief Engineer officer depending on ability and ambition. The routes are:

(a) Marine Traineeship: structured training for seafarers employed, usually, as ratings, in the deck or engineering departments in support of the officers of the watch. Entrants must show an aptitude to succeed to at least NVQ level 2. As a guide, they would be expected to have attained 3 GCSEs or equivalent.

(b) Marine Apprenticeship: provides an enhanced level of training for those employed initially as ratings in the deck or engineering departments whilst following a programme of learning leading to NVQ level 3 and qualification as officer of the watch. As a guide, entrants would be expected to have attained a minimum of four GCSEs, including English, mathematics and science (or equivalents).

(c) Officer cadet: provides structured learning for those aiming to progress to Captain (Master) or Chief Engineer officer and achieve qualifications at HND or degree level in addition to professional certificates of competency. Entry standards may vary from company to company and according to whether the degree or HND option is chosen. As a guide, candidates would be expected to have attained A levels and a minimum of four GCSEs at Grades A–C, or equivalents, including mathematics, English and science. Entry with GCSEs only may be possible for suitably motivated candidates.

(d) Postgraduate Entry: accelerated programmes have been developed for new entrants with suitable science-based degrees. This is similar to the cadet programme but recognises prior qualification and maturity of applicants.

Personal Qualities

All candidates must be in good health and pass a statutory medical examination, with a good standard of eyesight required for prospective deck personnel. The ability to get on well with other people and adapt to new conditions is also important.

Starting Salary

Starting salaries vary between sponsoring companies.

i

Careers in Shipping, Carthusian Court, 12 Carthusian Street, London EC1M 6EZ; general information on all merchant navy careers and list of shipping companies providing sponsorship; www.gotosea.org.uk

The Marine Society, 202 Lambeth Road, London SE1 7JW; a charity offering scholarship schemes for young people wishing to go to sea. Please send SAE for information; www.marine-society.org

Merchant Navy Training Board (MNTB), 12 Carthusian Street,
London EC1M 6EZ; www.mntb.org.uk;
e-mail: enquiry@mntb.org.uk
Listings of individual shipping companies

METALLURGIST

Metallurgists are involved with the extraction of metals from ores,
their purification, and with reclaiming them from scrap. They are
also concerned with developing new alloys and processing metals
during manufacture.

Qualifications and Training
GCSE passes in a science subject, maths and English or equivalent
are required for entry to Edexcel (BTEC) and SQA two-year
courses for a certificate or diploma in metallurgical studies.

Candidates who have successfully completed the two-year
course and those with A levels or equivalent in maths, physics or
chemistry may study for the Edexcel (BTEC)/SQA higher certificates and diplomas or qualify for entry to full-time, sandwich or
part-time courses leading to degrees in metallurgy.

Personal Qualities
Metallurgy demands an interest in scientific and technological
subjects, an ability to solve practical problems and work with
other people on specific projects.

Starting Salary
Salaries vary, but newly qualified graduates can expect
£15,000–£18,000 and earn over £30,000 once experienced.

The Institution of Mining and Metallurgy, Danum House, South
Parade, Doncaster DN1 2DY; 01302 320486; www.imm.org.uk;
e-mail: hq@imm.org.uk

METEOROLOGIST

The Meteorological Office is an executive agency within the
Ministry of Defence. It is a centre of excellence for the production

of numerical weather forecasts, climate prediction and related studies. It serves the different and varying needs of defence, other areas of government, civil aviation, industry, commerce and the general public.

Qualifications and Training
From time to time there are vacancies in administration for which a minimum of five GCSEs to include English are required. Most vacancies arise in the forecasting, research and IT areas for which a first or upper second degree is necessary in maths, one of the physical sciences, computer science or meteorology.

Personal Qualities
Candidates need to be adaptable and prepared to work in more than one specialist area. Good communication and computing skills are necessary.

Starting Salary
Graduates can expect a salary range of £15,500–£24,000.

Local Jobcentres and Careers / Connexions Centres
Meteorological Office, Scott Building, Eastern Road, Bracknell,
    Berkshire RG12 2PW; 220 St Vincent Street, Glasgow G2 5QD;
    32 College Street, Belfast BT1 6BQ; www.metoffice.gov.uk;
    e-mail: education@metoffice.com
Royal Meteorological Society, 104 Oxford Road, Reading,
    RG1 7LL; 0118 9568500; fax: 0118 9568571;
    www.royal-met-soc.org.uk

MICROBIOLOGIST

Microbiology is the study of tiny living organisms (bacteria, viruses, fungi, protozoa and algae) and the massive impact they have on almost every aspect of our lives. There are good job opportunities for microbiologists in the human and animal healthcare sector, medical research and the food production and agricultural industries. Microbiologists are employed in hospitals, research institutes, industrial research and development and manufacturing sites, universities and environmental companies.

Their skills and knowledge are vital to the rapidly growing biotechnology industry where gene technology, fermentation and bioprocessing play an important part in developing products of the future.

Qualifications and Training

Minimum requirements for entry to a full-time first degree course is usually five GCSE passes at grade C with A levels or equivalent in at least two, preferably three, sciences (biology, chemistry, maths or physics). Some courses concentrate on specific areas of microbiology, others are more general and allow specialization at a later stage. Some courses offer a period of industrial training. It is also possible to obtain qualifications via part-time study while working in a laboratory.

Personal Qualities

Microbiologists have enquiring minds, are good problem solvers and can work accurately. Good communication skills are vital as microbiologists have to describe their work to other people. Most scientists work in a multidisciplinary group so it helps to be a good team worker.

Starting Salary

Graduate starting salaries are usually in the range of £13,000 to £19,000, depending on the area chosen.

Society for General Microbiology, Marlborough House, Basingstoke Road, Spencers Wood, Reading RG7 1AG; www.biocareers.org.uk; e-mail: careers@sgm.ac.uk
Microbiologists Make a Difference (free leaflet from the above)
Your Career in Microbiology (free booklet from the above)

MIDWIFERY

(see also *Nurse*)

Midwives (who may be female or male) provide care and advice to mothers and fathers before, during and after birth; they are either employed by the NHS in hospital and/or community settings, including home births, by private hospitals, or work independently. The midwife provides care during normal pregnancy and birth, and up to 28 days following the birth. The midwife will also care for women who have complications. The midwife is an integral part of the multidisciplinary team responsible for delivering care, working closely with obstetricians and other health professionals in ensuring the well-being of mothers and babies.

Qualifications and Training

A three-year diploma or degree programme of midwifery education leading to qualification as a registered midwife (RM) is available at various centres nationwide. Candidates need to have a minimum of five GCSEs (grade A–C), or equivalent, including English and a science subject, and must be at least 17 and a half years old (17 in Scotland). Programmes are also available for those with general nursing qualifications. Both courses include theory and practical components. Students spend time on a variety of placements in hospitals and the community.

Personal Qualities

An understanding of people, practical ability, common sense and good interpersonal skills are essential. Midwives must engage in continuous professional development throughout their career to be able to provide safe and effective care to mothers and their babies.

Starting Salary

Midwives in the NHS earn between £15,000 and £23,000.

$\boxed{\text{i}}$

England: NHS Careers, PO Box 376, Bristol BS99 3EY; 0845 60 60 655; www.nhscareers.nhs.uk

Nursing and Midwifery Admissions Service (NMAS), Rosehill, New Barn Lane, Cheltenham, Gloucestershire GL52 3LZ; 01242 544949; www.nmas.ac.uk

National Board for Nursing, Midwifery and Health Visiting for Scotland, PO Box 21, Edinburgh EH2 1NT; 0131 247 6622; www.nbs.org.uk

Northern Ireland: School of Nursing and Midwifery, The Queen's
  University of Belfast, 97 Lisburn Road, Belfast BT9 7BL;
  www.qub.ac.uk/nur
Welsh National Board for Nursing, Midwifery and Health
  Visiting, 2nd Floor, Golate House, 101 St Mary Street, Cardiff
  CF10 1DX; 029 2026 1400; www.wnb.org.uk
Careers in Nursing and Related Professions (Kogan Page)

MILKMAN

A milkman delivers milk, fruit juice, eggs and bread to customers,
keeping accounts and taking payment for goods delivered. The
work begins early in the morning but a milkman may finish just
after lunch.

Qualifications and Training

Formal academic qualifications are not necessary but numeracy
and an ability to drive are essential. On-the-job training leading to
NVQs in Dairy Retailing is available.

Personal Qualities

Milkmen must be physically strong, prepared to be out of doors
and ready to drive in all weather conditions. They must also be
honest, friendly and reliable.

Starting Salary

Varies depending on size of round and services offered.

i

The Dairy Council, 5–7 John Prince's Street, London W1M 0AP;
  020 7499 7822; www.milk.co.uk
National Dairymen's Association, 19 Cornwall Terrace, London
  NW1 4QP; 020 7935 4562; www.dairymen.org.uk

MILLINER

(see also *Fashion* **)**
Expensive 'model' hats are designed by a milliner and made up by the workers in a small retail workroom or factory attached to a boutique or fashion house. Hats for the wholesale trade are mass produced by machine, though some may be hand finished. The designs used are bought from model milliners and passed on to copyists, who work out how the hat can be adapted to machine production.

Qualifications and Training
Training as a junior in a retail workroom or factory may be supplemented by evening classes. Academic qualifications are not necessary, except for designing millinery, when a full fashion training is required. Some fashion courses include modules on hat making.

Personal Qualities
Making hats in a retail millinery workroom needs manual skill and patience – a hat may take up to three days to complete. Senior posts in wholesale production require an understanding of technology. Designers and copyists should have fashion sense and artistic creativity.

Starting Salary
Varies according to experience and type of employer, from £10,000+.

CAPITB Trust, 80 Richardshaw Lane, Pudsey, Leeds LS28 6BN; 0113 239 3355; www.careers-in-clothing.co.uk
British Hat Guild, The Business Centre, Kimpton Road, Luton, Bedfordshire LU2 0LB; 01582 23456; www.hat-guild.org.uk

MINICAB DRIVER

Minicabs are private hire vehicles, which means drivers can only operate if they have first been contacted by the customer. Owner-drivers of private hire vehicles often obtain their business through a taxi firm, which passes on enquiries from customers and charges the owner-driver for the service. Drivers often stay on the taxi firm's premises waiting for calls, or receive them on their radio. Their outgoings include the taxi firm's charge plus bills for servicing and repairs to the vehicle.

Qualifications and Training
Not all areas require hire vehicles or their drivers to be licensed. Where this is necessary, the vehicle has to undergo testing and the driver must be over 21, with at least a year's driving experience and a group A licence. Normally people under 25 do not apply, because of the high cost of insurance. A character reference and medical test are also necessary.

Personal Qualities
Minicab drivers must be able to cope with long and unsocial hours, and get on with a wide range of passengers, dealing with difficult ones as necessary.

Starting Salary
Dependent on the number of hours worked, rates paid and passengers carried.

Local minicab firms and local newspapers

MINING ENGINEER

see *Engineering*

MODEL

Models work as 'live' or photographic models, generally showing clothes or accessories. Photographic and advertising models rely on an agent to get them work and handle the fees. Competition is intense and very few models get to the top of the profession.

Fashion
Models are employed full-time by couturiers, wholesalers or fashion stores as 'live' models. They have the garments draped

and pinned on them during the design stages, and show them to the public. Live models must be tall, at least 5 feet 10 inches (175 centimetres). Photographic modelling involves posing in garments chosen to be illustrated in magazines, newspapers, catalogues or on advertising posters. This work is often out of season for the type of garments being modelled – furs are photographed in August, for example – but some of the work is done abroad. Expenses include the provision of accessories, a good basic wardrobe and hairdressing.

Qualifications and Training
Private model schools run training courses for live and photographic modelling. Reputable schools will only take entrants whom they think will succeed, and will introduce them to agencies at the end of the training period (four to six weeks).

Personal Qualities
A model must be able to work hard, be punctual and reliable, get on well with people, and have a great deal of common sense. Competition is intense and only the more intelligent, who can interpret what the stylist and photographer want, will get to the top. A female model should be at least 5 feet 8 inches tall and more or less 34–24–34. A male model should be at least 6 feet tall, chest 38/40, waist 30/32, inside leg 33. They should have clear skin, good hands, nails and teeth, healthy hair and attractive features.

Starting Salary
Salaries vary from £50 a day to £500+ for top models. Agencies can charge fees of 20 per cent.

Association of Model Agents, 122 Brompton Road, London SW3
    1JE; (send sae for information)
Careers in Fashion (Kogan Page)

MODELMAKER

Models can be made to represent almost anything: towns, office blocks, oil terminals, shopping centres, motorways, houses, cars and planes. They are often scaled-down versions of the real thing, but sometimes they can be enlargements. They are used to show what the real thing will look like and, if they are working models, may be used as testers. Models are often used too in television and films. Modelmakers work for firms specializing in such work, or sometimes branch out on their own.

Qualifications and Training
Formal academic qualifications are not necessary. Modelmakers may teach themselves or learn at evening class; some large firms offer apprenticeships. Edexcel (BTEC) courses in modelmaking are available at some FE colleges and some art colleges

Personal Qualities
Patience, manual dexterity, a good sense of design, shape and colour are necessary. Modelmakers must be prepared to do one job for a considerable length of time; a project such as a model town could take up to a year to complete.

Starting Salary
Low when training; with experience £200+ a week; good modelmakers may earn much more.

Local Jobcentres and Careers / Connexions Centres

MOTOR BODY REPAIRER
(see also *Vehicle Technician*)

The motor body repairer works in a highly mechanised industry where most of the body parts are pressings, forgings or castings. Body-building and repairing are allied to the other specialist skills of painting, industrial finishing, and trimming. Often, a motor body repairer will specialise in several areas of work.

Qualifications and Training
No formal educational qualifications are necessary, but GCSEs or equivalent in maths, English and a science are advantageous.

Mechanics and body repairers usually follow apprenticeship training arranged through Retail Motor Industry Training (ReMIT). Related NVQs are available at levels 2 and 3.

Personal Qualities
A good standard of physical fitness, a sense of responsibility (since the safety of drivers and passengers is involved) and an aptitude for dealing with machinery and tools are required.

Starting Salary
Rates for trainees are set by ReMit. Once qualified, the average salary is £17,000

Retail Motor Industry Training (ReMIT), 201 Great Portland Street, London: W1N 6AB 0207 307 3413; fax: 0207 307 3425; www.remit.co.uk
MITC Motor Industry Training Council, 201 Great Portland Street, London W1N 6AB; 0207 436 6373; www.mitc.co.uk; e-mail: info@mitc.co.uk
Local Jobcentres and Careers / Connexions Centres

MUSEUM AND ART GALLERY WORK

Art galleries and museums of various kinds (general, archaeology, social history, natural history, transport, science, local history) are administered by the government, local authorities, universities, private organizations or individuals. Most staff enter as curatorial assistants and gain experience of caring for collections, research and interpretation through publications and exhibitions. They may be responsible for displays and publications as well as offering support to senior staff. They will also spend time on documentation, collection management, education programmes and answering public enquiries.

Qualifications and Training
Many of those working in museums are graduates in history, archaeology or art history but there are also opportunities for

those with qualifications in natural science, geography and technology. Increasingly, those with qualification and experience in marketing, finance, fund-raising, retail and visitor services may find work in this sector. There are also opportunities for those with technical or design skills.

Training courses at different levels, including postgraduate, are available as in-service training schemes for museum and art gallery work. Postgraduate courses are also available at some universities and colleges. A postgraduate qualification and experience through voluntary work can improve prospects of finding museum work.

Personal Qualities

Staff must have an interest in the objects under their care and should have the ability to make the information about them interesting and easily understood.

Starting Salary

Curatorial assistants are often in the £9,000–£11,000 range and assistant curator/curator posts requiring appropriate qualifications and experience can vary from £11,000 to £18,000.

Further Information

Cultural Heritage National Training Organization (CHNTO), 1st Floor, Glyde House, Glydegate, Bradford BD5 0UP; 01274 391056; fax: 01274 394890; www.chnto.co.uk

The Council for Museums, Archives and Libraries – Resource, 16 Queen Anne's Gate, London SW1H 9AA; 020 7273 1444; www.resource.gov.uk; e-mail: info@resource.gov.uk

MUSIC THERAPIST

Music therapy is an interactive, primarily non-verbal intervention. It provides a process though which clients can express themselves, become aware of their feelings and interact more easily. The therapist uses live, improvised music to draw the client into an interactive musical relationship. Therapists work with people of all ages, in a wide variety of settings, including special schools, psychiatric hospitals, hospices and day centres. Music therapy is used in many clinical areas, including communication disorders, developmental delay, learning disabilities, mental health problems, physical difficulties, emotional problems, challenging behaviour and terminal illness.

Qualifications and Training
Music Therapy is a State Registered profession. The training is a postgraduate diploma course lasting between 1 and 2 years. Some courses offer a part-time option. Before training as a music therapist, students need first to have completed a three-year musical training leading to a diploma or degree. People from related disciplines, such as psychology or education, may also sometimes be accepted onto a training course if they have sufficient practical musical skills.

Personal Qualities
Music therapists need to be highly skilled musicians, and be able to use music creatively. Therapists also need to develop an understanding of their own reactions and responses. For this reason, student therapists are required to have their own personal therapy during training. Training courses generally prefer students to be over 25 when they begin training.

Starting Salary
Starting salaries are in the region of £17,500 to £18,000.

i

The Association of Professional Music Therapists, 26 Hamlyn Road, Glastonbury, Somerset BA6 8HT; 01458 834919; www.apmt.org.uk

The British Society for Music Therapy, 25 Rosslyn Avenue, East Barnet, Herts EN4 8DH; 020 8368 8879; www.bsmt.org

MUSICAL INSTRUMENT TECHNOLOGIST
(see also *Piano Tuner*)

The instrument technologist is concerned with making and repairing instruments of all kinds, from pianos to guitars. Good training and practical skill are essential and ensure plenty of work for the technologist.

Qualifications and Training

The Department of Communications and Music Technology at the London Guildhall University offers courses in almost every aspect of instrument technology through their City and Guilds Certificate, BTEC National Diploma, HND and degree courses. Full- and part-time courses are also offered by Leeds College of Music, Morley College, West Dean College, Merton Technical College and Newark Technical College. The Institute of Musical Instrument Technology awards a diploma and can provide further advice and information.

Personal Qualities

Instrument technologists need some musical ability, at least an ear for tuning and relevant technical skills – woodwork, electronics and metalwork.

Starting Salary

Salaries vary greatly: the average is £250–£300 a week when trained, but lower without experience.

> [i]

Crafts Council, 44a Pentonville Road, London N1 9BY; 020 7278 7700; www.craftscouncil.org.uk
Institute of Musical Instrument Technology, PO Box 118, Southsea, Hampshire P04 9YP; www.imit.org.uk
National Association of Musical Instrument Repairers; www.namir.org.uk

MUSICIAN

A musical training, leading to a degree or equivalent qualification, opens the door to a wide range of careers in music, including performing, teaching, administration, management, broadcasting, recording, journalism, publishing, promotion, librarianship and the retail trade.

Performer

Many professional musicians work on a freelance basis as soloists, orchestral players, commercial session musicians and in a variety of chamber music ensembles including classical, rock, dance and jazz groups. A performer's working life often includes some teaching, masterclasses or community education work alongside regular and vital practice.

Some musicians arrange their own engagements, others have agents or use a diary service to find work. For all performers, membership of a professional association or union is desirable.

There are opportunities, particularly for those who already play an instrument, to join the Army, the RAF or Royal Marines as a bandsman.

Composer

Very few composers earn a living solely by composition; most also perform or teach. The most lucrative area of composition is writing music for TV, films, videos and the commercial market, but some composers also find time to write their own music and get it performed. Professional advice on copyright (from a solicitor or professional association) is essential.

Teacher

With music now placed as one of the foundation subjects in the National Curriculum there is an increasing demand for music teachers. Opportunities range from private instrumental teaching to class teaching at primary, secondary and tertiary levels. Class teachers and some visiting instrumental teachers working in state schools require Qualified Teacher Status.

Private teachers set up and develop their own independent, studio-based business. The Incorporated Society of Musicians (ISM) sets professional standards for members who are listed in their Register of Professional Private Music Teachers. They set minimum hourly tuition fees, so that a reasonable income can be assured, and advise on business matters such as tuition contracts.

Qualifications and Training

Entry to undergraduate courses of study usually requires a minimum of five GCSEs and one or more A levels, preferably including music. Full-time courses of study over three or four years, usually leading to a degree, are available at conservatoires (performance-based), universities (more academic) and colleges of higher education (more broad spectrum). Singers require a longer training, often over six years. Conservatoires and universities also offer a range of postgraduate courses. Teachers require an appropriate teaching qualification, such as a PGCE (Postgraduate Certificate in Education). Details of courses in performance, composition, musicology and teaching are available from the Incorporated Society of Musicians' Web site. The government has introduced a training scheme for the music industry under the 'New Deal' initiative; details are available from Jobcentres.

Personal Qualities

A love of music, a positive and persuasive personality, robust physical and mental health, stamina, patience and excellent communication skills are essential for any career in music. Competition is fierce for performers and only a very few talented musicians can establish a successful solo career. The ability to get on well with others helps to ensure good relationships with colleagues, managers and promoters to support career development.

Starting Salary

Salaries vary enormously. Guidance on rates of pay is available from the Incorporated Society of Musicians.

Incorporated Society of Musicians, 10 Stratford Place, London W1C 1AA; 020 7629 4413; www.ism.org
Local Jobcentres and Careers/Connexions Centres

N

NATUROPATH

Naturopathy is not offered by the NHS, so naturopaths work in private practice. They believe in treating the whole patient, and in encouraging the body to cure itself, so do not generally give drugs which, they feel, often treat the symptoms without dealing with the actual cause of a problem. A naturopath uses treatments designed to correct total body chemistry; diet is seen as a major factor and patients are encouraged to eat more natural and unspoilt food. Hydrotherapy is often used to stimulate the blood to a specific area of the body or to draw it away from another (by applying cold packs to combat throbbing headaches, for example).

Naturopaths also need to be skilled in psychology since they recognise that physiological complaints may frequently be caused by psychological problems. Any remedies used tend to be nutritional, herbal or homeopathic, and naturopaths may also be trained in acupuncture or other systems of alternative or complementary medicine. In the UK, naturopathy is closely linked to osteopathy and many naturopaths are qualified osteopaths using these skills in treating their patients.

Qualifications and Training

Two graduate courses are offered by the British College of Naturopathy and Osteopathy in London. One course is a BSc (Honours) degree in Osteopathic Medicine combined with a Naturopathic Diploma, and the second is the BSc (Honours) degree in Naturopathic Medicine.

The usual minimum entry requirements are three good A levels or equivalent, one of which should be chemistry. Mature students may be considered on an individual basis, taking into account their academic and life experiences.

Personal Qualities
Professional skills must be combined with a sympathetic and caring manner.

Starting Salary
Salaries vary depending on hours worked, number of patients and fee scales.

The British College of Naturopathy and Osteopathy, Lief House, 120–122 Finchley Road, London NW3 5HR; 020 7435 6464; fax: 020 7431 3630; www.bcno.ac.uk; e-mail: bcd@bcno.ac.uk
The General Council and Register of Naturopaths, Goswell House, 2 Goswell Road, Street, Somerset BA16 0JG; 01458 840072; www.naturopathy.org.uk; e-mail: admin@naturopathy.org.uk

NAVAL ARCHITECT

Naval architects are professional engineers who play a key role as project leaders and specialists in the design, building and marketing of all systems which have to move just above, on or under the sea, including merchant ships, warships, offshore structures, submarines, hovercraft, yachts and other small craft. They also have to ensure that a safe, economic and seaworthy design is produced. The workplace may be a large company, a small group, a consultancy or a government department.

Qualifications and Training
Naval architects who meet the education, training and experience requirements may become members of The Royal Institution of Naval Architects (RINA), the professional institution for all qualified naval architects. They need to have had an aggregate of at least seven years' engineering education, training and responsible experience. Students and graduates working towards meeting these requirements may also become members. It is possible to

register with the UK Engineering Council as a Chartered Engineer (CEng), an Incorporated Engineer (IEng) or as an Engineering Technician (EngTech) through RINA.

Personal Qualities

A naval architect requires a creative, enquiring and logical mind; the ability to communicate clearly in speech and writing with others inside and outside the engineering profession; sound judgement and qualities of leadership and the ability to work as a part of a team.

Starting Salary

£25,000–£30,000 per year, five years after qualifying.

The Royal Institution of Naval Architects (RINA), 10 Upper Belgrave Street, London SW1X 8BQ; 020 7235 4622; www.rina.org.uk; e-mail: hq@rina.org.uk

NEUROPHYSIOLOGY TECHNOLOGIST

A more familiar name for the neurophysiology technologist is the EEG (electro-encephalography) technologist, who is responsible for setting up and operating electronic equipment which records electrical activity in the brain and nervous system. These tests often include visual, auditory or other types of evoked potentials (EPs), which are the responses of the brain to specific stimuli. EEG and EP tests are performed to help in the diagnosis of patients with epilepsy, cerebral tumours, strokes, dementias or multiple sclerosis.

In many departments, the technologist is also required to assist the clinician with electromyography (EMG) and nerve conduction studies (NCS). These tests look at the way in which nerves and muscles in the body are working, and help in the diagnosis of diseases such as dystrophies and nerve dysfunction. All these procedures are carried out either in the department, wards, intensive care units or operating theatres. Both outpatients and in-patients come to the department and the tests are performed on all ages. Heart rate and respiration may also be recorded. The neurophysiology technologist works as part of the hospital team in the surgical, neurological or psychiatric department.

Qualifications and Training

Five GCSEs, grade C or above, are normally required, including maths, English and combined science. Many entrants have A levels or equivalent. There are two main ways of entering the profession: as a student technologist employed by a hospital in an EEG clinical neurophysiology department; or as a student super-numerary technologist employed by a regional health authority. Training takes place mostly on the job with day-release facilities to study for an Edexcel (BTEC) qualification/NVQ award, level 3.

Personal Qualities

A medical technologist needs to be willing to take responsibility, able to keep calm under pressure and must be meticulous. In addition, a pleasant manner to put patients at their ease is essential.

Starting Salary

Trainee £7,000+; once qualified £10,000–£13,000 potentially rising to £30,000+ for senior posts.

Electrophysiological Technologists' Association, EEG
  Department, Staffordshire General Hospital, Weston Road,
  Stafford ST16 3SA (enclose sae)

NOTARY PUBLIC

A Notary Public is an international lawyer, whose main duty it is to prepare and verify legal documents for use abroad. These can be certified translations, powers of attorney and all manner of mercantile documents. There are two types of notaries: general notaries who are usually full-time solicitors with a part-time notarial practice, or scrivener notaries who are full-time notaries with linguistic skills. The latter are usually to be found in central London, the former anywhere in the UK.

Qualifications and Training

There is a unified system for the initial stage of qualification for both branches of the profession. This consists of a diploma course administered by Cambridge University. A general notary, having obtained this diploma, can then apply for a faculty to practise to the Faculty Office of the Archbishop of Canterbury. A scrivener notary, however, would need to take additional examinations such as those testing knowledge of two languages and the law of the country of one such language, with a requirement also to spend two years in a scrivener notary's office.

Personal Qualities

A notary must be a person of discretion and integrity.

Starting Salary

A general notary will receive not only the remuneration earned as a notary but also any income earned as a solicitor. A scrivener notary, on the other hand, will only receive notarial income, and a starting salary upon qualification will be about £30,000.

i

The Notaries' Society, 23 New Street, Woodbridge, Suffolk
   IP12 1DN; 01394 384134; www.thenotariessociety.org.uk
The Society of Scrivener Notaries, 35 Piccadilly, London W1J 0LJ;
   www.scrivener-notaries.org.uk
The Worshipful Company of Scriveners, HQS Wellington,
   Temple Stairs, Victoria Embankment, London WC2R 2PN; 020
   7240 0529; fax: 020 7497 0645; www.scriveners.org.uk;
   e-mail: clerk@scriveners.org.uk

NURSE

Nurses are employed in a wide variety of situations in hospitals, institutions (such as prisons and colleges), the armed forces, schools, industry and in private organizations. A student nurse may choose to specialise from a number of different fields – adult nursing, children's nursing, mental health, learning disability or in specialities within those fields. Currently, a nurse qualifies (that is, becomes registered) on the Adult, Mental Health, Mental

Handicap or Children's Part of the Register. Nurses may work in the NHS, in private hospitals or in the community.

There are increasing opportunities for work in the community for all types of nurses. Community paediatric nurses take nursing care into the homes of children who are seriously ill or who have long-term conditions. Most people with a mental health problem will be allocated a community psychiatric nurse. People with learning disabilities now tend to live a supported life at home rather than in a hospital or home. Community nurses with specialist training support this group. Nurses offer support to the patients and their carers.

Qualifications and Training

Courses are offered at degree and diploma level. Entry to degree courses is through UCAS. For the diploma, entry is directly to the Colleges of Nursing and Midwifery in Northern Ireland and Wales and through central clearing houses in England (NMAS) and Scotland (CATCH). A minimum of five GCSEs or equivalent are required but candidates without such qualifications may sit an education test known as the DC test. The minimum age of entry to programmes is 17 and a half (17 in Scotland).

Courses are offered in colleges of nursing and midwifery (except for Northern Ireland – *see* Further Information), which may be linked with a university or college of higher education. The 18-month Common Foundation Programme gives a general introduction to nursing, followed by 18 months in one of four branches, chosen before the course begins: adult nursing, mental health nursing, nursing people with a mental handicap or children's nursing. The focus of the course is equally split between theory and practice. Students spend time in the hospital and the community, gaining experience.

Once registered, nurses practise in a wide variety of settings. Some take further courses to gain specialist knowledge in meeting the needs of patients in differing clinical specialities. Others may choose nurse teaching or management within the health services. Whatever the area chosen, the initial nursing qualification will be the first step in a lifetime of professional education.

Personal Qualities

Nursing is always about people: patients, their families, their friends and the team of colleagues working to deliver nursing care. The ability to get on with others and good communication skills are essential. As nursing is physically demanding, candidates will need to be fit. Nurses must be committed to developing their knowledge and skills throughout their careers, enhancing their ability to care.

Starting Salary

Newly qualified nurses £15,355 to £17,055; Sister/Charge Nurse £21,605 to £25,420; Nurse Consultants £29,450 to £43,440. There are additional allowances for those in London and the South. Nurses training via the Diploma route are entitled to a bursary of around £5,000; those undertaking a degree are entitled to a smaller grant.

Nursing and Midwifery Admissions Service (NMAS), Rosehill, New Barn Lane, Cheltenham, Gloucestershire GL52 3LZ; 01242 544949; www.nmas.ac.uk

National Board for Nursing, Midwifery and Health Visiting for Scotland, PO Box 21, Edinburgh EH2 1NT; 0131 247 6622; www.nbs.org.uk

Northern Ireland: School of Nursing and Midwifery, The Queen's University of Belfast, 97 Lisburn Road, Belfast BT9 7BL; www.qub.ac.uk/nur

Welsh National Board for Nursing, Midwifery and Health Visiting, 2nd Floor, Golate House, 101 St Mary Street, Cardiff CF10 1DX; 029 2026 1400; www.wnb.org.uk

University and Colleges Admissions Service (UCAS), Rosehill, New Barn Lane, Cheltenham, Gloucestershire GL52 3LZ; 01242 223707; www.ucas.com

NHS Careers, PO Box 376, Bristol BS99 3EY; 0845 6060 655; www.nhscareers.nhs.uk

Careers in Nursing and Related Professions (Kogan Page)

NURSERY NURSE

(see also *Pre-School Worker*)

A nursery nurse works with babies and children under eight in the public, private and voluntary sectors. This can include schools, nurseries and hospitals. In schools, nursery nurses work in nursery, reception and infant classes alongside the teacher, providing and supervising educational and play activities. They may also be involved in providing out of school care at after-school clubs and on holiday schemes. Nursery nurses in hospitals can work in maternity and special care units, and on children's wards. Day nurseries, both private and local authority, employ nursery nurses to care for children under five whose parents are unable to care for them during the day. Nursery nurses can also be employed in clinics, residential homes, the community, family centres and private homes as nannies.

Qualifications and Training

The Council for Awards in Children's Care and Education (CACHE) level 3 Diploma in Child Care and Education (previously known as the NNEB) is a prerequisite for many jobs and can be done as a two-year full-time course or part time up to five years. There are no minimum entry requirements, but many colleges ask for GCSEs at C or above, including English. The BTEC National Diploma in Early Years, a two-year course, requires four GCSEs at grade C or above. Modern Apprenticeships are available; apprentices are trained by their employers and work towards NVQ level 3 in Early Years Care and Education.

Nursery nurses in Scotland must register with the Scottish Child Care and Education Board; this requires completion of a one-year programme of SQA National Certificate units plus the one-year HNC in Child Care and Education or a programme of SVQ level 3 units in Early Years and Education.

Personal Qualities

A genuine love of children is essential, with the ability to work with patience, tolerance, imagination and energy. Good motivation skills and a sense of fun are important.

Starting Salary

£9,000–£11,000 as a nursery assistant, £11,000–£15,000 as a nursery nurse/officer, £17,000+ as a manager. Nannies working for private families can earn from £250 to £600 a week depending on location and experience.

i

Council for Awards in Children's Care and Education (CACHE), 8 Chequer Street, St Albans, Hertfordshire AL1 3XZ; 01727 847636; www.cache.org.uk

Professional Association of Nursery Nurses, 2 St James' Court, Friar Gate, Derby DE1 1BT; 01332 372337; www.pat.org.uk; e-mail: pann@pat.org.uk

Scottish Childcare and Education Board, 6 Kilnford Crescent, Dundonald, Kilmarnock, Ayrshire KA2 9DW; 01563 850440

Nursery World; www.nursery-world.com (for job vacancies)

NURSING AUXILIARY

see *Healthcare Assistant*

OCCUPATIONAL THERAPIST

Occupational therapists work with people who have physical, mental or social problems, either from birth or as the result of accident, illness or ageing. Their aim is to enable people to achieve as much as they can for themselves. They start with a thorough assessment of each client and their lifestyle, in order to establish what the person wants to achieve. Treatment can involve adapting living and working environments, teaching coping strategies and discovering the most beneficial therapeutic activities.

Although occupational therapists often work as part of a team, they have more autonomy than other healthcare workers in the way they apply their knowledge and expertise. They work in hospitals, social service departments, individual's homes, residential and nursing homes, schools, universities, charities and prisons. They may also work in private practice.

Employment and promotional opportunities are excellent and all UK-educated occupational therapists receive a qualification that is recognised by the World Federation of Occupational Therapists, giving them opportunities to work abroad.

Qualifications and Training

Entry to the profession is normally on completion of a full- or part-time degree in Occupational Therapy. Most courses require three A levels or equivalent; mature students will be considered without these academic requirements. Accelerated two-year full-time courses are also available to graduates of other disciplines. Part-time in-service programmes are also available for those employed as occupational therapy support workers or technical instructors. Some part-time courses can be studied irrespective of employment status. Although courses vary, all include the principles and practice of occupational therapy, behavioural, biological and medical sciences, and periods of clinical practice in a variety of hospital and community settings.

Personal Qualities

In addition to academic ability, potential occupational therapists require sensitivity, tolerance, problem-solving skills and the ability to work as part of a team. Reliability, honesty and patience are also important, as well as enthusiasm, dedication and the desire to help and care for others.

Starting Salary

£16,520 on entry for a graduate, rising to over £36,500 for the highest grade of occupational therapy managers. Additional allowances include London and fringe zone weightings, as well as stand-by and on-call payments.

College of Occupational Therapists, 106–114 Borough High Street, Southwark, London SE1 1LB; 020 7357 6480; www.cot.co.uk; e-mail: EPGroup.PA@cot.co.uk

Careers in Nursing and Related Professions (Kogan Page)

OCEANOGRAPHER

Oceanography is the study of the seas, the organisms within them and the sea floor and its sediments. Scientific and commercial interest in this field has increased considerably over the past few decades and researchers are investigating the possibilities of deriving energy sources, minerals and food from the sea.

Oceanographers are also concerned with the study of pollution and erosion, navigation and underwater work, climate change, submarine geology and satellite remote sensing of the land, air and sea interfaces.

Qualifications and Training

An honours degree in one of the sciences is usually essential. There are only a few universities (Liverpool, Plymouth, Southampton and the University of Wales at Bangor) which run first degree courses in oceanography itself. However, most oceanographers have a first degree in physics, maths, chemistry or biology, with a postgraduate qualification in their specialist area.

Personal Qualities

Candidates should have a scientific aptitude and training together with an enquiring mind. Many jobs involve going to sea in research ships and a few involve diving or the use of submersibles.

Starting Salary

Around £16,000.

i

The Society for Underwater Technology, 80 Coleman Street, London EC2R 5BJ; 020 7382 2601; fax: 020 7382 2684; www.sut.org.uk

Southampton Oceanography Centre, Empress Dock, Southampton SO14 3ZH; 023 8059 6666; www.soc.soto.org.uk

Scottish Association for Marine Sciences, Dunstaffnage Marine Laboratory, PO Box 3, Oban, Argyll PA34 4AD; www.sams.ac.uk

OIL/GAS RIG WORK

(see also *Diver, Geologist*)

There are various openings for personnel working on oil or gas drilling rigs, both onshore (on land) and offshore (such as those in the North Sea). Opportunities in all fields are generally limited to experienced and/or highly qualified applicants. An offshore rig has to be self-sufficient and is a combination of a factory, hotel and heliport. The catering and accommodation are similar to the provision onshore. Many of the routine factory tasks (such as cleaning and maintenance) are carried out by outside contractors and service companies.

Geologist

The oil companies employ technical experts such as geologists, geophysicists and drilling and petroleum engineers. Geologists collect and analyse data from a variety of sources to determine whether drilling might prove successful at a particular site and to optimise production from existing oilfields. There are opportunities around the world.

Geophysicist

Geophysicists use remote sensing to study the composition and structure of the sub-surface. A major element of this is computer-aided analysis of seismic data.

Drilling Crew

The drilling crew are responsible for the drilling of wells, and the operation and maintenance of a variety of heavy machinery. The crew consists of a toolpusher who manages the team and is responsible for the safety and integrity of the operation, and a team of people including a driller, assistant driller, derrickman, roughnecks and roustabouts. A typical drill crew will number around 10 people. Progression to the role of driller is hierarchical, with people working through general labouring jobs (roustabouts), working on the drill floor (roughnecks) or at the top of the derrick (derrickman). The work is physical, from the operation of the drilling equipment to the cleaning and maintenance of pumps and equipment. A graduate drilling engineer and a range of other specialists such as logging engineers, directional drilling specialists and mudloggers will also work with the drill crew.

Divers (see also Diver)

Divers are employed in exploration and production work, as well as underwater repair work such as welding.

Engineers (see also Engineering)

A production engineer supervises activities ranging from production and storage, gas compression and injection (to assist in the recovery of the oil), to tanker loading. The reservoir engineer is concerned with the behaviour of the oil accumulation or reservoir, and has to attempt to discover how much oil remains below ground and what are the most effective methods of recovery.

Economics plays an important role. The maintenance engineer must ensure that all equipment is functioning properly, selecting and monitoring the companies under contract.

Qualifications and Training

Geologist: a good honours degree is the minimum required; many companies prefer postgraduate training. Geophysicist: an honours degree in geology or geophysics or other numerate discipline, such as maths or physics. Postgraduate training may be an advantage. Drilling Crew: trainees are normally sponsored by drilling companies. Roughneck courses last four weeks. Drillers, toolpushers and drilling engineers will receive further training, including statutory well-control, safety and emergency response training. Divers: must be trained on courses approved by the Health and Safety Executive. Training is expensive; candidates may be sponsored by employers. Engineers: oil companies recruit engineering graduates for trainee posts.

Personal Qualities

Geophysicists need scientific aptitude, numeracy, a good eye for detail, an enquiring mind and the ability to work in a team under pressure. Drilling crewmembers must be physically fit, as the work is arduous. Good teamwork skills are essential. Divers must be physically fit and able to stay calm in a crisis.

Starting Salary

Salaries vary depending on position, but are often relatively high.

OPITO (National Training Organization oil and gas extraction), Minerva House, Bruntland Road, Portlethen, Aberdeenshire AB12 4QL; 01224 787800; www.opito.com; e-mail: info@opito.co.uk

The Institute of Petroleum, 61 New Cavendish Street, London W1G 7AR; 020 7467 7100; www.petroleum.co.uk; 'Energy – Careers in the Oil and Gas Industry' available from Web site

The Institution of Mining and Metallurgy, Danum House, South Parade, Doncaster DN1 2DY; 01302 320486; www.imm.org.uk; e-mail: hq@imm.org.uk

Engineering Careers Information Service, EMTA, 14 Upton Road,
Watford, Hertfordshire WD1 7EP; 0800 282 167;
www.emta.org.uk/enginuity; e-mail: ecis@emta.org.uk

OPTOMETRIST

(previously known as *Ophthalmic Optician*; see also *Dispensing Optician*)

Optometrist are trained to examine eyes and test sight, detect and measure defects in healthy eyes and prescribe spectacles, contact lenses or other appliances to correct or improve vision. They must carry out whatever tests are clinically necessary to detect signs of injury or disease to the eye or elsewhere and must refer these patients to a medical practitioner. Most optometrists work in general practice in a variety of arrangements, including independent businesses, partnership, as an employee of corporate bodies, as a franchisee or in the hospital eye service. There are also job opportunities in research organizations, academic departments, ophthalmic hospitals and clinics.

Qualifications and Training

Optometrists must be registered with the General Optical Council before being permitted to practise in the UK. To obtain registration they must pass the professional qualifying exam run by the College of Optometrists. The exam is in two parts. For Part I the candidate must gain a BSc honours degree in optometry after three years of study at an accredited institution (or four years in Scotland). Part II is taken after the candidate has completed a preregistration year of supervised practice. The professional qualifying exam combines practical and oral assessment of the candidate's ability to manage patients and practise safely as an independent optometrist.

For acceptance on to a university course students normally need three A levels, two of which must be maths or science. GCSEs should include English and physics if not gained at A level. Average entry grades vary but are usually 320 A level points.

Personal Qualities

Opticians need mathematical and scientific skills to make accurate observations and calculations. They also need an ability to get on with and communicate effectively with patients of all ages and backgrounds and to be able to put them at their ease.

Starting Salary

Salaries are from £25,000 to £35,000.

The College of Optometrists, 42 Craven Street, London WC2N
    5NG; 020 7839 6000; www.college-optometrists.org;
    e-mail: optometry@college-optometrists.org
General Optical Council, 41 Harley Street, London W1G 8DJ;
    020 7580 3898; www.optical.org; e-mail: goc@optical.org
Scottish Committee of Optometrists, 7 Queens Buildings,
    Queensferry Road, Rosyth, Fife KY11 2RA; 01383 419444;
    www.scottishoptometry.co.uk; e-mail: secretarysco@aol.com
'A Career in Vision Care' available for download from
    www.college-optometrists.org

ORDNANCE SURVEY WORK

(see also *Cartography*)

The Ordnance Survey is part of the Civil Service and responsible to the Department of Transport, Local Government and the Regions. It produces all kinds of official maps covering the whole of Britain. For example, large-scale computerised Ordnance Survey mapping is used by local authorities, estate agents, solicitors, architects, civil engineers and government departments, while leisure paper maps are popular with ramblers, riders and cyclists. Other Ordnance Survey maps show historical detail, such as Roman Britain, or statistical data (for example, population density).

Job opportunities are limited; the organization no longer employs cartographic draughtsmen or assistants as all maps are produced digitally. There are, however, sometimes opportunities for trainee surveyors. These are advertised in the locality of the vacancies. The work includes checking new features such as buildings, hedges, fences and roads, and noting any alterations since the map was last printed. These are input on hand-held computers.

Increasingly, Ordnance Survey work involves the use of information technology, ranging from base data for digital atlases and computer games to complex geographical databases. Ordnance Survey's head office is in Southampton and most employees are based there. Field surveyors, however, may be posted virtually anywhere in England, Scotland or Wales.

Qualifications and Training.
A good general education and five GCSE passes at grade C or above, including maths, English, geography or information technology, and a minimum of 18 months' experience working in a related field. Computer literacy and a driving licence are desirable. Candidates also take an aptitude test.

Personal Qualities
A willingness to work in an outdoor environment, excellent interpersonal skills and an ability to work with all sections of the community, as well as the confidence, initiative and motivation to work alone or as part of a small team.

Starting Salary
£11,500 for trainee surveyors.

Ordnance Survey, Romsey Road, Southampton SO16 4GU; 023 8079 2000; fax 023 8079 2452; www.ordnancesurvey.co.uk

ORTHOPTIST

Orthoptists diagnose and treat various abnormalities and weaknesses in the eye, such as a squint or double vision. Many patients are children and special equipment and exercises are used to help correct any defects while they are still young. They work closely with medical eye specialists and, where operations are necessary, with ophthalmic surgeons. Most orthoptists work within the

NHS, in hospitals and clinics (including school clinics). There are also opportunities in private practice and teaching.

Qualifications and Training
Qualification is via a degree; courses are available at the universities of Sheffield and Liverpool. Applicants must have five GCSEs to include at least one science, English language and maths, plus three A levels or equivalent.

Personal Qualities
Orthoptists have to be able to win the confidence of their patients (who are often very young), so need a sympathetic manner and a good deal of patience. Some mathematical and scientific ability is also called for.

Starting Salary
From £15,920 in the NHS, slightly more in private practice.

The British Orthoptic Society, Tavistock House North, Tavistock Square, London WC1H 9HX; 020 7387 7992 (information pack available); www.orthoptics.org.uk; e-mail: bos@orthoptics.org.uk

OSTEOPATH

Osteopathy is a system of diagnosis and treatment where the main emphasis is on conditions affecting the musculo-skeletal system. Osteopaths use predominantly gentle manual and manipulative methods of treatment to restore and maintain proper body function. They work in private practice and are increasingly being asked to work as part of mainstream medicine.

Qualifications and Training
Entry requirements are one of the following: a minimum of two A levels in biology and chemistry; a science access or foundation course; mature students with professional qualifications of a similar level to studying at undergraduate level or equivalent

qualifications from European and overseas applicants. Courses include the study of anatomy, physiology and biochemistry, together with a clinical course in the principles, diagnoses and techniques of osteopathy. Extensive hands-on clinical experience with patients is a key feature of any course. Studying for a degree at the British School of Osteopathy leads to a Bachelor degree in osteopathy (B.Ost).

Personal Qualities

Osteopaths require good manual dexterity plus a genuine desire to help and care for people. An ability to get on with and gain the confidence of their patients is also important.

Starting Salary

Within the first five years of practice new graduates can earn approximately £25,000–£30,000.

i

The British College of Naturopathy and Osteopathy, Frazer House, 6 Netherhall Gardens, London NW3 5RR; 020 7435 6464

The British School of Osteopathy, 275 Borough High Street, London SE1 1JE; 020 7407 0222; www.bso.ac.uk; e-mail: admissions@bso.ac.uk

Working in Complementary and Alternative Medicine (Kogan Page)

PACKAGING TECHNOLOGIST

The purpose of packaging is to protect, preserve, contain and present its contents. It also has a vital function in branding and brand awareness. Opportunities for work exist with manufacturers of raw packaging materials, with companies that produce packaging and companies that have a product to be packed. Many small firms will not have their own packaging adviser / technologist and will hire a consultant when the need arises.

Work opportunities exist in developing materials for packaging purposes, for designing equipment to manufacture or fill packaging, for structural design of parts, for graphic design on packs, for physical and chemical testing and quality assurance.

Qualifications and Training

Packaging modules are available in some first degree courses and two universities offer the MSc in Packaging Technology. The Diploma in Packaging Technology from the Institute of Packaging is internally recognized as a qualification of excellence. It can be studied in three ways: residential, part-time and by distance learning.

Personal Qualities

Technologists and scientists must be able to look at problems in a practical way and have the ability to communicate their ideas to others both verbally and on paper.

Starting Salary

This varies according to age and qualifications but falls in the region of £10,000 to £16,000.

The Head of Training, Institute of Packaging, Sysonby Lodge, Nottingham Road, Melton Mowbray, Leicestershire LE13 0NU; 01664 250 0055; fax: 01664 564164 (for details of available training and careers advice); www.iop.co.uk; e-mail: info@iop.co.uk

PAINTER AND DECORATOR

(see also *Interior Decorator*)

Painting and decorating involves much more than just hanging paper and applying paint. Appropriate paint for different surfaces must be chosen, surfaces must be prepared by filling holes and cracks and scaffolding may have to be erected. Specialist skills include graining – using paint to give the effect of wood; marbling – doing the same for marble; and gilding – the application of gold and silver leaf to wood, glass and other surfaces. Painters and decorators work for large firms, building contractors, local authorities and as self-employed craftsmen.

Qualifications and Training

No formal educational requirements are necessary, but good mathematical ability is useful. Training is on the job by three-year apprenticeship. During this time apprentices may work towards NVQs.

Personal Qualities

As well as the necessary practical skills, painters and decorators must have an artistic sense, be neat in their work, able to get on with people and prepared to work out of doors, standing most of the time.

Starting Salary

£12,000+ initially; average salaries are £16,000.

i

Construction Industry Training Board, Bircham Newton, King's
Lynn, Norfolk PE31 6RH; 01485 577577; www.citb.org.uk

PATENT AGENT/PATENT EXAMINER

Patent Agent

Patent agents advise individual clients and companies on matters relating to patent law and act on their behalf if they wish to patent an invention, or to register a trademark or a design in the UK or abroad. First, records are searched to gauge the likelihood of a patent being granted. The patent agent then draws up the particulars of the client's invention clearly and concisely, ensuring it neither infringes another patent nor is liable to be copied without infringing its own patent. In cases where a client's patent has been infringed, the agent advises as to the best course of action. Patent agents are employed by private practice firms of patent agencies, industrial companies with a patent department and the government.

Patent Examiner

These are Civil Servants who examine the applications for patents submitted by patent agents and others. The principal task is to establish the originality or otherwise of the invention, and whether or not the applicant is entitled to the protection claimed. There is some opportunity to work abroad in the European Patent Office.

Patent Officer

These are Civil Servants employed in protecting Crown rights in new inventions and developments, compensating the owners of patents used by the Crown and generally advising government departments on matters relating to patents.

Qualifications and Training

The minimum educational requirement for an agent is a degree in a science or a technology-related subject. It is usually necessary to register as a patent agent in the European Patent Office. This involves taking the European qualifying exams for which a degree is necessary.

Patent examiners and officers need a first or second class honours degree in engineering, physics, chemistry, maths or an equivalent professional qualification.

Personal Qualities

Curiosity, the ability to assimilate new ideas, good analytical and critical skills, clear and concise thinking and the capacity for logical and clear expression both in speech and writing are all essential.

Starting Salary

Trainees (no examinations passed) £15,000 to £20,000; technical assistants (close to qualification) £25,000 to £35,000; newly-qualified attorneys £35,000 to £45,000; attorneys with 3–5 years' post-qualification experience £50,000 to £65,000.

i

Chartered Institute of Patent Agents, Staple Inn Buildings, High Holborn, London WC1V 7PZ; 020 7405 9450; www.cipa.org.uk; e-mail: mail@cipa.org.uk

The Patent Office, Cardiff Road, Newport, Gwent NP9 1RH; 01633 814544 (Patent Examiners); www.patent.gov.uk; www.insidecareers.co.uk/patent/index.htm; downloadable guide to becoming a patent attorney

PATTERN CUTTER

see *Clothing Industry, Fashion*

PERSONAL ADVISER (Connexions)

(see also *Careers Adviser*)

The Connexions Service aims to provide a coherent system of support for young people in their transition to adulthood and working life. It will operate in all areas of England by 2003 and be staffed by a network of personal advisers whose aim will be to help 13 to 19-year-olds achieve their full potential by addressing barriers to learning. Some personal advisers may specialize in working with those who need additional support because of problems such as homelessness, mental illness or substance abuse.

The work of individual advisers will depend on their clients and involve work with other agencies to broker access to specialist services. Most of an adviser's time will be spent in direct contact with young people, but some time will also be spent liaising with other organizations, working with parents and carers and promoting links with the local community. There is also a certain amount of administrative work – producing accurate and up-to-date records to be shared with other professionals.

Personal advisers are based in a variety of settings, including schools, colleges, youth and community centres and Connexions offices. At times, advisers may be called out to deal with crises in young people's lives. Most jobs will involve evening and weekend work. Some Connexions Partnerships will provide services during the evening and overnight, to respond to the needs of young people.

Qualifications and Training

A number of courses are currently being developed, including an Access course for people with relevant experience and aptitude and an extension course for people already working in this field.

The usual entry requirement for people starting direct on the Diploma for Personal Advisers is a relevant professional qualification, for example in youth work or careers guidance, plus relevant experience and aptitude. The minimum age for entry to training is normally 21. A driving licence is usually required. All candidates undergo police checks, so anyone with a conviction for a crime against children is barred from this type of work.

Personal Qualities

Advisers need strong communication and relationship-building skills to engage the trust and respect of young people. They need to be able to listen carefully and respond appropriately; a non-judgemental approach is essential. Personal advisers need to empathize with young people's concerns whilst maintaining professional and emotional detachment. A sense of humour, reliability, flexibility, good time management and team-working skills are also important.

Starting salaries

Salaries vary between individual Connexions Partnerships. Trainees may start on £14,000 to £15,000; qualified staff with the Diploma for Personal Advisers between £19,000 to £21,000 (£23,000 to £25,500 in London).

Connexions Web site: www.connexions.gov.uk
Local Connexions Partnership

PERSONAL ASSISTANT

(see also *Secretary*)

A senior secretary or personal assistant (PA) may work with one or more senior executives. Accurate skills in shorthand, audio typewriting, word processing and information management and a knowledge of office-based software are desirable. The PA may also act as administrator, information centre, organizer of the manager's day, progress chaser, arranger of travel and meetings, receptionist and communicator (oral and written) internally and externally. A senior secretary or PA assumes responsibility without direct supervision and takes decisions within the scope of assigned authority.

Qualifications and Training

GCSEs (including English), A levels or a degree are all acceptable qualifications. (Numeracy and a second language are very useful.) NVQs in Administration are available. A secretary usually gains experience as a member of a management team, although some find jobs at a senior level following a postgraduate secretarial or secretarial/linguist course. Some secretaries progress to management through further study in personnel, administration, public relations, marketing or information technology.

Personal Qualities

Good secretaries are judged by what they do, but qualities such as self-motivation, discretion, tact, loyalty, personality, flexibility, communication skills and smart appearance are expected.

Starting Salary
£12,000–£20,000+, more in London.

Institute of Qualified Private Secretaries Ltd (IQPS), First Floor, 6
   Bridge Avenue, Maidenhead SL6 1RR; 01628 625007; fax: 01628
   624990; www.iqps.org; e-mail: office@iqps.org
Careers in Secretarial and Office Work (Kogan Page)

PERSONNEL OFFICER
see *Human Resource Adviser/Manager*

PEST CONTROLLER

Pest controllers control not only mice, rats, cockroaches and ants
that may be damaging foodstuffs in a factory, hotel, or private
home, but also rabbits, moles, birds and foxes that attack farmers'
crops. They work for local authorities and private firms. Service
staff are employed to lay traps and set poison. There are also
opportunities for graduates in research and management.

Qualifications and Training
Qualifications in pest control are usually preferred, although at
assistant level, full training is provided on the job, including day
or block release to achieve a recognized qualification, such as
British Pest Control Association courses. The Royal Society for the
Promotion of Health offers a Certificate in Pest Control and NVQs
are also available. Graduates should have a biology degree or a
relevant science degree.

Personal Qualities
This is not a job for the squeamish but also not for the vicious. The
work demands a mature outlook, an ability to get on with many
kinds of people, to work in varying conditions and to work alone.
The ability to drive is important.

Starting Salary
Salaries range from about £9,000 to £19,000+, the higher figure
being for graduates.

i

British Pest Control Association, Ground Floor, Gleneagles House,
Vernongate, Derby DE1 1UP; 01332 294288; www.bpca.org.uk
Local Government Careers; www.lgcareers.com
Royal Society for the Promotion of Health, 38A St. George's
Drive, London SW1V 4BH; 020 7630 0121; www.rsph.org;
e-mail: rshealth@rshealth.org.uk

PETROL PUMP ATTENDANT

see *Garage Work*

PHARMACIST

The main work of the pharmacist is the dispensing of doctors'
prescriptions. There are three branches of the profession:
Community Pharmacists, Hospital Pharmacists, and Industrial
and Research Pharmacists.

Community Pharmacist

Community pharmacists work from high street, health centre and
rural pharmacies as part of the NHS. They dispense prescriptions
and ensure that medicines ordered on prescription or bought over
the counter are correctly and safely supplied, with all necessary
advice on their use. They keep a poisons register and act as a link
between the doctor and the pharmaceutical manufacturer, being
prepared to discuss developments with both. They are readily
accessible health advisers to the public. In addition, they sell a
wide range of non-pharmaceutical articles.

Hospital Pharmacist

They dispense drugs for hospital in- and outpatients and work
side by side with nurses, doctors and other health professionals to
ensure NHS patients receive the most appropriate medicines in
the most effective way. In addition, in some hospitals, pharmacists manufacture their own products, take part in research work
and come into direct contact with in-patients by accompanying
medical staff on their ward rounds

Industrial and Research Pharmacist

They work as part of a team of scientists researching diseases, developing new drugs and carrying out clinical trials. Industrial pharmacists are also recruited to work in the areas of manufacturing, regulatory and medical affairs, sales and marketing and computer science/information technology.

Qualifications and Training

Pharmacists must complete a four-year Master of Pharmacy degree, followed by one year's paid competency-based training and a registration examination. Entry to degree courses is with A level chemistry plus two other A levels or equivalent; maths and biology are preferred.

Personal Qualities

Meticulous attention to detail, a sense of responsibility and an ability to get on with people are required.

Starting Salary

Pre-registration pharmacists in the NHS earn around £12,000 which rises to about £17,000 on qualification. Community and industrial pharmacists start on £23,000+.

i

The Association of the British Pharmaceutical Industry, 12 Whitehall, London SW1A 2DY; 020 7930 3477 (free booklet offering guide to careers for graduates); www.abpi.org.uk

Guild of Hospital Pharmacists, 40 Bermondsey Street, London, SE1 3UD; 020 7939 7000; www.ghp.org.uk

The National Pharmaceutical Association, Mallinson House, 38–42 St Peter's Street, St Albans, Hertfordshire AL1 3NP; 01727 832161 (trade association for community pharmacists); www.npa.co.uk; e-mail: npa@npa.co.uk

Royal Pharmaceutical Society of Great Britain, 1 Lambeth High Street, London SE1 7JN; 020 7735 9141; www.rpsgb.org.uk; e-mail: careers@rpsgb.org.uk, Scottish Department, 36 York Place, Edinburgh EH1 3HU; www.rpsgb.org.uk/scotland/index.html

NHS Careers, PO Box 376, Bristol BS99 3EY; Careers helpline: 0845 60 60 655; www.nhscareers.nhs.uk/home.html

'A Future in Pharmacy' (The Royal Pharmaceutical Society of Great Britain)

PHARMACY TECHNICIAN

Pharmacy technicians work as part of the pharmacy team and are supervised by a pharmacist. Their duties can include the dispensing of medicines from prescriptions, preparing sterile medicines, assessing stocks of drugs, patient counselling, advising on health promotion issues and collecting and collating information on drugs from a variety of sources. Pharmacy technicians can work in chemists, hospitals, the armed forces, the prison service, or within the pharmaceutical industry.

Qualifications and Training

A nationally recognized qualification is the NVQ Pharmacy Services at level 3 which is available from approved centres. Entry requirements for this are generally four GCSEs at grade C or above, including English, mathematics and chemistry plus one other science. Mature applicants are welcome, and previous education and work experience are considered.

Personal Qualities

Pharmacy technicians should be accurate in their work, reliable, careful and have high standards of hygiene. They should also enjoy working with other people and in teams.

Starting Salary

Once qualified, approximately £9,800 rising to £15,000+.

i

Education Officer, Association of Pharmacy Technicians, Stantons, 3 Castle Rise, Llanvaches, Newport, Gwent NP26 3BS; 029 2087 4784

Royal Pharmaceutical Society of Great Britain, 1 Lambeth High
   Street, London SE1 7JN; 020 7735 9141; www.rpsgb.org.uk;
   e-mail: careers@rpsgb.org.uk; Scottish Department,
   36 York Place, Edinburgh EH1 3HU;
   www.rpsgb.org.uk / scotland / index.html
NHS Careers, PO Box 376, Bristol BS99 3EY; Careers helpline 0845
   60 60655; www.nhscareers.nhs.uk / home.html

PHOTOGRAPHER

(see also *Medical Illustrator, Photographic Work*)

Photography is an international means of communication. Its
great advantage over the written word is that it does not need to
be translated for use in a different country. The uses of photography range from commercial and press to medicine and crime
detection. The use of digital equipment is changing the way
photographs are taken, edited and stored.

   Photography is also a popular hobby, providing jobs for many
in the photographic manufacturing, retailing, servicing and
photo-finishing trades.

Commercial Photographer

This work includes advertising, fashion, industrial and general
practice photography. Photographers in advertising, editorial and
fashion are nearly always freelance, employed for a particular
campaign or job. Industrial photographers may be freelance or
employed by large organizations where they take photographs
for brochures, catalogues, instruction manuals and in-house
magazines. General practice photographers are mainly involved
in portraiture and take wedding photographs.

Photojournalism and Press Photographer

Press photographers work for newspapers, magazines, periodicals and technical journals. All these media, particularly the last
three, employ freelance as well as in-house staff. Photojournalists
are photographers who are able to tell a story with pictures. They
are almost always freelance and the main market for their work is
Sunday colour supplements.

Institutional and Specialist Photography

Scientific photographers are used to provide information essential for research in a scientific or engineering field. This work may include aerial photography as well as the use of techniques such as holography, photomicrography and macrophotography. The main employers are the Civil Service, private industries and universities. The main uses for photography in hospitals are to satisfy clinical, research, publication and teaching requirements. Clinical photography in particular demands the use of specialist techniques: photomicroscopy, macrophotography, endoscopic photography and the use of infra-red and ultraviolet light sources.

Institutions that require photographers include museums, trade associations, national parks departments, charities, advisory councils, education authorities, libraries, auction houses and national galleries.

Photographers are also employed to teach photography in colleges and schools run by manufacturers and major retailers. There are opportunities to teach part-time photographic courses in many schools and colleges.

There are also opportunities to be a photographer in the Army, Royal Navy and Royal Air Force, but no one can join the Army or Royal Navy solely to be a photographer. The RAF alone recruits directly into ground photography. In police forces, most photographers are civilian employees.

Qualifications and Training

Formal educational qualifications are not always required but, for a place on a course, four to five GCSEs or equivalent are usually necessary. (*See* Medical Illustrator for the requirements for medical photography.) To be a trainee press photographer, five GCSEs at grades A, B or C are necessary, or four GCSEs and one A level, or two GCSEs and two A levels. English language is necessary. There are a number of HND and degree courses available and for entry to these five GCSEs plus two A levels or equivalent are necessary. Some establishments will accept individuals with a good portfolio of work.

The Royal Navy requires a good general education to GCSE level with particular attention to maths and English. In the police force requirements vary; some ask for City and Guilds qualifications and some for three GCSEs, including English, maths and a science.

Training is often on the job in photography, in a junior position; for example, a messenger or general assistant in an advertising studio or as a trainee assistant photographer in the police force. NVQs in Photography at levels 3 and 4 are available.

Personal Qualities

Photographers generally require a blend of artistic and technical skills, the ability to deal with people and to put them at their ease, and good eyesight and colour vision. Medical and police photographers must have the ability to remain 'outside' their work and not be too squeamish.

Starting Salary

Salaries vary enormously but the following are intended to give some indication: assistant photographers earn around £9,000; established photographers £20,000+. Medical photographers start around £13,500; social and wedding photographers are generally self-employed and earnings vary depending on number and type of clients.

i

Association of Photographers Ltd, 81 Leonard Street, London
    EC2A 4QS; 020 7739 6669; www.aophoto.co.uk
British Institute of Professional Photography, Fox Talbot House,
    Amwell End, Ware, Hertfordshire SG12 9HN; 01920 464011;
    www.bipp.com; e-mail: bipp@compuserve.com
National Council for the Training of Journalists, Latton Bush
    Centre, Southern Way, Harlow, Essex CM18 7BL;
    01279 430009; www.nctj.org.uk; e-mail: info@nctj.com
Great Careers in Video, Film and Photography (Kogan Page)

PHOTOGRAPHIC WORK

There are a range of jobs associated with the production of photographs and images.

Wholesale Photofinishing Laboratories

These cater for the amateur photographic markets, handling thousands of films a day. Sophisticated state-of-the-art printing, processing, finishing, pricing and hands-free dispatch equipment are used to ensure that service times are maintained. Most laboratories operate over a 24-hour cycle, staffed by skilled technicians and operators

Professional Laboratories/Imaging Centres

Professional laboratories/imaging centres can be divided into two major segments: social and commercial. The social laboratories cover printing (hand and machine), processing (paper and film), colour negative/colour transparency, black and white photography and mostly deal with wedding photographs and portraits. Digital imaging techniques have had a significant effect on the work of commercial laboratories and use of imaging software is now common.

Manufacturing, Retailing and Service Trades

Large quantities of film, photographic and non-photographic papers and chemicals are manufactured in the UK. Opportunities exist for technicians to research and develop new products; this sector of the industry also employs engineers and sales personnel.

Qualifications and Training

The industry has its own training organization, the Photography and Photographic Processing National Training Organization (PPPNTO). NVQs and apprenticeship schemes are well established for all aspects of the photographic, digital and allied services. There is an increasing requirement for personnel with degrees in the sciences.

Personal Qualities

Good colour vision is essential, especially for personnel engaged in colour coordination and equipment integration. Photo scientists must have an interest in discovering environmental improvements, technological advancements, product improvements and increased efficiency. Staff are handling other people's memories, which are often unique and carry commercial or sentimental value. All personnel must have a caring and responsible attitude to their work.

Starting Salary

Laboratory technicians start on £7,000–£10,000. Those with experience can earn £25,000+.

i

Imaging National Training Organization, Ambassador House, Brigstock Road, Thornton Heath, Surrey CR7 7JG; 020 8665 1110; www.photoimagingnto.org

Professional Photographic Laboratories Association (PPLA), 29 Hempfield Road, Littleport Ely, Cambridgeshire CB6 1NW; 01353 863255; fax: 01353 863522; www.pmai.org/sections/ ppla.htm

PHYSICIST

Physics deals with the interrelation of matter and energy. Physicists are needed wherever the physical properties of materials have to be studied. They are employed in the fields of electronics, nuclear power, computing, aerospace, optics, telecommunications, engineering and instrument manufacture. In addition, hospitals employ medical physicists whose work includes support for medical use of radiation and design and implementation of new equipment for diagnosis and treatment of disease. Some physicists lecture in universities or teach in schools. Physics technicians assist fully qualified physicists.

About one-third of all physicists work in public service industries; one-third in private industry and one-third in secondary and higher education. Some physicists work on problems at the frontiers of knowledge; others tackle the problems which arise in the application of physical ideas to industrial and engineering problems. Physics graduates also find themselves employed in occupations such as medicine, computing and even finance.

Qualifications and Training

To continue with science at A level, students must choose either a double award in science (England, Wales and Northern Ireland), which combines the three subjects and leads to two science GCSE qualifications or a combination of the individual sciences (biology, chemistry, physics) at GCSE, or a combination of the individual sciences (biology, chemistry, physics), at GCSE or equivalent.

Entry to most degree courses requires 2–3 A levels (or a suitable combination of A and AS-levels) or equivalent, including maths and physics. Since there is a shortage of applicants, grade requirements in some universities are not high but all departments will consider good grades in maths to be equally important with good grades in physics. A National Diploma with several merits and distinctions may be considered if it has suitable maths and physics content.

Junior technicians need a good education to GCSE level with particular attention to maths, a science and a subject showing the use of English in order to take an Edexcel (BTEC)/SQA national certificate. There are special certificate courses for medical junior physics technicians. For senior technicians an Edexcel (BTEC)/SQA HND award is available; the requirements are an A level in physics and GCSE maths, chemistry and English. An Edexcel (BTEC)/SQA NC or ND award is acceptable in place of A/H levels. Training for technicians is generally on the job, such as modern apprenticeships, with time off to attend courses.

Personal Qualities

Those working in physics must be able to recognize a problem and plan an experiment or set of experiments to solve it. They should be imaginative, persevering, have good powers of concentration and adopt a sound, logical approach. Technicians should have the practical skills necessary to carry out experiments, be responsible, accurate and caring in their attitude to work.

Starting Salary

Trainee technicians start between £8,000 and £10,000; the majority of senior technicians earn £12,000 to £18,000. Salaries for new graduates are variable, averaging £18,000. Civil Service researchers and teachers start on a salary of around £17,000.

i

The Institute of Physics, 76 Portland Place, London W1B 1NT; 020 7470 4800; www.iop.org; e-mail: physics@iop.org

Institute of Physics and Engineering in Medicine, Fairmount House, 230 Tadcaster Road, York YO24 1ES; 01904 610821; fax: 01904 612279; www.ipem.org.uk

'Physics – Just the Job; A Day in the Life; Smart Moves and Smart Facts', Institute of Physics

PHYSIOTHERAPIST

A Chartered Physiotherapist treats patients suffering from a wide variety of diseases, conditions or injuries by physical means. They help people who have had strokes to regain the use of lost functions, treat sports injuries and people with arthritis and help children with cerebral palsy to learn to walk. The techniques used include massage and manipulation, exercise, electrotherapy and hydrotherapy. Most physiotherapists work in the Health Service but there are many opportunities now for employment in industry, sports clinics, schools and private practice.

Qualifications and Training

A minimum of five GCSEs and three A levels or equivalent are normally required for a place on a three- or four-year course leading to a degree; entry to these courses is very competitive. Subjects at GCSE should ideally include English and two sciences and A levels should include a biological science.

Personal Qualities

Physiotherapists must be caring, patient, reasonably fit, good communicators and have the ability to inspire confidence in their patients.

Starting Salary

Newly qualified staff start around £15,500; senior staff can earn £30,000+.

The Chartered Society of Physiotherapy, 14 Bedford Row, London WC1R 4ED; career advice line: 020 7306 6600; www. csphysio.org.uk

NHS Careers, PO Box 376, Bristol BS99 3EY; Careers helpline 0845
   6060 655; www.nhscareers.nhs.uk/home.html
Careers in Nursing and Related Professions (Kogan Page)

PIANO TUNER

Piano tuners or technicians are able both to tune a piano evenly
throughout the scale and to discover and put right any fault. They
work with a kit of specialized tools, and are employed in piano
factories and by piano dealers. Some also work for themselves.

Qualifications and Training

Courses are available at three institutions: London Guildhall
University, Newark and Sherwood College and The Royal
National College for the Blind, Hereford. Entry requirements are
usually four GCSEs at grade C or above. The Piano Tuners'
Association will accept a candidate for membership after five
years from the start of training – at least two years' training and at
least two years' working as a piano tuner.

Personal Qualities

Musical ability, while not essential, is an advantage. Patience and
deftness are required, together with an aptitude to be able to use
woodworking, home-improvement and DIY tools. As tuners are
mostly self-employed, the ability to work alone, competence in
managing a small business and self-motivation are also important.

Starting Salary

Salaries vary greatly: the average is £250–£300 a week when
trained but lower without experience. Established, self-employed
piano tuners may earn up to £800 a week.

i

Pianoforte Tuners' Association, c/o 10 Reculver Road, Herne
   Bay, Kent CT6 6LD; 01227 368808;
     www.pianotuner.org.uk; e-mail: members@pianotuner.org.uk

PILOT

see *Civil Aviation*

PLASTERER

Plasterers are among the most skilled of the building craftsmen. They not only wet-plaster large wall areas but also may construct plaster fittings in a workshop and then fix them into place on a building site. Intricate details such as ceiling mouldings are also made wet by the plasterer or constructed in a workshop from fibrous plaster. Plasterers may also lay cement floors and carry out external finishes on houses. There are opportunities for work with building contractors and local authorities, and also for being self-employed.

Qualifications and Training

No formal educational requirements are necessary. Training is on the job as plasterer's mate, and by a three-year apprenticeship during which time it is possible to work towards NVQs.

Personal Qualities

Plasterers must be physically strong and have the ability to work very quickly. Defects in a wall or ceiling surface are often very obvious so high standards and a responsible attitude to work are important.

Starting Salary

Newly qualified plasterers earn around £12,000; average salaries are £16,000.

i

Construction Industry Training Board, Bircham Newton, King's Lynn, Norfolk PE31 6RH; 01485 577577; www.citb.org.uk

PLUMBER

Plumbers do work associated with the provision of water supply pipe work, including that used for fire fighting; all forms of space heating, gas installation, sanitary appliances, discharge pipe work and drainage. They also work on roofs fitting flashings and are responsible for putting up rainwater pipes and gutters. Plumbers may work on building sites and be employed by building contractors, property companies or local authorities. Many are self-employed, working mainly in private houses.

Qualifications and Training
No formal educational requirements are necessary. Training is on the job, and by a four-year apprenticeship during which time it is possible to work towards NVQs levels 2 and 3. NVQs levels 4 and 5 will be available in the future.

Personal Qualities
Plumbers must be agile, deft and able to work neatly, carefully and accurately. They must also be prepared to work outside and have a head for heights.

Starting Salary
£75 a week as a first-year apprentice; £248 week as a fourth-year apprentice. Average earnings for a qualified plumber are £17,500. Those who are self-employed often earn more.

i

Institute of Plumbing, 64 Station Lane, Hornchurch, Essex RM12 6NB; 01708 472791; www.plumbers.org.uk

British Plumbing Employers Council (Training) Ltd; England and Wales: 14/15 Ensign House, Ensign Business Centre, Westwood Way, Coventry CV4 8JA; 02476 470626; Scotland: 2 Walker Street, Edinburgh EH3 7LB; 0131 225 2255 www.bpec.org.uk

PODIATRIST

see *Chiropodist*

POLICE OFFICER

The purpose of the police is to uphold the law, fairly and firmly, to prevent crime, to pursue and bring to justice those who break the law, and to be seen to do all this with integrity, common sense and sound judgement. There are many different specialities within the police service, although everyone joins as a constable. These include the Criminal Investigation Department (CID); traffic police; dog handlers; mounted police; river police; and crime prevention officers.

There are 43 forces in England and Wales and 8 in Scotland plus three separate police forces – the British Transport Police, the Ministry of Defence Police, and the UK Atomic Energy Authority Constabulary.

Qualifications and Training

There are no minimum formal educational requirements, although applicants should have achieved a good all-round standard of education. All candidates sit a series of entrance tests which measure the ability to spell words and construct sentences correctly, the ability to check information quickly and correctly, the ability to solve numerical problems accurately, the ability to reason logically when given facts about events and the ability to observe scenes carefully and recall details accurately. All applicants undergo fitness tests which measure blood pressure, lung capacity, percentage body fat, suppleness, strength and stamina.

Normal entry is from 18 and a half. All recruits serve a two-year probation period as constables with training at a national police training centre. Each force recruits individually and entry requirements may vary. There is an Accelerated Promotion Scheme (APSG) for graduates.

Starting Salary

Constables begin on just under £18,000; this increases to around £20,000 on completion of initial training and to just over £21,000 after two years. There are extra allowances for those in Inner and Outer London forces.

i

England and Wales: Police Recruiting Department, Room
514 (graduate entry: Room 556), Home Office, Queen Anne's
Gate, London SW1H 9AT; 0845 6083 000;
www. policecouldyou.co.uk (for careers information and
interactive exercises); www.police.uk (for links to all police
forces and recruitment campaigns)

Scottish Executive Justice Department, Saughton House,
Broomhouse Drive, Edinburgh EH11 3XD;
www. scottish. police.uk;
www.tulliallan.police.uk (for graduate entry)

UKAEA Constabulary, Building E6, Culham, Abingdon,
Oxfordshire OX14 3DB; 01235 463315; fax: 01235 464204;
www.ukaea.org.uk

British Transport Police Recruitment; PO Box 260, 15 Tavistock
Place, London WC1H 9SJ; 020 7830 8871 (regular officers),
0800 389 9426 (Special Constables); www.btp.police.uk

Ministry of Defence Police; www.mod.uk

Careers in the Police Service (Kogan Page)

POLITICS

Politics is a career for relatively few; there are 659 Members of
Parliament, 129 Members of the Scottish Parliament, 60 Members
of the National Assembly for Wales and 87 British Members of the
European Parliament. MPs work long and late hours in parliament and generally spend at least one day a week in their
constituency. They may specialize in a particular subject, such as
health or education. Ministerial responsibilities impose extra
duties of national importance. All MPs must have another career
to support them while they are seeking election and to fall back on
if they lose their seats.

Constituency agents work for local party branches, organizing
publicity and acting as a link between the MP and the party. MPs
employ their own researchers and constituency staff. There are also
opportunities for administrative and office staff in the central party
offices. These central office staff, as well as carrying out general
office duties, are responsible for writing speech material for party
spokesmen and providing information to the national press.

Qualifications and Training

No formal educational requirements are necessary for political jobs, although most politicians have a good academic background. MPs are adopted by a constituency party because they are already well known to the party through their active voluntary work or, sometimes, because they have made a name for themselves in some other field.

Agents need an excellent knowledge of electoral law and party organization, for which on-the-job training is available. A background in Public Relations is increasingly regarded as useful because of the need to build good working relationships with the media. Head office staff are usually recruited from constituency agents and assistants.

Personal Qualities

It is necessary in politics to be hard working, persevering, resilient and, for agents and administrative staff, to have excellent organizational skills. MPs should also have a certain personal charisma and be able to put their ideas across clearly and persuasively.

Starting Salary

MPs' salaries are around £50,000; Cabinet Ministers are entitled to £118,000 and the Prime Minister is entitled to £163,000 but the highest paid is the Lord Chancellor at £172,279. All politicians receive extra allowances to cover other expenditure.

i

Local constituency parties

Conservative Central Office, 32 Smith Square, London SW1P
    3HH; 020 7222 9000; www.conservatives.com

The Labour Party, Millbank Tower, Millbank, London
    SW1P 4GT; 08705 900200; www.labour.org.uk

Liberal Democrats, 4 Cowley Street, London SW1P 3NB;
    020 7222 7999; www.libdems.org.uk

A list of all other UK political parties is available from
    http://bubl.ac.uk/uk/parties.htm

POST OFFICE

Consignia is the new name for the Post Office. In the UK Consignia has three major consumer brands: Royal Mail which delivers post, Parcelforce Worldwide providing a parcel services and the Post Office which has 18,000 branches. Opportunities for school leavers include administration, secretarial, postman/woman, counter clerk and retail assistant. For graduates there may be opportunities in commercial management, information technology, finance, logistics, marketing, human resources and e-business.

Qualifications and training

No formal educational qualifications are necessary for the school-leaver jobs, but they will be required to take an aptitude test. Training is provided for postmen/women, counter clerks and retail assistants and NVQs are available.

Graduate entrants should have studied a relevant degree. Useful subjects include business studies, information technology, maths, geography, transport and planning or engineering.

Personal qualities

All public-facing employees need to be good communicators, patient and prepared to help. Counter clerks and retail assistants should be numerate and have good interpersonal skills. Graduates should be numerate and possess good interpersonal and organizational skills.

Starting salary

School leavers from £150.32 a week, graduates from £18,500, plus London and other regional allowances.

i

School leavers should apply to the Human Resources manager at
the local Royal Mail, Parcelforce Worldwide or Post Office
(address and telephone number in local telephone directory)
Graduates should apply to Consignia Graduate Recruitment
Training and Development Centre, Coton House, Rugby
CV23 0BR; www.consignia.com;
e-mail: grad.recruitment@consignia.com

POTTER

Employees in the pottery industry make ordinary domestic china, earthenware, vases and ornaments, fine bone china, ceramic tiles, sanitary ware, industrial and electrical porcelain and huge insulators used in distributing electricity. Although the industry is mechanized, there is still a predominant demand for skilled workers: hand painters, fettlers and spongers, casting, lithographing, binding and lining, to name a few. Some potters work individually, hand throwing or casting their own pieces and selling them personally or through a shop or gallery.

Qualifications and Training
No formal educational requirements are needed for the industry and training is mainly on the job. Craftsmen potters sometimes become apprenticed to master potters but more commonly they take foundation courses followed by vocational or degree courses at an art school.

Personal Qualities
Potters need a good eye for shape and design, a steady hand and a delicate touch. Potters working for themselves must also be inventive and have business skills and marketing ability.

Starting Salary
Industry employees start at £80+ a week. Craftsmen set their own rates and, if they are selling their work through a gallery, must pay the owner a percentage.

i

Crafts Council, 44a Pentonville Road, London N1 9BY; 020 7278 7700 (send sae); www.craftscouncil.org.uk

The Craft Potters' Association, 25 Foubert's, London W1F 7QF

PRE-SCHOOL WORKERS

Those working in the early years sector are committed to providing high quality care and education for children. These include pre-school workers, who work with children every day and pre-school managers and leaders who have overall responsibility for the quality of their work. There are many different opportunities because different types of provision have developed to meet the varying needs of families. There include daycare nurseries where children attend all day, every week, and pre-schools and play-groups which offer morning and/or afternoon sessional care. Work in pre-schools is often part time. However, new services are developing, for example after-school care, so there may be opportunities for work at other times and with older children. The majority of groups are registered charities, managed by parents and volunteers from the local community. Groups may also be funded by local authorities or private concerns.

Qualifications and Training

Vocational training is provided by organizations like the Pre-School Learning Alliance through classroom-based and distance-learning courses awarded by The Council for Awards in Children's Care and Education (CACHE). A Certificate at level 2 and Diploma at level 3 in Pre-School Practice are available. In Scotland, a self-study pack called 'Basic Training in Playwork' provides the basic knowledge and skills needed to work with young children in a play setting.

Personal Qualities

Pre-school workers should have a genuine interest in how children learn and develop in order to develop a coherent curriculum for the children. They also need to have the ability to work well in a team, liasing with parents, other adults and other professionals. Pre-school leaders need to have the skills necessary to lead a team.

Starting Salary

Salaries vary for pre-school workers from one area of the country to another.

Council for Awards in Children's Care and Education (CACHE), 8 Chequer Street, St Albans, Hertfordshire AL1 3XZ; 01727 847636; www.cache.org.uk

Pre-School Learning Alliance, 69 Kings Cross Road, London
   WC1X 9LL; 020 7833 0991; fax: 020 7837 4942;
   www.pre-school.org.uk; e-mail: pla@pre-school.org.uk
Wales PPA, Ladywell House, Newtown, Powys Y16 1JB; 01686
   624573; www.walesppa.co.uk; e-mail: info@walesppa.org
Northern Ireland PPA, Information Centre, 6C Flower Way,
   Apollo Road, Belfast BT12 6TA; 02890 662825
Scottish Pre-School Play Association (SPPA), 14 Elliot Place,
   Glasgow G3 8EP; 0141 221 4148; fax: 0141 221 6043

PRINTING

The purpose of printing is communication, whether the printed
matter be books, magazines, newspapers, security documents or
bank cards. Printers are also involved in other products, from
wallpaper and floor coverings to advertising slogans on milk
cartons. The printing industry covers a wide range of jobs in both
factories and offices. Printing is the sixth largest UK industry,
employing 170,000 people in 12,000 companies.

Graphic Design
This is the most artistic job in the printing industry. Designers
liaise with clients, understand their needs and transform ideas
into high quality printed products. A mastery of computers,
complete understanding of processes, techniques, typography
and colour is required. Applicants normally enter the industry
after a national certificate diploma or higher level course in
graphic design.

Pre-Press Department
Most setting is via floppy disk or CD. The pre-press operator uses
a computer keyboard and mouse to set type and arrange the page,
which is output to film or direct to the printing plate. An error in
the pre-press department could result in the scrapping of thousands of books or products.

Proofreader
Proofreaders check customers' proofs for spelling mistakes and
incorrect typefaces before returning them. When setting to disk,
proofreading is done automatically.

Camera /Scanner Operator

The reproduction of colour photographs is largely done by electronic scanners, requiring technical ability rather than the craft skills of the past.

Planner/Platemaker

If the process is not completed electronically, make-up planning operators take the film and place the type and illustrations in the right place on the correct pages.

Printing Department

This is where ink is applied to paper or other materials, by a variety of large and small printing machines. Such machines are complex and often computer controlled. They are managed by one or more craftsmen who control the physics and chemistry of the press to ensure that each copy produced is perfect.

Finishing Department

Printed products are usually produced in large flat sheets or reels. To convert and finish sheets or reels into books, brochures or magazines, the material must be folded, stitched, sewn and trimmed. A range of specialized machinery is used to produce the finished product at high speed. Great care is needed at this stage to avoid faults, which could result in scrapping the product and financial loss to the company.

Office Jobs

Account executives look after individual printing jobs; they write instructions for each department and check the product's arrival into and departure from each section. Estimators work out how much a job will cost. Cost clerks go through the costs item by item and discover where and why the money was spent. Sales staff find customers.

In large companies production controllers manage a team of estimators and production control staff. They interpret sales orders, estimates costs, plan materials purchase, arrange time on appropriate machines, sets priorities and advise customers on the progress of their order.

Qualifications and Training

Academic qualifications are not mandatory for craft workers but the following subjects studied to GCSE level are preferred: English, maths, computer studies and science. Training is to NVQ levels 2 and 3, with time off to attend courses.

Office staff have qualifications ranging from GCSEs to a degree. GCSEs are preferred for junior clerks and there are opportunities to gain further qualifications through Edexcel (BTEC)/SQA or City and Guilds awards. To take the higher diploma in printing on a two- or three-year basis, four GCSEs to include English, maths and a science plus one A level are necessary, or an Edexcel (BTEC)/SQA or NC/ND in printing. There are in addition three print-related degree courses, for which two A levels are necessary.

NVQs at levels 2 and 3 are available in Print Production and Print Administration. Modern Apprenticeships are available for production and office trainees.

Personal Qualities

A responsible attitude and a pride in what is being produced are necessary. Production workers need good colour vision and manual dexterity. Applicants must provide evidence of careful work and attention to detail. They must possess dexterity and normal colour vision. The work requires images to be manually or computer manipulated to a high degree of accuracy. Applicants for jobs in the Finishing Department need physical strength, an affinity with machinery, concentration and the ability to work as a team.

Starting Salary

Salaries vary but are generally above average.

British Printing Industries Federation (BPIF), Farringdon Point, 29–35 Farringdon Road, London EC1M 3JF; 020 7915 8300; www.bpif.org.uk

Institute of Printing, The Mews, Hill House, Clanricarde Road, Tunbridge Wells, Kent TN1 1PJ; 01892 538118; www.globalprint.com/uk/iop

Scottish Print Employers Federation, 48 Palmerston Place,
    Edinburgh EH12 5DE; 0131 220 4353; www.spef.org.uk
Print and Graphic Communication NTO, Alliance House, 926
    Alum Rock Road, Ward End, Birmingham B8 2NS; 0121 789
    5100; www.printnto.org; e-mail: info@printnto.org

PRISON OFFICER

Prison officers are employed in prisons, detention centres, young-offender institutions and remand centres. The work involves supervising prisoners inside the place of detention, escorting them to courts and other prisons and, if relevant, teaching a skill or trade. Officers also deliver programmes which help prisoners address their offending behaviour. Some specialist prison officers are employed as hospital officers, dog handlers, security experts and caterers.

Qualifications and Training

Five GCSEs, including maths and English, are required and applicants must pass an aptitude test and an interview. Training is a mixture of time spent at a local prison and residential courses at an officers' training school. In Scotland, five standard grades (1, 2 or 3) or equivalent (including maths and English) or three years' experience managing people. A good level of physical fitness is required. NVQs in Custodial Care are available at levels 2 and 3. There is special training for caterers, dog handlers, physical education instructors and medical staff. An accelerated promotions scheme exists for graduate entrants.

Personal Qualities

Officers should be positive thinkers with humanity and common sense; they must be good listeners, assertive, have excellent communication skills and the ability to mix with a wide range of people.

Starting Salary

In England and Wales starting pay is around £16,000, rising to £22,000+ with extra allowances for officers in London. In Scotland the starting salary is £12,500. Having completed a successful probationary period and gained the appropriate SVQ, officers receive an increase of £1,000. The current maximum is £18,150 but this is under review.

┌───┐
│ i │
└───┘

Custodial Care NTO, Churchill House, 12 Mosley Street, Newcastle Upon Tyne NE1 1DE; 0191 230 8072; www.ccnto.com; e-mail: admin@ccnto.com

Prison Service HQ, Home Office, Cleland House, Page Street, London SW1P 4LN; 020 7217 3000; www.hmprisonservice. gov.uk

Scottish Prison Service, Carlton House, 5 Redheughs Rigg, Edinburgh EH12 9HW; 0131 556 8400; www.sps.gov.uk; e-mail: gaolinfo@sps.gov.uk

PROBATION OFFICER

(see also *Social Work and Social Care*)

The aims of the National Probation Service for England and Wales (NPS) are: protecting the public; reducing re-offending; the proper punishment of offenders in the community; ensuring offenders are aware of the effects of crime on the victims of crime and the public; and the rehabilitation of offenders.

All probation work with offenders combines continuous assessment and management of risk with the provision of expert supervision programmes designed to reduce re-offending. Approximately 70 per cent of offenders supervised will be on community supervision orders and 30 per cent in prison. Probation staff are regularly seconded to work in youth offending teams, prisons and with a range of crime prevention agencies.

In Scotland, the functions of the Probation Officer are performed by social work departments in local authorities.

Entry Requirements

Professional training in England and Wales is through the Diploma in Probation Studies which is managed by the 42 probation services working with nine regional consortia. This is an integrated programme of education and training that combines work- and university-based learning through a Community Justice NVQ level 4 award and an undergraduate degree. Trainee probation officers are appointed to probation areas following a rigorous recruitment and selection process and are paid a training salary. Programmes leading to the Diploma in Probation Studies are normally completed within 24 months. The minimum age for appointment as a probation officer is 22, so training cannot be undertaken by those under 20. Entry requirements for those under 21 are two passes at A level and three at GCSE or three at A level and one at GCSE; candidates over 21 but under 25 years need five passes at GCSE and candidates over 25 years may be accepted without formal qualifications but have to demonstrate academic potential. Experience of related work, though not necessarily with offenders, is essential and can be gained through volunteering.

Entry in Scotland is through a course of professional training leading to a Diploma in Social Work (DipSW); for details *see* Social Work and Social Care.

Personal Qualities

Probation officers need to be able to develop imaginative, relevant strategies to help offenders lead law-abiding lives. They need to be good listeners and have an understanding of different ethnic and cultural backgrounds. They also need to be assertive, able to exercise and maintain authority and cope with aggression.

Starting Salary

Trainee probation officers earn between £12,000 and £13,000; once qualified, the scale is £17,000–£23,000, with extra allowances for those in London.

i

C6 Division, Home Office, Room 442, 50 Queen Anne's Gate,
   London SW1H 9AT; 020 7273 3000;
      www.homeoffice. gov.uk / recruitment; 'Careers in the
      National Probation Service' can be downloaded from the site
Community Justice NTO, 344–354 Grays Inn Road, London
   WC1X 8BP; 020 7278 1366; www.cjnto.org.uk
Careers in Social Work (Kogan Page)

PSYCHOLOGIST

Psychologists study people: how they think, act, react and inter-act. They are concerned with all aspects of behaviour and the thoughts, feelings and motivation underlying such behaviour. The profession has many different specialities, from clinical psychology, concerned with reducing psychological distress and promoting psychological well-being, to market research where psychologists may research why and how consumers prefer one product to another. Psychologists work in the NHS, private hospitals, industry, for government and local authorities, in schools and in private practice.

The British Psychological Society maintains the Register of Chartered Psychologists, which has stringent entry require-ments. Anyone who wishes to become a Chartered Psychologist should ensure that their degree is accredited by the society as conferring the Graduate Basis for Registration (GBR). This is required for all BPS-accredited postgraduate training courses in applied psychology.

Clinical Psychology

Clinical psychologists use their knowledge of psychology when working with people with health problems or severe learning difficulties. They work alongside professionals such as doctors, nurses, social workers and counselling psychologists within NHS Trusts, hospitals, clinics, children's homes, and other community or related settings. They also work in private practice or research and academic institutions.

Qualifications and Training

Applicants must have an accredited psychology degree and some work or research experience, which should have clinical rele-vance. To register as a Chartered Clinical Psychologist candidates must obtain GBR and complete an accredited postgraduate train-ing course in clinical psychology.

Starting Salary

For newly graduated psychologists, approximately £16,500. For experienced psychologists with management responsibilities, salaries range from £27,500 to £32,000. Senior psychologists managing departments or specialist sections can earn from £36,000 to £60,000.

Counselling Psychologists

Counselling psychologists work with individuals, couples, families and groups such as people with disabilities or those who are discriminated against. They work to improve their client's sense of well-being, reduce stress and to help them resolve crises. They help people understand their problems and develop coping strategies and solutions. Counselling psychologists work in GPs' surgeries, NHS Trusts and hospitals, business institutions or specialist agencies.

Qualifications and Training

A degree in psychology and postgraduate professional training in counselling psychology is necessary for Chartered Counselling Psychologist status.

Starting Salary

This is based upon nationally agreed scales and should range between £15,000 and £60,000, depending on experience and level of responsibility.

Educational Psychologists

Educational psychologists work primarily in schools and colleges with teachers and lecturers, and with parents. They can work directly with a child or young person (up to the age of 19) or indirectly via parents and teachers. Educational psychologists are often involved in policy planning within the education departments of local authorities.

Qualifications and Training

An appropriate qualification in psychology, a teacher training qualification, teaching experience and a postgraduate qualification are all necessary to become registered as a Chartered Educational Psychologist in England, Wales and Northern Ireland. Teachers can retrain by undertaking an accredited qualification in psychology, postgraduate training and supervised experience. In Scotland, there is no requirement to become a fully qualified teacher.

Starting Salary

Educational psychologists in Britain are usually employed by LEAs as part of the psychological service. In Northern Ireland they are appointed by the Education and Library Boards. Main grade educational psychologists earn between £22,000 and £33,000. Senior principal educational psychologists earn £35,000 to £45,000.

Occupational Psychologists

Occupational psychologists focus on the performance of people at work and in training, how organizations function and how individuals and groups behave in the work environment. The services of occupational psychologists are increasingly in demand and this area of psychology is broader in scope and less formalized than others. The work of an occupational psychologist can include work with individuals, organizational consultancy, assessment and training, vocational guidance and counselling, ergonomics and health and safety.

Qualifications and Training

To register as a Chartered Occupational Psychologist it is necessary to obtain GBR, plus an accredited postgraduate course in occupational psychology, and to complete two to three years' supervised practice.

Starting Salary

Salaries vary enormously. The range for those in government departments is as follows: graduates £12,500–£14,000, senior psychologist £19,000–£23,000. Private sector and industry salaries can vary from £15,000 to £100,000, depending on experience and expertise.

Teaching and Research

There are no formal qualifications that are a preparation for teaching at university, although most universities encourage newly appointed staff to take a postgraduate certificate in higher education. All university lecturers are expected to be involved in developing their subject via research projects. For example, an educational psychologist may undertake research on how to teach concepts to blind children and an occupational psychologist may research the relationship of stress to work conditions.

Qualifications and Training
A degree in psychology is acceptable for teaching in further education but most individuals involved in teaching and research in higher education will have a PhD or have held a research post. A teaching qualification such as the Postgraduate Certificate in Education (PGCE) is also increasingly required.

Starting Salary
Salaries at further and higher education institutions range from £17,000 to £37,000 for lecturers, to £27,000 to £37,000 for senior lecturers and professors.

Health Psychology
This is an evolving area, which applies psychological methods to the study of behaviour relevant to health, illness and healthcare. Health psychologists may study why and when people seek professional advice about their health, how patients adapt to illness and how they interact with healthcare professionals.

Starting Salary
As for clinical psychologists.

Qualifications and training
To register as a Chartered Health Psychologist, an accredited degree must be followed by a one-year accredited postgraduate course in health psychology, followed by a minimum of two years' appropriate practice as a health psychologist under the supervision of a Chartered Health Psychologist.

Forensic Psychology
Is one of the fastest-growing areas of employment for psychology graduates. Work can be found in academic institutions, Prison

Services, the National Health Service, Probation Services and Social Services. Forensic psychologists undertake their work in the criminal and civil justice field.

Qualifications and training

To register as a Chartered Forensic Psychologist an accredited degree must be followed by either successful completion of Stages 1 and 2 of the Society's Diploma in Forensic Psychology or successful completion of a Society-accredited training course in forensic psychology followed by successful completion of Stage 2 of the Society's Diploma in Forensic Psychology.

Personal Qualities

All psychologists should have a genuine interest in people, their behaviour and have an empathy for their problems. They also need to be excellent communicators and have the skills to work with people from different backgrounds and social groupings.

Starting Salary

As for clinical psychologists.

| i |

The British Psychological Society, St Andrews House, 48 Princess Road East, Leicester LE1 7DR; 0116 254 9568; www.bps.org.uk; (the Society publishes free information leaflets on its Web site); e-mail: enquiry@bps.org.uk

Association of Educational Psychologists, 26 The Avenue, Durham DH1 4ED; www.aep.org.uk; The Association produces a Careers Information booklet which can be obtained from the Association's head office (please send an A4 size stamped-addressed envelope), or download from their Web site

PSYCHOTHERAPIST

Psychotherapy is a generic term, within which there are many specialist disciplines. People may practice as psychoanalytic psychotherapists, as cognitive or behavioural psychotherapists, or as counsellors with varying degrees of training and experience; however, there are plans to introduce greater regulation.

Psychotherapists may work with individuals of any age, couples and families, or groups resolving problems such as over-shyness, over-aggression, sleeping disorders, separation difficulties, behavioural problems, eating difficulties, self-harm and depression. They work in hospitals, in- and outpatient clinics, child and family consultation centres, GPs' surgeries, special schools for disturbed children and in private practice.

Qualifications and Training
Psychotherapists come from varying professional backgrounds, but will usually have a degree in medicine, psychology, social sciences or a qualification in one of the core professions of the health service plus appropriate experience of working with people with mental health problems. Training then takes a further four years and involves academic study, personal analysis, workshops and supervised therapeutic treatment. There are several different training organizations. Most courses lead to National registration with either the British Confederation of Psychotherapists (BCP) or the UK Council for Psychotherapy.

Personal Qualities
Psychotherapists must have a genuine interest in the problems of children and adults, and a desire to help. They must themselves be emotionally well balanced.

Starting Salary
Salaries vary depending on the experience and professional background of the individual therapist.

The Association of Child Psychotherapists, 120 West Heath Road, London NW3 4S8; 020 7458 1609

British Association of Psychotherapists, 37 Mapesbury Road, London NW2 4 HJ; 020 8452 9823; www.bap-psychotherapy.org; e-mail: mail@bap-psychotherapy.org

British Confederation of Psychotherapists, 37a Mapesbury Road, London NW2 4HJ; 020 8830 5173; www.bcp.org.uk

UK Council for Psychotherapy; 167–169 Great Portland Street, London W1N 5FB; 020 7436 3002; www.psychotherapy.org.uk

PUBLICAN

The licensee of a pub may be a manager who is paid a salary, a lessee or tenant who rents the property from a brewer, a pub company or a free trader who owns the premises. As well as the ever-popular traditional town and country pubs there is now a wide variety of pubs ranging from theme pubs, café bars and steak bars to pubs with gourmet restaurants and full entertainment facilities. Nearly all pubs serve food and an increasing number also offer accommodation.

Qualifications and Training

To hold a licence individuals generally need a National Licensee's Certificate – an entry-level qualification available from the British Institute of Innkeeping (BII), who also offer a number of other relevant qualifications. NVQs, diploma and degrees are available in Hotel, Catering and Licensed Retail Management. Brewery companies put their managers through a comprehensive training programme. Licensees could well be running businesses grossing more than half a million pounds a year. They must know how to market their services and devise new ideas to attract customers. They must also have a good knowledge of subjects such as bookkeeping, licensing laws, hygiene, staff motivation, customer care and cellar management.

Personal Qualities

Publicans should be ambitious and able to take responsibility. They should enjoy working with people, have a customer-care focus and good interpersonal skills.

Starting Salary

Salaries range form £18,500+ with participation in bonus schemes, to £35,500+. Accommodation, lighting and heating are normally provided.

British Beer and Pub Association, Market Towers, 1 Nine Elms Lane, London SW8 5NQ; 020 7627 9191; www.beerandpub.com; e-mail: mailbox@beerandpub.com

British Institute of Innkeeping, Wessex House, 80 Park Street,
  Camberley, Surrey GU15 3PT; 01276 684449; www.bii.org;
  e-mail: info@bii.org; www.barzone.co.uk (dedicated Web site
  for careers in licensed retailing)
Working in Hospitality (Kogan Page)
The Publican's Handbook (Kogan Page)

PUBLIC RELATIONS OFFICER

The chief aim of the public relations officer/executive is to ensure
that the correct information about their employer or client is made
known to the right people in order to establish and maintain
goodwill and mutual understanding between an organization
and its public. This is done by a variety of means, including media
relations, internal and external communication, company literature, exhibitions and events. Corporate PR work is concerned
with effectively putting across an organization's policy and activities to a variety of people, including government departments,
employees, shareholders and other stakeholders. Consumer PR is
concerned with giving information about a product; it is closely
allied with marketing and advertising. Other areas of PR include
community relations, sponsorship and financial PR. PR executives are employed by organizations, PR consultancies or work as
freelance consultants.

Qualifications and Training

Entrants to the profession are increasingly graduates. The
Institute of Public Relations (IPR) has approved 15 courses at
various levels as qualifications for associate membership. Entry
requirements for degree courses vary according to the institution,
but most require five GCSEs and A levels or equivalents. The IPR
runs its own postgraduate foundation and diploma courses, available in 8 centres across Britain.

Personal Qualities

Public relations officers must understand people and what moti-
vates them and have the ability to get on well with people from
different backgrounds. They must be imaginative, creative, reli-

able and have good managerial skills. Excellent written and oral communication skills are essential.

Starting Salary

Trainees in PR earn around £15,000. Salaries vary across the business sectors but the average for a PR account executive is £19,000.

The Institute of Public Relations, The Old Trading House, 15 Northburgh Street, London EC1V 0PR; 020 7253 5151; www.ipr.org.uk; e-mail: info@ipr.org.uk

The Public Relations Consultants Association (PRCA), Willow House, Willow Place, London SW1P 1JH; 020 7233 6026; fax: 020 7828 4797; www.prca.org.uk

Careers in Marketing, Advertising and Public Relations (Kogan Page)

PUBLISHING

(see also *Journalism*)

The publishing industry in the UK is estimated to employ over 184,000 people across the sectors of book, journal, newspaper, magazine, directory, database, and interactive publishing. There is no formal route into publishing, although an increasingly high percentage of new entrants are graduates. Those without publishing experience will generally be expected to start at the bottom and work their way up. Common entry posts are in editorial, production, and marketing/sales departments. In general, the editorial function is concerned with the development of content and evaluating the target audience of a publication. Those in senior editorial positions will ultimately be responsible for ensuring that the publication meets its financial objectives. The production department is responsible for delivering the end product in printed or electronic format, and the marketing and sales departments are responsible for promoting the end product to the customer.

Book publishing

There are over 100,000 books published each year. Aside from the general trade market, the industry can be broken down into the categories of children's publishing, scientific/technical/medical

(STM), academic, legal and educational. Book publishing is an ever-popular field and competition for entry-level posts is fierce. However, those willing to start as editorial, production, marketing or sales assistants can progress rapidly within the sector.

Directory and database publishing

There are over 2,500 companies in the UK publishing consumer, business, copy sales-based and ad sales-based directories from *Yellow Pages* to the *Good Food Guide*. The directory publishing team generally consists of production, editorial, advertising sales, marketing and customer relations departments. Directory publishing is often seen as a route into book publishing, but the sector can provide a wealth of opportunities in its own right.

Magazine publishing

With more than 8,000 magazine titles job opportunities are many and varied. The industry needs people with a range of skills and interests for jobs in sales, editorial, design, production, marketing and circulation. As well as the vast array of magazines on display at newsagents there are also business, professional and specialist titles that provide information and entertainment on a huge range of subjects. To this you can add the growing number of customer magazines which are produced under contract for companies who want to market their products and services to their customers.

Magazine publishers do much more than publishing magazines on paper; they provide readers with a package of products and services ranging from trade shows and exhibitions, to supplements, awards and licensed goods. They are also publishing widely on the Internet and provide an increasing range of information services online.

Newspapers

Over 8 per cent of adults read at least one newspaper on a regular basis. In addition to the national newspapers, there are large numbers of weekly and daily regional newspapers. Journalism remains the most popular career within newspaper publishing. However, in addition to reporting and writing, sub-editing, graphic design and press photography are all classed as journalism, and offer a wide number of alternative career paths.

Advertising sales are crucial to the majority of newspapers, and represent just one of the opportunities available to those who wish to work in newspaper publishing but are not seeking a job as a journalist.

Journal publishing

Journals disseminate new research findings and the latest new thinking to scholarly and professional organizations. There are hundreds of different journal publishers, ranging from global organizations to micro businesses. Within mid-to-large publishing houses, career opportunities exist in editorial, production, marketing, and sales and customer services. Owing to the specialist nature of journal publishing, many entering the field have a background in a particular academic area, but there are opportunities available to anyone with the relevant skills and personal qualities.

Qualifications and Training

Publishing is a fast-moving industry and technological advances have been reflected in the training and skills required by publishers. Computer literacy is essential for the majority of job roles. A number of universities and colleges offer degree or postgraduate courses in publishing, and, whilst it is possible to find work without doing one of these, it is often a competitive advantage. For details of courses available, contact sector specific organizations in further information.

Personal Qualities

Desirable attributes depend on department and sector, but most employers are looking for enthusiasm, determination and a commitment to working in publishing. It is often helpful to have gained some work experience in the field. A strong commercial awareness is crucial.

Starting Salary

Starting salaries vary enormously between organizations and sectors. However, new entrant salaries are usually in the region of £10,000–£15,000.

i

Association of Learned and Professional Society Publishers,
   South House, The Street, Worthing, West Sussex BN13 3UU;
   01903 871 686; www.alpsp.org
Directory and Database Association, PO Box 23034, London W6
   0RJ; 020 8846 9707; www.directory-publisher.co.uk
Institute of Publishing, 78 Manor Way, Guildford GU2 7RR;
   020 7233 0935; www.instpublishing.org.uk
Newspaper Society, Bloomsbury House, 74–77 Great Russell
   Street, London WC1B 3DA; 020 7636 7014;
   www.newspapersoc.org.uk; e-mail: ns@newspapersoc.org.uk
Periodicals Training Council, Queens House, 55–56 Lincoln's Inn
   Fields, London WC2A 3LJ; 020 7404 4168;
   www.ppa.co.uk/ptc; e-mail: careers@ppa.co.uk
Publishing National Training Organization, Queens House,
   55–56 Lincoln's Inn Fields, London WC2A 3LJ; 020 7405 0836;
   www.publishingnto.co.uk; e-mail: info@publishingnto.co.uk
The Publishing Training Centre, 45 East Hill, London SW18 2QZ;
   020 8874 2718; www.train4publishing.co.uk;
   e-mail: publishing.training@bookhouse.co.uk
The Publishers Association, 29B Montague Street, London
   WC1B 5BH; 020 7691 9191; www.publishers.org.uk;
   e-mail: mail@ publishers.org.uk
Society of Freelance Editors and Proofreaders, Mermaid House,
   1 Mermaid Court, London SE1 1HR; 0207 403 5141;
   www. sfep.demon.co.uk
*The Kogan Page Guide to Working in the Media, Careers in Publishing
and Bookselling, Careers Using English* (all Kogan Page)

PURCHASING OFFICER/BUYER

Purchasing careers exist in all large organizations – whether
profit-making or not. Essentially, purchasing and supply management involves identifying the requirements of the company's
internal customers and then obtaining the necessary products and
services by negotiation and agreement with suppliers. The
primary objective is to obtain value for money. This does not
always mean achieving the very lowest price – sometimes other
commercial considerations are more important. For example, the

flexibility and speed of response of the supplier might be the deciding factor, or the need to minimize risk by choosing a vendor with a good business record.

In a manufacturing environment such as a car plant, the purchaser would be directly involved in buying components such as wheels, lights and shock absorbers for the production line. In a financial services company, purchases might well be for telecommunications systems, catering services and marketing services, including advertising and design.

In retail purchasing the role is slightly different as buyers are more involved in merchandising, selecting product lines which appeal to the consumer and sell quickly.

Qualifications and Training

Most companies require a minimum of four or five GSCE passes. Graduates or individuals with A levels usually enter as trainee buyers, working with experienced personnel and continuing their training in the workplace. The minimum requirement for individuals wishing to study for the Foundation Stage of the CIPS Graduate Diploma is two A levels and three GCSEs (or equivalent). The Certificate in Purchasing and Supply Management is offered to those with no A levels.

Personal Qualities

Purchasers need to be innovative, able to manage change, have good networking and interpersonal skills and familiarity with ICT.

Starting Salary

Starting salaries for trainee buyers are £16,000–£18,000.

The Chartered Institute of Purchasing and Supply, Easton House, Easton on the Hill, Stamford PE9 3NZ; 01780 756777; www.cips.org

QUANTITY SURVEYING

see *Surveyor/Surveying Technician*

QUARRYING

The quarrying industry is concerned with the extraction from the ground of materials such as limestone, granite, slate, chalk, gravel, clay and sandstone. Some quarries also produce materials; for example, lime, ready-mixed concrete and coating stone needed for road building. The industry employs people at operative, craft, technician and management levels.

Qualifications and Training

Operatives need no formal qualifications, although NVQs are available in Mobile Plant and Process Operations in Drilling and Shotfiring Operations. Applicants can also enter an apprenticeship scheme to qualify for an NVQ in Engineering Maintenance.

A number of courses related to quarrying are available at Doncaster College; it has a long-standing close relationship with the industry which provides sponsorship and industrial placements. The University of Nottingham, Camborne School of Mines (University of Exeter), University of Leeds and the Royal School of Mines (Imperial College, University of London) offer degree-level courses related to quarry management and engineering.

Personal Qualities

Operative and craft employees must have good physical ability and possess the necessary mechanical skills to operate quarrying machinery such as loaders and dumptrucks. Supervisors must have the usual organizational skills combined with a knowledge of the technology and of the materials involved.

Starting Salary

Average salaries in the industry are £20,000+.

Institute of Quarrying, 7 Regent Street, Nottingham NG1 5BS; 0115 9411315; www.inst-of-quarrying.org/iq

EPIC (NTO), 36–38 London Road, St Albans, Hertfordshire AL1 1NG; 01727 869008; www.epicnto.com

R

RADIO

see *Broadcasting*

RADIOGRAPHER

Radiography is a caring profession which calls for considerable technological expertise. There are two branches: diagnostic radiography and therapeutic radiography. Diagnostic radiographers are responsible for producing high quality images on film and other recording materials which help doctors to diagnose disease and the extent of injuries. Therapeutic radiographers help to treat patients, many of whom have cancer, using X-rays, ionizing radiation and sometimes drugs.

Qualifications and Training

All radiography qualifying courses are now at degree level. Courses are normally based in a university or higher education institution affiliated to a university, with half the time spent on clinical education in hospital departments associated with the university.

On graduation, entrants are eligible for State Registration by the Radiographers Board of the Council for Professions Supplementary to Medicine, which is an essential requirement for employment in the NHS. The requirements for entry to radiography courses are two A levels and three GCSEs at grade C or above, or equivalent. Entry is also possible through validated Access courses and applications from mature candidates are welcomed by many radiography education centres.

Personal Qualities

As well as having an interest in science, radiographers should be caring and compassionate but sufficiently level-headed not to get upset when dealing with sick people. They need to be patient and calm when faced with patients who may be frightened or difficult. Good health and reasonable strength are needed for lifting people and heavy equipment. In addition, radiographers should be good-humoured, able to work well in a team and assume responsibility.

Starting Salary

Around £16,000 in the NHS.

College of Radiographers, 207 Providence Square, Mill Street, London SE1 2EW; 020 7740 7200; www.sor.org
NHS Careers, PO Box 376, Bristol BS99 3EY; Careers helpline: 0845 6060 655; www.nhscareers.nhs.uk/home.html
Careers in Nursing and Related Professions (Kogan Page)

RADIOTHERAPIST

see *Radiographer*

RAILWAY WORK

The rail industry employs a vast number of people: drivers, revenue protection inspectors, customer service assistants, signal operators, engineers, fitters, clerical workers, technicians, and managers. The latter are responsible for the day-to-day running of the railways or are in charge of departments such as planning, engineering, marketing and accounts.

Qualifications and Training

Train drivers do not require formal educational qualifications but are expected to have studied English, maths and a science. Training is on the job and a range of NVQs is available. Guards, signalmen, station attendants and general railmen are also trained on the job and work towards NVQs.

Technicians need four GCSEs, including maths, English and a science, and undertake apprentice training, working along-side experienced staff. NVQs at levels 2 and 3 are available in Rail Transport Engineering: Maintenance and Rail Transport Engineering.

Management recruitment is normally at graduate level, although trainees with A levels may be sponsored on sandwich degrees. Training for graduates varies depending on the nature of their work and lasts up to two years.

Personal Qualities

All rail staff must have a strong interest in providing an efficient service and in promoting and caring for passengers' needs. In addition, drivers need perfect vision without glasses. Managers need qualities appropriate to their departments plus managerial and administrative skills.

Starting Salary

Different train operating companies pay different amounts; drivers earn around £13,500 while training, £24,000+ once qualified; operatives earn £9,500+, technicians £12,000+, clerical staff £10,000+ and graduate recruits £15,000+. Free or reduced-price travel is usually offered as an extra benefit.

The National Training Organization for the Rail Industry, RITC Ltd, B118 Macmillan House, Paddington Station, London W2 1FT; 0870 2202773; fax: 0870 2202774; www.ritc.org.uk; enquiries@ritc.org.uk

RECEPTIONIST

(see also *Hotel Work*)
Receptionists work in hotels, large organizations and private firms, sometimes combining the job with the duties of telephonist. In hotels, they welcome the guests, make bookings and prepare the final accounts. They also deal with reservation correspondence and act as a general information office. In small hotels this can be handled by one person but in most, and especially the

larger, hotels, they work in a team headed by the Reception Manager. In large official organizations, such as a town hall or in firms with many staff, receptionists direct visitors to the correct department. In small firms the job is often combined with answering the phone, typing and franking the mail.

Medical receptionists work in a variety of environments. They need, in addition to the standard skills of a receptionist, a full understanding of the principles of medical ethics and confidentiality, knowledge of the NHS and social services, medical terminology and clinical procedures.

Qualifications and Training

Formal educational qualifications are not necessary, but proficiency in English and maths is an advantage. For some posts knowledge of other languages is important. Many further education colleges offer one-year full-time courses and a range of part-time courses in reception skills. A range of qualifications is available, including NVQs at levels 1, 2 and 3 and Modern Apprenticeships.

The AMSPAR diploma in health service reception is a nationally recognizeised professional qualification. It can be achieved by examination and is available from a wide network of approved centres throughout the UK.

Personal Qualities

Receptionists should be friendly, pleasant with a good phone manner and neat appearance. They also need stamina, as they are often expected to work shifts that include evenings and weekends. They should have a real liking for people and a good memory for faces. Computer literacy is increasingly important.

Starting Salary

From £7,500 to £14,000+, more in London.

Local Jobcentres and Careers / Connexions Centres

Association of Medical Secretaries, Practice Managers,
Administrators and Receptionists (AMSPAR), Tavistock
House North, Tavistock Square, London WC1H 9LN;
020 7387 6005; www.amspar.co.uk; e-mail: amspar@atlas.co.uk
Hotel and Catering Training Company, 26–28, Hammersmith
Grove, London W6 7BR; 0500 832 300; www.hctc.co.uk

RECORDING ENGINEER

see *Broadcasting, Engineering*

RECREATIONAL MANAGER

see *Leisure and Amenity Management, Sport and
Recreation Facility Management*

REFRIGERATION ENGINEER

see *Engineering*

RECRUITMENT CONSULTANT

The aim of recruitment/employment consultants is to fit people
to jobs. Agencies deal with all types of staff, from office and secretarial to highly complex and specialist technical roles. Much of the
work involves selling to potential users and matching clients'
demands. This includes interviewing prospective job candidates,
keeping records of their details and matching them to employers'
requirements.

Qualifications and Training

Many recruitment consultants have come into the industry after
some experience of another job, for example, sales, personnel or
office work. They are trained either in-house or on courses run by
the Recruitment and Employment Confederation (REC). The REC
offers two levels of qualification: the foundation award, suitable
for those in their first year in the industry, and the certificate in
recruitment practice for those with more than one years' experience. Both qualifications can be studied by distance learning or at
an evening class.

Personal Qualities

Recruitment consultants must be able to relate to people at different organizational levels, have good communication skills, work quickly and calmly under pressure and be organized and resilient.

Starting Salary

Varies greatly for trainees, but with experience consultants can earn a salary of £25,000+ with commission.

The Recruitment and Employment Confederation,
   36–38 Mortimer Street, London, W1W 7RG; 020 7462 3260;
   www.rec.uk.com

REGISTRAR

The local registration service (LRS) is a network of register offices in England and Wales which registers births, stillbirths, marriages and deaths. These are staffed by a mixture of statutory officers and local government employees. The latter are known as 'deputies' to the statutory officers. England and Wales is divided into 366 registration districts and each district has a Superintendent Registrar based at the register office. Some districts have outstations which are either visited or permanently manned.

Qualifications and Training

No formal requirements other than a good general education are necessary. Training is on the job but vacancies are few.

Personal Qualities

Registrars must be able to get on with people, giving advice calmly and sympathetically and be even-tempered. They should be able to do their job well in situations of excitement, emotion and distress. Confidentiality must be maintained at all times. Good handwriting is important, and the ability to drive may be necessary in rural locations. Entrants must be prepared for weekend work.

Starting Salary

£12,000+.

Local authorities

Local Jobcentres and Careers / Connexions Centres

Local Government Careers; www.LGcareers.com – for further careers information; www.LGjobs.com – for current job vacancy adverts in local councils all over the country.

Office of Population Censuses and Surveys, St Catherine's House, 10 Kingsway, London WC2B 6JP; 020 7242 0262; www.statistics.gov.uk

REMOVALS

Removers play a key role in the chain of events leading up to departure from one home and arrival in another – which can be around the corner or on the other side of the world. It is the remover's job to see that all the customer's belongings are professionally packed and transported to their destination. The work may involve packing fragile objects quickly and efficiently, as well as travelling long distances. Some large companies have their own storage facilities, so employees may be involved in ensuring that furniture is stored safely.

Estimators are the technical salespeople in a removals company. They visit customers' homes and estimate the amount of packing space needed, the time it will take and the price.

Qualifications and Training

Employees can work towards NVQs for the removals and storage industry. Progression is also possible to supervisory level. An LGV (Large Goods Vehicle) licence would be beneficial, but not essential when starting out. Estimators should have a good standard of education with good passes preferably in English, maths, geography and modern languages, hold a full car driving licence and be able to express themselves clearly and persuasively. Training is on the job.

Personal Qualities

Removers should be fit and strong. They must be honest and have a sense of responsibility towards other people's possessions. Common sense and the ability to work in a team are important.

Starting Salary

Salaries vary from region to region in the UK depending upon the market and competition in the area.

British Association of Removers (Training Services) Limited,
3 Churchill Court, 58 Station Road, North Harrow, Middlesex HA2 7SA; 020 8861 3796; www.removers.org.uk;
e-mail: info@bar.co.uk
Local Jobcentres and Careers / Connexions Centres

REPORTER

see *Broadcasting, Journalist*

REPRESENTATIVE – SELLING

A sales representative may work for a manufacturer, wholesale distributor or service industry, persuading potential customers to buy the firm's products and also looking after the needs of existing customers. The representative is usually assigned a geographical area and travels around it on the firm's behalf. It is possible to be a representative for any number of products, from soap powder and double glazing to office equipment, machine tools and beauty products.

Qualifications and Training

Requirements for trainees vary, but most firms would look for four GCSEs grades A – C or equivalent and in some companies recruitment is at graduate level. Sales reps may study for examinations set by such bodies as the Chartered Institute of Marketing or the Managing and Marketing Sales Association. Diplomas and certificates are also issued by various trade associations representing particular types of product. Technical sales representatives usually have a degree or equivalent in the relevant subject.

Personal Qualities

An outgoing, friendly personality, a manner that inspires confidence and the ability to speak forcefully and persuasively, plus persistence and stamina, are all important.

Starting Salary

£12,000–£18,000+, but this can be commission based. A car or petrol allowance is generally included in salary packages.

Chartered Institute of Marketing, Moor Hall, Cookham, Maidenhead, Berkshire SL6 9QH; 01628 427500; www.cim.co.uk

The Institute of Professional Sales, Moor Hall, Cookham, Maidenhead, Berkshire SL6 9QH; 01628 427372; www.iops.co.uk

The Managing and Marketing Sales Association, PO Box 11, Sandbach, Cheshire CW11 3GE; 01270 526 339; www.mamsasbp.com; e-mail: info@mamsasbp.com

RETAILING

The retailing industry covers a range of businesses: department stores, supermarkets, cash-and-carry and discount warehouses, mail order firms, local shops and some manufacturing companies which sell direct to the public. Work opportunities include shop assistants, warehousing staff, cashiers, visual merchandisers, cashiers, managers – store or department – and buyers. Larger concerns will also have administrators, personnel officers and transport and logistic departments. In some shops – in a profession such as pharmacy, or in a trade such as butchery – the owner or manager must have special training. Most people in the retail trade have to work on Saturdays and, increasingly, at least one late night a week, but there is often a rota system to make the working week more flexible. Sunday trading is becoming more common, and stores need full staffing. In large stores, bank holiday working is often recompensed by time off plus extra payment.

The growth in online shopping has affected all sectors of the retail industry and led to a growth of retail-related call centre work and work for packers and dispatchers to fulfil those orders.

Qualifications and Training

Sales staff generally do not need academic qualifications and training is on the job. Entrants may work towards NVQs levels 1 to 4. However, to be taken on as a junior trainee or trainee supervisor, three to four GCSEs or equivalent are required. Trainee managers and buyers need two A levels and increasingly companies recruit graduates as trainee managers.

Personal Qualities

Employees in retailing should enjoy meeting and helping people and have a pleasant manner. The ability to communicate in a friendly and helpful way is essential. Those involved with handling money and checking stock should be numerate and methodical.

Starting Salary

On average, sales assistants start on £8,500+, graduate management trainees on £16,000+.

Local Jobcentres and Careers / Connexions Centres
   Department stores/supermarkets, personnel departments
Distributive NTO, Mardall House, 9–11 Vaughan Road,
   Harpenden, Hertfordshire AL5 5HU; 01582 760809;
   www.dnto.com; www.inretail.co.uk;
   e-mail: enquiries@inretail.co.uk (for vacancies)

RIDING INSTRUCTOR

Riding instructors teach people, individuals or groups, how to ride. They may also accompany riders who hire horses by the hour and be required to help train horses and look after them, cleaning tack and stables. The work includes teaching in riding schools and clubs and in summer camps, training competition riders and, occasionally, sitting as a judge or examiner.

Qualifications and Training

To take the British Horse Society's Assistant Instructor certificate, candidates must be members of the society and, if under 18, have four GCSEs, one of which should be in English. On completion of Stages 1, 2 and 3, the Preliminary Teaching Test, an approved first aid certificate and 500 hours of teaching experience, they are awarded the Assistant Instructor's certificate.

There are several methods of training: at a riding school, paying fees for instruction, board and lodging – the courses can be as short as three months or as long as a year, depending on the type of course; or as a BHS Apprentice at a BHS approved riding centre, doing stable work while receiving instruction. This takes approximately one year. Pupils pay for their keep. For more information on the BHS apprenticeship scheme, contact the BHS Approvals Office. After being awarded the Assistant Instructor's certificate, candidates may take the Intermediate Instructor's exams after reaching the age of 20. At 22, Intermediate Instructors may go on to take the British Horse Society Instructor's certificate. The Fellowship may be taken from 25 years of age.

Personal Qualities

Patience and authority, but above all a love of horses, are essential for this work. A riding instructor must enjoy being out of doors and get on well with people, especially children.

Starting Salary

£8,000–£10,000 for an Assistant Instructor as a rough guide; the amount will vary depending on whether instruction is being provided, accommodation and stabling for the instructor's own horse and the instructor's age and experience.

i

The British Horse Society, Stoneleigh Deer Park, Kenilworth, Warwickshire CV8 2XZ; 08701 202244 or 01926 707700; www.bhs.org.uk

ROAD HAULAGE

see *Freight Forwarding, Lorry Driver, Road Transport, Vehicle Technician*

ROAD TRANSPORT

(see also *Bus and Coach Companies*)

This industry includes road haulage, plus passenger transport and commercial companies that have their own transport and delivery facilities. Passenger transport covers bus and coach services. Commercial companies need to plan the flow of materials or parts for manufacturing and the subsequent delivery of their products to their customers. Similarly, retail organizations need transport to bring merchandise to their outlets. The work divides into loading, moving and unloading, involving a wide range of operative and administrative staff: drivers, warehousemen, depot managers, mechanics, clerical staff, transport planners and many others. There is a variety of public-sector and private-sector employers.

Qualifications and Training

Jobs range from those needing few formal qualifications to those that require a degree. There are NVQs in Road Passenger and Road Freight Transport for operative staff; and Edexcel (BTEC)/SQA national certificates for those with four GCSEs or equivalent; the Institute of Logistics and Transport offers a range of professional qualifications from entry level upwards. Degrees in transport management are available at a number of universities.

Personal Qualities

Drivers need to be physically strong, responsible, careful and able to communicate effectively. Transport managers need good numeracy and ICT skills, be able to think analytically and plan effectively.

Starting Salary

A newly qualified driver will earn around £10,000–£12,000, while an experienced driver carrying dangerous goods can earn £25,000+. Graduate trainees start between £18,000 and £22,000.

i

Road Haulage and Distribution Training Council, 14 Warren Yard, Warren Farm Office Village, Stratford Road, Milton Keynes MK12 5NW; 01908 313360; www.rhdtc.co.uk; e-mail: info@rhdtc.co.uk

British International Freight Association, Institute of Freight Forwarders, Redfern House, Browells Lane, Feltham, Middlesex TW13 7EP; 020 8844 2266; www.bifa.org; e-mail: bifa@bifa.org

The Institute of Logistics and Transport, Logistics and Transport Centre, PO Box 5787, Corby, Northamptonshire NN17 4XQ; 01536 740100; www.iolt.org.uk; e-mail: careers@iolt.org.uk

Institute of Transport Administration, Mill House, 11 Nightingale Road, Horsham, West Sussex RH12 2NW; www.iota.org.uk

The Passenger Transport Forum for Employee Development (TRANSfED), Regency House, 43 High Street, Rickmansworth WD3 1ET; 01923 896607; www.transfed.org; e-mail: enquiries@transfed.org

ROOFER

This title covers a variety of jobs concerned with erecting a roof: laying down roofing felt, nailing down wooden battens to support tiles, tiling and slating. Other specialities include built-up felt roofing, when layers of felt are alternated with tar, then finished off with slabs of concrete or other materials; and roof sheeting, when large sheets of waterproof material are attached to roof frames. Some roof work includes working from scaffolding.

Qualifications and Training

Formal educational requirements are not necessary. Apprenticeship lasts for three years; training is on the job and at training centres, leading to NVQs levels 2 and 3.

Personal Qualities

A head for heights is essential, plus an ability to work out of doors in all weather conditions.

Starting Salary

£12,000 initially, rising to £16,000+.

Construction Industry Training Board, Bircham Newton, King's Lynn, Norfolk PE31 6RH; 01553 776677 (ext 2466)

ROV PILOT TECHNICIAN

Remotely operated vehicles (ROVs) were introduced into the military and offshore fields in the late 1970s and early 1980s and now offer a career path for well-educated technical staff. ROVs are operated by the Royal Navy, offshore companies, environmental agencies, police and salvage companies. These underwater robots carry out the work of a diver at depths where diving is impossible.

Qualifications and Training

Employers normally require ROV personnel to have a good background in electronics or hydraulics. Experience with pneumatics, plant maintenance or electrical engineering are also of interest. Candidates who do not have formal qualifications (academic, trade or in the services) in one of these areas, are unlikely to be considered. Training courses are available at a number of schools which allow newcomers to the industry to learn the basics; however, none of these courses is formally required and will not normally be accepted as a basis for employment unless the person has the right sort of background and qualifications. Details of courses are available from The International Marine Contractors Association Web site.

Personal Qualities

Initiative and ability to work in small close-knit teams and a willingness to work outside the UK are essential. To work offshore in any capacity it is necessary to undergo and pass a special medical examination.

Starting Salary

Starting salaries are £18,000+, rising to £28,000+.

The International Marine Contractors Association, Carlyle
House, 235 Vauxhall Bridge Road, London SW1V 1EJ;
www.imca-int.com / careers; e-mail: imca@imca-int.com
Local Royal Navy Careers Information Offices

ROYAL AIR FORCE

The Royal Air Force is responsible for the airborne defence of the
UK and its allies. It consists of a small flying force, almost exclusively officers, supported by non-commissioned airmen and
airwomen working in a variety of trades such as engineering,
communication and air traffic control work as well as supporting
jobs such as catering, medical and dental support workers,
photographers, security guards and musicians. A few non-
commissioned officer airmen and airwomen work as crew in
specialities such as air signallers, air electronics operators or air
loadmasters.

Ground opportunities for officers include air traffic and fighter
control, engineering, physical education, intelligence, catering,
administration, supply and education. There are also provost
(police) officers, medical officers, dental officers, nursing officers,
legal officers and chaplains.

Qualifications and Training

Officers

Minimum academic entry requirements are two A levels and five
GCSEs at A–C (including English and maths) or equivalent. The
normal upper age limit is 26 (24 for pilots) but qualified specialists
can apply up to the age of 39. Graduates are preferred for some
specialisms and student sponsorships are available. Those
wanting to train as pilots take aptitude tests to assess co-ordina-
tion and speed of reaction. Applicants must meet nationality and
residence requirements and pass a medical examination. For
some jobs good eyesight and colour vision is essential. Women
may apply to all branches except the RAF regiment.

Training for all new officers starts with an intensive 24-week course which covers operational and leadership skills. This is followed by training relevant to the chosen specialization, which varies in length from a few weeks to up to three years for pilots.

Non-Commissioned Personnel

For some jobs no academic qualifications are needed. For entry to scientific and technical trades, 3– 5 GCSEs, often including science and maths, are required. Musicians need to have passed Grade 8 or have a higher qualification; dental/nursing staff need the appropriate professional qualifications. The minimum age for entry to most trades is 16; the upper age limit is normally 30, but there is some variation between trades.

Ground recruits attend an initial seven-week course covering physical fitness and weapons training which is followed by specialist training. Aircrew have a twelve 12-week basic training course followed by specialist training. Many airmen and airwomen will work towards NVQs or other nationally recognized qualifications throughout their career.

Personal Qualities

Air Force personnel must enjoy teamwork and a disciplined regime and be willing to go into combat. They need physical fitness, dedication, commitment, initiative and a sense of responsibility.

Starting Salary

The following are intended to give an indication of salary: Pilot Officer £18,797, Flying Officer £22,597; Leading Aircraftman/woman £12,070, Junior Technician £15,461. In addition to basic salaries, there are many extra allowances, including travel, accommodation and overseas service.

i

Local RAF Careers Information Offices; www.raf-careers.com

ROYAL MARINES

The Royal Marines act as the emergency strike force of the Royal Navy. Its personnel are trained for amphibious assaults and commando operations on land. It has a well-deserved reputation for toughness, and training is arduous. Marines are sent at short notice to deal with emergency situations, which include natural disasters as well as military operations. There are six specialist areas in the Royal Marines. These are Ships Detachment (serving on Royal Navy ships), Air Squadron, Special Boat Squadron, Jungle and Arctic Warfare and Embarked Force (working at sea and forming part of the amphibious Task Force). Most commandos serve as Riflemen but there are some specialist and support trades. The Royal Marines is an all-male service.

Qualifications and Training

Officers

Full career entry is between 17 and a half and 23, and at least two A levels or equivalent are required. Undergraduates may be recruited on a cadetship scheme and sponsored at university. Graduates can enter up to the age of 25. Initial training is 15 months followed by nine months working in a specialist unit. Officers specialize in particular areas of work such as radio communications, amphibious operations or special reconnaissance work, but are trained in all the activities undertaken by the Marines.

Other Ranks

Entry to the Royal Marines is between 17 and a half and 28 and does not require formal qualifications but many recruits have GCSE and some have A levels. All candidates must pass the Royal Navy selection test. The minimum height requirement is 1.65 metres (5 feet 6 inches) with appropriate height to weight ratio. Initial training lasts 30 weeks and is followed by a period of more advanced training with the opportunity to work towards the appropriate qualifications. Before returning to civilian life marines can learn a new trade or supervisory and management skills at a Royal Navy vocational training centre.

Personal Qualities

The same basic qualities are needed as for the other services: discipline, dedication, fitness, initiative and an ability to work with others. Marines spend long periods away from home, often in difficult and dangerous locations with climates ranging from tropical to arctic. High standards of physical fitness and stamina are essential. Around 900 Marines are recruited each year and entry is competitive.

Starting Salary

Ratings' start on £10,344, increasing to £12,070 – £22,100 once trained. Officers earn from £20,000 – to £35,000.

Local Royal Navy Careers Information Offices; www.royal-navy.mod.uk

ROYAL NAVY

(see also *ROV Pilot Technician*)

Navy personnel work in the nation's combat fleet and at its land bases. Like the other services, the Navy uses many trades and skills. Royal Navy Ratings are non- commissioned servicemen and women working in one of six branches: warfare, engineering, supply, medical, fleet air arm and deep navy (submarines). Officers command and are responsible for the welfare of the ranks. They may work in warfare, engineering, supply, aviation or training. Special Officers work as doctors, dentists nursing officers or chaplains.

Qualifications and Training

Officers

There are two main entry routes – direct entry from school, university or civilian employment or by promotion from the ranks. Some scholarships are available for sixth formers and undergraduates. Minimum entry requirements are 2 two A levels or equivalent.

An increasing number of officers are graduates. Applicants must be under 23 (26 for graduates). Experienced engineers must be under 32 on entry; age limits for Special Officers can be up to 44.

All officers spend two to five terms at the Britannia Royal Naval College at Dartmouth, which will include some time spent at sea. After this they go on to further training which varies in length according to specialism.

Ratings

The minimum age for entry to most jobs is 16. Medical and dental assistants and nurses need to be slightly older. The upper age limit for communications technicians and artificer apprentices is 27; for other trades 32. Academic requirements vary according to the trade but are between two and five GCSEs or equivalent. Medical and dental assistants and nurses may need professional qualifications. All applicants have to pass a test in reasoning, English, numeracy and mechanical comprehension and a medical. Jobs in submarines are not open to women.

Initial basic training is eight weeks followed by specialist training relevant to the trade chosen. Some of this time will be spent at sea.

Personal Qualities

A liking for the sea is important. Other requirements are the same as for the other services: discipline, dedication, fitness, initiative and an ability to work with others. Different trades demand specific skills – languages are useful for those working in communications, while a knowledge of science and technology is needed by those working with sophisticated equipment.

Starting Salary

Ratings start on £10,344; a Leading Rating earns £19,812 – £25,342. Graduate officer entrants start on £18,798. A Lieutenant's salary is £28,813 – £34,270 and a Captain earns £59,280 – £65,521.

i

See contact details under Royal Marines

RSPCA INSPECTOR

Inspectors for the Royal Society for the Prevention of Cruelty to Animals (RSPCA) deal with complaints from the general public about the alleged ill-treatment of animals, and also perform more routine tasks. Inspectors have no power to take an animal from its owner unless the owner legally signs it over. They may caution people and, in some circumstances, the organization will ensure that cases go before the courts. Inspectors also visit boarding kennels, pet shops and riding schools. They can be involved in physical rescues, often working unsociable hours and driving considerable distances.

Qualifications and Training

Applicants require GCSEs or equivalent in English language and a science, a valid driving licence and the ability to swim 50 metres fully clothed. Experience of working with animals is desirable.

About 20 inspectors are recruited each year from over 2,000 applicants. Training lasts six months and covers animal welfare legislation, basic veterinary training, mountain and boat rescue techniques, investigation skills, interview techniques, court work, animal-handling techniques, media training and public speaking. After written examinations, students serve six months' probation before becoming fully qualified. Minimum age for entry is 22.

Personal Qualities

As well as having compassion for animals, inspectors must be firm, authoritative, tactful, persuasive and have good communication skills. Good interpersonal skills and the ability to manage confrontational situations are essential.

Starting Salary

Student inspectors start around £14,000; experienced inspectors earn £20,000+. Inspectors also receive an accommodation allowance.

| i |

Chief Superintendent, Training School, RSPCA Headquarters,
    Causeway, Horsham, West Sussex RH13 7WN; 01403 264181;
    www.rspca.org.uk
Scottish SPCA, Braehead Mains, 603 Queensferry Road,
    Edinburgh EH4 6EA; 0131 339 0222;
    www.scottishspca.org; e-mail: enquiries@scottishspca.org
Careers Working with Animals (Kogan Page)

SADDLER

Saddles are still made by hand, by craftsmen of considerable experience. They usually work in one of the many small companies which specialise in saddlery, making harnesses and other leather goods such as satchels and wallets. Saddlers' shops stock all these items and may also stock suitcases and sports goods and offer a repair service.

Qualifications and Training

The Society of Master Saddlers administers a four-year apprenticeship indenture scheme leading to certification by the Worshipful Company of Saddlers. Saddlery courses of varying lengths are available at the Capel Manor College at Enfield, Middlesex, Walsall College of Arts and Technology, Cambridge Saddlery Courses in Bury St Edmunds, Suffolk, and Cumbria School of Saddlery in Penrith, Cumbria. Cordwainers at Capel Manor College offers two courses in saddlery: a diploma in saddlery studies and an HND in saddlery technology. Both courses cover many aspects of running a small business, and both last for two years.

The Society of Master Saddlers administers the National Saddlery Skills Assessment Scheme by which those making saddles, bridles and harnesses may have their skills assessed and gain qualifications in each specialist area at levels 1, 2 and 3. These qualifications are recognised by other members of the trade.

Personal Qualities

Painstaking attention to detail and pride in craftsmanship are needed. Owners of saddlers' shops often have a strong interest in horses too.

Starting Salary
£125–£400+ per week with experience.

Cordwainers College at Capel Manor, Bullsmoor Lane,
Enfield, Middlesex EN1 4RQ; 020 8366 4442;
www.capelmanorcollege.co.uk;
e-mail: enquiries@capelmanorcollege.freeserve.co.uk
Walsall College of Arts and Technology, Leather Department,
Shelley Campus, Scarborough Road, Walsall WS1 1XN;
01922 720889; www.walcat.ac.uk
Cambridge and District Saddlery Courses (INT) Ltd, 31 St John
Street, Bury St Edmunds, Suffolk IP33 1SN; 01284 700640
Cumbria School of Saddlery, Unit 9, Redhills Business Park,
Penrith, Cumbria CA11 0DL; 01768 899919
The Society of Master Saddlers, Kettles Farm, Mickfield,
Stowmarket, Suffolk IP14 6BY; 01449 711642;
www.mastersaddlers.co.uk;
e-mail: enquiries@mastersaddlers.co.uk
Worshipful Company of Saddlers, Saddlers' Hall, 40 Gutter Lane,
London EC2V 6BR; 020 7726 8661; www.saddlersco.co.uk;
e-mail: clerk@saddlersco.co.uk

SALES REPRESENTATIVE

see *Representative – Selling*

SECRETARY

(see also *Personal Assistant, Receptionist*)

Secretaries work in all types of organizations. Sometimes they are
assigned to one person, sometimes they provide support services
for several people. Most secretaries need to have well-developed
ICT skills but there is still a demand for those with shorthand and
audio typing. As well as producing documents, secretaries undertake a range of organizational tasks such as arranging travel and
meetings. They may also work as receptionists and deal with
callers and queries by phone or e-mail. Those in senior positions
may make decisions on behalf of managers.

Bilingual Secretary

A bilingual secretary is fluent in a second or third language and may work in commerce, overseas or as an EU employee. The work will include composing, reading and translating documents in the foreign language. They may use speaking / listening skills in their languages for telephone work, receiving visitors and interpreting at meetings.

Farm Secretary

In addition to normal secretarial work, farm secretaries will be responsible for completing complex forms, keeping records and accounts and calculating wages. A farm secretary may work for one employer, be freelance or be sent out by an agency to smaller farms.

Legal Secretary

Accurate skills have always been paramount for legal paperwork, but word processors have made the job easier. Legal secretaries are employed by barristers and solicitors in professional practice and in large commercial organizations.

Medical Secretary

Medical secretaries are good administrators, keep records, handle correspondence and filing. They work in hospitals, for individual doctors / consultants and in health centres. Accuracy and confidentiality are essential, as is a thorough knowledge of medical terminology.

Qualifications and Training

There is a range of full- and part-time courses available. Courses usually include word processing, audio, shorthand and office procedures. There are training opportunities for young people leading to NVQ levels 1, 2 and 3 in Administration.

GCSEs are usually required to obtain a place on a full-time secretarial course. A good working knowledge of the English language is essential. Additional qualifications are needed to specialise as a legal, medical or farm secretary. There are a number of postgraduate diploma courses for graduates wishing to train as bilingual secretaries.

Personal Qualities

Good secretaries are judged by what they do, but qualities such as self-motivation, discretion, tact, loyalty, flexibility, excellent communication skills and smart appearance are expected.

Starting Salary

Varies from £8,000 to £20,000+ depending on experience, location and type of employer. Bilingual and legal secretaries are better paid.

i

Association of Medical Secretaries, Practice Managers, Administrators and Receptionists (AMSPAR), Tavistock House North, Tavistock Square, London WC1H 9LN; 020 7387 6005; www.amspar.co.uk; e-mail: amspar@atlas.co.uk

Institute of Qualified Private Secretaries Ltd (IQPS), First Floor, 6 Bridge Avenue, Maidenhead SL6 1RR; 01628 625007; fax: 01628 624990; www.iqps.org; e-mail: office@iqps.org

ILEX Paralegal Training, Kempston Manor, Kempston, Bedford MK42 7AB; 01234 841000; www.ilex.org.uk; e-mail: info@ilex.org.uk

The Institute of Para-legal Training, The Mill, Clymping Street, Clymping, Littlehampton, West Sussex BN17 5RN; 01903 714276

Institute of Linguists, Saxon House, 48 Southwark Street, London SE1 1UN; 020 7940 300; www.iol.org.uk

SECURITY WORK

There are many aspects of security work, including patrolling, guarding, monitoring CCTV, operating delivery services for documents and valuables, advising on burglary prevention and installing security systems. There is also work in other areas such as preventing industrial espionage, the personal protection of public figures and the supplying of store detectives. The industry has two main sections: in-house, where organizations have their own security force dealing with the protection of their property and assets; and contract guarding, in which guards, patrolmen, drivers of 'cash-in-transit' vans are supplied by another company.

Qualifications and Training

There are no specific entry requirements, although experience acquired in the armed forces or the police is a useful background. Training varies, but the relevant British Standard requires at least two days' induction training. Larger companies often provide additional training in areas such as the use of equipment, legal responsibilities and relations between the company, the police and the public.

The introduction of NVQs has provided recognised training standards and a career structure for employees.

Personal Qualities

It is essential to have an impeccable background for security work plus a fair amount of strength and common sense, initiative and reliability. Entrants may be asked to work night shifts. Good communication skills are now increasingly required in security officer roles, because of greater contact with the public.

Starting Salary

There is a great variety in payment, from National Minimum Wage to £7.50 an hour.

British Security Industry Association Limited, Security House, Barbourne Road, Worcester WR1 1RS; 01905 21464; www.bsia.co.uk; info@bsia.co.uk

Security Industry Training Organization, Security House, Barbourne Road, Worcester WR1 1RS; 01905 20004; www.sito.co.uk; info@sito.co.uk

The National Security Inspectorate, ISI Division, Orchard House, Victoria Square, Droitwich, Worcester WR9 8DS; 01905 773131; www.isi.org.co.uk; e-mail: info@tisi.demon.co.uk

SERVICE ENGINEER

see *Electrician*

SERVICE MECHANIC

Mechanics are needed to service and repair business machines such as photocopiers, as well as domestic machines such as washing machines and televisions. Service mechanics are employed by machine manufacturers. Although some work may be done in the company's workshop, more frequently the mechanic will visit offices or private homes. As office equipment and domestic appliances become increasingly dependent on computer technology the work is becoming more IT related.

Qualifications and Training

These vary, but formal academic qualifications are not always necessary. Some employers require City and Guilds certificates in mechanical, electrical or electronic engineering. Modern Apprenticeships and related NVQs are available.

Personal Qualities

Service mechanics spend a great deal of their time on other people's premises, so a polite and friendly manner plus the ability to work quickly and neatly are useful. A driving licence is often essential.

Starting Salary

For those with experience, £16,000+.

Local Jobcentres and Careers/Connexions Centres

SHEET-METAL WORKER/PLATER

Sheet-metal workers/platers are engaged in shaping, cutting and joining together pieces of metal. Sheet-metal workers work with thin metal sheet up to 3 millimetres thick, using a wide range of hand and power tools. They make such items as aircraft sections and car prototypes. Platers work with metal plates from 3 millimetres thick upwards. As well as hand and power tools, heavy presses are needed to bend the plate. Products include ship and submarine parts and industrial boilers.

Qualifications and Training

No formal educational qualifications are required but mathematical ability is necessary. It is possible to work without a formal apprenticeship. Training with an apprenticeship takes up to four years, during which time courses are available leading to NVQs.

Personal Qualities

Sheet-metal workers/platers must be strong, good at working with their hands, able to read technical drawings and to work as one of a team in a noisy atmosphere.

Starting Salary

Average salaries in the industry are £19,000 for those with experience.

Engineering Careers Information Service, 41 Clarendon Road, Watford, Hertfordshire WD1 1HS; 01923 238441; Freephone: 0800 282167; www.emta.org.uk; www.enginuity.org.uk (for careers information); e-mail: ecis@emta.org.uk

Local Jobcentres and Careers / Connexions Centres

SHIPBROKER

Shipbrokers act as go-betweens for shipowners, looking for cargo to fill their vessels, and charterers, seeking to ship their dry cargo and tanker requirements. Sale and purchase of vessels is also an important service offered to clients. Brokers are paid commission on the contracts arranged. The Baltic Exchange in London is the centre of the chartering market. It is a self-regulated market and the Exchange maintains a register of those seeking employment, which its member companies may consult. Vacancies are also advertised on the Web site. Additionally, shipbrokers/ship's agents in ports make arrangements when a ship calls for customs clearance – loading and discharging cargoes, meeting crew requirements, and so on. Port agents who attend to cargo liners may also be involved in marketing and documenting cargo. In order to maintain contact with the international scene, shipbrokers tend to work long hours and to travel abroad frequently.

Qualifications and Training

There are no specific academic qualifications needed for ship-broking beyond a good general educational background. However, members of a firm who wish to make a career in the shipping business usually study for the examination leading to membership of the Institute of Chartered Shipbrokers. Such study can be part-time or by correspondence course and covers not only shipping practice but more general studies in law, economics and international trade. The Institute also offers a foundation diploma in shipping for those just starting in the business.

Personal Qualities

A good business sense, the ability to learn through practical experience, and willingness to work long and irregular hours and to travel are all necessary.

Starting Salary

Earnings vary greatly.

The Baltic Exchange, 14–20 St Mary Axe, London EC3A 8BH; 020 7623 5501; www.balticexchange.com
The Institute of Chartered Shipbrokers, 3 St Helen's Place, London EC3A 6EJ; 020 7628 5559; fax: 020 7628 5445; www.ics.org.uk

SHIPPING

see *Merchant Navy*

SIGNWRITER

Signwriters design and hand paint company names and logos on to shop fronts and the sides of vans and lorries; they may also paint estate agents' signboards and a wide variety of other temporary signs and notices. Signwriters increasingly use a range of materials and techniques, including computer technology, to create signs. The letters are often formed from plastics, metal or wood and stuck on to the background.

Some signwriters are in business on their own; others work for commercial signwriting companies.

Qualifications and Training

There are no formal academic entry requirements for this type of work, but artistic talent combined with an interest in lettering is important. Some graphic design courses include typography and signwriting and provide wider training. Some commercial signwriting firms take on trainees and NVQs in Assembly, Fabrication and Manufacturing Processes and Signmaking are available at level 2.

Starting Salary

Many signwriters are self-employed and earnings vary greatly.

Local Jobcentres and Careers/Connexions Centres

SOCIAL WORK

Healthcare settings

Healthcare settings are managed by any branch of the health service, such as hospitals, GP practices, clinics, accident and emergency units and psychiatric hospitals. The list can also include hospices, clinics for the treatment of substance abuse, and so on. Social workers work in these areas and offer a range of services.

Mental Health Social Work

Social workers can also specialise in working with people with mental health problems. Anyone with two years' experience can train further to become an Approved Social Worker (ASW) and a Mental Health Officer (MHO). The role of the ASW or MHO is to try to ensure that people with mental health problems can be supported and treated in the community, or can go to hospital on a voluntary basis if they need treatment.

Qualifications and Training
Social Work – Healthcare Settings
The Diploma in Social Work (DipSW) is the recognised qualification for all social workers in the UK and for probation officers in Northern Ireland. The DipSW is designed and delivered by partnerships between colleges and social care agencies. It takes two to three years to complete. Approximately half the time is spent in the university or college and the remainder is spent in the workplace under the supervision of a qualified and experienced social worker. The DipSW is due to be replaced with a degree in 2003.

Mental Health Social Work
DipSW – as above, plus ASW/MHO training.

Personal Qualities
All individuals working in the area of social work need patience and a warm, sympathetic personality. They need to have excellent communication skills, be good listeners, trustworthy, and have compassion for others.

Starting Salary
£14,000 to £25,000.

The Central Council for Education and Training in Social Work (CCETSW) has been replaced by Social Care/Services Councils
General Social Care Council, Goldings House, 2 Hay's Lane, London SE1 2HB; 020 7397 5800; www.doh.gov.uk/gscc; e-mail: info@gscc.org.uk
Northern Ireland Social Care Council, 7th Floor, Millennium House, Great Victoria Street, Belfast BT2 7AQ; 028 02890 417600; www.dhsspsni.gov.uk/hss/niscc; e-mail: info@niscc.n-i.nhs.uk
Scottish Social Services Council, c/o Scottish Executive, James Craig Walk, Edinburgh EH1 3BA; 0131 244 1949; e-mail: info-scotland@sssc.uk.com
Care Council for Wales, 6th Floor, West Wing, South Gate House, Wood Street, Cardiff CF10 1EW; 029 2022 6257; e-mail: info@ccwales.org.uk
For information about a career in social work, visit www.socialworkcareers.co.uk or telephone 0845 6046404.

Home Carer

Home carers provide emotional and practical support for the elderly, people with physical disabilities, mental health problems and a range of other illnesses.

The role of the home carer includes housework, shopping, dressing, bathing, toileting and supervising medication. They are offered training and support by a Home Care Organiser, who also provides team supervision. Most home carers work for local authorities or private agencies.

Home Care Organiser

The Home Care Organiser undertakes assessment of a person's needs and their financial circumstances. They decide whether or not the person is eligible for support and exactly what financial support they need. They then arrange for home care provision. They work in teams alongside social workers and care managers, mainly in local authorities, the voluntary sector or private agencies.

Qualifications and Training

For home carers, NVQs in Care are available. For a Home Care Organiser, some relevant experience and NVQs in Care or Management, a diploma in domicillary care management, a certificate/diploma in management studies are all qualifications that are increasingly required.

Personal Qualities

All individuals working in the area of social work need patience and a warm, sympathetic personality. They need to have excellent communication skills, be good listeners, trustworthy, and have compassion for others.

Starting Salary

For home carers, salaries vary locally but are around Minimum Wage levels. A Home Care Organiser may earn £13,000 to £19,000 depending on qualifications and experience.

| i |

See Social Work – Healthcare Settings

SOCIAL WORK AND SOCIAL CARE – CHILDREN AND YOUNG PEOPLE

(see also *Personal Adviser, Youth Worker*)

Childminding

Childminders provide a service for parents who need to leave their children in a safe environment while they go to work. All childminders have to be registered. In September 2001, OFSTED became responsible for the regulation of childminding and daycare in England and for ensuring childminders are of an adequate standard and meet health and safety regulations. Most childminders are paid directly by the parents, although some are paid by the local authority. Details of local Children's Information Services can be obtained from the OFSTED helpline on 0845 601 4771.

Social Worker with Children and Families

Since 1995, social service departments have been required by law to identify and support children in need in their area and to protect children who may be at risk from harm. The workers in this area are qualified social workers, who can be employed by local authorities in children and family teams or in specialist agencies such as the NSPCC (National Society for the Prevention of Cruelty to Children) in England. The NSPCC is commissioned by the local authority to do this work.

Social workers work with children and their families to ensure that the child is in the most appropriate environment. They give advice and support on a range of issues, including housing, mental health, drugs, alcohol, abuse or neglect of children and relationship problems.

Qualifications and Training

Childminding

Childminders do not need any specific qualifications, although many do complete NVQs in Child Care. All childminders must register with their local authority. Registration includes checks on the safety of the childminder's home and on health and police records of the applicant, their partner and others living in the home.

Social Worker with Children and Families
The DipSW is an essential qualification for those wishing to work in this area.

Personal Qualities
All individuals working in the area of social work need patience and a warm, sympathetic personality. They need to have excellent communication skills, be good listeners, trustworthy and have compassion for others. Those who work with children and young people also need to communicate effectively with other adults who are involved with the child or young person.

Starting Salary
Childminding from £80+ per week, per child; Social Worker £16,000–£25,000.

i

See Social Work – Healthcare Settings
National Childminding Association, 8 Masons Hill, Bromley, Kent BR2 9EY; 020 8464 6164; www.ncma.org.uk; e-mail: info@ncma.org.uk

SOLICITOR

The role of the solicitor is to provide clients with skilled legal representation and advice. The clients can be individual people or companies, or any type of organization or group. A solicitor may work on all kinds of legal matters, from house purchases to defence of people accused of crimes; from selling a corporation to drafting a complicated will or trust. Solicitors may also represent clients in all courts but will often brief a Barrister (*see* Barrister) to represent the client, and then act as a liaison between them.

Scottish solicitors can appear in all courts and tribunals in Scotland up to and including the Sheriff Court. They can also gain rights of audience enabling them to appear in the higher courts by becoming a Solicitor-Advocate, or may brief an Advocate to represent their clients.

While some solicitors may deal with a variety of legal problems, others specialise in a particular area such as shipping, planning and construction, financial services or social security. Specialization within the profession is increasing. The majority of solicitors work in private practice with firms made up of several partners. Many others work as employed solicitors in commerce, industry, local and central government and other organizations.

Qualifications and Training

England and Wales: The Law Society governs the training of solicitors in England and Wales, which takes place in two stages – the academic and the professional. Most, but not all, entrants to the profession are graduates. Fellows of the Institute of Legal Executives over the age of 25 with five years' qualifying experience do not need to complete the academic stage. Non-law graduates take the Common Professional Examination (CPE) or a Postgraduate Diploma in Law; those with the qualifying law degrees are exempt from this. The next stage, the vocational stage, is taken via the legal practice course, available at a number of colleges or universities. It is a one-year full-time or two-year part-time course. The trainee solicitor then has to undertake a two-year training contract with an authorised firm or organization. During the course of this, a 20-day professional skills course is undertaken, usually on a modular basis.

Scotland: The Law Society of Scotland governs the training of solicitors in Scotland. It is possible to study for a Bachelor of Laws Degree at five Scottish universities: Aberdeen, Dundee, Edinburgh, Glasgow and Strathclyde. Alternatively, it is possible to take the Law Society's own examinations by finding employment as a pre-diploma trainee. After completion of the LLB degree or professional examinations, all graduates who would like to become solicitors must take the diploma in legal practice – a 26-week postgraduate course, which also offers training in office and business skills. After successful completion of the degree and the diploma, those who wish to become solicitors then serve a two-year training contract with a Scottish solicitor. Trainees must undertake a further two-week course of study, keep training records, which will be examined and monitored by the Society, and take a test of professional competence. The trainees can then apply to the Law Society of Scotland for a practising certificate. All Scottish solicitors must hold a Law Society of Scotland practising certificate.

Personal Qualities

A high level of academic achievement, integrity, good communication skills, patience, discretion, a good command of language and problem-solving skills are all required.

Starting Salary

Salaries vary but graduate trainees can receive up to about £20,000 in London and newly qualified solicitors can earn considerably more than this. Those working for provincial solicitors and for small firms may find the salaries slightly lower. The Law Society lays down minimum salaries below which trainees cannot be paid. On average, qualified solicitors earn £28,000–£30,000.

In Scotland, the Law Society does not lay down salaries, but recommends minimum salary rates for trainees, which are currently £10,300 for trainees in their first year and £13,905 for trainees in their second year.

$\boxed{\text{i}}$

The Law Society, 113 Chancery Lane, London WC2A 1PL;
020 7242 1222; www.lawsociety.org.uk;
e-mail: info.services@lawsociety.org.uk
The Law Society of Scotland, 26 Drumsheugh Gardens,
Edinburgh EH3 7YR; 0131 226 7411; fax: 0131 225 2934;
www.lawscot.org.uk; e-mail: legaleduc@lawscot.org.uk
Careers in the Law (Kogan Page)

SPEECH AND LANGUAGE THERAPIST

Speech and language therapists (SLTs) identify, assess and treat people who have communication and/or swallowing disorders. A large proportion of these will be children but SLTs also help adults who may have communication or swallowing problems caused by disease, accident or psychological trauma. Some SLTs may specialise in a particular patient group, for example in the areas of severe learning difficulties, hearing impairment or neurological disorders, while others choose more general, broad-based practice. The NHS is the largest employer of SLTs, working in community clinics, hospitals, special schools and homes for the mentally or physically disabled. Some of the larger voluntary organizations also employ SLTs. Often, the SLT works closely in a team which may include members of the medical, teaching, therapeutic, psychological and other caring professions.

Qualifications and Training

Speech and language therapy is a degree-entry profession. Courses leading to professional qualifications are offered at 15 universities and colleges of higher education throughout the UK. There are a number of two-year postgraduate diploma and master's courses available to candidates with relevant degrees.

Entry qualifications for courses vary from one institution to another, but the minimum is five GCSEs and two A levels or equivalent. A good balance of language and science is expected. Other equivalent qualifications are considered on merit. All courses will consider applications from mature students (over 21), who are encouraged to apply in the normal way.

Students who successfully pass all academic and clinical components of an accredited course are eligible to obtain a certificate to practise and to enter the professional register of the Royal College of Speech and Language Therapists as full professional members.

Opportunities also exist to work as a Speech Therapist's Assistant. An NVQ in Care at level 3 is available.

Personal Qualities

It is essential that speech therapists themselves should have clear speech, with a good ear. In addition, they must have an interest in people as individuals, as well as an enquiring mind, initiative, patience, imagination and a willingness to take responsibility.

Starting Salary

Around £15,800.

i

Royal College of Speech and Language Therapists, 2 White Hart Yard, London SE1 1NX; 020 7378 3012; www.rcslt.org; e-mail: postmaster@rcslt.org
NHS Careers, PO Box 376, Bristol BS99 3EY; Careers helpline: 0845 6060 655; www.nhscareers.nhs.uk

SPORT AND RECREATION FACILITY MANAGEMENT

(see also *Leisure and Amenity Management*)

Sport and recreation facility managers are responsible for the efficient running of leisure centres, swimming pools, sports halls and associated facilities. Managers usually start their careers as Recreation Assistants and progress through supervisory and Assistant Manager positions via on-the-job training and professional development.

Qualifications and Training

The Institute of Sport and Recreation Management (ISRM) offers a comprehensive programme of training and qualifications designed to cover all aspects of sport and recreation facility management and operation ranging from Recreation Assistant, NVQ level 2 and Supervisor, NVQ level 3, to Management, NVQ levels 4 and 5.

HND courses and a range of degrees in recreation management and sports sciences are available.

Personal Qualities

A liking for people, a strong interest in sport, and organizing skills are essential. Swimming and lifesaving ability are essential for swimming pool work.

Starting Salary

Recreation assistants at 18 years old, around £10,000; managers' salaries are variable depending upon level of responsibilities, type of facility, location, qualifications and experience and can range from £13,000 to £25,000.

i

Institute of Sport and Recreation Management, Giffard House, 36–38 Sherrard Street, Melton Mowbray, Leicestershire LE13 1XJ; 01664 565531; fax: 01664 501155; www.isrm.co.uk

Institute of Leisure and Amenity Management, ILAM House, Lower Basildon, Reading, Berkshire RG8 9NE; 01491 874800; www.ilam.co.uk; e-mail: education@ilam.co.uk

SPORTSPERSON

(see also *Coach, Jockey, Leisure and Amenity Management, Sport and Recreation Facility Management*)

There are opportunities in sport for professional sportspeople and for careers in coaching. Not all sports allow players to be professionals, and there are others, such as snooker, where there is room for only a very few professionals. Sports attracting professionals in relatively large numbers are football, cricket, golf, horse racing, rugby league and tennis.

Sportspeople's careers are generally short, but if, during their careers, they have made a name for themselves, there may be opportunities in journalism, broadcasting or consultancy.

Qualifications and Training

Professional sportspeople naturally need to be very good at their sport. Those in team games generally begin by playing for their school, town or county side. In this context, a young player may be noticed by professional selectors. In the case of football, it is not necessary to join a local football league club; apprentices are taken on from all over the country. Because a club apprentice has no guarantee that he will ever play for the first side, some clubs allow apprentices time off to obtain academic qualifications.

Coaches must gain recognised coaching qualifications, which are awarded by the governing bodies of the various sports and acquired either at evening class or weekend school.

Personal Qualities

As well as talent, professional sportspeople must possess dedication, perseverance, commitment and a degree of ruthlessness. Coaches and teachers also need perseverance, as well as patience, tact and the ability to inspire children or adults of very different abilities, often in less than ideal situations.

Starting Salary

Salaries for professionals are often low initially, but the rewards for top performers may be very high. The amount of money earned varies enormously depending upon the sport. Coaches' salaries vary according to whether the work is full- or part-time, what type of work they are doing and the number of hours.

Sport England, 16 Upper Woburn Place, London WC1H 0QP; 020 7273 1500; www.sportengland.org

Sport Scotland, Caledonia House, South Gyle, Edinburgh EH12 9DQ; 0131 317 7200; www.sportscotland.org.uk; e-mail: library@sportscotland.org.uk

The Sports Council For Wales, Sophia Gardens, Cardiff CF11 9SW; 029 2030 0500; www.sports-council-wales.co.uk; e-mail: scw@scw.co.uk

STAGE MANAGER

see *Theatre*

STATISTICIAN

Statisticians are concerned with the collection, analysis and inter-pretation of numerical data. They work in both central and local government, commerce and industry, universities and other research and teaching institutions.

Qualifications and Training

Most statisticians begin their careers by gaining a degree in statis-tics, or a maths degree with a specialization in statistics, or a post-graduate degree in statistics. Examinations up to Graduate Diploma level are also administered by the Royal Statistical Society. These are available on a part-time and distance-learning basis.

Personal Qualities

Skill at maths, a logical mind and the ability to select and interpret essential facts and figures are required, as is the ability to analyse problems and communicate the results.

Starting Salary

£16,000–£17,500 for graduates, rising to £30,000+ with experience.

i

The Professional Affairs Officer, Royal Statistical Society, 12 Errol
Street, London EC1Y 8LX; 020 7638 8998; www.rss.org.uk;
e-mail: prof.affairs@rss.org.uk
'Careers in Statistics' (The Royal Statistical Society)

STEEL ERECTOR

see *Building*

STEEPLEJACK

Steeplejacks are the mavericks of the building industry, able to
tackle any job at any height in any trade. While working high up,
safety chairs and harnesses are used and, sometimes, safety nets
and rescue lines. Steeplejacks are mostly employed on repair and
maintenance work, perhaps painting, pointing brickwork and
masonry. Basic electrical skills are needed on some jobs.

Some firms of steeplejacks specialise, for example, in power-
station chimneys, demolition work, restoration work and the erec-
tion and maintenance of lightning conductors.

Qualifications and Training

The Construction Industry Training Board offers a course for
those aged 16 and over. The course provides some work experience and is an entry to the industry's own apprenticeship scheme.
NVQs are available at levels 1, 2 and 3.

Personal Qualities

A head for heights is most important, plus the ability to work
quickly, neatly and carefully, and being prepared to work on
one's own.

Starting Salary

£10,700 per year, experienced steeplejacks earn £12,000+.

i

Construction Industry Training Board, Bircham Newton, King's
Lynn, Norfolk PE31 6RH; 01485 577577; www.citb.org.uk

National Federation of Master Steeplejacks and Lightning Conductor Engineers, 4D St Mary's Place, The Lace Market, Nottingham NG1 1PH; 0115 955 8818; www.nfmslce.co.uk; e-mail: info@nfmslce.co.uk

STOCKBROKER

Stockbrokers buy and sell securities on the Stock Exchange on behalf of investors, who may be individuals but are increasingly institutions, such as banks, insurance companies, pension funds or unit trusts. They also advise clients on shares they hold and suggest good times to sell or buy. Stockbrokers work from their offices using the phone and Internet to keep in touch with financial markets and news.

Qualifications and Training

A degree is desirable, but good A levels may be accepted. Before being allowed to trade, all staff must pass the Registered Representative Examination, administered by the Securities Institute. Stockbrokers train on the job, working alongside experienced brokers. Many employers expect their staff to study for the Securities Institute Diploma.

Personal Qualities

Entrants should be confident, numerate and able to express ideas clearly and concisely. Good interpersonal skills are essential, in order to ensure effective client relationships, as is the ability to work as part of a team.

Starting Salary

Depending on location, starting salaries vary from £16,000 to £25,000. Brokers' salaries depend on the amount of business carried out; top brokers can earn between £100,000 and £250,000.

The Securities Institute, Centurion House, 24 Monument Street, London EC3R 8AJ; 020 7645 0600; www.securities-institute.org.uk; e-mail: info@securities-institute.org.uk

STONEMASON

Stonemasons repair and restore stonework on old buildings and also provide stonework for new buildings, from walls, cladding and paving, to arches, staircases and fireplaces. The two kinds of masonry work are banking and fixing. Banker masons prepare the rough stone ready for use in a building and fixers assemble the stone where needed. In large firms the jobs are separate, but in smaller firms a mason may do both.

There are many different jobs for stonemasons: some specialise in monumental work – making and carving gravestones; others specialise in particular types of stone – for example, granite, marble, limestone.

Qualifications and Training

Formal academic qualifications are not required. Training is by a three-year apprenticeship supplemented by study through day or block release leading to NVQs, levels 2 and 3. The Building Crafts College also offers a one-year full-time City and Guilds course in advanced stonemasonry, covering basic traditional stonemasonry up to City and Guilds craft level (NVQ 3) and, additionally, stone carving, letter cutting and conservation and restoration techniques.

Personal Qualities

Manual skills are all-important in stonemasonry. Candidates must also be strong, prepared to work out of doors and possess great patience and accuracy.

Starting Salary

£12,000 for newly qualified stonemasons; experienced workers earn £20,000+.

Construction Industry Training Board, Bircham Newton, King's
    Lynn, Norfolk PE31 6RH; 01485 577577; www.citb.org.uk
Building Crafts College, 153 Great Titchfield Street, London
    W1P 7FR; 020 7636 0480
College of Masons, 42 Magdalen Road, London SW18 3NP;
    020 8874 8363

STORES SUPERVISOR
see *Purchasing Officer*

STRUCTURAL ENGINEERING
see *Engineering*

STUDIO MANAGER
see *Broadcasting*

SUB-EDITOR
see *Journalist*

SURVEYOR/SURVEYING TECHNICIAN
(see also *Estate Agent, Land Agent*)

Surveying
Surveying covers a wide variety of work within one profession, and a number of professional bodies offer qualifications in the different areas (*see* below). There are also technician qualifications. Surveying technicians work in all the same fields as surveyors but without being professionally qualified.

General Practice
This includes auctioneering, estate agency, valuation and estate management. People working in this area are responsible for the selling or letting, surveying, valuation and management of both urban and rural property. Qualifications in general practice are offered by the Association of Building Engineers (ABE), the Architecture and Surveying Institute (ASI), and the Royal Institution of Chartered Surveyors (RICS).

Aerial Surveying
A specialization of land surveying (*see* below), aerial surveying involves photogrammetry – the use of aerial photographs as a

basis for calculations. Qualifications are offered by the ASI and the Institute of Civil Engineering Surveyors.

Rural Practice
This is often combined with land agency and concerns the use and development of agricultural land. The qualifying bodies in this area are the ASI and the RICS.

Archaeological Surveying
This relatively new specialization involves working on an archaeological dig, making plans, maps and cross-sections of the excavations. It requires the skill of a cartographer as well as that of a land surveyor. The Architects' and Surveyors' Institute has members in this discipline.

Building Surveying
The structural surveying of properties and reporting on their condition and valuation is carried out by building surveyors/building engineers. They advise on necessary repairs and maintenance and prepare plans and specifications for alterations and improvements. Local and central government employ a large proportion of qualified building surveyors, although many are in private practice. Qualifications in this area are available from the ABE, the ASI and the RICS.

Hydrographic Surveying
The hydrographer surveys and charts underwater areas, such as ports and harbours and offshore areas where drilling for oil takes place. Hydrographic surveying qualifications are offered by the ASI and the RICS.

Land Surveying
The land surveyor measures and charts the Earth's physical features so that maps can be drawn. The scale of the work can range from a one-house building site to a whole region of Africa and there are opportunities in public services (the Ordnance Survey and the Ministry of Defence, for example), as well as in private practice or large commercial organizations. Qualifications are offered by the ASI and the RICS.

Minerals Surveying

Minerals surveyors assist in the design, development and surveying of quarries and underground mines, ensuring safety for the workers as well as optimum profitability for the company extracting the minerals. They also value mineral workings for rating and taxation and therefore need to be all-rounders with a knowledge of geology, the management of mineral workings, taxation and planning legislation. This area of surveying is unique in having its qualifications and duties laid down by law. Minerals surveyors must hold the surveyor's certificate granted on behalf of the Secretary of State for Industry by the Mining Qualifications Board. They must be at least 21 and have at least four years' practical experience (including 2,000 hours underground) in order to sit the exam for this certificate. Further qualifications are provided by the RICS, and the ASI.

Quantity Surveying

In private practice, quantity surveyors work with an architect to draw up design specifications in line with the client's budget. When the finished design is agreed, the quantity surveyor draws up a bill of quantities, detailing the materials and labour that will be needed. Building contractors work on this bill of quantities in preparing their tender for the job; they will use their own quantity surveyors to estimate their costs. Quantity surveyors also monitor costs as the work progresses and is completed. If they train for this work while employed by construction contractors, they usually take the qualification of the RICS. Professional qualifications are also offered by the ASI.

Qualifications and Training

The Royal Institution of Chartered Surveyors (RICS) offers a range of qualifications in the different areas of surveying. Normally entrants need three A-levels or equivalent for entry into an RICS approved degree or diploma course. An alternative is undertaking an HND or HNC in a related surveying discipline which can give advanced entry to those courses. On successful completion of an RICS approved degree or diploma, graduates enrol onto the Assessment of Professional Competence (APC), which is two years' practical training while in employment, concluding with an RICS professional assessment interview. Various degree backgrounds are valuable for surveying; one-year full-time and two-year part-time postgraduate conversion courses are available.

Technicians need a relevant HNC/HND or NVQ 4 followed by the Assessment of Technical Competence. This is two years' RICS structured training while working, which concludes with the RICS technical assessment interview. Those who have gained technical membership of RICS can take a bridging course to become a chartered surveyor.

Personal Qualities

Logical and orderly thinking, ability in figure work and detailed drawings are called for in this precision work. Communication skills and business acumen are essential. Good oral and written English is an asset and some areas may require specialised mathematical ability.

Starting Salary

The average starting salary for chartered surveyors is £14,000–£18,000. After qualification, salaries increase to £19,000–£24,000.

i

Architecture and Surveying Institute, St Mary's House, 15 St Mary Street, Chippenham, Wiltshire SN15 3WD; 01249 444505; www.asi.org.uk; e-mail: info@asi.org.uk

The Association of Building Engineers (ABE), Jubilee House, Billing Brook Road, Weston Favell, Northampton NN3 8NW; 01604 404121; www.abe.org.uk; e-mail: building.engineers@abe.org.uk

The Royal Institution of Chartered Surveyors (RICS), 12 Great George Street, London SW1P 3AD; 020 7222 7000; www.rics.org

The Royal Institution of Chartered Surveyors in Scotland, 9 Manor Place, Edinburgh EH3 7DN; 0131 225 7078; www.rics.org

TAX ADVISER/TECHNICIAN

Tax advisers/technicians work for private firms or independently, offering assistance to other firms/individuals who need guidance through the complications of the tax laws. A tax adviser would be able to advise clients on how to plan and present their taxable income so that they legally pay the least tax possible.

Tax technicians work for firms of accountants or solicitors, in clearing banks and for consultancy firms which offer a complete tax service to their clients. However, the largest area of work involves corporate tax in organizations that have their own tax department to prepare corporate tax and VAT returns on behalf of the company.

Qualifications and Training

Many tax advisers qualify first as accountants, but a growing number begin with A levels as tax trainees. The Chartered Institute of Taxation offers a qualifying exam for candidates already qualified as accountants or lawyers. The Association of Taxation Technicians is a starting point for all other tax trainees and offers an exam. This may be sufficient in itself for those candidates who do not expect to give detailed planning advice in their careers, or provide a stepping stone to the Institute's exam.

Personal Qualities

Tax advisers/technicians must be prepared for continuous professional development, be able to keep up to date with numerous tax changes, have an analytical mind, be able to apply lateral thinking and have good communication skills.

Starting Salary

The starting salary is similar to others in finance at £15,000+; those with experience earn high salaries.

The Chartered Institute of Taxation, 12 Upper Belgrave Street, London SW1X 8BB; 020 7235 9381; fax: 020 7235 2562; www.tax.org.uk; e-mail: post@tax.org.uk

The Association of Taxation Technicians, 12 Upper Belgrave Street, London SW1X 8BB; 020 7235 2544; fax: 020 7235 4571; www.att.org.uk; e-mail: info@att.org.uk

TAX INSPECTORS

Tax inspectors work for the Inland Revenue, the government department responsible under the direction of the Treasury for the efficient administration of income tax, tax credits, corporation tax, capital gains tax, petroleum revenue tax, inheritance tax, national insurance contributions and stamp duties. Inspectors are responsible for the tax affairs of businesses and individuals, ensuring they pay the right amount at the right time, helping them to obtain their entitlements and meet their obligations. Inspectors detect and deter non-compliance and encourage voluntary compliance by carrying out enquiry work.

Qualifications and Training

Training as a tax inspector takes between four and six years. To apply to the Revenue's graduate training programme a second class honours degree or better is needed. The training combines formal training and study with on-the-job experience, including investigation and interviewing techniques, bookkeeping, tax law and practice. It is also possible to enter through the clerical grades and apply to train as an inspector through internal programmes. No formal qualifications are needed to join the Inland Revenue at the clerical grades.

Personal Qualities

Tax inspectors need to have an open mind and be able to use their imagination and analytical ability to spot and solve complicated issues. They also need well-developed interpersonal skills and to be able to get on with a wide variety of people, both customers and colleagues. Also needed is a good standard of written and verbal communication.

Starting Salaries

On the graduate programme starting salaries are dependent on qualifications and work experience but range between £18,600 and £19,850 in London and £16,000 and £17,250 elsewhere. On completing the programme inspectors earn a minimum of £33,000.

---

i

Inland Revenue, Graduate Recruitment, 3rd Floor, Mowbray
  House, PO Box 55, Castle Meadow Road, Nottingham
  NG2 1BE; 0115 974 0606;
  www.inlandrevenue.gov.uk/recruitment

TAXI DRIVER

(see also *Minicab Driver*)

A 'taxi' is a traditional hackney carriage (like the famous black London taxis). The hackney carriage driver is allowed to 'ply for hire' – drive around the streets looking for passengers – and can be flagged down by a 'fare' (passenger). They may also operate from taxi ranks (known as 'standing for hire') in the streets. A private hire vehicle, on the other hand, has to be booked over the telephone or in person at the office from which it operates. Drivers therefore spend a good proportion of their time waiting around for passengers. Hours for both types of driver are generally long and unsocial (since there is a good deal of evening or night work, as well as weekend and public holiday work). Drivers may be owner-drivers or work for a company.

Qualifications and Training

Taxi drivers must be at least 21 years of age to be granted a licence, although in practice, because of insurance requirements, most are over 25. A valid Group A driving licence and relevant driving experience are also necessary. Hackney carriage drivers are legally bound to take the shortest or quickest route to a passenger's destination. Trainee drivers usually have to pass special tests, known as 'Knowledge Tests', to prove that they know their way about sufficiently well. These tests are generally oral, the most demanding being the Knowledge of London Test, which is required before drivers may operate in the capital. This usually takes some 18 months to two years to complete. Specialised training schools exist and there are also special training schemes for the disabled and for people who have been in the forces. In London, too, an additional driving test must be passed before a licence is granted.

Personal Qualities
Driving in traffic demands a calm, unflappable personality, with lots of patience. Drivers also need to have a good memory. In addition, a taxi driver must be 'of good character', as a licence will not be granted to anyone who has committed certain offences.

Starting Salary
Almost all taxi drivers are self-employed and have to pay tax and national insurance out of their earnings. Owner-drivers generally earn more than drivers employed by a company (who are often on a fixed rate), although they must also finance the repairs and servicing costs incurred by their own vehicles. Average earning are around £14,000.

Local taxi companies
Licensed Taxi Drivers Association, 9–11 Woodfield Road, London
    W9 2BA; 020 7286 1046

TEACHER

Teaching offers a wide variety of openings working with children and young people of all ages and backgrounds. Teachers do not merely stand in front of a chalkboard and teach facts to their particular class, nor does a teacher's day end when the final bell rings. They are expected to take a full and active part in their pupils' development as well as covering the relevant academic

courses for routine examinations. They will also have the opportunity to devise projects, extra-curricular activities, special
outings, and so on. A good deal of time out of school hours is
spent marking work and preparing lessons, and keeping up with
new developments in specific subjects or in education as a whole
(and this applies to the relatively long holidays, too).

Teachers' work varies according to the age group being
taught. Nursery teachers take the under-fives, infant teachers the
five- to seven-year-olds. Secondary education starts at 11 and
continues (in some cases) to 18 or 19. In addition, teachers are
needed in sixth-form colleges and the numerous further and
higher education establishments. Teachers at primary and junior
(8 to 11) level generally teach a variety of basic subjects and
specialist-subject teachers are not introduced until secondary
level, although specialist music or sports teachers may be
brought in at an earlier age.

Teaching has undergone radical changes in recent years and a
large part of secondary education in comprehensive schools is
now directed at mixed-ability classes, which makes great
demands on teachers. The majority of pupils attend state schools,
although there are also openings in private education. There are
also opportunities for teachers in special schools: for the handicapped (either boarding or day establishments), for disturbed
children (in community homes or approved schools), for those
with learning difficulties (such as deafness, or dyslexia) and in
children's hospitals, where long-term patients are expected to
take lessons. Such schools often make even greater emotional
demands on their staff than normal.

Anyone wishing to teach in a state-maintained school in
England and Wales must normally hold Qualified Teacher
Status (QTS), obtained by completing an approved course of
initial teacher training (ITT). The two main routes to achieving
QTS are: the Bachelor of Education (BEd) degree (some
institutions offer a BA or BSc degree with QTS) – usually four
years; *or* a subject degree appropriate for the national curriculum subject to be taught, followed by a postgraduate certificate
in education (PGCE) – three years plus one year. Most BEd
courses are for primary teaching, and most PGCE courses are for
secondary teaching.

Graduate and Registered Teacher Programmes (GRTP) enable schools to employ people who are not yet qualified to teach and undertake training leading to QTS whilst working. The GTP involves one year of postgraduate training and requires a first degree to qualify. The RTP requires applicants to have successfully completed two years of higher education (or the part-time equivalent) and to complete a degree whilst training. Applicants must be over 24 and need to find a school willing to employ them.

All applications for all training routes, regardless of subject or teaching level, must have attained the standard equivalent to at least grade C in both GCSE English language and maths. GCSE science is also required from those born after 1 September 1979 wanting to teach primary or middle school pupils. Entry requirements for BEd courses are five subjects at GCSE grades A to C, two of which must be at A level or equivalent.

While there are significant similarities between teaching in Scotland and teaching in England and Wales, there are also many differences – from entry into the profession to pay and conditions and continuing professional development. There are six teacher education institutions in Scotland: University of Paisley at the Ayr campus, University of Edinburgh, University of Glasgow, University of Strathclyde, Northern College at the Aberdeen and Dundee campuses (Dundee offers Primary courses only).

Courses are at undergraduate and postgraduate level. All teachers in local authority schools in Scotland must be registered with the General Teaching Council for Scotland (GTCS). The GTCS is responsible for making the decision as to whether a teaching qualification attained outside of Scotland is acceptable. The process is called Exceptional Admission.

Personal Qualities

Teachers do not merely need good academic ability; they must also be able to communicate their knowledge clearly and in an interesting fashion. They must also be able to establish a good relationship with their pupils and be prepared to take on considerable responsibility. Infinite patience and a sense of humour are great assets. It is important to have had some experience of working with children before training.

Starting Salary

In England and Wales salary is determined by a 14-point pay scale ranging from £16,500 to £32,500; advanced skills teachers are paid on a 27-point scale, salaries range from £27,939 to £44,571; head teacher's salaries range from £33,375 to £78,783. There are extra allowances in London.

In Scotland new teachers start on £18,000 and the 7-point scale goes to £28,707; Principal Teachers are on an 8-point scale ranging from £31,299 to £40,401; head teachers can earn up to £69,300.

Teaching Information Line, PO Box 3210, Chelmsford, Essex
  CM1 3WA; 0845 6000 991 (for English speakers),
  0845 6000 992 (for Welsh speakers);
  www.canteach.gov.uk; e-mail: teaching@ttainfo.co.uk
The General Teaching Council for Scotland, Clerwood House,
  96 Clermiston Road, Edinburgh EH12 6UT; 0131 314 6000;
  www.gtcs.org.uk; e-mail: gtcs@gtcs.org.uk
The Scottish Executive Education Department SS13, Area 2A,
  Victoria Quay, Edinburgh EH6 6QQ; www.scotland.gov.uk;
  www.teachinginscotland.com; e-mail: teaching@scotland.gov.uk
Northern Ireland: Department of Education, Rathgael House,
  Balloo Road, Bangor, Co Down BT19 7PR; 028 91 279000;
  www.deni.gov.uk; e-mail: deni@nics.gov.uk

TECHNICAL ILLUSTRATOR

The job involves the drawing of technical subjects, free hand and in accurate detail. The subjects illustrated include car engines, the insides of machinery and other scientific, mechanical and technical equipment.

Qualifications and Training

Four GCSEs are preferred. Art is not essential but some artistic ability is necessary. Training is on the job and by attendance at courses. A number of HNDs and degrees in technical illustration are available. Many courses require the student to have completed a foundation course in art and design. Some firms may offer apprenticeships. A portfolio of work is desirable when applying for jobs or courses.

Personal Qualities

Accuracy, neatness, good concentration and the ability to work alone are required.

Starting Salary

New entrants start around £13,000, but with experience a salary of £18,000 upwards may be earned.

Local Jobcentres and Careers/Connexions Centres

TECHNICAL WRITER

see *Writer*

TELECOMMUNICATIONS

The telecommunications industry continues to change and develop rapidly. Although there have been job cuts in this sector, there are still a large range of career opportunities. Deregulation of the industry around the world has resulted in many mergers and alliances to take advantage of the greater need for communications in business, as well as home use of the Internet, digital TV and WAP cell phones.

The sector recruits large numbers of hardware technicians and software engineers but telecommunications companies also employ people in accountancy, sales and marketing, training, finance, human resources and production planning. The move to broader bandwidth will increase the capacity of networks, allowing them to carry more traffic and a wider range of services. This is likely to mean continued growth for telecoms companies. Much hope is placed in the development and uptake of third generation (3G) phones which will allow high speed, multimedia access on mobile devices.

Technicians in the industry are involved in finding faults in telecommunications systems and ensuring that networks and equipment are working properly. This includes installing, setting up, testing and repairing equipment in businesses or people's homes, such as phones, cable, satellite or digital TV, fax machines or computers. Some technicians install and maintain the communications links for power and rail companies. There are also opportunities for such work in the Armed Services. Engineers and IT specialists combine technical expertise with strategic vision to enhance existing services, particularly in mobile and Internet technologies.

Qualifications and Training

Technicians normally need at least four GCSEs grades A–C or equivalent in maths, English, science and technology. Many have other qualifications such as a national certificate or diploma in electronics or telecommunications technology. Modern Apprenticeships are available, as are NVQs in Testing and Approval, Fitting, Maintenance and Operation of Telecommunications Switching, Transmission, Radio (or Mobile Telephones), Cabling and Power Systems.

Engineers and IT specialists are normally graduates with relevant degrees in Computer Science, Telecommunications or Electronics. Graduates from a range of degree backgrounds are recruited as trainees to commercial posts.

Personal Qualities

An interest in technological developments, good communication and interpersonal skills and the ability to work as part of a team.

Starting Salary

Technicians start around £11,000 to £15,000 and with experience can earn from £20,000 to £30,000. Graduate trainees' salaries are around £18,000+.

British Telecom, 81 Newgate Street, British Telecom Centre, London EC1A 7AJ; 0207 356 5000; www.bt.com
Vodafone; www.vodafone.co.uk
Orange; www.orange.co.uk
e-skills NTO, 1 Castle Lane, London SW1E 6DR; 020 7963 8920; www.e-skillsnto.org.uk; e-mail: info@e-skillsnto.org.uk

TELEPHONIST
see *Call Centres, Receptionist*

TELEVISION
see *Broadcasting*

THATCHER

Thatchers are self-employed craftsmen who roof, re-roof or repair thatched buildings with long straw, combed wheat straw, reed and other materials. The materials and methods they use have to preserve the building in its original form. A thatched roof gives good insulation against heat and cold and lasts 20 to 50 years. A roof is thatched by taking off the old thatch and then pegging down layers of new straw or reed.

Qualifications and Training
Academic qualifications are not essential. Thatching can be learned on the job as an apprentice to a Master Thatcher. Training takes four to five years. The Countryside Agency runs a training scheme for people of all ages, leading to NVQ level 2 in Thatching.

Personal Qualities
Thatchers need to be robust, good with their hands and not mind bad weather or heights. They also need common sense, the ability to make decisions and deal with customers.

Starting Salary
About £100 a week as an apprentice, thereafter depending on amount of work and individual charges.

> [i]

National Society of Master Thatchers, 20 The Laurels, Tetsworth, Thame, Oxfordshire OX9 7BH; 01844 281568; http://nsmt.hypermart.net
The Countryside Agency, John Dower House, Crescent Place, Cheltenham GL50 3RA; 01242 531381; www.countryside.gov.uk; e-mail: info@countryside.gov.uk

THEATRE

(see also *Actor*)

Theatre comprises much more than the actors and directors who receive the publicity. Many other people are involved in a theatrical production. Lighting and sound effects are created and handled by electricians; scenery and props are built, arranged and moved by technicians; the practical aspects of the production are organised and run by the stage manager and assistants. The designer creates the sets; the wardrobe mistress makes the costumes and the director or producer is responsible for the production as a whole. Other staff include the publicity officer, house manager and box office staff.

Producer

The producer chooses the play, rents the theatre, engages the director and actors and is responsible for paying the bills. The producer is responsible for raising the money for the production.

Production Manager/Technical Director

They are responsible for budgets, contracting and scheduling. This is a project management role and is usually a promotion from stage manager posts.

Director

The director is in charge of the actors, dancers, designers, singers and technicians, working within the managerial brief and, in consultation with producer and playwright, responsible for casting. The director's main work is in taking rehearsals and in turning the play into a theatrical production. The casting director auditions actors and arranges financial details with the actors and their agents.

Designer

The designer is responsible for sets and costumes, working closely with the director, and produces drawings of sets and costumes. The scenery and costume departments will work from these drawings and also from scale models of the sets.

Stage Manager

The stage manager is responsible for the smooth running of rehearsals and productions, ensuring that properties and costumes are ready when required, that actors know when they are needed, for supervising lighting, scene-making and scene changes and responsible for effects, music, curtain calls and prompting. A stage manager will often have assistants (ASMs and DSMs) and will also be helped by scene shifters. A stage manager may sometimes become a producer or director.

Lighting Designer

The theatre electrician may be in sole charge of the lighting or, in a large company with sophisticated equipment, be part of a team headed by an expert who will design a lighting plan. Appropriate electrician' qualifications are needed.

Production Staff

A large theatre may have a series of production workshops; smaller theatres may combine several jobs in one:

Armoury: the armoury is responsible for making armour or weapons, for special effects like gunfire and shells and for decorative metalwork. The members of the team are experts, for example gunsmith.

Metal workshop: here the heavy metalwork is designed and manufactured, for example for steel supports and complex trees. A welding qualification is useful.

Carpenters' workshop: technical drawing and carpentry skills come in useful for building sets. RADA offers a course for theatre carpentry.

Paint workshop: this is where the sets are painted. Knowing how to create the right textures and effects is part of the scene painter's skill.

Property-making shop: properties are often bought but in many productions, some props – for example, a throne or special upholstery – have to be specially made. An enthusiasm for research and an eye for detail are needed.

Wardrobe and wigs: although costumes and wigs may be hired, many are made by the wardrobe department. A good knowledge of period fashion and skills in dressmaking and tailoring are needed. Casual help is also needed when there is much sewing for a new production. Special hats are usually produced by a free-lance milliner. Accessory-making is another specialist job, as is wig- and beard-making, for which a City and Guilds certificate is a useful qualification. The wardrobe department is also responsible for looking after costumes and repairing and cleaning them.

Box Office

The box office is in charge of ticket sales. The manager is responsible for promotion and marketing, for hiring his or her staff and for checking the takings. Experience of accounts or general management is useful. This office makes a good starting place for anyone interested in arts administration.

Press Office/Marketing

These departments deal with publicity for the theatre. Press officers provide editorial content and liaise with the press, arrange for photo sessions and interviews. Staff often have a background in journalism or advertising. The marketing department produces posters, advertisements and programmes. An arts graduate with secretarial training may find work here. Tact, self-confidence and a pleasant voice are useful qualities.

Theatrical Agent

Agents try to find work for the actors on their books. Experience and good contacts are essential. Payment is usually 10 to 15 per cent of the client's fee.

Qualifications and Training

Director

A thorough grounding in the dramatic arts is essential. A degree in drama is useful. There are a few trainee director posts, mostly under the auspices of the Arts Council. A director will have had extensive experience of the theatre, probably as a stage manager or acting. Some directors come to the theatre from film or television, which also offer training.

Designer
Most designers will have completed a full-time art and design course.

Stage Manager
A full-time stage management course is provided at drama school for one to two years.

Production
NVQs are available at levels 1, 2 and 3 for theatre technicians.

Personal Qualities

Producer
Tact, persuasiveness, sound business sense, flair for organization and knowledge of what 'sells' in the theatre are all necessary.

Director
Directors need creativity, strong character, the ability to direct and weld together a team of people and a strong sense of the theatre. The casting director needs tact and the ability to cope with crises.

Designer
A theatre designer needs a thorough knowledge of period settings and costumes, and what looks effective on stage, as well as a sense of style and an ability to work within a budget and adapt to a variety of stage shapes.

Stage Manager
Managers need organizing ability, tact, calmness in a crisis, a good memory, an eye for detail, a practical approach and an interest in the literary and technical aspects of theatrical production.

Starting Salary
Salaries in the theatre are not high. The range varies according to location and level of responsibility.

$\boxed{\text{i}}$

Royal Academy of Dramatic Art (RADA), 62 Gower Street,
    London WC1E 6ED; 020 7636 7076; www.rada.org;
    e-mail: enquiries@rada.ac.uk
Association of British Theatre Technicians, 47 Bermondsey Street,
    London SE1 3XT; www.abtt.org.uk; e-mail: careers@abtt.org.uk
The Society of British Theatre Designers, 47 Bermondsey Street,
    London SE1 3XT; 020 7403 3778; www.theatredesign.org.uk;
    e-mail: webmaster@theatredesign.org.uk
National Council for Drama Training, 5 Tavistock Place,
    London WC1H 9SS; 020 7387 3650; www.ncdt.co.uk;
    e-mail: ncdt@lineone.net
Conference of Drama Schools, 1 Stanley Avenue, Thorpe,
    Norwich NR7 0BE; 01603 702021; www.drama.ac.uk;
    e-mail: enquiries@cds.drama.ac.uk
British Actors Equity Association, Guild House, Upper
    St Martin's Lane, London WC2H 9EG; 020 7379 6000;
    www.equity.org.uk
Careers in the Theatre (Kogan Page)

THEATRICAL AGENT

see *Theatre*

THERAPIST

see *Art Therapist, Dental Therapist (Dentistry), Drama Therapist, Music Therapist, Occupational Therapist, Physiotherapist, Speech and Language Therapist*

TOOLMAKER

Toolmakers work in engineering making a wide range of jigs, used to guide cutting tools and to hold the work in position; fixtures, to hold metal for bending or welding or to hold parts together; press tools in different shapes and sizes for cutting parts; mould tools to make items such as fridge interiors or mobile phone cases and measuring gauges. Toolmakers are often involved in making small quantities of a new product when it is at the design and development stage. Toolmaker machinists make the tools, often specializing in just one kind. Toolmaker fitters work on large structures that are constructed from many parts. They check all the parts, number them and then fit them together.

Qualifications and Training

Formal educational requirements are not essential for those wishing to undertake a modern apprenticeship but GCSEs or equivalent in English, maths and a science are recommended, particularly for those who want to take the Edexcel (BTEC) certificate course. Edexcel (BTEC) higher certificate courses are available for those with a certificate or with education to A level standard in maths and a science.

Training is on the job by three-year apprenticeship; time off is allowed for course attendance leading to City and Guilds or Edexcel (BTEC) qualifications. Modern apprenticeships are available.

Personal Qualities

Toolmakers must be deft and accurate in their work. The ability to read drawings is part of the training and not a requirement to begin an apprenticeship; some aptitude for learning the work is required and a brief aptitude test is carried out at interview.

Starting Salary

About £75–£80 a week at 16, and over £400 when qualified.

Engineering Careers Information Service, 41 Clarendon Road, Watford, Hertfordshire WD1 1LB;
 01923 238441; www.emta.org.uk
Local Jobcentres and Careers / Connexions Centres

TOURIST INFORMATION OFFICER

Tourist information officers work for national or regional tourist boards and local authorities with the aim of attracting visitors to Britain or to a particular region. The work includes promoting attractions, working with press and public relations agencies, designers and photographers to advertise local features, researching local history to develop new attractions, and participating in exhibitions both nationally and overseas to promote the area. They work closely with businesses in attracting holidaymakers, tour operators, exhibitions and conferences to the area and research future trends and needs. They are also responsible for overseeing the council's tourist information offices.

Qualifications and Training

Having a degree or HND in a business- or tourism-related subject can be an advantage, but personal qualities and proven business skills are just as important. NVQs in Tourist Information at levels 2–3 are available.

Previous tourist information centre experience, paid or voluntary, is invaluable. Marketing, travel agency or other retail experience is advantageous.

Personal Qualities

Good communication skills are essential, as are marketing and promotional experience and skills, including the ability to be creative, and write snappy copy to promote the area and various events. Excellent organizational skills and the ability to get on with a wide cross-section of people, from business leaders and councillors to residents and visitors, are important. A knowledge of languages, geography, history or archaeology can be an advantage for some posts.

Starting Salary

£12,000–£14,000 for graduate entrants.

Local Government Careers; www.LGcareers.com – for further careers information; www.LGjobs.com – for current job vacancy adverts in local councils all over the country

National and local tourist boards

Institute of Travel and Tourism, 113 Victoria Street, St Albans, Hertfordshire AL1 3TJ; 01727 854395; www.itt.co.uk

The Travel and Tourism and Events Sector National Training
Organization, The Cornerstone, The Broadway, Woking,
Surrey GU21 5AR; 01483 740854; www. ttento.com
Careers in the Travel Industry (Kogan Page)

TOUR MANAGERS

Tour managers are employed by major tour companies as official
guides for parties of tourists travelling with them. The manager is
responsible for the welfare of the tourists and must deal with any
worries or complaints. In addition, they are responsible for all the
paperwork necessary when the party stays overnight in a hotel or
crosses a border. Much of their work is seasonal and generally
only senior staff are employed on a permanent basis.

Qualifications and Training
A good general education including GCSE passes in English,
geography and maths is usually required by the travel trade.
Qualifications in relevant languages and experience of living and
working abroad are an obvious advantage; a manager on a particular tour will need an insight into local customs and fluency in the
relevant languages. Most training takes place on the job and there
are NVQs available.

Personal Qualities
Tour managers must have patience, tact and a pleasant personality. They need to be able to get on with a wide variety of people of
all nationalities and from all walks of life, without becoming flus-
tered or panic-stricken in a crisis.

Starting Salary
Around £150+ a week with full accommodation. There are also
opportunities to earn more money by organizing extra trips for
the tourists.

Institute of Travel and Tourism, 113 Victoria Street, St Albans,
Hertfordshire AL1 3TJ; 01727 854395; www.itt.co.uk

The Travel and Tourism and Events Sector National Training Organization, The Cornerstone, The Broadway, Woking, Surrey GU21 5AR; 01483 740854; www.ttento.com

TTC Training, The Cornerstone, The Broadway, Woking, Surrey GU21 5AR; 01483 727321; www.ttctraining.co.uk

Major tour operators

Careers Using Languages (Kogan Page)

Careers in the Travel Industry (Kogan Page)

TOWN AND COUNTRY PLANNER

Planners are concerned with reconciling the needs of the population for buildings, shopping centres, schools and leisure centres with the necessity of preserving and enhancing the natural and built environment. They collect information about the present use of land, the position of roads and other features, as well as drawing up plans for new schemes. Planners in development control ensure that buildings or developments intended for a particular area are suitable and do not conflict with existing buildings or the surrounding environment. Planners work for local and central government, environmental agencies and, to an increasing extent, in private practice. There are also varied opportunities for planning support staff.

Qualifications and Training

To enter a degree or diploma course in town planning, five GCSE passes and two A levels are desirable. Useful subjects include maths, English language, geography and history or a foreign language. Those with Royal Town Planning Institute (RTPI) accredited degrees or diplomas in town planning have satisfied the academic requirement for election to corporate membership of the Institute. To achieve membership, these candidates would also need to be able to demonstrate two years' experience in town and country planning. Planning courses are available at undergraduate and postgraduate levels, full- and part-time and on a distance-learning basis.

Planning Support staff are normally expected to have good GCSE grades in English, maths and other appropriate subjects, but relevant experience might be a deciding factor for more mature candidates. There are colleges that offer courses for support staff on a part-time or block-release basis. Qualifications gained are the Edexcel (BTEC) certificate, higher certificate or higher diploma in planning or the SQA certificate or higher certificate in planning. An NVQ at level 3 in Town Planning Support is also available for support staff.

Personal Qualities

Town planners and support staff need to have a knowledge of many subjects: economics, sociology, architecture and geography. Planners must be able to work in a team and cooperate with experts in other subjects. Planners need to take advice and opinions from many different people and, therefore, need to be able to reconcile the conflicting views of various interest groups. They must be good communicators and have imagination and an interest in and understanding of both people and the environment.

Starting Salary

Qualified planners about £12,000–£19,000, support staff £9,000–£15,000 upwards depending upon qualifications and experience.

> | i |

The Royal Town Planning Institute, 41 Botolph Lane, London
   EC3R 8DL; 020 7929 9494; www.rtpi.org.uk;
   e-mail: careers@rtpi.org.uk

TRADING STANDARDS OFFICER

Trading standards officers are employed by local authorities and responsible for enforcing a very wide range of legislation aimed at protecting consumers and traders. Laws relate to food and consumer product safety, credit, descriptions of goods and services, prices, animal health and welfare. While most operations are carried out through random inspections, officers are also required to investigate complaints and where appropriate, take matters to court.

Qualifications and Training

The principal qualification is the Diploma in Trading Standards (DTS), which may be obtained through accreditation of prior learning or through completion of an approved degree course in Consumer Protection.

Personal Qualities

Officers will need to be able to apply their training and knowledge in a fair, open and common sense manner. An ability to communicate clearly, to appreciate the demands of business, and to ensure that consumers are not deprived of their legal rights are all component parts of the duties. The wide variety of interests provided by the job is frequently quoted as a main attraction.

Starting Salary

£18,000–£20,000 for newly qualified officers.

Institute of Trading Standards Administration, 3–5 Hadleigh Business Centre, 351 London Road, Hadleigh, Essex SS7 2BT; 01702 559922; www.tradingstandards.gov.uk; e-mail: institute@tsi.org.uk

Local Government Careers; www.LGcareers.com – for further careers information; www.LGjobs.com – for current job vacancy adverts in local councils all over the country.

TRAFFIC WARDEN

Traffic wardens are civilians who work in conjunction with local police forces. They check parking meters and penalise drivers parking on double yellow lines or in other illegal places. They may also be required to do school crossing patrols or traffic control duty, as well as receiving vehicles towed into the police pound and looking out for out-of-date car licences.

Qualifications and Training

No formal educational requirements are necessary; training is on the job.

Personal Qualities
Traffic wardens must be responsible, self-confident, good communicators and able to deal effectively with aggression and confrontation.

Starting Salary
This varies according to area, ranging from £11,000 to £15,000; wardens in London receive more.

Local police forces; www.police.uk provides links to all police forces

TRAINING OFFICER/MANAGER

Training officers work in medium-sized firms and organizations, national and local government, emergency services and voluntary organizations. They are responsible for identifying training requirements, designing training programmes, delivering training to individuals or groups and evaluating the success of training.

Qualifications and Training
This is an area of work that people move into after gaining experience in other posts or following general personnel experience. A professional qualification is advisable. The Chartered Institute of Personnel and Development (CIPD) offers a certificate in training practice for those new to the profession or with limited experience. NVQs in Training and Development at levels 3–5 are available.

Personal Qualities
Training officers should have good communication, presentation, diagnostic, organizational and negotiation skills. They need to be able to set realistic targets, meet deadlines and plan ahead.

Starting Salary
New entrants earn from £13,000 to £17,00; managers between £26,000 and £40,000.

Chartered Institute of Personnel and Development, CIPD House, Camp Road, Wimbledon SW19 4UX; 020 8971 9000; www.cipd.co.uk

TRANSLATOR

Translators work freelance from home or as staff translators, within a commercial organization whose main business is not translation, or within a translation agency. Normally, they only translate from another language into their mother tongue. The work translated varies from whole books to business letters and documents. Translators, especially those who specialise in work for publication, must be able to express themselves very well. In areas where the subject matter of the text is specialised, for example computing, maths or mountaineering, expert knowledge is required of the translator. A broad-based general knowledge is always an advantage. Translators may be responsible for finding their own work but may also be registered with a translation company or agency.

Qualifications and Training

Proficiency in a foreign language is obviously necessary, as is the ability to write well in the target language. An understanding of the culture of the relevant countries is important. Increasingly, there is a need to be computer-literate. Most translators have a postgraduate qualification or a diploma in translation. First degree courses in translation are available at a number of universities.

Personal Qualities

Translators must be meticulous, conscientious, creative and persistent. The ability to carry out research as and when necessary, and good interpersonal skills are also required.

Starting Salary

Freelance translators sometimes own the copyright in their work and strictly the payment they receive is for granting others the right to use their translation. Published translators may also receive royalties. Translators are usually paid per 1,000 words. The ITI's Rates and Salaries Survey is a useful source of salary details (*see* below).

| i |

Institute of Linguists, Saxon House, 48 Southwark Street, London SE11 1UN; 020 7940 3100; fax: 020 7940 3101; www.iol.org.uk; e-mail: info@iol.org.uk

Institute of Translation and Interpreting (ITI), Exchange House, 494 Midsummer Boulevard, Milton Keynes, Buckinghamshire MK9 2EA; 01908 255905; fax: 01908 255700; www.iti.org.uk; e-mail: info@iti.org.uk

'Average Rates for Translation' (Institute of Linguists)

Careers Using Languages (Kogan Page)

Great Careers for People Interested in Languages (Kogan Page)

'Some courses in translation and Interpreting in the UK', factsheet from ITI (address above)

'2001 Rates and Salaries Survey', available from ITI (address above)

TRANSPORT ENGINEERING

see *Engineering*

TRAVEL AGENT

Travel agents sell tickets for travel by air, land and sea on behalf of transport organizations. They make hotel bookings for individual travellers, business people or holidaymakers. Some travel companies deal only with business travel and are also involved in arranging conferences and trade fairs. However, travel agents are best known for selling package holidays on behalf of tour operators. Many travel agents will also advise travellers on visas, foreign currency and necessary injections.

Qualifications and Training

Modern apprenticeships and NVQ qualifications are available. No specific qualifications are asked for but GCSEs in maths, English and geography are an advantage. Computer literacy is becoming increasingly important.

Personal Qualities

Travel agents must enjoy dealing with the general public, have a responsible attitude regarding the accuracy of information given and good administrative and ICT skills.

Starting Salary

Varies according to job; assistants earn £8,000–£13,000, managers £15,000+.

Local Jobcentres and Careers/Connexions Centres

Institute of Travel and Tourism, 113 Victoria Street, St Albans, Hertfordshire AL1 3TJ; 01727 854395; www.itt.co.uk

The Travel and Tourism and Events Sector National Training Organization, The Cornerstone, The Broadway, Woking, Surrey GU21 5AR; 01483 740854; www.ttento.com

TTC Training, The Cornerstone, The Broadway, Woking, Surrey GU21 5AR; 01483 727321; www.ttctraining.co.uk

Careers in the Travel Industry (Kogan Page)

TRICHOLOGIST

Trichologists treat hair and scalp disorders, the most common being hair loss. Electrical and heat treatments, massage and special lotions and ointments are used. Trichologists practise on their own behalf; some of their patients are referred to them from doctors, but trichology is not available on the NHS.

Qualifications and Training

Basic academic qualifications are necessary. Training may be by a three-year pupillage with a practising trichologist. The necessary theoretical instruction is available at technical colleges, evening classes or by correspondence. It is also necessary to have some practical experience of working in a recognised clinic.

Personal Qualities

Trichologists must understand the necessary biological principles and have a knowledge of nutrition, plus an interest in helping people. They must have high standards of personal hygiene.

Starting Salary

This is dependent upon number of patients, hours worked and fees charged.

Institute of Trichologists, 20–22 Queensberry Place, London SW7 2DZ; 020 7491 7253

TRUCK DRIVER

see *Lorry Driver*

UNDERTAKER

see *Funeral Director*

UNDERWRITER

see *Insurance*

UPHOLSTERER

(see also *Furniture and Furnishing*)

The upholstery industry in the UK has a long tradition of supplying and repairing seating. Whilst competition from cheap imports is fierce, the UK's reputation for quality has helped sustain the industry. Companies range from small businesses supplying a local market to large undertakings making suites for the major retailers. The job may entail anything from providing modern chairs and sofas for large hotel chains to the restoration of antique furniture in private homes or museums.

There are three main roles within the sector: the cutter, the sewer and the upholster. Often within smaller companies all three roles are carried out by all staff but with some specialization. Upholsterers measure up, prepare and fit the fabric components in all kinds of furniture. It is highly skilled work and includes not only the visible top coverings (which can vary from velvet to leather), but also the preparation and supports below, such as padding, stuffing, springing or webbing.

Qualifications and Training
Craft training is generally gained through a three- to four-year Modern Apprenticeship including NVQs at level 3. Other training is available, from beginner-level courses (City and Guilds/OCN Craft Certificates) through more advanced knowledge-based programmes (City and Guilds Progression Awards) to HNDs, foundation and full degrees.

Personal Qualities
Upholsterers need to have nimble fingers, good eyesight and infinite patience, and must enjoy working on individual projects.

Starting Salary
Salary rates vary but pay is generally good, with apprentices at 16 earning £70+ a week. By 19 many are earning in excess of £300 a week. Qualified and experienced staff can earn a lot more. Individual craftsmen working for themselves set their own rates.

The Furniture, Furnishings and Interiors National Training Organization, The Poplars, Off Wollaton Rd, Beeston, Nottinghamshire NG9 2PD; 0115 9221200; fax: 0115 9223833; www.ffinto.org; e-mail: info@ffinto.org

VALUER

(see also *Auctioneer, Estate Agent, Land Agent, Surveyor/Surveying Technician*)

Valuers are employed by a wide variety of firms to assess the worth of goods and property (including land, buildings, fine arts, chattels, machinery and livestock). They may work for building societies, estate agents, insurance companies, property companies or any commercial, financial or industrial organization that has to know true commercial values for selling, renting, investment or taxation purposes. Some valuers are also surveyors, auctioneers or land agents.

Qualifications and Training

There are two components to qualifying as a Chartered Surveyor or Valuer. First, successful completion of a degree or diploma approved by the Royal Institution of Chartered Surveyors (RICS), followed by enrolment onto the Assessment of Professional Competence (APC). This is two years' practical training while in employment, concluding with an RICS professional assessment interview. Postgraduate conversion courses are also available.

Professional qualifications in rating and valuations are awarded by the Institute of Revenues, Rating and Valuation (IRRV). Courses leading to IRRV examinations are available on day release or block release and by distance learning.

Personal Qualities

A valuer needs discretion combined with aptitude to understand the various economic factors involved in commerce.

Starting Salary

Trainees £10,000–£13,000 depending on age and qualifications, with higher salaries in London; £13,000–£19,000 when qualified.

Institute of Revenues, Rating and Valuation, 41 Doughty Street, London WC1N 2LF; 020 7691 8980; www.irrv.org.uk

Royal Institution of Chartered Surveyors (RICS), 12 Great George Street, Parliament Square, London SW1P 3AD; 020 7222 7000; www.rics.org/afa

VEHICLE TECHNICIAN

(see also *Garage Work, Road Transport*)

Apart from working in garages, maintaining and repairing cars belonging to the general public, vehicle technicians are also employed to maintain heavy goods vehicles, buses and coaches owned by large road transport operators, motorcycles, agricultural machinery or 'performance' cars. The areas of work are varied, including the maintenance of aero engines and a number of jobs in industry, involved with machinery of all kinds.

Industry

Categories include: metal-working machine tools, industrial pumps, valves and compressors, textile machinery, construction and earth-moving equipment, office machinery, refrigeration machinery, industrial plant and steelwork. The machinery is designed by the mechanical engineer, and maintained by the technician.

Agriculture

As farming becomes increasingly mechanised, technicians are more in demand for the maintenance of such equipment as tractors, crop harvesters of all kinds, seed drills, even automated revolving milk parlours.

Qualifications and Training

Training for school leavers, normally via a Modern Apprenticeship leading to NVQs at level 2 and 3, is available for a range of vehicle technician occupations. Apprenticeships are generally arranged through Retail Motor Industry Training (ReMIT). Some manufacturers run their own training courses.

Edexcel (BTEC) national and higher national certificates in mechanical engineering course are available at many further education colleges. Entry to the national certificate is with four GCSEs or equivalent. For HND courses an A level or equivalent in maths, chemistry or physics or completion of the national certificate is required. Courses can be done full- or part-time.

Personal Qualities
Mechanical aptitude, the ability to diagnose faults with the aid of a workshop manual and to work responsibly without supervision and undertake routine tasks are all essential

Starting Salary
Rates for trainees are set by ReMIT (see below); once qualified, average salary is £17,000.

$\boxed{i}$

The Passenger Transport Forum for Employee Development (TRANSfED), Regency House, 43 High Street, Rickmansworth WD3 1ET; 01923 896607; www.transfed.org; e-mail: enquiries@transfed.org

Retail Motor Industry Training (ReMIT), 201 Great Portland Street, London W1W 5AB; 0207 307 3413; fax: 0207 307 3425; www.remit.co.uk

MITC Motor Industry Training Council 201, Great Portland Street London W1N 6AB; 0207 436 6373; www.mitc.co.uk; e-mail: info@mitc.co.uk

VETERINARY NURSE

Nurses assist vets during operations and X-rays, sterilise instruments, look after animals recovering from surgery and keep the animals and their cages clean. After qualification, the work of a veterinary nurse can include practice management, staff supervision, teaching and training other nurses or support staff. Some VNs choose to work outside veterinary practice in research establishments, colleges, zoos and breeding or boarding kennels.

Qualifications and Training

Entry requirements are five GCSEs at grade C or above, including English language and two passes in a physical or biological science and maths. Equivalent qualifications are accepted at the discretion of the Royal College of Veterinary Surgeons Review Officer. Alternatively, the British Veterinary Nursing Association's pre-veterinary nursing course, approved by the RCVS, enables the holder to enrol on to the veterinary nursing scheme without other GCSEs. A qualified nurse can go on to study for an advanced diploma in veterinary nursing (surgical and medical).

A BSc degree in Veterinary Nursing is available at Middlesex University. Entry requirements are at least two A levels or equivalent. A science subject is preferred

Personal Qualities

A love of animals is essential, plus patience, a calm manner and good health.

Starting Salary

Salaries for new entrants are around £6,000. Experienced veterinary nurses earn between £10,500 and £17,000.

i

British Veterinary Nursing Association (BVNA), Level 15,
   Terminus House, Terminus Street, Harlow, Essex CM20 1XA;
   01279 450567; fax: 01279 420866; www.bvna.org.uk;
   e-mail: bvna@bvna.co.uk
The Royal College of Veterinary Surgeons, Belgravia House,
   62–64 Horseferry Road, London SW1P 2AF; 020 7222 2001;
   www.rcvs.org.uk
Careers Working with Animals (Kogan Page)

VETERINARY SURGEON

Most vets work in private practice, usually starting out as a veterinary assistant and working their way up into a partnership or into their own business. Some specialise in small-animal treatment, including pets such as dogs, cats and birds, while others work with particular kinds of animals such as farm animals, racehorses or the more exotic zoo animals. Other vets go into research or industry. The Ministry of Agriculture, for instance, employs a substantial number to work on disease control, monitoring such epidemics as foot and mouth or swine vesicular disease. Others are employed by animal welfare organizations, such as the PDSA, in animal hospitals. Vets are also needed in the food-processing industries where their job is concerned with checking that conditions are humane and hygienic.

Qualifications and Training

A veterinary surgeon must hold a degree from one of the six veterinary schools in the UK. The six universities offering the course set their own entrance requirements but all demand an extremely high standard of A passes or equivalent. Chemistry is essential, and other useful subjects are physics, maths, biology or zoology. The course lasts five years (six at Cambridge), and covers a formidable amount of academic and practical work, comparable to that needed to be a doctor.

Personal Qualities

Vets need sympathy combined with detachment, endless patience and physical fitness (particularly if dealing with larger animals). They must also be self-reliant and prepared to work unsocial hours. Some business sense and the ability to keep accounts are also important.

Starting Salary

Assistants (less than five years qualified) in general practice start at £16,000–£18,000 rising to £25,000–£31,000 with a few years' experience.

The Royal College of Veterinary Surgeons, Belgravia House, 62–64 Horseferry Road, London SW1P 2AF; 020 7222 2001; www.rcvs.org.uk

'Training to Become a Veterinary Surgeon' available for download from the RCVS Web site – or from The Administrative Officer (Education) at the above address

VISION MIXER

see *Broadcasting*

W

WAITING

see *Catering and Accommodation Management, Hotel Work*

WARDEN

see *Caretaker, Conservation (Environmental), Leisure and Amenity Management*

WATCH AND CLOCK MAKER/ REPAIRER

Watch and clock makers make timepieces by hand, sometimes to a design of their own.

Repairers receive watches and clocks from customers for servicing and repair. They must be able to examine a timepiece thoroughly for worn-out parts, clean and regulate a watch or clock, and repair or replace faulty parts. The work involves the use of precision tools and electronic equipment. Restoration is carried out on antique clocks and watches.

Qualifications and Training

The British Horological Institute (BHI) coordinates all watch and clock training organizations. A two-year HND in Horology is available from the University of Central England. Applicants need three GCSEs, including maths and English, or to have completed the preliminary year of the BHI course. A one-year course in antique clock repair and restoration is offered by West Dean College in Chichester. St Loye's College in Exeter provides residential training in horology for students with disabilities.

The BHI also offers correspondence courses at Preliminary, Intermediate and Final level which cover all aspects of horology from watch repairs, clocks, electric, electronic to heavy turret and master clocks. These courses lead up to internationally recognized qualifications.

Personal Qualities

Mathematical and drawing ability as well as dexterity are important. Applicants must have good eyesight, the physical skill and patience to do the intricate work required, and be able to work alone.

Starting Salary

Many horologists are self-employed and earnings vary enormously, starting from £8,000 to over £20,000 for those who have experience and a specialism.

The British Horological Institute, Upton Hall, Upton, Newark, Nottinghamshire NG23 5TE; 01636 813795; www.bhi.co.uk

WATER ENGINEERING

see *Engineering*

WEB SITE DESIGNER

see *Computing*

WEB SITE PROGRAMMER

see *Computing*

WELDER

Welders join pieces of metal together by applying intense heat and melting the edges so that two pieces become one. The sorts of items welded are metal sections of aeroplanes, ships, oil rigs, cars and power turbines. Welders work in light- and heavy-engineering firms, in foundry work and in shipbuilding. Some plastics are also welded.

Welders work on all types of fabrication from the manufacture of metal-frame chairs, to high quality, complex applications such as building a submarine.

Qualifications and Training

Formal academic qualifications are not necessary, but GCSEs in English, maths and a science are preferred. Modern Apprenticeships are available leading to NVQs in Engineering Production or Engineering Construction. Once qualified, welders must undertake regular retesting to demonstrate competence.

Personal Qualities

A welder must have a steady hand and excellent powers of concentration. Workers must be careful and follow safety instructions, as the work is potentially dangerous.

Starting Salary

Around £12,000, rising to £20,000–£25,000; higher for specialist welders.

i

Engineering Careers Information Service, EMTA, 14 Upton Road, Watford, Hertfordshire WD1 7EP; 0800 282 167;
www.emta.org.uk/enginuity; e-mail: ecis@emta.org.uk
Engineering Construction Industry Training Board, Blue Court, Church Lane, Kings Langley, Hertfordshire WD2 8JP;
01923 260000; www.ecitb.org.uk
Welding Institute, Granta Park, Abington Hall, Abington, Cambridge CB1 6AL; 01223 891162; www.twi.co.uk;
e-mail: twi@twi.co.uk

WINDOW DRESSER

see *Display Designer*

WINE TRADE

The wine trade has grown beyond the small merchant or importer and most opportunities are now with large companies which import, retail and deal with the licensed trade, hotels and catering, off-licences, supermarkets and multiple stores. There are posts in marketing, advertising, packaging, promotion, market research, buying and quality control.

Qualifications and Training

Opportunities exist at GCSE, A and degree level for entry into the wine trade. On-the-job training is provided by the Wine and Spirit Education Trust (WSET), a registered educational charity set up by the drinks industry. They offer Certificate, Higher Certificate and Diploma courses. The University of Brighton offers a two-year full-time HND in wine studies.

Personal Qualities

These depend on the area entered, but a love and knowledge of wine are obviously important, plus relevant knowledge about the chief wine-growing areas, and their type of soil and climate. Tasters need a discriminating sense of taste and smell. Language skills can be an advantage.

Starting Salary

Experienced merchants and managers earn between £12,000 and £20,000+.

Wine and Spirit Education Trust, Five Kings House, 1 Queen
Street Place, London EC4R 1QS; 020 7236 3551;
fax: 020 7329 8712; www.wset.co.uk
Harpers Wine and Spirit Weekly, Harling House, 47 Great Suffolk
Street, London SE1 1RQ (job advertisements);
www.harpers-wine.com

WRITER

(see also *Journalist*)

Some authors exist solely on the proceeds of their writing, but for many it is a part-time occupation, additional to a full-time job. The field of creative writing is probably the most difficult in which to succeed. It is also the area which contains some of the best-known writers, the authors of popular fiction bestsellers. It is probably slightly easier to make a living by non-fiction writing, producing text on a specialist or technical subject, or writing textbooks.

There are a few posts as writer in residence, where writers work for regional authorities developing writing projects with people living in the region. There are also opportunities of a journalistic nature for non-journalists. Writers may contribute to specialist journals or submit short stories to magazines interested in fiction.

Qualifications and Training

Generally, writers are born, not made. However, it is possible to take courses in both creative and technical writing.

Personal Qualities

Writers must be self-disciplined, able to work on their own, highly motivated and persevering.

Starting Salary

Earnings vary enormously, but the majority of writers do not support themselves by their writing alone. Writers in residence can expect about £14,000–£20,000.

Society of Authors, 84 Drayton Gardens, London SW10 9SB; 020 7373 6642; www.societyofauthors.org; e-mail: info@societyofauthors.org

Writers' and Artists' Yearbook (A&C Black)

The Writers' Handbook (Macmillan)

YOUTH AND COMMUNITY WORKER

(see also *Social Work and Social Care – Children and Young People* **and** *Personal Adviser Connexions***)**

Youth work promotes young people's personal and social development, provides support to help them achieve and progress into independence and enables young people to have a voice in their communities and in society. This is accomplished through work with individuals, work with and in groups, and with communities. In many instances youth workers work in partnership with professionals from other sectors, such as schools and colleges, careers, health organizations, the police and social services.

Youth and community workers work in a range of settings, including youth clubs, schools, colleges, community centres, as personal advisers within the Connexions Service and other specialist agencies offering information, advice and counselling. Some workers also work in mobile centres and with young people on the streets and in cafés. There are currently around 3,000 full-time youth workers employed in England and a far larger number of part-time and volunteer youth workers. The introduction of the Connexions Service in England, which offers advice, information and guidance to young people aged 13–19, is likely to lead to substantial numbers of new posts for people with youth work skills.

In Scotland, youth and community work is combined with adult education under the generic term 'community education'.

Qualifications and Training

For those seeking qualification as a full-time, nationally qualified youth worker, various routes, including full-time and part-time diploma and degree courses, postgraduate courses, and distance learning exist. Detailed information on courses can be obtained from the National Youth Agency, directly or via their Web site. Details of training and employment in Scotland and Wales can be obtained from Community Learning Scotland and the Wales Youth Agency, respectively.

NVQs in Community Work are available at levels 2/3 and 4. There is normally a minimum age requirement varying from 19 to 21 (18 for some degree courses) and applicants are usually expected to have substantial experience of work with young people or adults in community settings. This can be paid or unpaid. Mature entrants may be accepted without formal academic qualifications.

Personal Qualities

An interest in and understanding of the issues that affect people's lives, plus patience, stamina and a sense of humour are all qualities demanded of youth and community workers. They must also be able to plan, record and evaluate their work.

Starting Salary

Ranges from £13,600 to £23,000.

i

The National Youth Agency, 17–23 Albion Street, Leicester LE1 6GD; 0116 285 3700; www.nya.org.uk; e-mail: nya@nya.org.uk
'NYA Guide to Becoming a Youth Worker' (National Youth Agency, £1.00), 'What is the Youth Service?' (National Youth Agency, £1.00)
Community Learning Scotland, Rosebery House, 9 Haymarket Terrace, Edinburgh EH12 5EZ; 0131 313 2488; www.communitylearning.org
Wales Youth Agency, Leslie Court, Lon-y-Llyn, Caerphilly CF83 1BQ; 029 2055700; wya.newi.ac.uk
PAULO: The National Training Organization for Community-based Learning and Development, Springfield House, Springfield Business Centre, Springfield Road, Grantham NG31 7BQ; 01476 514628; www.paulo.org.uk/paulo; e-mail: info@paulo.org.uk

Z

ZOO KEEPER

Keepers look after animals in zoos, mucking out their living quarters, preparing their food, feeding them and engaging in all other aspects of animal husbandry. There is increasing emphasis on education, public relations and research. Keepers work long hours – from 8am to as late as 7pm – much of the time outdoors and the work is often physically demanding.

Qualifications and Training

No specific qualifications are needed; on-the-job training is by a correspondence course followed by a City and Guilds qualification. However, many applicants for posts in zoos have done courses in Animal Care or Welfare. These are available at First, National and Higher National Diploma level and there are also related degree courses. Graduates are more likely to enter posts in education and research. Applications for such jobs far exceed the number of places available, and zoos prefer people to enquire only when a vacancy is advertised.

Personal Qualities

Affection and respect for animals, combined with an unsentimental approach, are essential. Keepers must have practical common sense, an interest in education and conservation and the ability to communicate effectively with the public.

Starting Salary

Salaries range from about £8,000+ to £13,000+.

i

The Association of British Wild Animal Keepers;
www.abwak.co.uk (Contact details for members of the
Association can be found on the Web site)
Careers Working with Animals (Kogan Page)

ZOOLOGIST

Zoologists work in either research or teaching. A very small
number find jobs in industry, mainly in pharmaceutical and
animal foodstuff companies. Research zoologists will probably
work in one of the many government-backed centres on a variety
of projects, including animal behaviour, pest control and the
population ecology of birds.

Qualifications and Training

A degree in zoology, available at some universities, is needed for
a career as a zoologist. Postgraduate training in specializations
such as entomology or nematology is also available.

Personal Qualities

Zoologists should have a scientific mind and an interest in
research.

Starting Salary

£15,000 upwards.

The Institute of Biology, 20–22 Queensberry Place, London SW7
2DZ; 020 7581 8333; www.iob.org.uk

INDEX

For professional associations see under subject, eg Incorporated Society of Musicians *see* Musicians, Incorporated Society of.

Index of Advertisers